Programmer's Guide to Fortran 90

Springer
New York
Berlin
Heidelberg
Barcelona
Hong Kong
London
Milan
Paris
Singapore
Tokyo

Walter S. Brainerd
Charles H. Goldberg
Jeanne C. Adams

Programmer's Guide to Fortran 90

Third Edition

Springer

Walter S. Brainerd
Charles H. Goldberg
Jeanne C. Adams
Unicomp, Inc.
1874 San Bernardino Ave. NE
Albuquerque, NM 87122
USA

Cover image © Michael Tcherevkoff

Library of Congress Cataloging-in-Publication Data
Brainerd, Walter S.
    Programmer's guide to Fortran 90 / Walter S. Brainerd, Charles H.
Goldberg, Jeanne C. Adams. — 3rd ed.
      p.   cm.
    Includes index.
    1. FORTRAN 90 (Computer program language)   I. Goldberg, Charles
H.   II. Adams, Jeanne C.   III. Title.
QA76.73.F25B735   1995
005.13'3 — dc20   95-34368

Printed on acid-free paper.

Production managed by Robert Wexler; manufacturing supervised by Jacqui Ashri.
Camera-ready copy prepared by the authors.
Printed and bound by Hamilton Printing Co., Rensselaer, NY.
Printed in the United States of America.

9 8 7 6 5 4

ISBN 0-387-94570-9   SPIN 10836372

Springer-Verlag   New York Berlin Heidelberg
A member of BertelsmannSpringer Science+Business Media GmbH

Preface

The new standard version of Fortran, informally known as Fortran 90, has many excellent new features that will assist the programmer in writing efficient, portable, and maintainable programs. However, because Fortran 77 is contained completely within Fortran 90, new features may be learned at whatever pace seems appropriate, and older Fortran programs will still run under Fortran 90. For example, scientific programmers might choose to concentrate initially on the new array processing features, saving for later the methods to encapsulate data types using the new global data feature, modules.

Programmer's Guide to Fortran 90 is organized so that it may be read from beginning to end, but it also is organized so that particular topics may be studied by reading some chapters before previous ones are mastered. To a reasonable extent, all of the material about one topic is presented together, making the book suitable as a reference work, as well as a tutorial.

All of the important features of the Fortran programming language are covered with examples, beginning with the simplest constructs. The book concentrates to some extent on the new features of the Fortran 90 programming language, because the new features often provide the best facilities to accomplish a particular programming task. Both the style of the many example programs and the selection of topics discussed in detail guide the reader toward acquiring programming skills to produce Fortran programs that are readable, maintainable, and efficient.

Case studies are used to illustrate the practical use of features of Fortran 90 and to show how complete programs are put together. There are also simple problems to enable the reader to exercise knowledge of the topics learned.

An unusual feature of the book is that the first chapter contains a complete discussion of all the basic features needed to write complete Fortran programs: the form of Fortran programs, data types, simple expressions and assignment, and simple input and output. Subsequent chapters contain detailed discussions of control constructs, procedures, arrays, character strings, data structures and derived types, modules, and pointer variables.

From the beginning, Fortran has had extensive facilities for input and output; however, this is a topic that is not explored fully in many books because it is a little more difficult than other features and perhaps just not as interesting as some features. The use of these facilities is very important in production programs, so this book contains, in Chapter 9, an extensive discussion of the excellent input/output facilities in Fortran.

Fortran is old for a programming language. It is natural that, as the language evolves, there are features that are redundant in the sense that, in most situations, better equivalent features are available. Many such features are covered briefly in Chapter 10. These features should seldom be used when writing a new program or modifying an old one; they are presented so that someone who must maintain an old program will understand enough about how they work to read and modify these statements.

No knowledge of Fortran 77 is assumed. However, footnotes indicate some important differences between Fortran 77 and Fortran 90; these will be of special interest to the Fortran 77 programmer. Readers familiar with Fortran 77 may skip immediately to Chapter 2 after looking over some of the examples in Chapter 1 to learn about kind parameters and to see what the new source form and declarations look like.

Appendices A and B give descriptions of the many intrinsic functions and the complete syntax specifications for the language, but there still will be occasions when an obscure property of the language must be learned. In these cases it will be necessary to consult the official standard, published by the International Standards Organization and the American National Standards Institute, or the reference work *The Fortran 90 Handbook*, by Adams, Brainerd, Martin, Smith, and Wagener, McGraw-Hill, 1992.

The Second Edition

The significant changes in the second edition are

- All the programs have been run on the NAGWare f90 compiler; they should contain very few errors of a clerical nature.

- The chapters covering procedures and modules have been rewritten completely.

- Chapter 10 has been renamed to more closely reflect its contents.

- A few features, such as certain redundant input/output formatting edit descriptors, have been moved to Chapter 10. External procedures constitute a major feature that has been moved to Chapter 10. It is much simpler to use either internal or module procedures and it is quite simple to convert an external procedure to a module procedure, thereby enabling compiler verification of argument compatibility.

The philosophy behind the division of material between Chapters 1–9 and Chapter 10 perhaps needs a little clarification. The first nine chapters provide a reasonably complete description of a fully functional subset of Fortran 90. The subset chosen consists of those features that we feel are the most useful, efficient, and reliable in Fortran 90, and which tend to produce the most readable, maintainable, and efficient programs. For the most part, the descriptions of these features are self contained.

Chapter 10 contains features that, however useful they might once have been as the best (and, in some case, the only) way to do something in Fortran, are now largely redundant second cousins of features presented in Chapters 1-9. For the most part, the newer features in Chapters 1-9 provide at least the full functional capability of the redundant features in Chapter 10. Some of the redundant features are, or have become, incompatible with other features of Fortran, and have awkward, unsystematic restrictions on their use. The rules that describe interactions between features in Chapter 10 and those in other chapters are not given, except perhaps briefly in Chapter 10. For example, the section in Chapter 9 on internal files does not say that using namelist with an internal file is illegal, even though this assertion is true, and is one of the reasons why namelist input/output is covered in Chapter 10.

Of course, it is necessary for a good Fortran programmer to know the entire Fortran 90 language, but if new program development is done using only the features described in this book, it will be more important to be able to read the other parts of the language than to use it extensively to write programs. If you are already familiar with Fortran 77, it is all there to use in a Fortran 90 system. If you are new to Fortran programming, this book covers the features of Fortran 90 that should be learned first; the "outmoded" features can be learned later as necessary.

The Third Edition

One of the things that makes Fortran programs look old-fashioned to some people is that they are typically written using uppercase letters. This was required if Fortran 77 programs were to be portable because the Fortran 77 standard did not include the use of uppercase letters.

The Fortran 90 standard allows uppercase letters, but does not require compilers to accept them. For this reason, the first two editions used uppercase letters in order to ensure that the programs would run on any Fortran 90 systems. Now that there are many Fortran 90 compilers available, it is possible to say that every existing Fortran 90 compiler accepts lowercase letters and there is every reason to expect that all Fortran 90 compilers will accept programs written using lowercase letters.

Thus, the main change from the second to the third edition is that all programs use lowercase letters. We hope this will make the programs a bit easier to read and give the book a much more modern appearance.

Several people have pointed out errors in earlier editions and offered suggestions for improvements. We would like especially to thank Hank Lauson, Brian Smith, Richard Maine, Mike Metcalf, and Chris Smith.

Walter S. Brainerd
Charles H. Goldberg
Jeanne C. Adams

July 1995

Contents

1

Introduction to Programming in Fortran 90

The best way to learn a programming language is to start reading and writing programs immediately. If a computer is available, we encourage you to write and *run* programs modeled on the simple sample programs in this chapter. In addition to this book, you will need a short set of directions to show you how to enter and run a program at your local installation.

1.1 Programs that Calculate and Print

Since computers are very good at arithmetic and Fortran is designed to be very good at expressing numerical computations, one reasonable thing to learn first about Fortran 90 is how to tell a computer to do the sort of arithmetic that otherwise might be done by hand or with the aid of a hand calculator. This section describes how to write programs to calculate and to print the answer.

1.1.1 Simple Calculations

The first example is a program that prints the result of an addition.

```
program calculation_1
    print *, 84 + 13
end program calculation_1
```

The program `calculation_1` tells the computer to add the numbers 84 and 13 and then to print the sum, 97.[1] When the computer is told to run `calculation_1`, it does precisely that: it adds the two numbers and prints their sum. The execution output will look something like this.

```
run calculation_1

97
```

1.1.2 The run Command

The line

```
run calculation_1
```

is not a part of Fortran but a command or script to the local operating system, telling it to compile (that is, translate) and run the program `calculation_1`. Details of the `run` command vary widely because any experienced system command writer can tailor it to taste. Often the local command will contain the characters "f90" in the command verb, the program file name, or both to distinguish it from run commands for other languages available on the system.

1.1.3 Default Print Format

The asterisk following the keyword `print` tells the computer that the programmer will not be specifying the exact **format** or layout for the printed answer. Therefore, the Fortran system will use a **default format**, also called a list-directed format (9.8.19), designed to be satisfactory in most cases. The Fortran standard allows some freedom in the design of default formats, so your output may differ slightly from the sample execution shown above.

---

1. Fortran 77 programmers will notice that, at long last, the 6-character limit on identifiers has been changed to a 31-character limit.

1.1.4 Printing Messages

If you want the computer to print the exact typographic characters that you specify, you enclose them in quotation marks (double quotes) or apostrophes (single quotes), as illustrated by the program quotes.[2] The quotes are not printed in the output.

```
program quotes
    print *, "84 + 13"
end program quotes

run quotes

84 + 13
```

In a Fortran program, a sequence of typographic characters enclosed in quotes or apostrophes is a **character string**. A character string may contain alphabetic characters as well as numeric characters and may contain other special characters such as punctuation marks and arithmetic symbols.

Printing both exact literal characters and a computed numeric value produces the following easy-to-read output.

```
program calculation_1_v2
    print *, "84 + 13 =", 84 + 13
end program calculation_1_v2

run calculation_1_v2

84 + 13 = 97
```

In the program calculation_1_v2 (calculation 1 version 2), there are two items in the list in the print statement, a **character constant** "84 + 13 =" to be printed exactly as written (but without the delimiting quotation marks) and an arithmetic expression whose value is first calculated and then printed. Although the two items may look similar, they are treated quite differently. Enclosing the character string in quotes means that it is to be transcribed *character for character*, including the three blank characters (spaces, in ordinary typing), while the same expression written without quotes or apostrophes is to be evaluated so that the sum can be printed. Commas are used to separate the items in the list of a print statement.

---

2. Previous versions of Fortran accepted only single quotes as character string delimiters.

1.1.5 The program Statement

Each Fortran program may begin with a **program statement**. It consists of the keyword program followed by a **program name** of the programmer's choosing. The name must start with a letter and consist of at most 31 letters, digits, and underscores. The program name calculation_1 has no significance except to the human reader.

1.1.6 The end Statement

The **end statement** begins with the keyword end. It may be followed by the keyword program, which may in turn be followed by the name of the program. Every Fortran program must have an end statement as its last statement.

> *Style Note:* Don't be lazy. Include the keyword program and the name of the program on every program end statement.

1.1.7 Exercises

1. Write and run a program that prints your name.

2. Write and run a program that computes the sum of the integers 1 through 9, preceded by a short message, explaining what the output is.

3. What computer output might be expected when the following program is run?

```
program simple
    print *, 1, "and", 1, "equals", 1 + 1
end program simple
```

1.2 Intrinsic Data Types

The five intrinsic (i.e., built-in) **data types** in Fortran are integer, real, complex, logical, and character. Each data type has a set of values that may be represented in that type and operations that can be performed on those values. We already have seen examples of the use of two of these data types. "84 + 13" (including the quotation marks) is a character string constant, and 84 + 13 is an expression whose value is of type integer.

The following subsections discuss each of the five intrinsic types and the way that constants of those types are written in Fortran.

1.2.1 Integer Type

The **integer type** is used to represent values that are whole numbers. In Fortran, integer constants are written much like they are written in ordinary usage. An **integer constant** is a string containing only the digits 0 to 9, possibly followed by an underscore (_) and another integer constant or named integer constant, which designates the kind parameter as described in Section 1.2.9. The following are examples of integer constants.

         23   0   1234567   42_1   42_short   42_long

A **signed integer constant** is an integer constant optionally preceded by a + or - sign. A signed integer constant may be considered a restricted kind of expression, but often may be used where an integer constant may be used.

Every Fortran system must have at least one integer kind, although the kind number used for this kind may vary from one computer to another. Many Fortran systems have several integer kinds, with different kind numbers corresponding to different ranges of representable values.

1.2.2 Real Type

There are two forms of a **real constant** in Fortran. The first is called **positional form** because the place value of each digit is determined by its position relative to the decimal point. The positional form of a real constant consists of an integer followed by a decimal point followed by a string of digits representing the fractional part of the value, possibly followed by an underscore and a kind parameter. Assuming that `double` and `quad` are names of integer constants that are permissible real kinds on the Fortran system being used (see Section 1.2.9), all the following are real constants written in positional form.

         13.5   0.1234567   123.45678   00.30_double   3.0
         3.   12345.   .0   .1234567_quad

A real constant written in the positional form may have no digits to the left of the decimal point or it may have no digits to the right of the decimal point, but a decimal point by itself is not a legal real constant.

The **exponential form** of a real number consists of either an integer or a real number written in positional form followed by the letter e and an optionally signed integer (without a kind parameter) and optionally followed by an underscore and kind parameter. The letter e is read as "times 10 to the power" and the integer following the e is a power of 10 to be multiplied by the number preceding the e. Exponential notation is useful for writing very large or very small numbers. For example, 2.3e5 represents 2.3 times 10 to the power 5, 2.3×10^5, or $2.3 \times 100{,}000 = 230{,}000$. The integer power may contain a minus or plus sign preceding it, as in the real constant 2.3e-5, which is 2.3×10^{-5} or $2.3 \times 0.00001 = 0.000023$. Two more examples are 1e9_double, which is one billion with kind parameter double, and 1e-3, which is one one-thousandth.

Every Fortran system must have at least two real kinds,[3] although the kind numbers used for these kinds and the precision (roughly, the number of significant digits) and exponent range implemented by these kinds may vary from one computer to another. Many Fortran systems have several real kinds, with different kind numbers corresponding to different precisions or ranges of values.

1.2.3 Complex Type

The Fortran **complex type** is used to represent the mathematical complex numbers, which consist of two real numbers and often are written as $a + b\,i$. The first real number is called the **real part** and the second is called the **imaginary part** of the complex number. In Fortran, a **complex constant** is written as two (possibly signed) integer or real numbers, separated by a comma and enclosed in parentheses. Examples of complex constants are

```
(1, -1)
(3.14_double, -7)
(-1.0, 3.1e-27_quad)
```

If the two parts are type integer, the kind parameter of the complex constant is the default complex kind. If one part is integer and the other is real, the kind parameter of the complex constant is the kind of the real. If both parts are real, the kind parameter of the complex constant is the same as the part with the greater precision.

---

3. The two required kinds of real representations correspond to the Fortran 77 real and double precision data types, which now have alternative descriptions in terms of kind parameters.

1.2.4 Arithmetic Operators

The operators that may be used to combine two numeric values (that is, integer, real, or complex) include +, -, *, /, and **. Except for **, these symbols have their usual mathematical meaning indicating addition, subtraction, multiplication, and division. The two asterisks indicate exponentiation; that is, the value of 2 ** 4 is 16 computed as 2 raised to the power 4 or 2^4 in mathematical notation. The symbols + and - may be used as unary operators to indicate the identity and negation operations, respectively.

Integer division always produces an integer result obtained by chopping off any fractional part of the mathematical result. For example, since the mathematical result of 23/2 is 11.5, the value of the Fortran arithmetic expression

```
23.0 / 2.0
```

is 11.5, but the value of the expression

```
23 / 2
```

which is the quotient of two integer constants, has the value 11. Similarly, the value of both the expressions

```
-23 / 2      23 / (-2)
```

is - 11.

1.2.5 Relational Operators

Numeric values may be compared with **relational operators**. The two forms for each relational operator are given in Table 1-1.[4]

Complex values may be compared only with the relational operators == and /=. However, due to roundoff error, in many cases it is not appropriate to compare either real or complex values using either the == or the /= operator. In such cases, it is better to test for approximate equality instead.

The result of a relational operator is type logical (Section 1.2.7).

1.2.6 Mixed Mode Expressions

Mathematically, the integers are a subset of the real numbers and the real numbers are a subset of the complex numbers. Thus, it makes sense to combine two numeric values, even if they are not the same Fortran type. The two operands of a numeric operator do not have

---

4. Note that the Fortran 77 relational operators each have new equivalents in Fortran 90.

Table 1-1 The relational operators.

Fortran 90 forms		Meaning
<	.lt.	less than
<=	.le.	less than or equal to
==	.eq.	equals
/=	.ne.	is not equal to
>=	.ge.	greater than or equal to
>	.gt.	greater than

to be the same data type; when they are different, one is converted to the type of the other prior to executing the operation. If one is type integer and the other is type real, the integer is converted to a real value; if one is type integer and the other is type complex, the integer is converted to a complex value; if one is type real and the other is type complex, the real is converted to a complex value. As an example, the value of the expression

        23.0 / 2

is 11.5, because the integer 2 is converted to a real value and then a division of two real values is performed.

The two operands of a numeric operand also may have different kind parameter values. In this case, if the two operands have the same type or one is real and one complex, the result has the kind parameter of the operand with the greater precision. For example, if kind 5 has greater precision than kind 2, the value of

        1.0_2 + 3.0_5

is 4 with kind parameter 5. Assuming that kind 4 has greater precision than either kind 2 or kind 3, the value of

        1.1_4 + (2.2_2, 3.3_3)

is $3.3 + 3.3i$ with kind parameter 4. If one operand is type integer and the other is real or complex, the kind parameter of the result is that of the real or complex operand.

1.2.7 Logical Type

The Fortran **logical type** is used to represent the two truth values "true" and "false". A **logical constant** is either .true. or .false.

The operators that may be used to combine logical values are .not., .and., .or., .eqv., and .neqv. They are all binary operators except the unary operator .not. The value resulting from the application of each logical operator is given in Table 1-2.

Table 1-2   Values of the logical operators.

x_1 x_2	$.\text{not}.x_2$	$x_1.\text{and}.x_2$	$x_1.\text{or}.x_2$	$x_1.\text{eqv}.x_2$	$x_1.\text{neqv}.x_2$
true true	false	true	true	true	false
true false	true	false	true	false	true
false true	false	false	true	false	true
false false	true	false	false	true	false

To give one simple example, the value of

.false. .eqv. .false.

is true.

1.2.8   Character Type

The **character type** is used to represent strings of characters. The form of a **character constant** is a sequence of any characters representable in the computer delimited by either quotation marks (double quotes) or apostrophes (single quotes). If the delimiting character is to occur in the character string, it is represented by two of the delimiters with no intervening characters. A character constant may be preceded by a kind parameter and an underscore. Note that the kind parameter for a character constant (ascii in the second example below) goes in front of the constant, rather than after it, as is the case for kind parameters on all other types of constants. The following are examples of character constants.

```
"Joan"
ascii_'John Q. Public'
"Don't tread on me."
'He said, "Don''t tread on me."'
```

There is only one character operator that produces a character result, **concatenation**. The symbol used is // and the result of the binary operator is a string of characters consisting of those in the first string followed by those in the second string. For example, the value of "John Q." // "Public" is the string "John Q.Public". Note that there is no blank after the period, although there could have been; the value of "John Q. " // "Public" is the string

"John Q. Public". The kind parameter of the two operands must be the same.

Relational operators (Section 1.2.5) may be used to compare character values, which is done using the character collating sequence (Sections 5.1.8 and 5.1.11).

1.2.9 Kind Parameters

Kind parameters provide a way to parameterize the selection of different possible machine representations for each of the intrinsic data types. If the programmer is careful, this provides a mechanism for making selection of numeric precision and range portable. For the character data type, it permits the use of more than one character set, such as Japanese, Chinese, and chemistry symbols, within a program.

Each intrinsic data type (integer, real, complex, logical, and character) has a parameter, called its **kind parameter**, associated with it. A kind parameter is intended to designate a machine representation for a particular data type. As an example, an implementation might have three real kinds, informally known as single, double, and quadruple precision.

The kind parameter is an integer. These numbers are processor dependent, so that kind parameters 1, 2, and 3 might be single, double, and quadruple precision, or on a different system, kind parameters 4, 8, and 16 could be used for the same things. The only requirements are that there must be at least two real and complex kinds, representing default real and double precision, and at least one kind for the integer, logical, and character data types. Note that the value of the kind parameter has nothing to do with the number of decimal digits of precision or range.

You need to check your Fortran manual for the computer system being used to determine which kind parameters are available for each type and which kind parameters are the default for each type. Kind parameters are optional in all cases, so it is possible to always use the default kind if that is sufficient for your application.

The intrinsic functions `selected_int_kind` and `selected_real_kind` may be used to select an appropriate kind for a variable or a named constant (Section 1.3.10). These functions provide the means for making a program portable in cases where values need to be computed with a certain specified precision that may use single precision on one machine, but require double precision on another machine. They are described in Section 1.5.1.

For the logical data type, an implementation may have representations with the property that logical values are packed one per bit; or it may be that due to the type of addressing and instruction set, putting one logical value per byte turns out to be more efficient. These representations can be selected by the programmer by specifying a kind parameter value.

When a kind parameter is a part of another constant, it may be either an integer constant (which does not have a sign) or a named integer constant (parameter). In integer, real, and logical constants, it follows the underscore character (_) at the end.

```
12345_4
1.345_2
.true._1
```

In character constants, it occurs at the front and is followed by an underscore.

```
ascii_"abcde"
greek_"αβγδε"
```

The kind of a complex constant is determined by the kinds of the two real components as described in Section 1.2.3.

1.2.10 Exercises

1. Convert the following type real numbers from positional notation to exponential notation.

    ```
    48.2613     .00241_4    38499.0
    0.2717      55.0        7.000001_quad
    ```

2. Convert the following type real numbers from exponential notation to positional notation.

    ```
    9.503e2     4.1679e+10_double    2.881e-5
    -4.421e2    -5.81e-2_8           7.000001e0
    ```

3. Write a program that prints the sum $.1 + .2 + .3 + \cdots + .9$.

4. Determine the kind number of one real kind that has precision greater than that of the default real kind on your computer system.

5. Print the value of selected_int_kind and selected_real_kind for about a dozen different argument values to see which kind values are available on the computer you are using. Check your results with the Fortran manual for your system.

6. Write a program that prints the sum of the complex numbers
    $(.1+.1i) + (.2+.2i) + (.3+.3i) + \cdots + (.9+.9i)$.

7. Write a program that prints the logical value of each of the following expressions:

```
2 > 3
2 < 3
.1 + .1 == .2
.5 + .5 /= 1.0
```

8. Write a program that computes and prints the concatenation of all of your names (e.g., first, middle, and last).

1.3 Variables and Input

One benefit of writing a computer program for doing a calculation rather than obtaining the answer using pencil and paper or a hand calculator is that when the same sort of problem arises again, the program already written can be reused. The use of **variables** gives the programs in this section the flexibility needed for such reuse. The programs in Section 1.1 direct the computer to perform the indicated arithmetic operations on numeric constants appearing in the print statements. The sample program add_2 finds the sum of any two integers supplied as input. The numbers to be added do not appear in the program itself. Instead, two integer variables x and y are reserved to hold the two values supplied as input. Because Fortran statements can operate on variables as well as constants, their sum can be calculated and printed. The first sample run shows how this new program could be used to find the sum of the numbers 84 and 13, calculated by the program calculation_1 in Section 1.1.

```
program add_2
   integer :: x, y
   read *, x
   print *, "Input data  x:", x
   read *, y
   print *, "Input data  y:", y
   print *, "x + y =", x + y
end program add_2
```

```
run add_2
```

```
Input data  x: 84
Input data  y: 13
x + y = 97
```

After declaring that the variables x and y will hold integer values, the program add_2 tells the computer to read a number from an input device and call it x, then to read another number and call it y, and finally to print the value of x + y, identified as such. Two additional print statements that echo the values of the input data complete the program add_2. During the execution of this program, the two numbers which are the values for x and y must be supplied to the computer, or the computer cannot complete the run (Section 1.3.3).

1.3.1 Declaration of Variables

Type statements appear between the program statement and the beginning of the executable part of the program. Each declaration consists of a keyword specifying a Fortran intrinsic type, followed by two colons and a list of variable names separated by commas. For example, the program add_2 uses the type declaration

```
integer :: x, y
```

Corresponding to the integer, real, complex, logical, and character constants introduced in Section 1.2, there are integer, real, complex, logical, and character variables. For example, if the variables q, t, and k are to be real variables in a program and the variables n and b are to be integer variables, then the following lines contain the necessary declarations.[5]

```
real :: q, t, k
integer :: n, b
```

Variables may be declared to have a particular kind parameter by putting kind = followed by the kind parameter value in parentheses after the keyword representing the data type. For example, if more significant digits are needed than your system keeps in the

---

5. Fortran 77 programmers will note the new syntax for type declarations. Older forms of type declarations (see Chapter 10) are accepted by Fortran compilers, but it is good programming practice to use the new forms in all new programs.

default real type and the kind parameter for extra precision is 2, the variables dpq, x, and long may be declared to be extra precision reals by the following declaration.

```
real (kind = 2) :: dpq, x, long
```

In the case of character variables, the keyword character should be followed by len = and an integer indicating the number of characters in the character string in parentheses after the keyword character. If the character variable is to have a kind parameter other than the default, that too can be specified inside the same parentheses. If the variable name is to be a string of 20 characters, it may be declared as follows.

```
character (len = 20) :: name
```

If, in addition, the variable name is to be of kind kanji, assumed to be the name of an integer constant, the declaration might be

```
character (len = 20, kind = kanji) :: name
```

Style Note: As a matter of good programming practice, every variable that is used in a Fortran program should be listed in a type declaration.

It is possible to give a variable an **initial value** when it is declared. For example the variable count may be declared to be type integer and set to 0 by the statement[6]

```
integer :: count = 0
```

and the variables a, b, and c may be declared type real and set initially to the values 1.1, 2.2, and 3.3, respectively, by the statement

```
real :: a = 1.1, b = 2.2, c = 3.3
```

The value of a variable initialized in this way may be changed during execution of the program.[7]

----

6. In Fortran 77, data initialization was done with a separate data statement (Section 10.2.4).

7. If a variable is given an initial value in a subroutine or function, its value is saved between executions of the subprogram and not reinitialized.

1.3.2 Implicit Typing

In its earliest days, the Fortran language did not have type declarations. Instead, variables were assigned a type by **implicit typing** based on the first letter of their names. Only real and integer variables were permitted. Variables whose names started with the letters I–N were type integer. All other variables were type real. Although it is now common practice to declare all variables, those that accidentally or intentionally remain undeclared are still assigned the default types based on the first letter of the variable name. Implicit typing can be turned off with the statement

    implicit none

With implicit typing turned off, misspelled or mistyped variable names are detected and flagged as errors (undeclared variables); with implicit typing on, they are accepted as new implicitly declared variables, but usually have unexpected values or types.

Style Note: Every program and procedure should contain the

    implicit none

statement to turn off implicit typing. *Note:* it is acceptable to break this style rule in very short programs.

1.3.3 Supplying Input Data

The two input values 84 and 13 for the variables x and y, shown in the sample execution of the program add_2, did not appear in the computer by magic. They were typed in by the user. To run the program, it is assumed that there is a command "run" that compiles and runs a Fortran program, reading input from a file whose name is the same as the program, but with the characters "_in" appended. Thus, the command

    run add_2

compiles and runs the program add_2 and reads the input data from the file add_2_in. For the Fortran system used to run this execution of add_2, an input file named add_2_in must be prepared. The file contains the two lines

84
13

1.3.4 File Names

The rules for naming files are determined by the operating system, not by the Fortran language. It is usually possible to create a command file run that follows the file naming conventions of this book; however, local traditions vary. For example, Fortran 90 program files often have names ending with the characters ".f90" and the Fortran 90 compiler is often named "f90". In such a case, a run script on a Unix system could consist of the following two lines.

```
f90 -o $1 $1.f90
$1 < $1_in > $1_out
```

In Unix, $1 stands for the first word on the command line after the script name run, that is, the program name, add_2. Substituting add_2 for $1, the first line directs the operating system to apply the compiler f90 to the program file add_2.f90 and place the executable output (-o $1) in the file add_2. The second line directs the operating system to execute add_2 ($1) using input ($1< _in) from the file add_2_in and placing output (> $1_out) in the file add_2_out.

1.3.5 Echo of Input Data

In Fortran, as well as most other programming languages, it is good programming practice for the user to provide an **echo of the input data** using print statements, so that the output contains a record of the values used in the computation. Each read statement in the program add_2 is followed by an echo of the input data just read.

> *Style Note:* It is good programming practice to echo all input data. However, it will be impractical to follow this rule in some cases, such as when there is a large amount of input data.

1.3.6 Rerunning a Program with Different Data

The program add_2 contains echoes, whose importance is demonstrated when the program is rerun using different input data. The echoes of input data help identify which answer goes with which problem. Other important uses of input echoes will appear later. In showing another sample run of the program add_2, this time adding two different numbers, we don't repeat the program listing. The program does not change; only the input data change. This time, the data file add_2_in had the following two lines.

```
4
7
```

The execution output might look like

```
run add_2

   Input data  x: 4
   Input data  y: 7
   x + y = 11
```

The final print statement of add_2 refers to the variables x and y. As the execution output for the two sample runs shows, what actually is printed is the value of the character string constant "x + y = " followed by the value of the expression x + y at the moment the print statement is executed.

The program add_2_reals is obtained from the program add_2 simply by changing the keyword integer in the variable declaration to the keyword real, which causes the type of the variables x and y to be real. The program add_2_reals can be used to add two quantities that are not necessarily whole numbers. This execution of the program also illustrates that the input data values may be negative. The input file add_2_reals_in for this sample execution contains two lines

```
97.6
-12.9
```

The program file contains the following lines:

```
program add_2_reals
   implicit none
   real :: x, y
   read *, x
   print *, "Input data  x:", x
   read *, y
   print *, "Input data  y:", y
   print *, "x + y =", x + y
end program add_2_reals
```

and the run command creates an output file add_2_reals_out.

```
run add_2_reals
```

```
Input data  x:   97.5999985
Input data  y: -12.8999996
x + y =   84.6999969
```

Some Fortran systems habitually print real quantities in exponential format. On such a system, the sample execution will more closely resemble the following:

```
run add_2_reals
```

```
Input data  x:   0.975999985E+02
Input data  y: -0.128999996E+02
x + y =   0.846999969E+02
```

We assume that the reader will become familiar with how to prepare and edit program and input files and how to view output files on their local computer system. Details and naming conventions vary, and although it is possible to create run scripts duplicating the examples in this book, local traditions may dictate otherwise.

1.3.7 Reading Several Values

The read statement may be used to obtain values for several variables at a time, as shown in the program average, that calculates the average of any four numbers. The four numbers to be averaged are supplied as data, rather than appearing as constants in the program. This permits the same program to be used to average different sets of four numbers.

```
program average
   implicit none
   real :: a, b, c, d
   read *, a, b, c, d
   print *, "Input data  a:", a
   print *, "            b:", b
   print *, "            c:", c
   print *, "            d:", d
   print *, "Average =", (a + b + c + d) / 4
end program average
```

The input data file in the sample execution has one line:

```
58.5 60 61.3 57
```

When we run the program average using this data file, the following
output is produced.

```
run average

Input data  a:   58.5000000
            b:   60.0000000
            c:   61.2999992
            d:   57.0000000
Average  =  59.2000008
```

This program does a computation more complicated than any discussed so far, but the meaning of the program should be obvious.

As shown in the sample execution, the data are supplied to the
variables in the order they are listed in the read statement. Note that
the four variables in the read statement are separated by commas and
that there is a comma between the asterisk and the first variable in
the input list. Although it is not required in Fortran, it is often desirable to put all input data for a read statement on one line in the
input file, creating a correspondence between read statements and
data lines. However, the input data file

```
58.5
60
61.3
57
```

also would have produced the same execution output.

Execution of each read *statement normally reads data from a new line
in the input file.* Thus, if four separate read statements were to be
used to read the variables a, b, c, and d, the four input values must be
on four separate data lines in the input file.

1.3.8 Default Input Format

The asterisk in the read statement indicates that the format of the
input data is left to the preparer of the input file, except that the
individual values must be separated by at least one blank character or
a comma.

> *Style Note:* Whenever possible, use the default input format.
> It makes preparation of data much easier and less prone to
> error.

1.3.9 Rules for Names

x and y are **names** of variables used in the program with the name add_2; the variable names a, b, c, and d are used in the program with name average. The following are the rules for names of variables as well as most other kinds of things with names in a Fortran program:

1. The first character of the name must be a letter.

2. The remaining characters may be any mixture of letters, digits, or underscore characters (_).

3. There may be at most 31 characters in a name.

These rules allow ordinary names like lisa, pamela, and julie to be used as names. They also allow ordinary English words like sum and area and more technical-looking names like x3j3 and wg5 to be used as names. The underscore allows longer names to be more readable, as in distance_to_the_moon, vowel_count, and number_of_vowels_in_the_text.

All names in Fortran, including names of programs, follow the these rules.

1.3.10 Parameters/Named Constants

The program meters_to_inches that converts a length in meters to the equivalent length in inches illustrates the use of a **parameter**, which is a **named constant**. Parameters are declared much like variables, except that the keyword parameter is added after the type and the value of the parameter follows the name of the parameter and an equals sign (=). Parameter names are subject to the same rules as variable names. For example,

    real, parameter :: pi = 3.14159

declares pi to be a real parameter with the value 3.14159.

The value of a parameter is fixed by its declaration and cannot change during execution. On the other hand, if the keyword parameter is omitted, the objects being declared become variables and their values can be changed at any time, even if they are given an initial value. Thus,

    integer :: count = 0

declares count to be an integer variable with the initial value 0.

A parameter name may be used any place in a Fortran program the corresponding constant may be used; this is why it is also called a named constant.

Style Note: It is good programming practice to declare quantities to be parameters whenever possible. Assigning a constant value to a parameter rather than a variable tells the reader of the program that the value corresponding to that name will never change when the program is running. It also allows the computer to provide a diagnostic message if the programmer inadvertently tries to change its value.

Since parameters are named constants, use of a parameter name instead of the corresponding constant makes a program more readable. It is easy to forget what role an unnamed constant plays in a program.

Perhaps the most important reason for using a parameter declaration is that the program can be modified very easily if the particular value represented by the parameter name needs to be changed. The programmer can then be sure that the constant will be correct whenever it is used throughout the program.

```
program meters_to_inches
! Converts length in meters to length in inches

    implicit none
    real :: meters
    real, parameter :: inches_per_meter = 39.37

    read *, meters
    print *, meters, "meters =", &
        meters * inches_per_meter, "inches."
end program meters_to_inches

run meters_to_inches

    2.0000000 meters =  78.7399979 inches.
```

The ampersand indicates that a Fortran statement is continued on the next line; it is explained in Section 1.4.1.

1.3.11 Reading and Writing Character Strings

Since computers can process character data as well as numeric information, computer languages provide for the reading and printing of character strings. The somewhat facetious program who shows how this is done in Fortran.

```
program who
   implicit none
   character (len = 20) :: whats_his_name

   print *, "Do I remember whatshisname?"
   read *, whats_his_name
   print *, "Of course, I remember ", whats_his_name
end program who

run who

Do I remember whatshisname?
Of course, I remember Roger Kaputnik
```

When the default input format, indicated by the asterisk, is used to read a character string, it is best to enclose the string in quotes or apostrophes, the same as a character constant used within a program. Neither delimiting quotes nor apostrophes appear in the printed output when using the default output format unless the delim= specifier indicates otherwise (Section 9.4.3). The input file for the execution of the program who shown above consists of one line.

```
"Roger Kaputnik"
```

1.3.12 Input Data from a Terminal

We close this section with a version of the program meters_to_inches designed to be run on a Fortran system in which input data is supplied for the read statements by typing the data at a computer terminal *during* the execution of the program. This is called **interactive input.**[8] The only change we make to the Fortran program is to add a print statement prompting the user about what data to type. This **input prompt** immediately precedes the read statement.

```
program meters_to_inches
! Converts length in meters to length in inches.
! The length in meters is typed
! when prompted during execution.
```

---

8. For interactive execution, the run script is modified to specify input from the standard input device (usually the keyboard) and output to the standard output device (usually the screen).

```
      implicit none
      real :: meters
      real, parameter :: inches_per_meter = 39.37

      print *, "Enter a length in meters."
      read *, meters
      print *, meters, "meters =", &
         meters * inches_per_meter, "inches."
   end program meters_to_inches
```

```
run meters_to_inches
```

```
 Enter a length in meters.
   2.0000000 meters =  78.7399979 inches.
```

On most systems, the characters typed at the keyboard also appear on the screen.

1.3.13 Exercises

1. Which of the following are valid names for variables?

   ```
   name      address   phone_#     phoney     real
   iou       iou_2     4gotten     packet     _laurie
   ```

2. The program inches_to_feet is similar to the program meters_to_inches described in this section. What output is produced when inches_to_feet is run using 110 inches as the input value?

   ```
   program inches_to_feet
      implicit none
      real :: inches
   !  there are 12 inches per foot
      real, parameter :: inches_per_foot = 12.0

      read *, inches
      print *, inches, "inches =",  &
            inches / inches_per_foot, "feet."
   end program inches_to_feet
   ```

3. In the program rhyme, both jack and jill are parameters. What does a computer print when this program is run?

```
program rhyme
   implicit none
   integer, parameter :: jack = 1, jill = 2
   print *, jack + jill, "went up the hill."
end program rhyme
```

4. Write a program that reads in a first name, a middle initial, and a last name as the values of three different character variables and prints out the full name.

1.4 The Form of a Fortran Program

A Fortran program consists of a sequence of statements; these statements are written on lines that may contain from 0 to 132 characters.

1.4.1 Continued Statements

Often there is one Fortran statement on one line, but a statement can be continued onto more lines if the last character of the line to be continued is an ampersand (&).

```
print *,  &
       "I hope this is the right answer."
```

A statement may not have more than 40 lines.

If the first nonblank character on the continued line is also an ampersand, the leading blanks are ignored. This permits a long characters string to be split across more than one line, for example.

```
print *,  &
       "This is a line that contains a really, really, &
       &really, really, long answer."
```

This even allows names and other types of constants to be split across lines, but this is almost never necessary and not recommended. A character string can also be split using the concatenation operator as illustrated in examples in Section 5.2.1.

1.4.2 Multiple Statements Per Line

Conversely, more than one statement can occur on a line, provided the statements are separated by a semicolon (;).

```
a = 0; b = 0
```

The important fact is that, in the absence of a continuation symbol, the end of a line marks the end of a statement.[9]

Each Fortran statement except the assignment statement (and the statement function statement discussed in Chapter 10) begins with a **keyword**, such as `print`, that identifies the kind of statement it is.

1.4.3 Significant Blank Characters

Blank characters are significant in a Fortran program.[10] In general, they must not occur within things that normally would not be typed with blanks in English text, such as names and numbers. On the other hand, they must be used between two things that look like "words". An example is that in the first line of a program the keyword `program` and the name of the program must be separated by one or more blanks, as in the example

```
program add_2
```

Keywords and names such as `print` and `number` must contain no blank characters, except that keywords that consist of more than one English word may contain blanks between the words, as in the Fortran statement

```
    end do
```

Two or more consecutive blanks are always equivalent to one blank unless they are in a character string.

On the other hand, there are places where blank characters are not significant, but can and should be used to improve the readability of the program. For example, all of the programs in this book have blanks surrounding operator symbols, such as + and -, and have a blank after each comma in an input/output list or procedure argument list.

---

9. The form of a Fortran program described here is the Fortran 90 free source form. Conversion to free source form from Fortran 77 fixed source form is described in Section 10.5.1; it is simple and recommended. Each Fortran program unit must conform entirely either to free source form or to fixed source form.

10. Significant blank characters in Fortran 90 are a big change from previous versions of Fortran in which no blanks were significant within the statement part of a program line. The old source form with fixed columns and insignificant blanks is still legal; it is described in Chapter 10. Even when using old source form, it is a good idea to use blanks to improve the readability of a Fortran program.

Style Note: Blank characters and blank lines should be used freely in a Fortran program to make it easier to read.

1.4.4 Comments

Any occurrence of the exclamation symbol (!) other than within a character string or a comment marks the beginning of a **comment**. The comment is terminated by the end of the line. All comments are ignored by the Fortran system.

Since comments are ignored, it is permissible to place a comment after the ampersand (&) continuation symbol without impairing the continuation.

```
real :: x, &    ! measured value
        xbar    ! smoothed value
```

1.4.5 The Fortran Character Set

A Fortran statement is a sequence of characters. The characters of the Fortran character set consist of the uppercase letters A to Z, the lowercase letters a to z, the digits 0 to 9, the underscore _ , and the special characters in Table 1-3,

Table 1-3 The Fortran special characters.

Character	Name of character	Character	Name of character
	Blank	:	Colon
=	Equals	!	Exclamation point
+	Plus	"	Quotation mark or quote
–	Minus	%	Percent
*	Asterisk	&	Ampersand
/	Slash	;	Semicolon
(	Left parenthesis	<	Less than
)	Right parenthesis	>	Greater than
,	Comma	?	Question mark
.	Decimal point or period	$	Currency symbol
'	Apostrophe or single quote		

The default character kind must contain all required characters of the Fortran character set and may contain additional nonprintable characters such as *tab* or *line feed* or additional printable characters, such as {, ♥, or characters from a language other than English, such as ü. These additional characters can appear in a Fortran program only within a comment or character constant.

If both uppercase and lowercase letters are supported, corresponding uppercase and lowercase letters are considered equivalent in a Fortran program except within a character constant. This means, for example, that a print statement could be written

```
PRINT *, 84 + 13  ! Uppercase letters
```

or

```
PriNt *, 84 + 13 ! Mixed uppercase and lowercase letters
```

and the effect would be the same. It is possible that some systems do not allow lowercase letters.

Two of the Fortran characters, $ and ?, have no special use, and the currency symbol need not display or print as $ in all implementations.

1.4.6 Exercise

1. What does the following program print? Its style is *not* recommended.

```
                    program &
        ugh
                    print &
          *     ,            &
                  12.0       +&
        34.6
              end
```

1.5 Some Intrinsic Functions

There are many **built-in** or **intrinsic functions** in Fortran. To use these functions, simply type the name of the function followed by the arguments to the function enclosed in parentheses. For example, abs (x) produces the absolute value of x and max (a, b, c) yields the maximum of the values of a, b, and c.

There are also some built-in subroutines, such as date_and_time and random_number. Appendix A contains a list of all the intrinsic procedures.

1.5.1 Kind Intrinsic Functions

The kind function returns the kind parameter value of its argument. For example, kind (x) is the kind parameter of the variable x. kind (0) is the default integer kind; kind (0.0) is the default real kind; kind (.false.) is the default logical kind; and kind ("a") is the default character kind.

There is an intrinsic function selected_real_kind that produces a kind value whose representation has at least a certain precision and range. For example, selected_real_kind (8, 70) will produce a kind (if there is one) that has at least 8 decimal digits of precision and allows values between -10^{70} and $+10^{70}$. This permits the programmer to select representations having required precision or range.

For the integer data type, there is an intrinsic function selected_int_kind with only one argument. For example, selected_int_kind (5) produces an integer type allowing representation of all integers between (but not necessarily including) -10^5 and $+10^5$.

1.5.2 Numeric Type Conversion Functions

There are built-in functions that convert any numeric value to each of the numeric types. These functions are named int, real, and cmplx. For example the value of int (4.7) is the integer 4, the value of real ((2.7, -4.9)) is 2.7, the real part of the complex number $2.7 - 4.9i$, and the value of cmplx (2) is $2 + 0i$. These functions are essential in some situations, such as when it is necessary to convert an integer to a real to avoid an integer division or when the type of a procedure actual argument must match the type of a dummy argument. For example, if a variable sum holds the sum of a bunch of integer test scores and it is necessary to divide by the integer variable number_of_scores to find the average, unless one or both are converted to type real, the result will be an integer, which is probably not what is desired. The expression

```
real (sum) / number_of_scores
```

will produce a real result with the fractional part of the average retained.

In other cases, explicit conversion is not required, but can improve the clarity of the program. For example, if i is an integer variable and r is a real variable, the assignment of the value of r to the variable i can be done with the statement

```
i = r
```

When this is done, any fractional part of the value of r is dropped, so that if r were 2.7, the value of i would be 2 after execution of the assignment. That this is happening can be made clearer to the reader of the program if the statement

i = int (r)

is used instead.

> *Style Note:* In a context that requires conversion from complex to integer or real or requires conversion from real to integer, use the intrinsic type conversion functions, even if they are not required.

The numeric type conversion functions also may be used to convert from one kind to another within the same data type or to specify the kind parameter of the result of conversion between data types. For example, int (x, kind = short) converts the real value x to an integer with kind parameter short and, if z is complex, the value of real (z, kind (x)) has the same kind parameter as x and has a value equal to the real part of z.

1.5.3 The logical Function

The function named logical converts from one logical kind to another. For example, if l is type logical and packed is an integer named constant, logical (l, packed) is the truth value of l represented as a logical with kind parameter packed and logical (l) is the value of l represented as a logical with default kind parameter.

1.5.4 Mathematical Functions

There are several functions that perform common mathematical computations. The following is a list of some of the most useful ones. Appendix B should be consulted for a complete list with descriptions of each of the functions. Most of them do what would be expected, but the functions max and min are a little unusual in that they may be used with an arbitrary number of arguments. The mathematical functions are

abs	cos	min
acos	cosh	modulo
aimag	exp	sin
asin	floor	sinh
atan	log	sqrt
ceiling	log10	tan
conjg	max	tanh

Some of these functions will be used in the case studies at the end of this chapter. Other intrinsic functions, such as those for array processing and character processing, will be discussed in relevant chapters.

1.5.5 Exercises

1. Write a program that prints the kind of each of the constants

    ```
    0
    0.0
    (0.0, 0.0)
    .false.
    "a"
    ```

    These are the default kinds.

2. Using the fact the `selected_real_kind` and `selected_int_kind` return a negative value when asked to produce a kind number for a precision or range not available on the system, determine all the possible kind numbers for reals and integers on your system.

1.6 Expressions and Assignment

A Fortran **expression** can be used to indicate many sorts of computations and manipulations of data values. So far we have seen simple examples of expressions as values to be printed using the print statement. We now discuss in more detail just what can appear in this list of things to be printed.

1.6.1 Primaries

The basic component of an expression is a **primary**. Primaries are combined with operations and grouped with parentheses to indicate how values are to be computed. A primary is a constant, variable, function reference (Section 3.2.2), array element (Section 4.1.2), array section (Section 4.1.6), structure component (Section 6.3.1), substring (Section 5.1.12), array constructor (Section 4.1.4), structure constructor (Section 6.3.2), or an expression enclosed in parentheses. Note that this is a recursive definition because the definition of an expression involves expressions in parentheses. Examples of primaries are

```
5.7e43_2              ! constant
number_of_bananas     ! variable
f (x, y)              ! function value
(a + 3)               ! expression enclosed in parentheses
```

Primaries can be combined using the operators discussed in Section 1.2 as well as with user-defined operators discussed in Section 7.3.4 to form more complicated expressions. Any expression can be enclosed in parentheses to form another primary. Examples of more complicated expressions are

```
-a + d * e + b ** c
x // y // "abcde"
(a + b) /= c
1a .and. 1b .eqv. .not. 1c
a + b == c * d
```

1.6.2 The Interpretation of Expressions

When more than one operation occurs in an expression, parentheses and the **precedence** of the operations determines the operands to which the operations are applied. Operations with the highest precedence are applied first to the operand or operands immediately adjacent to the operand. For example, since * has higher precedence than +, in the expression a + b * c, the multiplication is first applied to its operands b and c; then the result of this computation is used as an operand by adding it to the value of a. If the programmer intends to add a and b and multiply the result by c, parentheses must be used as in the expression (a + b) * c.

When two operators have the same precedence, they are applied left-to-right, except for exponentiation, which is applied right-to-left. Thus, the value of 9 - 4 - 3 is 5 - 3 = 2, but the value of 2 ** 3 ** 2 is $2^9 = 512$.

Table 1-4 shows the operations with the highest precedence at the top of the list and the ones with the lowest precedence at the bottom.

1.6.3 The Evaluation of Expressions

Once it is determined by use of parentheses and precedence of operations which operations are to be performed on which operands, the computer may actually evaluate the expression by doing the

Table 1-4 Operator precedence.

Operator	Precedence
User-defined unary operation	Highest
**	.
* or /	.
unary + or −	.
binary + or −	.
//	.
.eq., .ne., .lt., .le., .gt., .ge.	.
==, /=, <, <=, >, >=	.
.not.	.
.and.	.
.or.	.
.eqv. or .neqv.	.
User-defined binary operation	Lowest

computations in any order that is mathematically equivalent to the one indicated by the correct interpretation, *except that it must evaluate each subexpression within parentheses before combining it with any other value*. For example, the interpretation of the expression a + b + c indicates that a and b are to be added and the result added to c. Once this interpretation is made, it can be determined that a mathematically equivalent result will be obtained by first adding b and c and then adding this sum to a. Thus, the computer may do the computation either way. However, if the programmer writes the expression (a + b) + c, the computer must first do the computation as required by the parentheses. Note that the expression (a + b) + (c + d) can be done by first adding c and d but then the computer must add a and b and add that result to the first sum obtained. To evaluate this expression, the computer must not first add b and c or any other pair in which one operand is taken from (a + b) and the other is taken from (c + d), because doing this would violate the integrity of parentheses.

Note that integer division is an oddity in that it does not satisfy the rules of arithmetic for ordinary division. For example, (i / 2) * 2 is not equal to i if i is an odd integer. Thus, a computer may not make this substitution to optimize the evaluation of the expression.

Table 1-5 contains examples of expressions with allowable alternative forms that may be used by the computer in the evaluation of those expressions. a, b, and c represent arbitrary real or complex operands; i and j represent arbitrary integer operands; x, y, and z represent arbitrary operands of any numeric type; and 11, 12, and 13 represent arbitrary logical operands.

Table 1-5 Allowable alternative expressions.

Expression	Allowable alternative form
x + y	y + x
x * y	y * x
-x + y	y - x
x + y + z	x + (y + z)
x - y + z	x - (y - z)
x * a / z	x * (a / z)
x * y - x * z	x * (y - z)
a / b / c	a / (b * c)
a / 5.0	0.2 * a
i > j	j - i < 0
l1 .and. l2 .and. l3	l1 .and. (l2 .and. l3)
abs (I) > -1 .or. logical (l1)	.true.

Table 1-6 contains examples of expressions with forbidden alternative forms that must not be used by a computer in the evaluation of those expressions.

Table 1-6 Forbidden alternative expressions.

Expression	Nonallowable alternative form
i / 2	0.5 * i
x * i / j	x * (i / j)
(x + y) + z	(x + y + z)
i / j / a	i / (j * a)
(x + y) + z	x + (y + z)
(x * y) - (x * z)	x * (y - z)
x * (y - z)	x * y - x * z

The same sort of evaluation rules apply to the character data type; a computer needs to evaluate only as much of a character expression as is needed in the context in which it occurs. For example, the statements

```
character (len = 2) :: c1, c2, c3, cf
c1 = c2 // cf (c3)
```

do not require the function cf to be evaluated, because only the two characters making up the value of c2 are needed to determine the value of c1, because c1 contains only two characters. It is not necessary to know whether or not a function is evaluated if you simply avoid writing functions with side effects (i.e., those that print values or change variables that are not local to the function).

1.6.4 Assignment

The **assignment statement** is the most common way of giving a variable a value. An assignment statement consists of a variable, an equals sign (=), and an expression. The expression is evaluated and assigned to the variable. An example of an assignment statement is

```
x = a + 2 * sin (b)
```

Note for later that the variable on the left-hand side may be an array, an array element, an array section, a substring, or a structure component.

Complete agreement of the variable and expression type and kind is not always required. In some cases the data type or kind parameter of the expression may be converted in order to assign it to the variable. If the variable on the left-hand side is any numeric type, the expression may be any numeric type and any kind. If the variable is type character, the expression must be type character and have the same kind parameter. If the variable is type logical, the expression must be type logical but may be any kind. If the variable is a derived type (Section 6.2), that is, a user-defined type, the expression must be the same derived type.

All of these rules apply to assignment as provided by the system (intrinsic assignment); it is possible to extend the meaning of assignment to other cases as described in Section 7.3.2.

1.6.5 Exercises

1. What computer output might be expected when the following program is run?

    ```
    program calculation_2
        print *, (201 + 55) * 4 - 2 * 10
    end program calculation_2
    ```

2. The program calculation_3 uses a confusing sequence of arithmetic operations whose meaning would be clearer if written with parentheses. What computer output might be expected when it is run? Insert parentheses in the print statement in a way that does not change the value printed, but makes it easier to understand.

    ```
    program calculation_3
        print *, 343 / 7 / 7 * 2
    end program calculation_3
    ```

3. What computer output might be expected when `calculation_4` is run?

    ```
    program calculation_4
       print *, 2 * (3 * (5 - 3))
    end program calculation_4
    ```

4. What computer output might be expected when the program `power_of_2` is run?

    ```
    program power_of_2
       print *, 2 * 2 * 2 * 2 * 2 * 2 * 2 * 2 * 2 * 2
    end program power_of_2
    ```

5. Write an expression that rounds the value of the variable x to the nearest tenth.

6. When is `int (x / y)` equal to x / y for real values x and y?

7. If x and y are type integer and both are positive, the value of the intrinsic function `modulo (x, y)` is the remainder when x is divided by y. For example, `modulo (17, 5)` = 2. Rewrite the following expression using the built-in function `modulo`. Assume n is type integer with a positive value.

    n - (n / 100) * 100

8. Write an expression using the built-in function `modulo` that has the value 1 when n is odd and 0 when n is even.

9. Write an expression using the built-in function `modulo` that is true if the value of the variable n is even and is false if n is odd.

10. Write a program to compute the quantity $e^{i\pi}$. The constant π can be computed by the formula $\pi = 4 *$ `atan (1.0)` since tan $(\pi/4) = 1$. The complex constant i can be written (0, 1). The built-in function `exp (z)` is used for raising the mathematical constant e to a power. The sample output should look like

    ```
    run eipi
    ```

    ```
    The value of e to the power i*pi is ___
    ```

1.7 Introduction to Formatting

Fortran has extremely powerful, flexible, and easy-to-use capabilities for output formatting. This may seem surprising since Fortran is often considered a scientific programming language, but Fortran has always had better formatting facilities than many commercial languages. This section describes the basic formatting features that enable you to produce really good looking output, if you like. If the default formatting on your Fortran system is good enough, there is no necessity to learn formatting right away. This section appears early because some Fortran systems do not have satisfactory default formats, especially for reals. On such systems, the techniques of this section are essential.

1.7.1 Roundoff

Just as 1/3 cannot be represented exactly as a decimal, though .333333 comes very close, 1/10 and 1/100 cannot be represented exactly when the representation uses a number base two instead of ten. The base two or **binary system** of notation is used internally in most computers for storage and calculation of numeric values. As a result, when reals are converted from input represented in decimal notation to the computer's internal representation and back again during execution of a program, the original numbers may not be recovered precisely.

Perhaps you have already seen this in your own output, in the form of a tell-tale sequence of 9s in the last decimal digits printed. For example, using the program add_2_reals in Section 1.3.6 to add 97.6 and −12.9, the following output resulted.

```
run add_2_reals

Input data  x:  97.5999985
Input data  y: -12.8999996
x + y =  84.6999969
```

The value of the variable x prints as 97.5999985 although the value supplied in the input file is 97.6. The difference between the intended and calculated values is **roundoff** or **roundoff error**. It is normally of no consequence in practical calculations because it is virtually impossible to distinguish between such nearly equal values as 97.5999985 and 97.6.

Similarly, the printed value of the variable y is −12.8999996 instead of −12.9. The printed value of x + y is 84.6999969 differing by 0.000031 from the sum of the intended values, a hint to the expert that the computer being used probably does not use decimal arithmetic for its internal calculations.

Minor cases of roundoff are hidden easily by rounding values before printing. For example, if the unexpected echoes of input data above are rounded to four decimal places before printing, the results will appear precisely as expected: 97.6000 + (– 12.9000) = 84.7000.

Depending in large measure on whether the default format for reals rounds answers to fewer decimal places than are actually calculated, you rarely see any trace of roundoff on many computer systems. These extra guard digits may actually contain roundoff, but rounding answers before printing guarantees that the user will not see small roundoff errors. We mention roundoff at this point to forewarn the beginner whose Fortran system shows such behavior in output. Roundoff is not a malfunction of the computer's hardware, but a fact of life of finite precision arithmetic on computers.

In the remainder of this section we introduce the simplest forms of user-specified print formatting, including the facility for rounding real values to a specified number of decimal places before printing.

1.7.2 Format Specifications

Extremely flexible and versatile control over the appearance of printed output is available in Fortran if you are willing to forego the convenience of the default format. In place of the asterisk denoting the default format, you write a format specification or some alternative means of locating a format specification in the program. A **format specification** is basically a list of **edit descriptors**, separated by commas and enclosed in parentheses. An example is

```
(f5.1, a, i4)
```

For each expression to be printed, one of the edit descriptors in the format specification is used to determine the form of the output. For example if $x = 6.3$ is type real and $n = -26$ is type integer, then

```
print "(f5.1, a, i4)", x, " and ", n
```

would produce the output line

```
  6.3 and  -26
```

This example shows the three most frequently used edit descriptors, f (floating point) for printing of reals, a (alphanumeric) for character strings, and i (integer) for integers. The edit descriptor f5.1 means that a total of five positions are reserved for printing a real value rounded to one place after the decimal point. The decimal point occupies a position and a minus sign, if needed, occupies another position, so the largest number printable in f5.1 format is 999.9 and −99.9 is the smallest.[11] i4 editing reserves four positions for printing an integer. The minus sign takes up one of the four positions. The a edit descriptor reserves space for character output. The actual length of the character constant to be printed or the declared length of the character variable determine how many positions are used. It is also possible to reserve a specific number of positions for a character string. The edit descriptor a10, for example, reserves 10 positions, regardless of the data to be printed. See Section 9.8.13 for details.

1.7.3 Placement of Format Specifications

In the preceding example, the format specification is in the form of a character constant. Now the necessity of the comma after the asterisk or other format specifier in the print statement becomes apparent. It is the means of separating the format specifier from the first item in the list of expressions to be printed.

Since the format is a character expression, in the simplest case it is simply a character constant that appears in the input/output statement. For example, the following two sets of statements would produce the same output. It is assumed that x is real, n is integer, and fmt is character.[12]

```
print "(f5.1, a, i4)", x, " and ", n

fmt = "(f5.1, a, i4)"
print fmt, x, " and ", n
```

1.7.4 Tab and Line Feed Edit Descriptors

The slash (/) edit descriptor starts a new line in the printed output. Thus, a single print statement can produce several lines of output. For example

```
print "(a, /, a, /, a)", "These character strings", &
      "all appear", "on separate lines."
```

produces the three lines of output

---

11. If the number to be printed is outside these bounds, the specified field will be filled with asterisks.

12. It is also possible to give a format in the format statement, but this method is somewhat old fashioned and requires a label, and so is described in Chapter 10 with the redundant features.

```
These character strings
all appear
on separate lines
```

Commas may be omitted around slash edit descriptors.

The t (tab) edit descriptor is used to skip to a specified position of the output line for precise control over the appearance of the output. Tabs may be either forward or backward on the current line. For example,

```
print "(t30, i5, t50, i5, t10, i5)", a, b, c
```

will print the integer values of c in positions 10-14, a in positions 30-34, and b in positions 50-54. Some printing devices do not print position 1 of any output line. Instead, the character appearing in position 1 is used to control single and double spacing, overprinting, and skips to the top of a new page. If you have such a printer on your system, a t2 edit descriptor will skip to position 2 to get single spacing, or a t1 edit descriptor will skip to position 1 to use one of the line feed codes described in Section 9.1.5.

1.7.5 Repeated Edit Descriptors

If one or more edit descriptors are to be repeated, they may be enclosed in parentheses and preceded by the positive integer representing the number of repetitions.

```
3(i4) is equivalent to 3i4 or i4,i4,i4
5(/) is equivalent to /,/,/,/,/ or /////
2(a4,/,t2) is equivalent to a4,/,t2,a4,/,t2
```

The parentheses may be omitted if there is only one a, e, f, or i edit descriptor inside the parentheses. The e edit descriptor is used for printing reals in exponential notation. For example, the e10.3 descriptor uses 10 positions and prints the mantissa rounded to three decimal places. For more details, see Section 9.8.8.

1.7.6 Examples of Formatted Output

The following examples illustrate how formatted output works. If these lines are printed on many printers, the first character may not appear, but may affect the vertical spacing as described in Section 9.1.5.

```
print "(3i2)", 2, 3, 4

 2 3 4
```

```
x = 7.346e-9
print "(a, e10.3)", " The answer is ", x

The answer is  0.735E-08
```

```
q1 = 5.6
q2 = 5.73
q3 = 5.79
f123 = "(a, 3(/, t2, a, i1, a, f3.1))"
print f123, " Here come the answers--", &
           " q", 1, "=", q1, &
           " q", 2, "=", q2, &
           " q", 3, "=", q3

Here come the answers--
 q1=5.6
 q2=5.7
 q3=5.8
```

1.7.7 Formatted Input

A format specification can be used with the read statement to indicate how the positions of the input line are to be interpreted. Formatted input is not as essential as formatted output because most
natural arrangements of input data are accepted by the default read
formats. However, there are two major exceptions, which sometimes
make the use of input formatting desirable. First, default formats for
character input usually require quotes or apostrophes around the
input strings; character input read under an a edit descriptor does
not. Second, it is a small convenience not to have to separate numbers with commas or blanks when large amounts of data are read by
a program. For example, it is much harder to type 10 one-digit integers on a line of input with separating commas than without them.
Rather than discuss the rules in detail for using formatted input, one
example is given.

```
real :: x1, x2, x3
integer :: j1, j2, j3
character (len = 4) :: c
read "(a, 3 (f2.1, i1))", c, x1, j1, x2, j2, x3, j3
```

If the input line is

1234567890123

then executing the read statement is equivalent to executing the following assignment statements. Notice that quotes or apostrophes for
a format input data must be omitted and that decimal points for f
format input data are assumed when they are omitted.

```
c = "1234"
x1 = 5.6
j1 = 7
x2 = 8.9
j2 = 0
x3 = 1.2
j3 = 3
```

Style Note: It is good programming practice to use the
default read format whenever possible. Explicit input format specifications demand strict adherence to specified
positions for each value in the input data. The slightest
misalignment of the input data usually results in incorrect
values assigned to the variables. By comparison, the
default input format is usually relatively tolerant of varia-
tions in alignment and is user-friendly.

1.7.8 Exercises

1. If the variable x has value 2.5, what does the output for the following statement look like? Show blank positions with a "b".

   ```
   print "(f6.3, e11.1)", x, x ** 2
   ```

2. What are the largest and smallest values that can be printed by
   the statement

   ```
   print "(f8.3)", value
   ```

3.   What does the following statement print? Use "*b*" for blank positions.

```
print "(a, f9.5, a)", "!", 1.0/3.0, "!"
```

1.8 Case Studies: Quadratic Formula

A quadratic equation is an equation involving the square of the unknown x and no higher powers of x. Algorithms for solution of quadratic equations equivalent to the quadratic formula are found in Old Babylonian texts dating to 1700 B.C. It is now routinely taught in high school algebra. In this section, we show how to write a Fortran program to evaluate and print the roots of a quadratic equation. We also discuss improving the efficiency of the calculation by isolating common subexpressions. There are better ways to solve a quadratic equation, particularly in cases where roundoff might be a problem. Also the programs in this section do not handle the case when a, the coefficient of the x^2 term, is zero.

1.8.1 The Problem

The most general quadratic equation has the form

$$ax^2 + bx + c = 0$$

where a, b, and c are constants and x is the unknown. The quadratic formula says that the roots of the quadratic equation, that is, the values of x for which the equation is true, are given by the formula

$$x = \frac{-b \pm \sqrt{b^2 - 4ac}}{2a}$$

This means that one root is obtained by adding the square root term and the other root is obtained by subtracting the square root term.

The problem is to write a program that reads as input the three coefficients, a, b, and c, and prints as output the values of the two roots. Since there is very little input, and we wish to discuss the answers as they are computed, we write the program for interactive execution with input from a terminal keyboard and output to the display screen or printing element.

1.8.2 The Solution

Experienced programmers may regard the following pseudocode solution as obvious, as indeed it is, but the three steps of the pseudocode solution must be thought, if not necessarily written down.

```
Read the coefficients a, b, and c
Calculate the two roots by the quadratic formula
Print the two roots
```

It is but a small step to the Fortran program that implements the pseudocode solution.

```
program quadratic_equation_solver
!  Calculates and prints the roots
!  of a quadratic equation

!  Variables:
!     a, b, c: coefficients
!     x1, x2: roots

   implicit none
   real :: a, b, c, x1, x2

!  Read the coefficients
   print *, "enter a, the coefficient of x ** 2"
   read *, a
   print *, "enter b, the coefficient of x"
   read *, b
   print *, "enter c, the constant term"
   read *, c

!  Calculate the roots by the quadratic formula
   x1 = (-b + sqrt (b ** 2 - 4 * a * c)) / (2 * a)
   x2 = (-b - sqrt (b ** 2 - 4 * a * c)) / (2 * a)

!  Print the roots
   print *, "The roots are"
   print *, "x1 =", x1
   print *, "x2 =", x2
end program quadratic_equation_solver
```

In the input section, each read statement is preceded by an input prompt, that is, a print statement telling the user at the computer terminal what input is expected. In the calculation section, the quadratic formula illustrates the use of the intrinsic function sqrt.

1.8.3 Program Testing

To test the program quadratic_equation_solver, we made up several quadratic equations with known roots. Since all variables are type real, our first test case has simple real roots. The solutions of the quadratic equation

$$x^2 - 5x + 6 = 0$$

are 2 and 3.

```
run quadratic_equation_solver

 Enter a, the coefficient of x ** 2
1
 Enter b, the coefficient of x
-5
 Enter c, the constant term
6
 The roots are
 x1 =    3.0000000
 x2 =    2.0000000
```

The next quadratic equation has negative and fractional roots to test whether the program will work in these cases. The solutions of the quadratic equation

$$4x^2 + 8x - 21 = 0$$

are −3.5 and 1.5, testing both possibilities.

```
run quadratic_equation_solver

 Enter a, the coefficient of x ** 2
4
 Enter b, the coefficient of x
8
 Enter c, the constant term
-21
```

```
The roots are
x1 =    1.5000000
x2 =   -3.5000000
```

Notice that x1 is always the greater of the two roots because its formula adds the square root term.

The next case tests irrational roots of the quadratic equation. The golden ratio is a ratio famous from Greek mathematics. Renaissance artists thought that the golden ratio was the most pleasing ratio for the sides of a rectangular painting or the facade of a building. The spiral shells of snails and the arrangement of seeds in a sunflower are related to it. The golden ratio also is the limit of the ratio of successive terms of the Fibonacci sequence. The two roots of the following equation are the golden ratio and the negative of its reciprocal.

$$x^2 - x - 1 = 0$$

```
run quadratic_equation_solver

 Enter a, the coefficient of x ** 2
1
 Enter b, the coefficient of x
-1
 Enter c, the constant term
-1
 The roots are
 x1 =    1.6180340
 x2 =   -0.6180340
```

The exact solutions are $(1 + \sqrt{5}) / 2$ and $(1 - \sqrt{5}) / 2$, which check with the output of the program using a hand calculator. The golden ratio has many interesting properties, including the fact that $1 / 1.6180339 = .6180339$.

The quadratic equation

$$x^2 - 6x + 9 = 0$$

has only one solution, $x = 3$. You might wonder what a program designed to find two roots will do with this equation.

```
run quadratic_equation_solver

 Enter a, the coefficient of x ** 2
1
 Enter b, the coefficient of x
-6
 Enter c, the constant term
9
 The roots are
 x1 =    3.0000000
 x2 =    3.0000000
```

Mathematicians call the solution of this quadratic equation a *double root*. For this equation, the quantity $b^2 - 4ac$ is zero, so it doesn't matter whether its square root is added or subtracted in the calculation of a root. The answer is the same for both roots.

Next we try the equation

$$x^2 - 1000001\,x + 1 = 0$$

Running the program produces the results

```
run quadratic_equation_solver

 Enter a, the coefficient of x ** 2
1
 Enter b, the coefficient of x
-1000001
 Enter c, the constant term
1
 The roots are
 x1 =    1.0000010E+06
 x2 =    0.0000000E+00
```

The smaller root is not accurate because b and $\sqrt{b^2 - 4ac}$ are nearly equal. Cancellation of the significant digits occurs during the subtraction leaving an answer severely contaminated by rounding errors. A way to cope with this situation is discussed in most introductory texts on numerical computation.

Finally, we try a test case which we know the program quadratic_equation_solver will not handle. The quadratic equation

$$x^2 + 1 = 0$$

has no real roots. Instead, the roots are

$$x = \pm\sqrt{-1}$$

$$= \pm i$$

+i and –i are complex numbers with no real part. We still try it anyway, just to see what happens.

```
run quadratic_equation_solver

 Enter a, the coefficient of x ** 2
1
 Enter b, the coefficient of x
0
 Enter c, the constant term
1
 *** Attempt to take square root of negative quantity ***
 *** Execution terminated ***
```

Since $b^2 - 4ac$ is –4, the error message is right on the money. One way to cope with this situation is discussed in Section 1.8.5.

1.8.4 Common Subexpressions

The arithmetic expressions for calculating the roots x1 and x2 both involve the same subexpression, sqrt (b ** 2 - 4 * a * c). As written, the program quadratic_equation_solver asks the computer to recalculate this subexpression as part of the calculation of x2. We can force the computer to calculate this subexpression only once by assigning it to a new intermediate variable sub_expression, and then calculating both roots in terms of the variable sub_expression.

```
program quadratic_equation_solver_2
!  Calculates and prints the roots
!  of a quadratic equation

!  Variables:
!      a, b, c: coefficients
!      sub_expression: value common to both roots
!      x1, x2: roots

   implicit none
   real :: a, b, c, x1, x2, sub_expression
```

```
!  Read the coefficients
   print *, "enter a, the coefficient of x ** 2"
   read *, a
   print *, "enter b, the coefficient of x"
   read *, b
   print *, "enter c, the constant term"
   read *, c

!  Calculate the roots by the quadratic formula
   sub_expression = sqrt (b ** 2 - 4 * a * c)
   x1 = (-b + sub_expression) / (2 * a)
   x2 = (-b - sub_expression) / (2 * a)

!  Print the roots
   print *, "The roots are"
   print *, "x1 =", x1
   print *, "x2 =", x2
end program quadratic_equation_solver_2
```

Some optimizing Fortran compilers will recognize that the program quadratic_equation_solver, in its original form, calls for the calculation of the same subexpression twice without change of any of the variables in the subexpression. Such a compiler would produce the more efficient machine language code corresponding to the second version, quadratic_equation_solver_2, even when the programmer writes the less efficient first version.

1.8.5 Complex Roots of a Quadratic Equation

The quadratic formula was used in the program quadratic_equation_solver to calculate the roots of a quadratic equation. The program worked well when the two roots were real, but it failed in the test case of a quadratic whose roots were imaginary. In that case, the quadratic formula calls for taking the square root of a negative number, a function evaluation with no real answer. In the next program, quadratic_equation_solver_3, we use complex values to compute the correct answer whether the roots of the quadratic are real or complex.

The subexpression

$$d = b^2 - 4ac$$

is called the **discriminant** because it discriminates between the cases of two real roots, a double real root, and two complex roots. If d is positive, then there is a real square root of d and the quadratic formula gives two real roots, one calculated by adding the square root of d and the other by subtracting it. If d is zero, then so is its square root. Consequently, when d is zero the quadratic formula gives only one real root, $-b/2a$.

When d is negative, on the other hand, its square root is imaginary. The complex square root of a negative number is obtained by taking the square root of its absolute value and multiplying the result by i, the basis of the complex number system. For example, if $d = -4$, then $\sqrt{d} = 2i$. Thus when d is negative, the two roots of the quadratic equation are given by the formulas

$$x_1 = \frac{-b}{2a} + \frac{\sqrt{|d|}}{2a}\, i$$

and

$$x_2 = \frac{-b}{2a} - \frac{\sqrt{|d|}}{2a}\, i$$

However, with the use of the complex data type, the formula for calculating the roots looks just like it does when the roots are real. The only thing that makes quadratic_equation_solver_3 look different from the real version is that the discriminant is converted to a complex value and all the remaining computations are done with complex values. The two sample executions show one case where the roots are complex and one case where they are both real.

```
program quadratic_equation_solver_3

!  Calculates and prints the roots
!  of a quadratic formula even if they are complex

!  Variables:  a, b, c = coefficients
!              z1, z2 = roots

    implicit none
    real :: a, b, c
    complex :: z1, z2

!  Read the coefficients
    read *, a, b, c
    print *, "Input data  a:", a
    print *, "            b:", b
    print *, "            c:", c
```

```
! Calculate the roots
  z1 = (-b + sqrt (cmplx (b**2 - 4*a*c))) / (2*a)
  z2 = (-b - sqrt (cmplx (b**2 - 4*a*c))) / (2*a)

! Print the roots
  print *, "The roots are:"
  print *, "z1 =", z1
  print *, "z2 =", z2

end program quadratic_equation_solver_3

run quadratic_equation_solver_3

Input data   a:   1.0000000
             b:   0.0000000E+00
             c:   1.0000000
The roots are:
z1 = (  0.0000000E+00,  1.0000000)
z2 = (  0.0000000E+00, -1.0000000)

run quadratic_equation_solver_3

Input data   a:   4.0000000
             b:   8.0000000
             c: -21.0000000
The roots are:
z1 = (  1.5000000,  0.0000000E+00)
z2 = ( -3.5000000,  0.0000000E+00)
```

1.8.6 Exercise

1. All of the programs in this section ignore the possibility that the value of a is zero, or is close to zero. What will happen if quadratic_equation_solver is run with input a = 0? Modify the program to handle this case. If a = 0, what happens if b is also zero? Modify the program to handle this case also. (Section 2.3 explains how to test if a = 0.)

1.9 Case Study: Debugging Pendulum Calculations

The time it takes a pendulum to complete one swing is virtually independent of the amplitude or maximum displacement of the pendulum at the height of its swing, as long as the swing is relatively small compared with the length of the pendulum. For this reason, pendulums have long been used to keep accurate time. The problem in this section is to write a program to calculate the frequency f (the number of swings per second) of a pendulum, and its period T (the time it takes to complete one swing). The input data is the length of the pendulum in meters.

The formula for the frequency of a pendulum is

$$f = \frac{1}{2\pi} \sqrt{\frac{g}{L}}$$

where g is the gravitational acceleration constant 9.80665 meters/sec² for bodies falling under the influence of gravity near the surface of the earth, L is the length of the pendulum in meters, and π is the mathematical constant 3.14159. In addition, the formula for the period T is

$$T = \frac{1}{f}$$

The solution to this problem uses everything we learned in this chapter: it has variables, input data, computational formulas, and even the built-in square root function. Nevertheless, it seems to be a straightforward calculation for which a Fortran program can be written quite easily. Here is the first attempt.

```
program pendulum
!  Calculates the frequency and period
!  of a pendulum of length L

   implicit none
   real :: L, f, T
   real, parameter :: pi = 3.14159,
                      g = 9.80665

   read *, L
   print *, "Input data L: ", L
   f = (1.0 / 2.0 * pi) sqrt (g / L)
   T = 1.0 / f
end program pendulum
```

When this program is entered into the computer, it will not compile and run. The error messages we show below are illustrative approximations of the messages we get from actual Fortran compilers. The quality and amount of useful information contained in error messages varies widely. We suggest comparing the error messages shown here with the messages your system produces for the same errors.

```
run pendulum
   *** Error -- syntax error in real statement ***
   real, parameter :: pi = 3.14159,
   *** Missing parameter assignment ***

   *** Error -- undeclared variable: g ***
   g = 9.80665

   *** Error -- syntax error in assignment statement ***
   f = (1.0 / 2.0 * pi) sqrt (g / L)
   *** Expecting operator when sqrt found ***

   *** Severe errors -- no execution ***
```

Only three syntax errors isn't too bad for a first attempt. The first error message is puzzling. What missing parameter assignment? The assignment pi = 3.14159 is right there, echoed in the error message, and the parameter assignment g = 9.80665 clearly is there in the next line. Why can't the compiler find them? The second error message is even more puzzling. g was supposed to be a parameter, not a variable, and besides, it is declared right in the line flagged by the error message. The crucial clue is before us, but as in a good detective mystery, only the practiced eye can see it. When the compiler detects an error in a real statement, it prints the offending real statement, the whole real statement, and nothing but the real statement. Looking back at the first error message, we now see that the compiler does not consider the line g = 9.80665 to be a part of this real statement. Now the problem is clear. Both error messages are related, and both are caused by the same mistake. There is no continuation character at the end of the first line of the statement declaring the parameters. It should read

```
real, parameter :: pi = 3.14159, &
                   g = 9.80665
```

The compiler sees the comma, and therefore expects another parameter assignment but, in the absence of the continuation character, it finds the end-of-statement instead; so it says that there is a missing parameter assignment. Sometimes, when a compiler gets confused, it gets very confused. It would take a very clever compiler to print the error message

```
*** Error -- missing continuation character ***
```

The third error message said that the compiler was expecting an operator such as +, -, or * when sqrt was found instead. The rule is that the asterisk for multiplication cannot be omitted in Fortran in places where a multiplication sign can be omitted in ordinary algebraic notation. We correct this assignment statement to the following.

```
f = (1.0 / 2.0 * pi) * sqrt (g / L)
```

1.9.1 The Second Compilation and Run

Since all known errors have been corrected, we rerun the program. This is what happens.

```
run pendulum
    *** Execution error -- file pendulum_in not found
    *** Severe error -- no execution ***
```

What went wrong this time? First, note that the situation is actually much improved over the first attempt. There are no syntax errors. This means that the current version is a syntactically correct Fortran program that compiled successfully and died during execution. Recalling that on this system, the file pendulum_in is the default input file associated with the program pendulum, the cause of the error message is clear. We never prepared the input file for this program.

1.9.2 Choice of Input Data for Testing

The data in the input file should consist of one number, the length of the pendulum in meters. Visualizing the size of a grandfather clock, and rounding the length of its pendulum to the nearest whole meter, we will use an input length of one meter. We now prepare an input data file with the single line

```
1
```

and run the program again.

1.9.3 The Third Compilation and Run

This time, there are no error messages.

```
run pendulum

Input data  L:    1.0000000
```

Unfortunately, there is only one line of output, and that line is the echo of the input data. At least we know that the input data was read correctly. But why didn't the computer print the answers? The reason is very simple and embarrassing. The computer didn't print the answers because we didn't provide print statements for them. It is clear to most people reading the program that we calculated values for the variables f and T for a purpose, but nothing is clear to the computer. If we include statements to print the answers, we obtain the following version of the program pendulum.

```
program pendulum
!  Calculates the frequency and period
!  of a pendulum of length L

   implicit none
   real :: L, f, T
   real, parameter :: pi = 3.14159, &
                      g = 9.80665

   read *, L
   print *, "Input data  L:", L
   f = (1.0 / 2.0 * pi) * sqrt (g / L)
   T = 1.0 / f
   print *, "The frequency of the pendulum is", &
                  f, "swings/sec."
   print *, "Each swing takes", T, "sec."
end program pendulum
```

1.9.4 The Fourth Compilation and Run

Assuming we have not introduced any syntax errors in the two new print statements, we expect the program pendulum to run, and this time, to print the correct answers. Here is what the fourth run produces.

```
run pendulum

Input data  L:    1.0000000
The frequency of the pendulum is    4.9190345 swings/sec.
Each swing takes    0.2032919 sec.
```

The program does run to completion; it prints the echo of the input data and it prints the answers, but they are wrong! The pendulum of a grandfather clock does not make almost five complete swings per second. One swing every two seconds is more like it, with each half of the swing producing a tick at one second intervals. Just because the computer prints an answer, it doesn't necessarily mean that the answer is right. The computer's arithmetic is almost certainly perfect, but the formula it was told to compute might be in error.

All the evidence seems to be pointing a finger at the assignment statement to calculate the frequency *f*:

```
f = (1.0 / 2.0 * pi) * sqrt (g / L)
```

or, if that statement is correct, at the statements that assign values to the variables and parameters that appear on the right in that statement. The assignment statement for f seems at first glance to be the Fortran equivalent of the algebraic formula for the frequency, so we shift our attention to the assignment of the parameters pi and g and the reading of the variable L. The echo of input data shows that L is correct. The parameter statement assigning pi and g seems to be correct, so we shift our attention back to the assignment statement calculating f. The error must be in this statement. If we still don't believe that it is wrong, we could print the values of pi and g just before this statement to further narrow the focus.

Remember the rule that a sequence of multiplications and divisions is executed from left to right. Thus, the assignment statement executes as though it were written

```
f = (( 1.0 / 2.0) * pi) * sqrt (g / L)
```

The correct Fortran version of the statement is

```
f = (1.0 / (2.0 * pi)) * sqrt (g / L)
```

1.9.5 The Fifth Compilation and Run

This time, the answers look correct. We expected a pendulum one meter long to swing once every two seconds.

```
run pendulum

Input data  L:   1.0000000
The frequency of the pendulum is   0.4984032 swings/sec.
Each swing takes   2.0064075 sec.
```

To check it we calculate the algebraic formulas on a hand calculator and get the same answers, and we could also try other pendulum lengths in the computer.

1.9.6 Post Mortem Discussion

The authors are really not incompetent enough to make all of the errors shown in this 14-line program, at least not in one grand *tour de force*. However, even experienced programmers will make each of these errors, one at a time or in combination, over the course of writing several dozen longer programs. Thus, it is vital for programmers not only to know how to write programs, but also to have effective strategies for debugging programs when the inevitable bugs appear. The techniques illustrated above: compiler error messages, echoes of input data, well-chosen test cases worked by hand, and diagnostic printed output will serve the programmer in good stead throughout a career.

2

Control Constructs

The programs in Chapter 1 performed simple calculations and printed the answers, but each statement in these programs was executed exactly once. Almost any useful program has the properties that some collections of statements are executed many times, and different sequences of statements are executed depending on the values of the input data.

The Fortran statements that control which statements are executed, together with the statements executed, are called **control constructs**. There are three kinds of control constructs, the **if construct**, the **case construct**, and the **do construct**. These constructs will be discussed in this chapter. The **stop** statement also is discussed briefly.

2.1 Statement Blocks

A collection of statements whose execution is controlled by one of the control constructs is called a **block**. For example, the statements between an **if** statement and the next matching **else if** statement form a block (Section 2.3). Transferring control into a block from outside is not permitted, but it is permitted to leave a block with a transfer of control, such as an `exit` or `cycle` statement. Any block may contain a complete `if`, `case`, or `do` construct, so that these constructs may be nested to any level.

Indentation of the blocks of a construct improves the readability of a program. The subordinate placement of the controlled blocks visually reinforces the fact that their execution is conditional or controlled.

> *Style Note:* The statements of each block of a construct should be indented some consistent number of spaces more than the statements that delimit the block.

2.2 Construct Names

Any `if`, `case`, or `do` construct may have a **construct name** on its first statement. It consists of an ordinary Fortran name followed by a colon. The `end if`, `end select`, or `end do` statement that ends the construct must be followed by the same construct name. This permits more complete checking that constructs are nested properly and, in the case of the `do` construct, provides a means of exiting or cycling more than one level of nested loop. In the following examples, `find_month` is a construct name. Construct names are particularly useful when there are nested constructs.

2.3 The `if` Construct and `if` Statement

The `if` construct is a simple and elegant decision construct that permits the selection of one of a number of blocks during execution of a program. The general form of an `if` construct is

```
if (logical expression) then
  block of statements
else if (logical expression) then
  block of statements
else if (logical expression) then
  block of statements
else if . . .

       .

       .

       .

else
  block of statements
end if
```

The else if and else statements and the blocks following them may be omitted. The end if statement must not be omitted. Some simple examples follow.

```
if (a == b) then
   c = a
   print *, c
end if


dice_test: if (dice <= 3 .or. dice == 12) then
   print *, "You lose!"
else if (dice == 7 .or. dice == 11) then
   print *, "You win!"
else
   print *, "You have to keep rolling until you get"
   print *, "either a 7 or a", dice
end if dice_test


!  30 days has September, April, June, and November
find_month: if (month == 9 .or. month == 4 .or. &
   month == 6 .or. month == 11) then
   number_of_days = 30
!  All the rest have 31, except February
else if (month == 1 .or. month == 3 .or. &
   month == 5 .or. month == 7 .or. &
   month == 8 .or. month == 10 .or. &
   month == 12) then
   number_of_days = 31
else if (month == 2) then
   if (leap_year) then
      number_of_days = 29
   else
      number_of_days = 28
   end if
else
   print *, month, "is not the number of a month."
end if find_month
```

The if-then statement is executed by evaluating the logical expression. If it is true, the block of statements following it is executed. Execution of this block completes the execution of the entire if construct. If the logical expression is false, the next matching else if, else, or end if statement following the block is executed. The execution of an else if statement is exactly the same; the difference is that an if statement must begin an if construct and an else if statement must not. The else and end if statements merely serve to separate blocks in an if construct; their execution has no effect.

The effect of these rules is that the logical expressions in the if statement and the else if statements are tested until one is found to be true. Then the block following the statement containing that test is executed, which completes execution of the if construct. If all of the logical conditions are false, the block following the else statement is executed, if there is one.[1]

2.3.1 Case Study: Escape Velocity of a Rocket

If a rocket or other object is projected directly upward from the surface of the earth at a velocity v, it will reach a maximum height h above the center of the earth given by the formula

$$h = \frac{R_E}{1 - v^2 / 2gR_E}$$

where R_E is the radius of the earth (6.366×10^6 m) and g is the acceleration due to gravity at the surface of the earth (9.80 m/s^2). This formula is not an unreasonable approximation, since a rocket reaches its maximum velocity within a relatively short period of time after launching, and most of the air resistance is confined to a narrow layer near the surface of the earth.

A close examination of this formula reveals that it cannot possibly hold for all velocities. For example, if the initial velocity v is such that $v^2 = 2gR_E$, then $1 - v^2/2gR_E$ is zero and the maximum height h is infinite. This velocity $v = 1.117 \times 10^4$ m/s (approximately 7 mi/s) is called the **escape velocity** of the earth. Any object, either rocket or atmospheric gas molecule, attaining this vertical velocity near the surface of the earth will leave the earth's gravitational field and not return. A particle starting at the escape velocity will continue rising to arbitrarily great heights above the earth. As it does so, it will slow to practically, but not quite, zero velocity.

At initial velocities greater than the escape velocity, the particle or rocket's velocity will not drop to zero. Instead it will escape from the earth's gravitational field with a final velocity v_{final} given by the formula

---

1. The usage of the term "block" has changed from Fortran 77. In Fortran 77 the term "if block" referred to the entire Fortran if construct from the if-then statement to the end if statement; a Fortran 90 block of statements was called a "clause" in Fortran 77.

$$v_{final} = \sqrt{v^2 - 2gR_E}$$

The original formula for the maximum height h gives negative answers in these cases and should not be used. The maximum height is infinite.

2.3.2 The Problem

We wish to write a Fortran program that reads an initial velocity of a rocket or molecule (in meters per second) and prints an appropriate description of the fate of the rocket or molecule. That is, if the rocket reaches a maximum height before falling back to earth, the maximum height should be printed. On the other hand, if the rocket escapes the earth's gravitational field, the final velocity with which it escapes should be printed.

2.3.3 The Solution In Pseudocode

From the preceding discussion, we see that the fate of the rocket or molecule can be determined by comparing the initial velocity to the escape velocity of the earth, or equivalently, by comparing v^2 to $2gR_E$. If v^2 is smaller, then a maximum height h is reached before the rocket or molecule falls back to earth. If the initial velocity is greater, then the object in question escapes with a nonzero final velocity given by the second formula. In the pseudocode solution below, the control structure is modeled exactly on the Fortran if construct.

```
Read the initial velocity v
Echo the input data
If (v² < 2gRₑ) then
    Calculate maximum height h above center of earth
    Print that the object attains maximum height h - Rₑ
        above the surface of the earth before returning
        to earth
else if (v² == 2gRₑ) then
    Print that the initial velocity is
        the escape velocity
else
    Calculate the final velocity
    Print that the object escapes earth
        with the calculated final velocity
end if
```

The if construct extends from the keyword if that begins the if construct to the keyword end if that ends the construct. The two lines of pseudocode between the keyword then and the keyword else if constitute a block. They are executed if and only if $v^2 < 2gR_E$. The line of pseudocode between the second keyword then and the keyword else is the first and only block controlled by an else if statement in this if construct. It is executed whenever $v^2 = 2gR_E$. Finally, the two lines of pseudocode between the keyword else and the keyword end if are the else block. They are executed in case none of the preceding if or else if conditions are true.

2.3.4 The Fortran Solution

Little remains to be done to refine the pseudocode solution to an executable Fortran program except to choose names for the Fortran variables and parameters that most nearly resemble the variable names in the formulas and to translate the pseudocode to Fortran nearly line by line.

```
program escape
!  Accepts as input an initial velocity v
!  Prints maximum height attained,
!      if object does not escape earth
!  Prints final escape velocity, vfinal,
!      if object escapes

!  Parameters
!    g  = acceleration of gravity near earth's surface
!              in meters / sec ** 2  (m/s**2)
!    RE = radius of the earth (in meters)

    implicit none
    real :: v, h, vfinal
    real, parameter :: g = 9.80, RE = 6.366e6

    read *, v
    print *, "Initial velocity of object =", v, "m/s"
    if (v ** 2 < 2 * g * RE) then
        h = RE / (1 - v ** 2 / (2 * g * RE))
        print *, "The object attains a height of", &
                  h - RE, "m"
        print *, "above the earth's surface " // &
                  "before returning to earth."
```

```
      else if (v ** 2 == 2 * g * RE) then
         print *, "This velocity is the escape " // &
                  "velocity of the earth."
         print *, "The object just barely escapes " // &
                  "from earth's gravity."
      else
         vfinal = sqrt (v ** 2 - 2 * g * RE)
         print *, "The object escapes with velocity", &
                  vfinal, "m/s."
      end if
end program escape

run escape

   Initial velocity of object =    1.0000000E+03 m/s
   The object attains a height of    5.1432500E+04 m
   above the earth's surface before returning to earth.

run escape

   Initial velocity of object =    2.0000000E+04 m/s
   The object escapes with velocity   1.6589949E+04 m/s.

run escape

   Initial velocity of object =    1.1170000E+04 m/s
   The object attains a height of    1.6871994E+11 m
   above the earth's surface before returning to earth.
```

2.3.5 Testing an if Construct

The goal in testing an if construct is to design test cases that exercise each alternative in the if construct. The first sample execution shows an initial velocity of 1.0×10^3 m/s (1 km/s), which is well below the escape velocity of the earth. The sample execution shows that the rocket reaches a maximum height of 5.14×10^4 m (51.4 km) before falling back to earth. Calculating the appropriate formula using a hand calculator gives the same answer.

The second sample execution shows an initial velocity of 2.0×10^4 m/s (20 km/s), which is well above the escape velocity. As expected, the printed output shows that the rocket will escape from the earth's gravitational field, so the correct block in the if construct is executed. It may seem surprising at first that the final velocity on escape is such a large fraction of the initial velocity. We rechecked it using a hand calculator and got the same answer. The explanation is that an initial velocity of nearly twice the escape velocity carries with it an initial kinetic energy (energy of motion) of nearly four times the energy of the escape velocity. So it is not really surprising that nearly three-fourths of the initial kinetic energy is retained and carried away with the rocket in the form of a large final velocity.

The third sample execution is designed to test the program using the escape velocity 1.117×10^4 m/s (11.17 km/s) as the initial velocity. Unfortunately, there is a little bit of roundoff in the calculations, and the middle block in the if construct is not executed. The printed answer is not bad. It says that the rocket will rise to a height of 1.69 $\times 10^{11}$ m above the surface of the earth before returning. Since this height is farther than the distance to either Mars or Venus at their nearest approach to earth, for all practical purposes the program has reported that the rocket will escape.

2.3.6 Roundoff Error in Tests for Equality

You must expect some roundoff in any calculation using reals. The largest source of roundoff in this problem is the fact that the physical constants, the radius of the earth and the gravitational acceleration, are given to only three or four significant digits, as is the escape velocity. Even if the physical constants were given and used to more digits, each arithmetic calculation in the computer is calculated to a fixed number of digits. If you run this program on your computer, you will probably notice that the last one or more digits of your computer's printed answers differ from the ones shown. This is to be expected. We suggest that you try initial velocities slightly larger than 1.117×10^4 m/s in an attempt to hit the escape velocity exactly on the nose. Quite likely there is no computer-representable number on your machine to use as input to cause execution of the middle alternative in the if block. *Equality tests for reals are satisfied only in special circumstances.* The best you can reasonably expect is even larger maximum heights or extremely low final escaping velocities. To avoid this test for equality, test for *approximate equality* instead. In our case, the two values v^2 and $2gR_E$ probably should be considered equal if they agree to within three significant digits because G is given to only three significant digits. This test for approximate equality can be used to replace the else if statement in the program escape.

```
else if (abs ((v**2 - 2*g*RE) / (2*g*RE)) < 1.0e-3) then
```

2.3.7 Flowchart for an if Construct

In standard flowcharting conventions, a diamond-shaped box is used to indicate a decision or fork in the flow of the program execution. A rectangular box represents processing of some sort. Using these standard conventions, the flowchart in Figure 2-1 indicates how an if construct is executed.

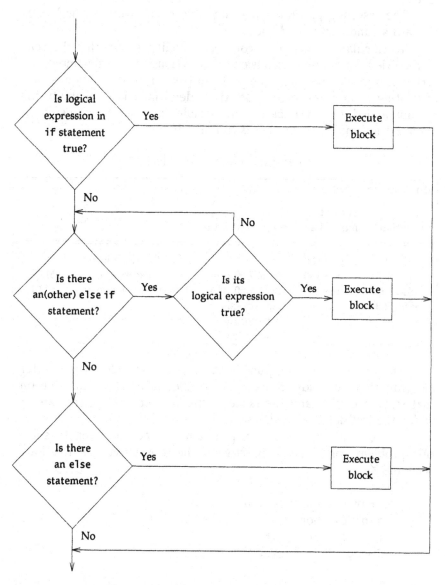

Figure 2-1 Flowchart for the if construct.

2.3.8 Case Study: Graduated Income Tax

The U.S. federal income tax is a graduated or progressive tax, which means that each income level is taxed at a different rate. After all deductions, progressively higher incomes are taxed at increasing rates. A program to calculate federal income tax uses a multi-alternative if block to select the correct tax computation formula for each income level.

The resulting program illustrates the use of some of the logical operators .and., .or., and .not.

To calculate a person's income tax liability, income for the year is modified by various exclusions, deductions, and adjustments to arrive at a taxable income. The problem treated in this section is that of writing a program to compute the federal income tax liability for an unmarried taxpayer based on taxable income. Schedule X in Table 2-1 indicates how the tax is computed.

Table 2-1 Schedule X tax table.

If taxable income is			
more than	but not more than	then income tax is	
$0	$17,850	15% of taxable income	
$17,850	$43,150	$2,677.50 plus 28% of excess over	$17,850
$43,150	$81,560	$9,761.50 plus 33% of excess over	$43,150
$81,560	. . .	Use worksheet to figure your tax.	

The input to the program is the person's taxable income, after all deductions and adjustments. The output is both the tax due on that taxable income and the person's tax bracket, that is, the rate at which the last dollar earned is taxed.

The central section of the program tax_computation to solve this problem corresponds directly to the alternatives in Tax Rate Schedule X.

```
program tax_computation
    implicit none
    real :: income, tax
    integer :: bracket
```

```
read *, income
print "(a, f15.2)", "Input data  income:", income

check_limits: &
if (income < 0) then
   print *, "Income cannot be negative."
else if (income > 81560) then
   print *, "Tax must be figured using worksheet."
else
!  Find appropriate range and compute tax
   select_range: &
   if (income==0) then
      tax = 0
      bracket = 0
   else if (income>0 .and. income<=17850) then
      tax = 0.15 * income
      bracket = 15
   else if (income>17850 .and. income<=43150) then
      tax = 2677.50 + 0.28 * (income - 17850)
      bracket = 28
   else if (income>43150 .and. income<=81560) then
      tax = 9761.50 + 0.33 * (income - 43150)
      bracket = 33
   end if select_range
!  End of tax computation section
   print "(a, f8.2, a, f8.2)", &
         "The tax on $", income, " is $", tax
   print "(a, i2, a)", "This income is in the ", &
         bracket, "% tax bracket."
end if check_limits

end program tax_computation
```

Each line in Tax Rate Schedule X corresponds to an if or else if test and a corresponding block in the tax computation if construct with construct name select_range. If income lies in the indicated range for that if test, then the variables tax and bracket are calculated by the formula in the following block. The conditions describing the ranges for income follow the form of Schedule X exactly. They guarantee that only one range and one tax computation formula applies for each possible value of income less than or equal to $81,560.

To be more specific, let us look at a few sample executions of tax_computation, in which the computer is supplied with different values as input for the variable income.

```
run tax_computation

Input data  income:          1000.00
The tax on $ 1000.00 is $   150.00
This income is in the 15% tax bracket.

run tax_computation

Input data  income:          20850.00
The tax on $20850.00 is $ 3517.50
This income is in the 28% tax bracket.

run tax_computation

Input data  income:          63150.00
The tax on $63150.00 is $16361.50
This income is in the 33% tax bracket.

run tax_computation

Input data  income:          95000.00
 Tax must be figured using worksheet.
```

Consider the second run with a taxable income of $20,850. The only condition in the tax computation section which this taxable income satisfies is

```
income > 17850 .and. income <= 43150
```

The tax is computed by the formula in the following block.

```
tax = 2677.50 + 0.28 * (income - 17850)
```

so that the tax computed is $2677.50 + .28 \times (20850 - 17850) = 2677.50 + .28 \times 3000 = 2677.50 + 840 = 3517.50$. The second assignment statement of this block assigns a tax bracket of 28 (percent) to the variable bracket. The remaining else if test in the select_range if construct is skipped. Then the two print statements that complete the else block of the if construct named check_limits are executed. Note that a complete if construct may be part of a block controlled by another if construct.

In the last of the sample executions, using a taxable income of $95,000, the condition in the else if statement of the if construct check_limits is satisfied, the variables tax and bracket are not assigned values at all, and the computer prints a statement that the tax cannot be computed using Schedule X.

Style Note: It is good programming practice to warn the user when a situation occurs that the program is not designed to handle.

2.3.9 Nonexclusive if Conditions

Because the tax computation if construct in the program tax_computation is based so closely on Tax Rate Schedule X, the alternative if and else if conditions are mutually exclusive. Just as one and only one line of Tax Rate Schedule X applies to each taxable income, one and only one condition in the tax computation if construct select_range is true (up to $81,560).

The test conditions in an if construct need not be mutually exclusive. Fortran permits more than one condition to be true. However, even if several conditions are true, only the first such condition selects its block for execution. The remaining conditions are not even tested. Executing the selected block completes execution of the entire if construct.

Using this rule for breaking ties when several conditions are satisfied, we may rewrite the inner if block of the program tax_computation with shorter test conditions.

```
!  Find appropriate range and compute tax
   select_range_2:  &
   if (income == 0) then
      tax = 0
      bracket = 0
   else if (income <= 17850) then
      tax = 0.15 * income
      bracket = 15
   else if (income <= 43150) then
      tax = 2677.50 + 0.28 * (income - 17850)
      bracket = 28
   else
      tax = 9761.50 + 0.33 * (income - 43150)
      bracket = 33
   end if select_range_2
!  End of tax computation section
```

What is to be gained by shortening the if tests? Certainly, there is less typing to enter the program. In addition, since the if tests are simpler, they will execute more rapidly. Just how much more rapidly is not clear. Not only is the correspondence between the length of the Fortran source program and the speed of execution of the compiled machine language program rather loose, but input and output operations tend to be very time consuming when compared to computational statements. Thus, it is possible that most of the execution time is spent in the read and print statements, and even a significant improvement in the speed of the if tests produces very little change in the total execution time.

What is lost? The most important thing that is lost is the closeness of the correspondence between the program and Tax Rate Schedule X. The original program tax_computation obviously implements Tax Rate Schedule X. If the if construct select_range were replaced by select_range_2, the new program also would implement Tax Rate Schedule X, but this fact would not be so obvious.

Another difference is that the second if construct is slightly more fragile or less robust. This means that although it works perfectly in its present form, it is slightly more likely to fail if it is modified at a later date. For example, if the order of the alternatives in the program tax_computation is scrambled, perhaps listed in decreasing rather than in increasing order of taxable income, the tax computation if construct select_range in tax_computation still works properly. The alternatives in the replacement if construct select_range_2 must remain in increasing order or the if construct will fail to compute taxes properly. On balance, the slight gain in efficiency and the slightly fewer keystrokes needed do not justify the less robust program.

> *Style Note:* Don't sacrifice clarity of the program to shorten the execution time by a few nanoseconds. Not only is the program harder to get right and maintain, but with a good optimizing compiler the improvement in execution time may be smaller than anticipated or even nonexistent.

2.3.10 The if Statement

There is a special form of test that is useful when there are no else if or else conditions and the action to be taken when the condition is true consists of just one statement. It is the **if statement**. The general form of an if statement is

    if (logical expression) statement

The statement to be executed when the logical expression is true must not be anything that does not make sense alone, such as an end if statement. Also, it must not be another if statement, and it may not be the first statement of a control construct.

When the if statement is executed, the logical expression is evaluated. If the result is true, the statement following the logical expression is executed; otherwise, it is not executed.

Using this form of testing has the drawback that if the program is modified in such a way that the single statement if is no longer adequate, the if statement must be changed to an if construct. If an if construct were used in the first place, the modification would consist of simply adding more statements between the if-then statement that begins the if construct and the end if statement. However, in the cases where the computation to be done when a certain condition is true consists of just one short statement, using the if statement probably makes it a little easier to read. Compare, for example

```
if (value < 0) value = 0
```

with

```
if (value < 0) then
    value = 0
end if
```

2.3.11 Exercises

1. Write an if construct that prints the word "vowel" if the value of the variable letter is a vowel (i.e., A, E, I, O, or U) and the word "consonant" if the value of letter is any other letter of the alphabet. Only uppercase letters can appear as values of letter.

2. Hand simulate the programs example_1 to example_4 using the values 45, 75, and 95 as input data (12 simulations in all). Check your answers with a computer, if possible. *Caution:* These simulations are tricky, but each program is syntactically correct. No indentation has been used in order not to give any hints about the structure of the if constructs. We suggest correctly indenting each program before hand simulating it.

```
program example_1
    integer :: x
    read *, x
```

```
            if (x > 50) then
            if (x > 90) then
            print *, x, " is very high."
            else
            print *, x, " is high."
            end if
            end if
        end program example_1

    program example_2
        integer :: x
        read *, x
        if (x > 50) then
        if (x > 90) then
        print *, x, " is very high."
        else
        end if
        print *, x, " is high."
        end if
    end program example_2

    program example_3
        integer :: x
        read *, x
        if (x > 50) then
        if (x > 90) then
        print *, x, " is very high."
        end if
        else
        print *, x, " is high."
        end if
    end program example_3

    program example_4
        integer x
        read *, x
        if (x > 50) then
        end if
        if (x > 90) then
        print *, x, " is very high."
        else
        print *, x, " is high."
        end if
    end program example_4
```

3. A toll bridge charges $3.00 for passenger cars, $4.00 for buses, $6.00 for trucks under 10,000 pounds, and $10.00 for trucks over 10,000 pounds. The problem is to write a program to compute the toll. Use interactive input if it is available. The input data consists of first the letter C, B, or T for car, bus, or truck, respectively. Either uppercase or lowercase letters are permitted. If the class is T (truck), then prompt the user for another character which is either "<" (meaning less than 10,000 pounds) or ">" (meaning greater than 10,000 pounds). The following are sample executions:

```
Enter vehicle class (C, B, or T)
t
Enter < or > to indicate weight class
<
The toll is $6.00

Enter vehicle class (C, B, or T)
c
The toll is $3.00
```

4. The Enlightened Corporation is pleased when its employees enroll in college classes. It offers them an 80 percent rebate on the first $500 of tuition, a 60 percent rebate on the second $400, and a 40 percent rebate on the next $300. The problem is to compute the amount of the rebate. The input data consists of one number, the amount of tuition paid by the employee. A sample execution might produce the following:

```
run tuition_rebate

Input data  tuition:  600
The employee's rebate is $  460
```

2.4 The case Construct

The case construct is somewhat similar to the if construct in that it permits selection of one of a number of different alternative blocks of instructions, providing a streamlined syntax for an important special case of a multiway selection. The general form of a case construct is

```
select case (expression)
  case (case selector)
    block of statements
```

```
case (case selector)
   block of statements
   .
   .
   .
case default
   block of statements
end select
```

The value of the expression in the select case statement must be a single integer, character (of any length), or logical value. The case selector in each case statement is a list of items, where each item is either a single constant or a range of the same type as the expression in the select case statement. A **range** is two constants separated by a colon and stands for all the values between and including the two values. The case default statement and its block is optional.

The case construct is executed by evaluating the expression in the select case statement. Then the expressions in the case statements are examined until one is found with a value or range that includes the value of the expression. The block of statements following this case statement is executed, completing execution of the entire case construct. No more than one case statement may match the value of the expression. If no case statement matches the value of the expression and there is a case default statement, the block following the case default statement is executed. The case default statement is optional in a case construct.

Any of the items in the list of values in the case statement may be a range of values, indicated by the lower bound and upper bound separated by a colon (:). The case expression matches this item if the value of the expression is greater than or equal to the lower bound and less than or equal to the upper bound.

A flowchart indicating how a case construct is executed appears in Figure 2-2.

Some simple examples follow.

```
select case (dice)
   case (2:3, 12)
      print *, "You lose!"
   case (7, 11)
      print *, "You win!"
   case default
      print *, "You have to keep rolling until you get"
      print *, "either a 7 or a ", dice
end select
```

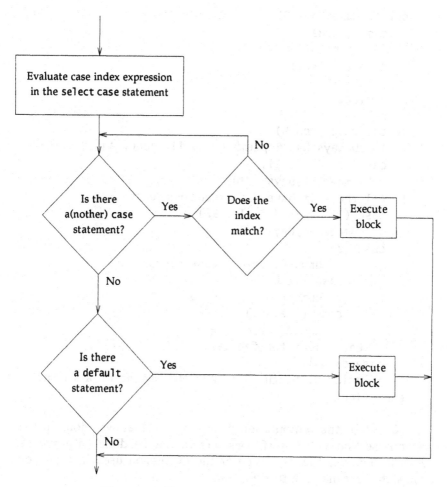

Figure 2-2 Flowchart for the case construct.

```
light: select case (traffic_light)
   case ("red")
      print *, "Stop"
   case ("yellow")
      print *, "Caution"
   case ("green")
      print *, "Go"
   case default
      print *, "Illegal value:", traffic_light
end select light
```

```
select case (b > 0)
   case (.true.)
      a = b
   case (.false.)
      a = -b
end select

select case (month)
   !  30 days has September, April, June, and November
   case (9, 4, 6, 11)
      number_of_days = 30
   !  All the rest have 31, except February
   case (1, 3, 5, 7:8, 10, 12)
      number_of_days = 31
   case (2)
      for_february: select case (leap_year)
         case (.true.)
            number_of_days = 29
         case (.false.)
            number_of_days = 28
      end select for_february
   case default
      print *, month, " is not the number of a month."
end select
```

Note that the computation of income tax that was done in the previous section with an if construct cannot be done with a case construct because the data type of the expression used in a select case statement may not be type real.

2.4.1 Exercises

1. Write a case construct that prints the word "vowel" if the value of the variable letter is a vowel (i.e., A, E, I, O, or U), prints the word "consonant" if the value of letter is any other letter of the alphabet, and prints an error message if it is any other character. Write a complete program that reads one character and uses the case construct to print the appropriate classification of the character.

2. A toll bridge charges $3.00 for passenger cars, $2.00 for buses, $6.00 for trucks under 10,000 pounds, and $10.00 for trucks over 10,000 pounds. The problem is to write a program to compute the toll using a case construct. Use interactive input if it is available. The input data consists of first the letter C, B, or T

for car, bus, or truck, respectively. Either uppercase or lower-case letters are permitted. If the class is T (truck), then prompt the user for another character which is either "<" (meaning less than 10,000 pounds) or ">" (meaning greater than 10,000 pounds). The following are sample executions:

```
Enter vehicle class (C, B, or T)
t
Enter < or > to indicate weight class
<
The toll is $6.00

Enter vehicle class (C, B, or T)
c
the toll is $3.00
```

2.5 The do Construct

All of the programs so far suffer from the defect that each instruction is executed at most once. At the enormous speed at which computers execute instructions, it would be difficult to keep a computer busy for very long using this type of program. By the simple expedient of having the computer execute some instructions more than once, perhaps a large number of times, it is possible to produce a computer program that takes longer to execute than to write. More important is the fact that a loop increases the difficulty of writing a program very little, while it greatly increases the amount of useful data processing and calculation done by the program.

The only looping construct in Fortran is the **do construct**. The general form of the do construct is

```
do loop control
   block of statements
end do
```

The block of statements, called the **loop body** or do construct body, is executed repeatedly as indicated by the loop control. Figure 2-3 shows a flowchart showing the execution of a do construct.

There are three types of loop control. In one case the loop control is missing, in which case the loop is executed until some explicit instruction in the do body such as an exit statement terminates the loop. In the second type of loop control, a variable takes on a progression of values until some limit is reached, In the third type, the loop is executed as long as a logical expression is true. After a very

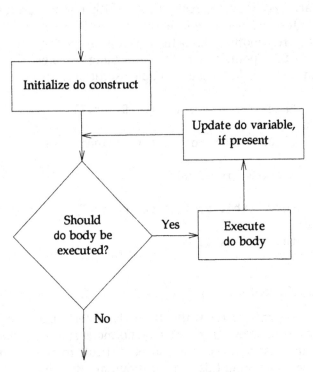

Figure 2-3 Flowchart for the do construct.

brief discussion of the exit statement and cycle statement, we will look at examples of the different types of loop control.

2.5.1 The exit Statement

The **exit statement** causes termination of execution of a loop. If the keyword exit is followed by the name of a do construct, that named loop (and all loops nested within it) is exited.

2.5.2 The cycle Statement

The **cycle statement** causes termination of the execution of *one iteration* of a loop. In other words, the do body is terminated, the do variable (if present) is updated, and control is transferred back to the beginning of the block of statements that comprise the do body. If the keyword cycle is followed by the name of a do construct, all loops nested within that named loop are exited and control is transferred back to the beginning of the block of statements that comprise the named do construct.

2.5.3 Loops with No Loop Control

For a do construct with no loop control, the block of statements between the do statement and the matching end do statement are executed repeatedly until an exit statement causes it to terminate. Suppose we wish to print out all powers of two that are less than 1000. This is done with a simple do construct with no loop control and an exit statement.

```
program some_powers_of_2

    implicit none
    integer :: power_of_2

    power_of_2 = 1   ! The zero power of 2
    print_power: do
        print *, power_of_2
        power_of_2 = 2 * power_of_2
        if (power_of_2 >= 1000) exit print_power
    end do print_power
end program some_powers_of_2
```

As another example, suppose a file contains integers, one per line. All of the integers are nonnegative, except the last integer in the file, which is negative. The following program reads the file and computes the average of the integers, treating the first negative integer it finds as a signal that there is no more data.

```
program average
!  This program finds the average of a file of
!  nonnegative integers, which occur one per line
!  in the input file.  The first negative number
!  is treated as the end of data.

    implicit none
    integer :: number, number_of_numbers, sum

    sum = 0
    number_of_numbers = 0
    do
        read *, number
        if (number < 0) exit
```

```
            print *, "Input data  number:", number
            sum = sum + number
            number_of_numbers = number_of_numbers + 1
        end do

        print *, "The average of the numbers is",  &
                real (sum)  / number_of_numbers
    end program average
```

To illustrate a simple use of the cycle statement, suppose a file of integers similar to the one used above is presented and the task is to count the number of odd numbers in the file prior to the first negative number in the file. The following program accomplishes this.

```
program odd_numbers
!   This program counts the number of odd numbers
!   in a file of nonnegative integers,
!   which occur one per line in the input file.
!   The first negative number is treated as end of data.

    implicit none
    integer :: number, number_of_odd_numbers

    number_of_odd_numbers = 0
    do
        read *, number
        print *, "Input data  number:", number
        if (number < 0) then
            exit
        else if (modulo (number, 2) == 0) then
            cycle
        else
            number_of_odd_numbers =  &
                    number_of_odd_numbers + 1
        end if
    end do

    print *, "The number of odd numbers is",  &
            number_of_odd_numbers
end program odd_numbers
```

These last two programs have a structure similar to that of the heart of many programs, both simple and complicated. In pseudocode, that structure is

```
do
    Attempt to read some data
    If all data have been processed, then exit
    Process the data
end do
```

For this kind of loop, a do construct with no loop control and an exit statement are just right.

2.5.4 Loop Control with a do Variable

Quite frequently, the successive values taken by a variable follow a simple pattern, like 1, 2, 3, 4, 5, 6, 7, 8, 9, 10, or 9, 7, 5, 3. Because these sequences occur so often in programming, there is a simple means of assigning successive values to a variable in Fortran using the do construct and variable loop control. A simple example that prints the squares and cubes of the integers 1 to 20 follows:

```
do number = 1, 20
    print *, number, number ** 2, number ** 3
end do
```

The block of this do construct consists of a single print statement. The first time the print statement is executed, the **do variable** number has the value of 1, and this number is printed as the first output line, followed by its square and its cube. Then the do variable number takes on the value 2, which is printed on the next line, followed by its square and its cube. Then the do variable takes on the values 3, 4, 5, up to 20 for successive repetitions of the print statement. At this point, the possible values for the do variable number specified in the do statement are exhausted and execution of the do construct terminates.

The general forms of loop control using a do variable are

variable = *expression*, *expression*

and

variable = *expression*, *expression*, *expression*

The three expressions specify the starting value, the stopping value, and the step size or **stride** between successive values of the do variable. The do statement in the do construct above used constants 1 and 20 for the starting and stopping values. When the step size expression is omitted, as it is in the do construct above, a step size of one is used.

The data type of a do variable must be either integer or real.

Style Note: Do not use a real do variable because of round-off error. Problems include systematic drift of successive values and the fact that one cannot always guarantee that the do block will be executed with the real do variable equal to the stopping value.

The number of times the loop is executed (unless terminated by an exit statement, for example) is given by the formula

$$\max\left(\left\lfloor\frac{m_2-m_1+m_3}{m_3}\right\rfloor, 0\right)$$

where m_1 is the starting value, m_2 is the stopping value, and m_3 is the step size. $\lfloor x\rfloor$ denotes the floor function, the greatest integer less than or equal to x.

For example, the following do loop is executed $\lfloor(10-2+2) / 2\rfloor =$ 5 times with the do variable assigned the values 2, 4, 6, 8, and 10.

```
do number = 2, 10, 2
    print *, number
end do
```

If the do statement were changed to

```
do number = 2, 11, 2
```

The do loop would be executed $\lfloor(11-2+2) / 2\rfloor = 5$ times, as before, and the values of the do variable number would be the same: 2, 4, 6, 8, and 10. The do statement

```
do number = 1, upper_limit
```

causes its do block to be executed no times if the value of the variable upper_limit is less than or equal to zero.

2.5.5 Counting Backward

If the step size is negative, the do variable counts backwards. Thus, it is possible to print the complete words to the popular camp song "Ninety-Nine Bottles of Beer on the Wall" using a do statement with a negative step size. The program beer, which tells the computer to print the verses, is given below. In the program, a print statement with no print list is used to print a blank line between verses.

```
program beer
!  Prints the words of a camp song

    implicit none
    integer :: n

    do n = 99, 1, -1
        print *
        print *, n, "bottles of beer on the wall."
        print *, n, "bottles of beer."
        print *, "If one of those bottles " // &
                "should happen to fall,"
        print *, "there'd be", n - 1,  &
                "bottles of beer on the wall."
    end do
end program beer

run beer
```

```
99 bottles of beer on the wall.
99 bottles of beer.
If one of those bottles should happen to fall,
there'd be 98 bottles of beer on the wall.

98 bottles of beer on the wall.
98 bottles of beer.
If one of those bottles should happen to fall,
there'd be 97 bottles of beer on the wall.

97 bottles of beer on the wall.
97 bottles of beer.
If one of those bottles should happen to fall,
there'd be 96 bottles of beer on the wall.
           .
           .
           .
1 bottles of beer on the wall.
1 bottles of beer.
If one of those bottles should happen to fall,
there'd be 0 bottles of beer on the wall.
```

A short name n is chosen for the do variable to make it easier to sing the program listing. The execution output shown is abbreviated after three full verses, with the last verse also given to show how the loop ends.

2.5.6 Case Study: Approximating a Definite Integral

The value of a definite integral is the area of a region of the plane bounded by the three straight lines. $x = a$, $y = 0$, $x = b$, and the curve $y = f(x)$ as shown in Figure 2-4. The better part of a semester in any calculus sequence is spent seeking analytic solutions to the area problem, that is, expressing the area by an algebraic or trigonometric expression. At the conclusion, the calculus student acquires a modest repertoire of useful functions that can be integrated in "closed form".

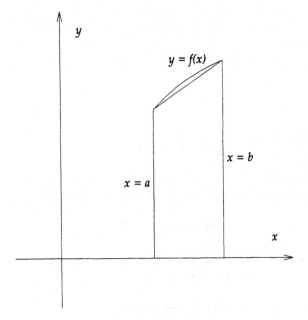

Figure 2-4 Trapezoidal approximation to the area under a curve.

It turns out to be easier to approximate the area of such regions numerically, if you have a computer available. Moreover, the numerical approximation method works even for functions that cannot be integrated in closed form. If we replace the curve $y = f(x)$ by a straight line with endpoints a and b, the region in question is converted to a trapezoid, a simple four-sided figure whose area is given by the formula

$$A = (b - a) \times \frac{f(a) + f(b)}{2}$$

Of course, the area of this trapezoid is not exactly equal to the area of the original region with curved boundary, but the smaller the width of the trapezoid, the better the approximation.

Specifically, the problem we wish to solve is to find the area of one arch of the curve $y = sin(x)$, that is, the area under this curve for x from 0 to π radians (180°) as shown in Figure 2-5. We will do it by writing a program to calculate trapezoidal approximations to the area, choosing a number of trapezoids sufficient to give the answer to three decimal places.

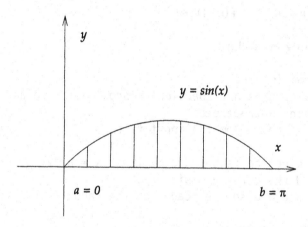

Figure 2-5 Approximating the area under the curve $y = sin(x)$.

If we call the width of each trapezoid h, we have the relationship

$$h = \frac{b - a}{n}$$

After a little algebra, the sum of the areas of the n trapezoids may be expressed by the formula

$$T_n = h \left[\frac{f(a)}{2} + f(a+h) + f(a+2h) + \cdots + f(b-h) + \frac{f(b)}{2} \right]$$

In the following program integral, the sum is formed by first computing

$$\left[\frac{f(a)}{2} + \frac{f(b)}{2}\right] = 0.5 \times [f(a) + f(b)]$$

To compute the remaining terms, it would be possible to use a real do variable x to take on the values

$$a+h,\ a+2h,\ ...,\ b-h$$

but we shall follow our style suggestion and use an integer variable i that counts 1, 2, ..., $n-1$ and compute the expression a + i * h to obtain the sequence of values

$$a+h,\ a+2h,\ ...,\ a+(n-1)h = b-h$$

The program follows.

```
program integral
!  Calculates a trapezoidal approximation to an area
!  using n trapezoids.
!  n is read from the input file.

!  The region is bounded by lines x = a, y = 0, x = b,
!  and the curve y = sin (x).
!  a and b also are read from the input file.

   implicit none
   real :: a, b, h, sum
   integer :: i, n
   intrinsic sin

   read *, n
   print *, "Input data  n:", n
   read *, a, b
   print *, "Input data  a:", a
   print *, "              b:", b

   h = (b - a) / n
!  Calculate the sum f(a)/2+f(a+h)+...+f(b-h)+f(b)/2
!  Do the first and last terms first
   sum = 0.5 * (sin (a) + sin (b))
   do i = 1, n - 1
      sum = sum + sin (a + i * h)
   end do
```

```
    print *, "Trapezoidal approximation to the area =", &
               h * sum
end program integral

run integral

Input data  n: 100
Input data  a:    0.0000000E+00
            b:    3.1415901
Trapezoidal approximation to the area =    1.9998353

run integral

Input data  n: 1000
Input data  a:    0.0000000E+00
            b:    3.1415901
Trapezoidal approximation to the area =    1.9999995
```

Since these two answers differ by only one in the fourth decimal place, we may conclude that the approximation using 100 trapezoids is sufficiently accurate for our purposes, and that the approximation using 1000 trapezoids is accurate to more than four decimal places. There is no need to rerun the program using more trapezoids to meet the limits of accuracy specified in the problem statement. The answer is 1.9999995 rounded to three decimal places to get 2.000.[2]

2.5.7 Exercises

1. Hand simulate the execution of the following statements, keeping track of the value of n and prod after the execution of each statement.

   ```
   integer :: n, prod
   prod = 1
   do n = 2, 4
      prod = prod * n
   end do
   ```

---

2. The alert reader may have noticed that the 6th and 7th decimal places in the echo of the input variable b are not the correct digits of π. The input data for b was given using five decimal places as 3.14159 and the last two places echoed represent roundoff.

2.   What output is produced by the following program?

```
program exercise
   implicit none
   integer :: m
   do m = 1, 20
      if (modulo (m, 2) /= 0) then
         print *, m
      end if
   end do
end program exercise
```

3.   What is the value of the variable sum at the conclusion of each of the following loops?

```
integer :: n, sum

sum = 0
do n = 1, 10
   sum = sum + 1
end do

sum = 0
do n = 1, 5
   sum = sum + n * n
end do

sum = 0
do n = 1, 14, 2
   sum = sum + n * n
end do

sum = 0
do n = 5, 1, -1
   sum = sum + n
end do
```

4.   An integer is a perfect square if it is the square of another integer. For example, 25 is a perfect square because it is 5 × 5. Write a program to selectively print those numbers less than 100 that are not perfect squares. Sample output for this program should look like the following.

```
run not_squares

    2
    3
    5
    6
    7
    8
    10
    .
    .
    .
    99
```

5. Read integers from input until the value zero is read. Then print the number in the file just before the zero value. Sample input data might be

```
    3
    7
    2
    10
    0
    9
    4
    0
    5
```

Sample output for this input data is

```
run last_number_before_first_zero

    Input data:  buffer  3
    Input data:  buffer  7
    Input data:  buffer  2
    Input data:  buffer  10
    Input data:  buffer  0
    The last number before the first zero is 10
```

6. Write a program that prints the smallest power of 3 that exceeds 5000.

7. In 1970, the population of New Jersey was 7,168,192 and it was increasing at the rate of 18% per decade. The area of New

Jersey is 7521 square miles. On the basis of the 18% growth rate continuing indefinitely into the future, predict the population of New Jersey every decade from 1980 on. Stop the predictions when the average number of square feet per person is less than 100. Print out all estimates. Execution of the program should produce something like the following.

```
run population_of_nj

    year      population    sq ft / person
    1980       8458466.         24789.6
    1990       9980990.         21007.3
      .            .               .
      .            .               .
      .            .               .
```

For partial confirmation of the validity of the prediction model, look up the 1980 and 1990 census data for New Jersey and compare the actual data with your program's predictions.

8. The mathematical expression

$$\left(1+\frac{1}{n}\right)^n$$

produces better and better approximations to the famous mathematical constant $e = 2.718281828459045...$ as n gets large. However, the computed result of this expression may be disappointingly inaccurate if the selected real kind does not permit many significant digits of $1/n$ to be retained in the sum $1+1/n$. Write a program to calculate the expression

$$\left(1+\frac{1}{n}\right)^n$$

for n taking on successive powers of two: 1, 2, 4, 8, 16, ... and successive powers of three: 1, 3, 9, 27, 81, ... Run this program using each of the real kinds available on your computer.

2.6 The stop Statement

The **stop statement** causes execution of a program to stop. With the use of modern control constructs, a program usually should stop by coming to the end of the program. However, there are some occasions where it is very convenient to use. For example, when print statements are inserted for debugging, it is often desirable to stop the program after a few such statements are executed or after the first few iterations of a loop are executed. Also, when severe errors are detected in the middle of a procedure that is being executed, it is much easier to execute a stop statement than exit out through what may be many layers of nested subroutine calls or function references.

3

Procedures

The original release of Fortran did not have independent procedures, but within a year, six new statements were added to the language, all having to do with subroutines and functions. Thus, as early as 1958, it was realized that large programs were extremely difficult to debug and maintain unless they could be split into independent modules. Modern programming practice has gone even further. Even relatively short programs are greatly improved when their component parts are refined as procedures.

There are two kinds of **procedures**: **functions** and **subroutines**. A function looks much like a Fortran program, except that it begins with the keyword function instead of the keyword program. Once written, a function is used just like the built-in functions discussed in Section 1.5 to compute a value that may be used in any expression. A subroutine also looks like a Fortran program or a function, except that the first line begins with the keyword subroutine. A subroutine may be used to perform any computation and is invoked by executing a call statement.

Both subroutines and functions are classified as either **internal procedures** or **module procedures**.[1] Very simply, an internal procedure is contained within a program or another procedure and a module procedure is contained in a module. Both kinds of procedures may use names of objects declared by the program or procedure that contains it. Internal procedures are treated in this chapter; module procedures are discussed in Chapter 7.

Functions and subroutines whose first statements begin with the keyword `recursive` are permitted to call themselves directly or indirectly; this technique is used to write clear and simple programs for what might otherwise be difficult programming tasks.

Style Note: Self-contained subtasks should be written as procedures.

3.1 Subroutines

Suppose the task at hand is to read in three real numbers and print them in ascending order. We will revisit this problem several times, improving the program in the process. The main steps needed to accomplish this task are: (1) read in the numbers, (2) sort them, and (3) print them. The program `sort_3` does this.

```
program sort_3

    implicit none
    real :: n1, n2, n3, temp

    ! Read the numbers
    read *, n1, n2, n3
    print *, "Input data  n1:", n1
    print *, "            n2:", n2
    print *, "            n3:", n3
```

---

1. In Fortran 77, all procedures were in a third category, **external procedures** (Section 10.4.3). As much as external procedures were an improvement over the unspeakable devices available in original Fortran, module procedures are a Fortran 90 improvement making external procedure unnecessary, except for procedures written in another programming language. It is usually very simple to convert a Fortran 77 external procedure to a module procedure, eliminating the need for all but the simplest interface blocks (Section 10.4.4) in the process.

```
! Sort the numbers
if (n1 > n2) then
    temp = n1; n1 = n2; n2 = temp
end if
if (n1 > n3) then
    temp = n1; n1 = n3; n3 = temp
end if
if (n2 > n3) then
    temp = n2; n2 = n3; n3 = temp
end if

! Print the numbers
print *, "The numbers, in ascending order, are:"
print *, n1, n2, n3

end program sort_3
```

This is not a very complicated program, but it is not immediately obvious (unless you believe the comments) that it performs the three steps described above needed to solve the problem. It would be nice to write commands that directly reflect those three steps and put the details somewhere else. This can be done with subroutines and illustrates one of the important uses of subroutines: to exhibit the overall structure of a program and put the details in another place. Here is what the program sort_3 looks like when it is rewritten using internal subroutines.

```
program sort_3

    implicit none
    real :: n1, n2, n3, temp

    call read_the_numbers
    call sort_the_numbers
    call print_the_numbers
        . . .

end program sort_3
```

This is certainly easier to understand than the first version. The ellipses (. . .) indicate that the computations that actually do the three steps are missing. These computations will each be done with a subroutine.

3.1.1 The call Statement

The **call statement** is used to indicate that the computation represented by a subroutine is to be performed. The keyword call is followed by the name of the subroutine and, often, by a list of arguments (Section 3.3) in parentheses. The program sort_3 contains
three call statements.

3.1.2 Writing a Subroutine

A subroutine is almost exactly like a program except that it begins
with the keyword subroutine and may have arguments that are written in the **subroutine statement**. The last statement of a subroutine
is the **end subroutine statement**, which contains the name of the subroutine.

The subroutine read_the_numbers consists of the subroutine
statement, the statements that read and echo the numbers, and the
end subroutine statement that terminates the internal subroutine.

```
subroutine read_the_numbers
    read *, n1, n2, n3
    print *, "Input data  n1:", n1
    print *, "            n2:", n2
    print *, "            n3:", n3
end subroutine read_the_numbers
```

It is not necessary to have an implicit none statement in the
internal subroutine because the implicit none statement in the host
program also takes effect within the subroutine. Similarly, it is not
necessary to declare the variables n1, n3, and n3 because they are
declared in the main program.

The other two subroutines are constructed in a similar way, just
copying the text from the original version of the program sort_3 and
adding the subroutine and end subroutine statements.

3.1.3 The contains Statement

When procedures are internal to a program, another procedure, or
they are in a module, they are preceded by a contains statement.[2]
The procedures must appear just before the last end statement of the
program, procedure, or module containing them. Thus, to complete
our example above, the contains statement is used and the subroutines follow.

---

2. External procedures are not preceded by a contains statement.

```
program sort_3

    implicit none
    real :: n1, n2, n3, temp

    call read_the_numbers
    call sort_the_numbers
    call print_the_numbers

contains

subroutine read_the_numbers
    read *, n1, n2, n3
    print *, "Input data  n1:", n1
    print *, "            n2:", n2
    print *, "            n3:", n3
end subroutine read_the_numbers

subroutine sort_the_numbers
    if (n1 > n2) then
       temp = n1; n1 = n2; n2 = temp
    end if
    if (n1 > n3) then
       temp = n1; n1 = n3; n3 = temp
    end if
    if (n2 > n3) then
       temp = n2; n2 = n3; n3 = temp
    end if
end subroutine sort_the_numbers

subroutine print_the_numbers
    print *, "The numbers, in ascending order, are:"
    print *, n1, n2, n3
end subroutine print_the_numbers

end program sort_3

run sort_3

 Input data  n1:    2.2000000
             n2:    7.6999998
             n3:    5.5000000
 The numbers, in ascending order, are:
   2.2000000    5.5000000    7.6999998
```

3.1.4 Subroutines with Arguments

Something that is worth noticing is that there are three lines in the subroutine sort_the_numbers, all doing the same kind of operation, namely, swapping the values of two variables if they are in the wrong order. This illustrates the second good reason to use a procedure: to write some statements once and use them many times, either within the same program or in different programs. In this case, the computation that is performed three times is represented the first time by the line containing three Fortran statements:

```
temp = n1; n1 = n2; n2 = temp
```

However, each time this swapping operation occurs in the program, different named variables are involved. This is no obstacle if a subroutine with arguments is used as illustrated by the subroutine named swap.

```
subroutine swap (a, b)
   real :: a, b, temp
   temp = a
   a = b
   b = temp
end subroutine swap
```

To call this subroutine values must be passed to it by placing them in parentheses after the name of the subroutine in the call statement. Thus, to swap the values of n1 and n2, use the statement

```
call swap (n1, n2)
```

n1 and n2 are called **arguments**. Argument passing applies to both subroutines and functions and so is described in Section 3.3.

Because the subroutine swap is used only by the other subroutine sort_the_numbers, it might seem natural to make swap internal to the subroutine sort_the_numbers. This is not permitted. Internal procedures may not be nested; that is, internal procedures may not contain other internal procedures.

swap appears to be a generally useful subroutine. If it is internal to the program sort_3 it cannot be used by other programs; however, if it is put into a module, it can be used by other programs. Module procedures are described in Chapter 7.

With the subroutine swap available, the program sort_3 now appears as follows:

```fortran
program sort_3

    implicit none
    real :: n1, n2, n3

    call read_the_numbers
    call sort_the_numbers
    call print_the_numbers

contains

subroutine read_the_numbers
    read *, n1, n2, n3
    print *, "Input data  n1:", n1
    print *, "            n2:", n2
    print *, "            n3:", n3
end subroutine read_the_numbers

subroutine sort_the_numbers
    if (n1 > n2) then
       call swap (n1, n2)
    end if
    if (n1 > n3) then
       call swap (n1, n3)
    end if
    if (n2 > n3) then
       call swap (n2, n3)
    end if
end subroutine sort_the_numbers

subroutine print_the_numbers
    print *, "The numbers, in ascending order, are:"
    print *, n1, n2, n3
end subroutine print_the_numbers

subroutine swap (a, b)
    real :: a, b, temp
    temp = a
    a = b
    b = temp
end subroutine swap

end program sort_3
```

```
run sort_3

Input data  n1:    2.2000000
            n2:    7.6999998
            n3:    5.5000000
The numbers, in ascending order, are:
   2.2000000    5.5000000    7.6999998
```

In this case, the resulting program is not any shorter because the subroutine call replaces only three statements on one line, but even in this simple case, the purpose of the program is quite a bit easier to understand, in part because of the self-documenting subroutine name swap and the hiding from the calling program sort_3 of inessential details of how the swapping actually is done.

3.1.5 Dummy Arguments and Local Variables

There are two new variables a and b in the subroutine swap that serve as place holders for the two numbers to be swapped. These are **dummy arguments** and must be declared in the subroutine even if they have the same name as a variable declared in the containing program. Passing arguments is described in more detail in Section 3.3.

The variable temp is used only in the subroutine swap. By declaring temp to be type real within the subroutine swap, we make this variable **local** to the subroutine, so that its value will not be confused with any value outside the subroutine. When this is done, it is not necessary to declare this variable in the main program.

3.1.6 Exercises

1. Write a subroutine sort_4_numbers that arranges the four integer variables i1, i2, i3, and i4 into ascending order. Test the subroutine by putting it in a main program that reads four numbers, calls the subroutine, and prints the sorted values.

2. Write a subroutine that reads in values for a loan principal amount p, an annual interest rate r, and the number of months m in which the loan is to be paid off. The monthly payment is given by the formula

$$pay = \frac{r \times p\,(1+r)^m}{(1+r)^m - 1}$$

The subroutine should print out a monthly schedule of the interest, principal paid, and remaining balance. Note that if the annual interest rate is r, the monthly interest rate is $r/12$. Test the subroutine with a program that calls it with $p = \$106,500$, $r = 7.25\%$, and $m = 240$ months.

3.2 Functions

If the purpose of a procedure is to compute one value (which may be a compound value consisting of a whole array or structure), a function is the kind of procedure to use.[3] The value of a function is computed when the name of the function, together with its arguments, is placed anywhere in an expression.

To illustrate a simple use of a function, suppose the task is to print out a table of values of the function

$$f(x) = \left[1 + \frac{1}{x}\right]^x$$

for values of x equal to 1, 10, 100, ..., 10^{10}. A program to do this is

```
program function_values

    implicit none
    real :: x
    integer :: i
    integer, parameter :: largest_power = 10
    integer, parameter :: kind_needed = &
        selected_real_kind (largest_power + 1)

    do i = 0, largest_power
        x = 10.0 ** i
        print "(f15.1, f15.5)", x, f (x)
    end do

contains

function f (x)  result (f_result)

    real :: f_result, x
```

---

3. Fortran 90 greatly extends the power of function procedures by allowing the function result to be an array or structure and by allowing recursive functions. Older versions of Fortran permitted only simple scalar integer, real, complex, character, and logical values.

```
    f_result = (1 + 1 / real (x, kind_needed)) ** x

end function f

end program function_values

run function_values
```

1.0	2.00000
10.0	2.59374
100.0	2.70481
1000.0	2.71692
10000.0	2.71815
100000.0	2.71827
1000000.0	2.71828
10000000.0	2.71828
100000000.0	2.71828
1000000000.0	2.71828
10000000000.0	2.71828

In this program the evaluation of the function occurs once for each execution of the do construct, but the expression that evaluates the function occurs only once. In this case, a function is used to submerge the details of evaluating the function to another place, making the program a little easier to read. When this is done, there is also the advantage that if the same table is needed, but for a different function, the main program does not need to be changed; only the procedure that evaluates the function needs to be changed.

This function illustrates a significant use of the selected_real_kind intrinsic function. The value $1 + 1/x$ is computed to get the desired answers. For $x = 10^{10}$, this value has 11 significant digits, so a kind of real must be used that will hold this many digits. If a real kind with fewer significant digits is used, the expression $1 + 1/x$ may evaluate as 1.00000, yielding an incorrect value for f_result. Both the largest power of x used and the kind needed to compute the function for this largest power are provided as parameters (named constants) in the program.

The type conversion

```
real (x, kind_needed)
```

converts the already real value x to a real kind of greater precision, and the rules for mixed mode arithmetic guarantee that this greater precision is used throughout the calculation.

3.2.1 Writing a Function

A function is almost like a program or subroutine except that its first statement uses the keyword function. It also may have arguments that are written in parentheses in the **function statement**. The last statement of a function is the **end function statement**, which contains the name of the function.

A difference between a subroutine and a function is that a function must provide a value that is returned as the value of the function. This is done by assigning a value to a **result variable** during execution of the function. This result variable is indicated by placing its name in parentheses at the end of the function statement following the keyword result. The result variable is declared within the function and is used just like any other local variable, but the value of this variable is the one that is returned as the value of the function to the program using the function.[4]

> *Style Note:* Use a result variable in every function procedure because it is easier to remember always to use the result clause than to remember the special cases when it is needed.

The function f computes the values required in our example and uses the result variable f_result to hold the result.

3.2.2 Invoking a Function

A programmer-defined function is called by writing its name, followed by its arguments, in any expression in the same manner that a built-in function (Section 1.5) is invoked.

3.2.3 Exercises

1. Write a function median_of_3 that selects the median of its three integer arguments. If all three numbers are different, the median is the number that is neither the smallest nor the largest. If two or more of the three numbers are equal, the median is one of the equal numbers.

2. Write a function average_of_4 that computes the average of four real numbers.

3. Write a function cone_volume (r, h) that returns the volume of a cone. The formula for the volume of a cone is $V = \pi r^2 h/3$, where r is the radius of the base and h is its height.

---

4. When the result keyword and variable are omitted, the function name is used as the result variable and must be declared in the function, just as it was in Fortran 77.

4.   Write a function round (x, n) whose value is the real value x
     rounded to the nearest multiple of 10ⁿ. For example, round
     (463.2783, -2) should be 463.28, which has been rounded to the
     nearest hundredth.

3.3 Argument Passing

One of the important properties of both functions and subroutines is
that information may be passed to the procedure when it is called
and information may be returned from the procedure to the calling
program when the procedure execution ends. This information passing is accomplished with procedure **arguments**. A one-to-one correspondence is set up between **actual arguments** in the calling program
and **dummy arguments** in the procedure. The corresponding arguments need not have the same name, and the correspondence is temporary, lasting only for the duration of the procedure call.

3.3.1 Agreement of Arguments

Fortran 77 required complete agreement of actual and dummy argument types. With the introduction of the new language features of
optional arguments, keyword-identified arguments, generic procedures, and assumed-shape arrays, the rules for agreement of actual
and dummy arguments are not as simple.[5] In this subsection, we try
to emphasize general principles, but for the sake of having all the
important rules in one place, we list exceptions needed to implement
these language features along with forward references to the sections
where they are discussed.

Except for dummy arguments declared as optional (Section
3.3.7), the number of actual and dummy arguments must be the same.
Each actual argument corresponds to a dummy argument. The
default correspondence is the first actual argument with the first
dummy argument, the second with the second, etc. However,
keyword-identified arguments (Section 3.3.6) can be used to override
the default, and provide clear, order-independent specification of the
correspondence between actual and dummy arguments.

The data type and kind parameter of each actual argument must
match that of the corresponding dummy argument. The shapes

---

5. The new procedure features of Fortran 90, optional arguments, keyword-identified
arguments, generic procedures, and assumed-shape arrays are so powerful and useful
that the Fortran 77 programmer should make the effort to learn them and use them.

(Section 4.1.3) also must agree;[6] that is, if the dummy argument is an array, the corresponding actual argument must be an array of the same shape (Section 4.1.3), and if the dummy argument is character, the corresponding actual argument must have the same length. Both of these rules are easy to satisfy if assumed-shape (Section 4.1.3) dummy arrays are used and assumed-length (Section 5.1.6) dummy character variables are used.

Additionally, if the dummy argument is a pointer (Chapter 8), the actual argument must be a pointer.

If the subroutine or function is generic (Section 7.3.1), there must be exactly one specific procedure with that generic name for which all the above rules of agreement of actual and dummy arguments are satisfied (however, keyword actual arguments also can be used to determine which procedure is specified). For given actual arguments, Fortran selects that specific procedure for which there is agreement of actual and dummy arguments.

3.3.2 Reference Arguments

An actual argument that is a variable (which includes an array name, an array element, an array substring, a structure component, or a substring) is passed **by reference**. Any reference to the corresponding dummy argument in the subroutine causes the computer to behave as if the reference were to the corresponding actual argument supplied by the calling program. Statements in the subroutine causing changes to such a dummy argument cause the same changes to the corresponding actual argument. It is bad programming practice to have such changes take place within a function procedure.

Style Note: Do not change the values of any dummy arguments in a function procedure.

3.3.3 Value Arguments

An actual argument that is a constant (either literal or named) or an expression more complicated than a variable can pass only a value to the corresponding dummy argument. This is known as pass **by value**. The dummy argument then must not have its value changed during execution of the procedure. There is no way to pass a value back to the calling program using such an argument.

---

6. For compatibility with Fortran 77, the rules for argument matching are not as strict as described here, and they are much more complicated. No functionality is lost by observing these rules.

3.3.4 An Example of Pass by Reference

Let us look again at the subroutine swap discussed earlier and how it is used in the program sort_3 in Section 3.1.4. In the subroutine statement, the subroutine name swap is followed by a list (a, b) of variables enclosed in parentheses. The variables a and b in that list are the dummy arguments for the subroutine swap.

Suppose that in executing the first read statement of the program sort_3, the computer reads and assigns to the variable n1 the value 3.14, assigns to the variable n2 the value 2.718, and assigns to the variable n3 the value 1.414. Since 3.14, the value of n1, is greater than 2.718, the value of n2, the computer executes the call statement

```
call swap (n1, n2)
```

During this execution of the subroutine swap, it is as if every occurrence of the dummy argument a in swap were replaced by the variable n1, and every occurrence of the dummy argument b in swap were replaced by the variable n2, as shown below.

```
              n1 n2
subroutine swap (a, b)
          n1 n2
  real :: a, b, temp
          n1
  temp = a
  n1   n2
  a = b
  n2
  b = temp
end subroutine swap
```

For example, in executing the statement

```
temp = a
```

of the subroutine swap, the computer assigns to the variable temp the value 3.14 of the variable n1 in the program sort_3, just as if the statement were written

```
temp = n1
```

In executing the statement

```
a = b
```

of the subroutine swap, the computer assigns to the variable n1 the value 2.718 of the variable n2, as though the statement were written

```
n1 = n2
```

Finally, the value 3.14 that is saved as the value of the variable temp is assigned to the variable n2 by the statement

```
b = temp
```

as though it were written

```
n2 = temp
```

The variables n1 and n2 in the statement

```
call swap (n1, n2)
```

are the actual arguments of the subroutine call. Whatever the names of the dummy arguments, during the execution of the subroutine, it is as if the names of the actual arguments were available in place of the dummy arguments.

At this point, execution of the call statement is complete and control returns to the main program sort_3, which continues by testing whether the new value 2.718 of n1 is greater than the value 1.414 of n3. Because it is, the computer is directed to execute a second call to the subroutine swap

```
call swap (n1, n3)
```

with the actual arguments n1 and n3. This time the subroutine swap is executed as if every occurrence of the first dummy argument a were replaced by the first actual argument n1 and every occurrence of the second dummy argument b were replaced by the second actual argument n3.

3.3.5 An Example of Pass by Value

Suppose a function is to be written that computes the following sum of certain terms of an arithmetic progression:

$$\sum_{i=m}^{n} (s + d\,i)$$

The arguments to this function are m, n, s (the starting value), and d, the difference between terms. A function to do this computation is contained in the program `series`

```
program series

    implicit none
    print *, series_sum (400, 700, 100.0, 0.1)

contains

function series_sum (m, n, s, d)  &
        result (series_sum_result)

    integer :: m, n, i
    real :: s, d, series_sum_result

    series_sum_result = 0
    do i = m, n
        series_sum_result = series_sum_result + s + i * d
    end do

end function series_sum

end program series
```

which produces the answer 46,655. All four actual arguments in the call of `series_sum` are constants and therefore passed by value.

3.3.6 Keyword Arguments

With the use of **keyword arguments**, it is not necessary to put the arguments in the correct order, but it is necessary to know the names of the dummy arguments.[7] The same computation may be made using the statement

```
print *,  &
        series_sum (d = 0.1, m = 400, n = 700, s = 100.0)
```

It is even possible to call the function using keywords for some arguments and not for others. In this case, the rule is that all actual

---

7. The Fortran 77 programmer is cautioned that the rules given here for keyword arguments and optional arguments apply only to internal and module procedures. The rules for using these features with external procedures involve interface blocks (Section 10.4.4) and are much more complicated.

arguments prior to the first keyword argument must match the corresponding dummy argument correctly and once a keyword argument is used, the remaining arguments must use keywords. Thus, the following is legal:

```
print *, series_sum (400, 700, d = 0.1, s = 100.0)
```

3.3.7 Optional Arguments

In our example computation of an arithmetic series, a common occurrence would be that the value of m is 0. It is possible to indicate that certain arguments to a procedure are **optional arguments** in the sense that they do not have to be present when the procedure is called. An optional argument must be declared to be such within the procedure; usually, there would be some statements within the procedure to test the presence of the optional argument on a particular call and perhaps do something different if it is not there. In our example, if the function series_ sum is called without the argument m, the value of m is to be set to zero. To do this, the intrinsic function present (A.4) is used to test whether an argument has been supplied for the dummy argument m, and if an actual argument is not present, the lower bound for the sum is set to zero. To handle both cases with the same do loop, a different variable, temp_m, is used to hold the lower bound. The reason a different variable is used is that a dummy argument corresponding to an actual argument that is not present must *never* be given a value within the procedure.

```
function series_sum (m, n, s, d)  &
        result (series_sum_result)

    integer, optional :: m
    integer :: n
    real :: s, d
    real :: series_sum_result
    integer :: i, temp_m

    if (present (m)) then
        temp_m = m
    else
        temp_m = 0
    end if
```

```
    series_sum_result = 0
    do i = temp_m, n
        series_sum_result = series_sum_result + s + i * d
    end do

end function series_sum
```

This new version of the function can now be called with any of the following statements, all of which compute the same sum:

```
print *, series_sum (0, 700, 100.0, 0.1)
print *, series_sum (0, 700, d = 0.1, s = 100.0)
print *, series_sum (n = 700, d = 0.1, s = 100.0)
print *, series_sum (d = 0.1, s = 100.0, n = 700)
print *, series_sum (m = 0, n = 700, d = 0.1, s = 100.0)
```

3.3.8 Argument Intent

It is possible, and good programming practice, to indicate the **intent** of use of each dummy argument of a subroutine or function. The intent may be in, which means that the dummy argument must not be changed within the procedure; it may be out, which means that the actual argument must be given a value by the procedure; or it may be inout, which means that the dummy argument is expected both to receive an initial value from and to return a value to the corresponding actual argument. Thus, for dummy arguments with intent out or inout, the corresponding actual argument is passed by reference and must be a variable.

Except in very rare cases, all arguments to a function should have intent in to avoid problems with side effects.

The intent is an attribute given to an argument when it is declared within the procedure. In our series summation example, all arguments can be given intent in by changing the function's declarations.

```
    function series_sum (m, n, s, d)  &
        result (series_sum_result)

    real :: series_sum_result
    integer, intent (in), optional :: m
    integer, intent (in)  :: n
```

```
real, intent (in) :: s, d
integer :: i, temp_m
      . . .

end function series_sum
```

The intent attribute is provided to make the program more easily understood by a human reader and to allow the compiler to catch some possible errors when the programmer violates the stated intent.

Style Note: Always indicate the intent attribute for procedure arguments.

3.3.9 Procedures as Arguments

An actual argument and the corresponding dummy argument may be a procedure. The actual argument may be a module procedure, a dummy procedure, or the specific name of an intrinsic procedure. Some specific intrinsic functions may not be passed as actual arguments; see Section A.12. When an intrinsic function is passed, it should be declared in an intrinsic statement. The intrinsic statement consists of the keyword intrinsic followed by a list of intrinsic procedure names. It can be used to indicate the use of any intrinsic procedure. An intrinsic function is used as an actual argument in the example numerical integration function in Section 3.6.

Procedures that are not intrinsic can be passed only if they are module procedures.[8] The numerical integration example is revisited in Section 7.2 where a module function is passed as the function to be integrated.

3.3.10 Exercises

1. Write a program that tests cone_volume (Exercise 3 of Section 3.2) as an internal function using keywords to call the function with arguments in the wrong order.

2. Rewrite the function cone_volume (Exercise 3 of Section 3.2) to make the radius an optional argument with a default value of 1 if it is not present. Test the revised function by using it both with the argument present and with the argument missing.

---

8. An external procedure also may be an actual argument in Fortran 77 and Fortran 90; the rules are the same as those for module procedures.

3.4 Scope

The **scope** of a name is the set of lines in a Fortran program where that name may be used and refer to the same variable, procedure, or type. In general, the scope of a variable or type name declared in a program extends throughout that program from the program statement to the end program statement. Any name that is declared is known in all procedures contained in the one in which it is declared, that is, in all procedures following the contains statement. However, the scope of a declared name does not include any internal or module procedure in which the name is redeclared.

A name declared in an internal procedure has scope extending only from the beginning to the end of that procedure, not to the program or procedure that contains it, nor to any other internal procedure. Recall that internal procedures cannot contain other procedures, so there is no further inheritance of a name declared in an internal procedure.

These ideas are illustrated by the following program segment.

```
program p
   implicit none
   integer :: a, b
   . . .
contains

subroutine s
   real b
   . . .
   print *, a, b
   . . .
```

The values of a and b are printed in the subroutine. a is the integer variable declared in the main program; its scope includes the subroutine because it is not redeclared. However, it is a real value that is printed for b, which is the b declared in the subroutine s. The scope of the integer b declared in the main program does not include the subroutine s. That is, there are two variables with the name b, an integer variable b, whose scope is the main program and does not include the subroutine, and a real variable b, whose scope consists of the subroutine s only.

A similar rule applies to implicit statements. The implicit typing (including none) is passed along to any internal procedures, so it is not necessary to put an implicit none statement in an internal procedure.

The name of an internal procedure, its number and type of arguments, their names for use only in keyword actual arguments, as well as the type of its result variable if it is a function, are considered as declared in the containing program or procedure, and their scope therefore extends throughout the containing program and all other internal procedures of the containing program. Therefore, an internal procedure can be called from the containing program or procedure or any of its internal procedures.

Modules (Chapter 7) follow a different paradigm. A module contains declarations of names of variables, parameters, types, kinds, etc., between the module statement and the contains statement, followed by full source code of the procedures internal to the module between the contains statement and the end module statement. When a module is used in a program, procedure, or another module, it is as if all declarations made in the module (except those declared private in the module or not available because of a use only option, Section 7.1.2) were made at the place where the use statement appears. Thus, names declared in a module have as scope the full extent of any program that uses the module. However, the scope of a name declared in a module does not include any internal or module procedure in which the name is redeclared. Similarly, procedures declared in a module may be called by any program that uses the module and by its internal procedures. A variable name declared in a module references the same variable in every program or external procedure that uses the module.[9]

3.5 The save Attribute

Unless something special is done by the programmer, the value of a variable that is local to a procedure may not be saved between calls to the procedure. Suppose it is desirable to have a variable in a subroutine that counts the number of times the subroutine is called; this might be useful for debugging, for example.

```
subroutine s
    implicit none
    integer :: count = 0
```

---

9. Modules provide a much better way to share values than common, the error-prone mechanism used in Fortran 77.

```
        count = count + 1
        print *, "This is execution #", count,  &
                "of subroutine s."
        . . .
    end subroutine s
```

In this case, the value of the local variable count is saved between calls of the subroutine because *initialized variables are saved.*

Initializing a local variable causes it to be saved. The other way to indicate that a variable is to be saved is to give it the save attribute.

```
    real, save :: p, q
```

It is not necessary to indicate the save attribute very often because most variables that are saved are also initialized.

3.6 Case Study: Numerical Integration

In Section 2.5.6, we wrote a program integral to approximate the definite integral

$$\int_a^b f(x)\,dx$$

by dividing the interval from a to b into n equal pieces, approximating the curve with straight lines, and computing the sum of the areas of the n trapezoids with the formula

$$T_n = h\left[\frac{f(a)}{2} + f(a+h) + f(a+2h) + \cdots + f(b-h) + \frac{f(b)}{2}\right]$$

In the program integral, the values for a, b, and n were read as input data. Now that we have procedures, a better approach is to write a function integral with arguments a, b, and n. The other problem with the program integral is that the name of the function to be integrated (sin, in the example), was "hard-wired" into the source code and could not be changed without rewriting and recompiling the program. Since it is possible to pass a procedure as an argument, we can make the name of the function an additional argument f to our function integral.

All of these changes so far affect only the declarative part of the program integral. The executable statements of the program are modified to use the dummy function argument f in place of the particular function sin, resulting in the following program integrate.

```
program integrate

implicit none

intrinsic sin

print *, integral (sin, a=0.0, b=3.14159, n=100)

contains

function integral (f, a, b, n)  result (integral_result)
!  Calculates a trapezoidal approximation to an area
!  using n trapezoids.

!  The region is bounded by lines x = a, y = 0, x = b,
!  and the curve y = f (x).

   real :: integral_result, f
   real, intent (in) :: a, b
   integer, intent (in) :: n
   real :: h, sum
   integer :: i

   h = (b - a) / n
!  Calculate the sum f(a)/2+f(a+h)+...+f(b-h)+f(b)/2
!  Do the first and last terms first
   sum = 0.5 * (f (a) + f (b))
   do i = 1, n - 1
      sum = sum + f (a + i * h)
   end do

   integral_result = h * sum

end function integral

end program integrate

run integrate

   1.9998353
```

The only sorts of functions that can be passed to a procedure such as `integral` are intrinsic and module procedures. The same example is revisited in Section 7.2 where a module procedure is passed to an integration function.

3.7 Case Study: Calculating Probabilities

Consider the problem of calculating the probability that a throw of two dice will yield a 7 or an 11. One way to solve this problem is to have a computer simulate many rolls of the dice and count how many times the result is 7 or 11. The probability of throwing 7 or 11 is then the number of successful throws divided by the total number of times the throw of the dice was simulated.

3.7.1 The Built-In Subroutine `random_number`

The heart of a probabilistic simulation program is a procedure that generates pseudorandom numbers. In Fortran 90, such a procedure is built in; it is a subroutine named `random_number`. The subroutine places uniformly distributed real numbers greater than or equal to 0 and less than 1 in the actual argument. The argument may be a single real variable or a real array. In this section, we will use `random_number` to generate one value at a time; in Section 4.6.1, we will use the same subroutine with an array as the argument to generate a whole array of random numbers with one subroutine call.

3.7.2 Computing the Probability of a 7 or 11

Using the subroutine `random_int`, the program to estimate the probability of rolling 7 or 11 with two dice is not difficult. To simulate the roll of one die, we need a subroutine that returns an integer from 1 to 6. The subroutine `random_int` has three arguments. The first is used to store the result, which is, with approximately equal probability, any integer that is greater than or equal to `low`, the second argument, and that is less than or equal to `high`, the third argument. For example, the statement

```
call random_int (digit, 0, 9)
```

assigns to `digit` one of the 10 one-digit integers 0, 1, 2, ..., 9. `random_int` is written as a subroutine, rather than a function for two reasons:

1.   It calls the subroutine `random_number`, which has the side effect of modifying the "seed" of the random generator; hence

`random_int` itself has side effects. A function should never have a side effect.

2. It it were a function, it would be tempting to set the value of the variable `dice` with the statement

```
dice = random_int (1, 6) + random_int (1,6)
```

A smart optimizing compiler might change this into the statement

```
dice = 2 * random_int (1, 6)
```

and each roll of the dice would produce an even number!

The program `seven_11` simulates the event of rolling the dice 1000 times and computes a pretty good approximation to the true answer, which is $6/36 + 2/36 = 22.22\%$.

```fortran
program seven_11

    implicit none
    integer, parameter :: number_of_rolls = 1000
    integer :: die_1, die_2, dice, i, wins

    wins = 0
    do i = 1, number_of_rolls
        call random_int (die_1, 1, 6)
        call random_int (die_2, 1, 6)
        dice = die_1 + die_2
        if ((dice == 7) .or. (dice == 11)) wins = wins + 1
    end do

    print "(a, f6.2)", &
        "The percentage of rolls that are 7 or 11 is", &
            100.0 * real (wins) / real (number_of_rolls)

contains

subroutine random_int (result, low, high)

    integer, intent (out) :: result
    integer, intent (in) :: low, high
    real :: uniform_random_value
```

```
      call random_number (uniform_random_value)
      result = &
          int ((high - low + 1) * uniform_random_value + low)

end subroutine random_int

end program seven_11

run seven_11

The percentage of rolls that are 7 or 11 is 22.40
```

3.7.3 Exercises

1. Write a program that determines by simulation the percentage of times the sum of two rolled dice will be 2, 3, or 12. You might want to use a case construct (Section 2.4).

2. Two dice are rolled until a 4 or 7 comes up. Write a simulation program to determine the percentage of times a 4 will be rolled before a 7 is rolled. What was the largest sequence of rolls before the issue was decided?

3. Write a simulation program to determine the percentage of times exactly 5 coins will be heads and 5 will be tails, if 10 fair coins are tossed simultaneously.

4. Use the subroutine random_int to create a program that deals a five-card poker hand. Remember that the same card cannot occur twice in a hand. Use a character valued function face_value (n) that returns "Ace" for 1, "2" for 2, ..., "10" for 10, "Jack" for 11, "Queen" for 12, and "King" for 13.

5. Modify the subroutine random_int so that the arguments low and high are optional. If low is not present, use the value 1. If high is not present, use the value low + 1. Test the subroutine with many different calls in which the optional arguments are omitted, arguments are called with keywords, and the arguments are in different orders.

3.8 Recursion

Recursion may be thought of as a mechanism to handle flow of control in a program, but its implementation requires dynamic storage allocation; that is why it was not in Fortran 77. Each time a recursive function or subroutine is called, there must be space for the variables that are local to the procedure. There is no way to tell at compile time how many times the routine will call itself, hence there is no way to determine the amount of storage needed to store copies of the variables local to the procedure.

The use of recursion is a very powerful tool for constructing programs that otherwise can be quite complex, particularly if the process being modeled is described recursively. However, depending on the implementation available, recursion can require a substantial amount of runtime overhead. Thus, the use of recursion illustrates the classic tradeoff between time spent in constructing and maintaining a program and execution time. In some cases, a process described recursively can be transformed into an iterative process in a very straightforward manner; in other cases, it is very hard and the resulting procedure is very difficult to follow. It is in these cases that recursion is such a valuable tool. We will illustrate some examples that fall into each category. A recursive version of the numerical integration program is discussed in Section 7.2.

3.8.1 The Factorial Function

First, let's look at the mathematical definition of the factorial function $n!$ defined for nonnegative integers. It is a simple example that will illustrate many of the important ideas relating to recursion.

$$0! = 1$$

$$n! = n \times (n-1)! \quad \text{for } n > 0$$

To use this definition to calculate 4!, apply the second line of the definition with $n = 4$ to get $4! = 4 \times 3!$. To finish the calculation we need the value of 3!, which can be determined by using the second line of the definition again. $3! = 3 \times 2!$, so that $4! = 4 \times 3 \times 2!$. Using the second line of the definition two more times yields $2! = 2 \times 1!$ and $1! = 1 \times 0!$. Finally, the first line of the definition can be applied to compute $0! = 1$. Plugging all these values back in produces the computation

$$4! = 4 \times 3 \times 2 \times 1 \times 1 = 24$$

From this, it is pretty obvious that an equivalent definition for $n!$ is

$$n! = n \times (n-1) \times (n-2) \times \cdots \times 3 \times 2 \times 1$$

for integers greater than zero. So this is an example for which it should be quite easy to write an iterative program as well as a recursive one, but to illustrate the recursive technique, let's first look at the recursive version. It should be easy to understand because it follows the recursive definition very closely.

```
recursive function factorial (n)  &
      result (factorial_result)

    integer, intent (in) :: n
    integer :: factorial_result

    if (n <= 0) then
       factorial_result = 1
    else
       factorial_result = n * factorial (n - 1)
    end if

end function factorial
```

The function is called using its name in an expression as shown by the simple program that computes 12!.

```
program test_factorial

implicit none

print*, "12! =", factorial(12)

contains

recursive function factorial (n)  &
      result (factorial_result)

    . . .


end function factorial

end program test_factorial

run test_factorial

 12! = 479001600
```

For a recursive function or subroutine, the keyword **recursive** must be placed on the procedure heading line. The **result** clause is absolutely essential in this program; otherwise, there would be no way to distinguish the use of `factorial` as a result variable from the use of `factorial` as a function, as is done in the `else` block in the procedure. This version of the function returns a result of 1 for a negative value of n for which the mathematical factorial function $n!$ is undefined. Another alternative is to treat a negative argument as an error, but returning 1 keeps the example simple.

This program illustrates something often called **tail recursion**, which means that the only recursive call occurs as the very last step in the computation of the procedure. It is always easy to turn a process involving only tail recursion into an iterative process. Here is the iterative version of the factorial function. Although not strictly necessary, the result clause is still used in accordance with the style rules suggested in Section 3.2.1.

```
function factorial (n)  result (factorial_result)

   integer :: factorial_result
   integer, intent (in) :: n
   integer :: i

   factorial_result = 1
   do i = 2, n
      factorial_result = i * factorial_result
   end do

end function factorial
```

Note that the do loop will be executed zero times for any value of n that is less than 2, so that the value of 1 will be returned in these cases.

3.8.2 The Fibonacci Sequence

This next example illustrates not only the use of recursion when an iterative program would do as well, but a case in which a decision to implement a program based on a recursive definition yields an algorithm that has very poor running time even if recursive function calls had no overhead.

The **Fibonacci sequence** 1, 1, 2, 3, 5, 8, 13, 21, 34, ..., arises in such diverse applications as the number of petals in a daisy, the maximum steps it takes to recognize a sequence of characters, and the most pleasing proportions for a rectangle, the "golden section" of Renaissance artists and mathematicians. It is defined by the relations

$f(1) = 1$

$f(2) = 1$

$f(n) = f(n-1) + f(n-2)$ for $n > 2$

Starting with the third term, each Fibonacci number is the sum of the two previous Fibonacci numbers. Naive incorporation of the recurrence relation in a recursive function program produces an execution time disaster for all but the smallest values of n.

```
recursive function fibonacci (n) &
        result (fibonacci_result)

    integer, intent (in) :: n
    integer :: fibonacci_result

    if (n <= 2) then
        fibonacci_result = 1
    else
        fibonacci_result = fibonacci (n - 1) + &
                            fibonacci (n - 2)
    end if

end function fibonacci
```

If the function is used to calculate $f(7)$, for example, the recursive calls request computation of $f(6)$ and $f(5)$. Then the computation of $f(6)$ again calls for the computation of $f(5)$ as well as $f(4)$. Thus, values of f are computed over and over with the same argument. In fact, the number of recursive function calls resulting from a single call to fibonacci (n) exceeds the answer, which is approximately 0.447×1.618^n. The execution time of this function is called **exponential** because it depends on a number greater than 1 raised to the nth power.

To make this computation much more efficient, values of f must be saved and reused when needed, rather than being recomputed. The next function to compute the Fibonacci sequence is iterative rather than recursive. It uses the variables f_i and f_i_minus_1 to hold the two most recently computed values of f and is iterative rather than recursive.

```
function fibonacci (n)  &
     result (fibonacci_result)

  integer :: fibonacci_result
  integer, intent (in) :: n
  integer :: f_i, f_i_minus_1, i

  if (n <= 2) then
     fibonacci_result = 1
  else
     f_i_minus_1 = 1
     f_i = 1
     do i = 3, n
        f_i = f_i + f_i_minus_1
        f_i_minus_1 = f_i - f_i_minus_1
     end do
     fibonacci_result = f_i
  end if

end function fibonacci
```

This program, although containing two statements that take a little time to understand, is by far more time and space efficient than the previous version. The increases are so dramatic that it is worth having a couple of lines of code that are not completely obvious.

3.8.3 The Towers of Hanoi

According to legend, there is a temple in Hanoi that contains a ritual apparatus consisting of 3 posts and 64 gold disks of graduated size that fit on the posts. When the temple was built, all 64 gold disks were placed on the first post with the largest on the bottom and the smallest on the top, as shown schematically in Figure 3-1. It is the sole occupation of the priests of the temple to move all the gold disks systematically until all 64 gold disks are on the third post, at which time the world will come to an end.

There are only two rules that must be followed:

1. Disks must be moved from post to post one at a time.

2. A larger disk may never rest on top of a smaller disk on the same post.

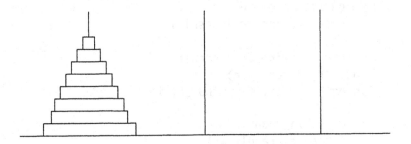

Figure 3-1 The towers of Hanoi.

A smaller version of this apparatus with only eight disks made of plastic is sold as a recreational puzzle. The sequence of moves necessary to solve the simpler puzzle is not obvious and often takes hours to figure out. We propose to write a simple recursive procedure hanoi that prints complete directions for moving any number of disks from one post to another. It is much more difficult to write a nonrecursive procedure to print these directions.

The recursive procedure hanoi is based on the following top-down analysis of the problem. Suppose n disks are to be moved from a starting post to a final post. Because the largest of these n disks can never rest on a smaller disk, at the time the largest disk is moved, all $n - 1$ smaller disks must be stacked on the free middle post as shown in Figure 3-2.

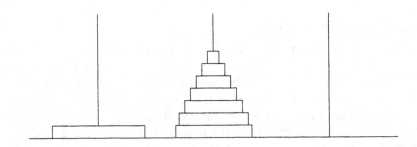

Figure 3-2 Locations of the disks when the largest disk is to be moved.

For the number of disks $n > 1$, the algorithm has 3 steps.

1. Legally move the top $n - 1$ disks from the starting post to the free post.

2. Move the largest disk from the starting post to the final post.

3. Legally move the $n - 1$ disks from the free post to the final post.

The middle step involves printing a single move instruction. The first and third steps represent simpler instances of the same problem— simpler in this case because fewer disks must be moved. Therefore, the first and third steps may be handled by recursive procedure calls. In case $n = 1$, only the second step should be executed, and this provides a nonrecursive path through the procedure for the simplest case. The Fortran subroutine hanoi, its test program test_hanoi, and a sample execution output for four disks are shown. It is not easy to write an iterative version of this program.

```fortran
program test_hanoi

    implicit none
    integer :: number_of_disks

    read *, number_of_disks
    print *, "Input data  number_of_disks:", &
            number_of_disks
    print *
    call hanoi (number_of_disks, 1, 3)

contains

recursive subroutine hanoi (number_of_disks, &
        starting_post, goal_post)

    integer, intent (in) :: &
    number_of_disks, starting_post, goal_post
    ! all_posts is the sum of the post values 1+2+3
    ! so that the free post can be determined
    ! by subtracting the starting_post and the
    ! goal_post from this sum.
    integer :: free_post
    integer, parameter :: all_posts = 6

    if (number_of_disks > 0) then
        free_post = &
        all_posts - starting_post - goal_post
        call hanoi (number_of_disks - 1, &
                    starting_post, free_post)

        print *, "Move disk", number_of_disks, &
                "from post", starting_post, &
                "to post", goal_post
```

```
          call hanoi (number_of_disks - 1,  &
                      free_post, goal_post)
      end if
  end subroutine hanoi

  end program test_hanoi

  run test_hanoi

   Input data   number_of_disks: 4

  Move disk 1 from post 1 to post 2
  Move disk 2 from post 1 to post 3
  Move disk 1 from post 2 to post 3
  Move disk 3 from post 1 to post 2
  Move disk 1 from post 3 to post 1
  Move disk 2 from post 3 to post 2
  Move disk 1 from post 1 to post 2
  Move disk 4 from post 1 to post 3
  Move disk 1 from post 2 to post 3
  Move disk 2 from post 2 to post 1
  Move disk 1 from post 3 to post 1
  Move disk 3 from post 2 to post 3
  Move disk 1 from post 1 to post 2
  Move disk 2 from post 1 to post 3
  Move disk 1 from post 2 to post 3
```

3.8.4 Indirect Recursion

It is possible for procedures a and b to be indirectly recursive in the sense that a calls b and b calls a. An example of this kind of recursion occurs in the function term in Section 5.3.

3.8.5 Exercises

1. Write a recursive function bc (n, k) to compute the binomial coefficient $\begin{pmatrix} n \\ k \end{pmatrix}$, $0 \le k \le n$, using the relations

$$\begin{pmatrix} n \\ 0 \end{pmatrix} = 1 \qquad \begin{pmatrix} n \\ n \end{pmatrix} = 1$$

$$\binom{n}{k} = \binom{n-1}{k-1} + \binom{n-1}{k} \quad \text{for } 0 < k < n$$

2. Write an efficient program to compute the binomial coefficient $\binom{n}{k}$.

3. The following recurrence defines $f(n)$ for all nonnegative integer values of n.

$$f(0) = 0$$

$$f(1) = f(2) = 1$$

$$f(n) = 2f(n-1) + f(n-2) - f(n-3) \quad \text{for } n > 2$$

Write a function f to compute $f(n)$, $n > 0$. Also have your program verify that for $0 \le n \le 1000$, $f(n) = [(-1)^{n+1} + 2^n]/3$.

4. For positive integers a and b, the greatest common divisor of a and b satisfies the following recurrence relationship:

$$\gcd(a, b) = b \quad \text{if } a \bmod b = 0$$

$$\gcd(a, b) = \gcd(b, a \bmod b) \quad \text{if } a \bmod b \ne 0$$

Write a recursive function gcd (a, b) using these recurrences. Test the program by finding $\gcd(24, 36)$, $\gcd(16, 13)$, $\gcd(17, 119)$, and $\gcd(177, 228)$.

3.9 The return Statement

The **return statement** causes execution of a procedure to terminate with control given back to the calling program. With the use of modern control constructs, a procedure usually should terminate by coming to the end of the procedure. However, there are situations in which it is better to use a return statement than introduce a complicated set of nested if constructs. Most of the programs in this book are too simple to require use of the return statement.

4

Arrays

In ordinary usage, a **list** is a sequence of values, usually all representing data of the same kind, or otherwise related to one another. A list of students registered for a particular course and a list of all students enrolled at a college are examples.

In Fortran, a collection of values of the same type is called an **array**. We will also refer to a one-dimensional array as a **list**.

Frequently, the same operation or sequence of operations is performed on every element in an array. On a computer that performs one statement at a time, it makes sense to write such programs by specifying what happens to a typical element of the array and enclosing these statements in a sufficient number of do constructs (loops) to make them apply to every element. Fortran 90 also has powerful intrinsic operations and functions that operate on whole arrays or sections of an array. Programs written using these array operations are often clearer and are more easily optimized by Fortran compilers. Especially on computers with parallel or array processing capabilities, such programs are more likely to take advantage of the special hardware to increase execution speed.

4.1 Declaring and Using Arrays in Fortran

We introduce the use of arrays with an example involving credit card numbers.

4.1.1 A Credit Card Checking Application

As an example of a problem concerned with a list, suppose that a company maintains a computerized list of credit cards that have been reported lost or stolen or that are greatly in arrears in payments. The company needs a program to determine quickly whether a given credit card, presented by a customer wishing to charge a purchase, is on this list of credit cards that can no longer be honored.

Suppose that a company has a list of 8262 credit cards reported lost or stolen, as illustrated in Table 4-1.

Table 4-1 Lost credit cards.

Account number of 1st lost credit card	2718281
Account number of 2nd lost credit card	7389056
Account number of 3rd lost credit card	1098612
Account number of 4th lost credit card	5459815
Account number of 5th lost credit card	1484131
.	.
.	.
.	.
Account number of 8262nd lost credit card	1383596

Since all of the 8262 numbers in the list must be retained simultaneously in the computer's main memory for efficient searching, and since a simple (scalar) variable can hold only one value at a time, each number must be assigned as the value of a variable *with a different name* so that the computer can be instructed to compare each account number of a lost or stolen card against the account number of the card offered in payment for goods and services.

4.1.2 Subscripts

It is possible to use variables with the 8262 Fortran names

```
lost_card_1
lost_card_2
lost_card_3
      .
      .
      .
lost_card_8262
```

to hold the 8262 values. Unfortunately, the Fortran language does not recognize the intended relationship between these variable names, so the search program cannot be written simply. The Fortran solution is to declare a single object name lost_card that consists of many individual integer values. The entire collection of values may be referenced by its name lost_card and individual card numbers in the list may be referenced by the following names:

```
lost_card (1)
lost_card (2)
lost_card (3)
     .
     .
     .
lost_card (8262)
```

This seemingly minor modification of otherwise perfectly acceptable variable names opens up a new dimension of programming capabilities. All the programs in this chapter, and a large number of the programs in succeeding chapters, use this form.

The numbers in parentheses that specify the location of an item within a list are **subscripts**, a name borrowed from mathematics. Although mathematical subscripts are usually written below the line (hence the name), such a form of typography is impossible on most computer input devices. A substitute notation, enclosing the subscript in parentheses or brackets, is adopted in most computer languages. It is customary to read the expression x (3) as "x sub 3", just as if it were written x_3.

The advantage of this method of naming the quantities over using the variable names lost_card_1, lost_card_2, ..., lost_card_8262 springs from the following programming language capability: *The subscript of an array variable may itself be a variable,* or an even more complicated expression.

The consequences of this simple statement are much more profound than would appear at first sight.

For a start in describing the uses of a subscript that is itself a variable, the two statements

```
i = 1
print *, lost_card (i)
```

produce exactly the same output as the single statement

```
print *, lost_card (1)
```

namely, 2718281, the account number of the first lost credit card on the list. The entire list of account numbers of lost credit cards can be printed by the subroutine `print_lost_cards`.

```
subroutine print_lost_cards (lost_card)

    integer, dimension (1:8262), intent (in) :: lost_card
    integer :: i

    do i = 1, 8262
       print *, lost_card (i)
    end do

end subroutine print_lost_cards
```

As an example of an array feature in Fortran, the collection of card numbers as a whole can be referenced by the one statement

```
print *, lost_card
```

The replacement just made actually creates a different output. The difference is that using the do loop to execute a `print` statement 8262 times causes each card number to be printed on a separate line. The new version indicates that as many as possible of the card numbers should be printed on one line, which might not produce acceptable output. Adding a simple format for the `print` statement instead of using the default produces a more desirable result, printing four card numbers per line.

```
print "(4i8)", lost_card
```

This is a little better, but another problem is that the number of lost and stolen cards varies daily. The subroutine will not be very useful if it makes the assumption that there are exactly 8262 cards to be printed. This can be fixed easily by changing the declaration to

```
integer, dimension (:), intent (in) :: lost_card
```

The colon indicates that the size of the array `lost_card` is to be assumed from the array that is the actual argument given when the subroutine is called. Also, this passed-on size is used in the `print` statement to determine how many credit card numbers are to be printed. Thus, we have created a general subroutine for printing a list of integers. However, it is so simple that it can be done with a single statement, so it is not worth showing it.

4.1.3 Array Declarations

The name of an array must obey the same rules as an ordinary variable name. Each array must be declared in the declaration section of the program. A name is declared to be an array by putting the dimension attribute in a type statement followed by a range of subscripts, enclosed in parentheses. For example,

```
real, dimension (1 : 9) :: x, y
logical, dimension (-99 : 99) :: yes_no
```

declares that x and y are lists of 9 real values and that yes_no is a list of 199 logical values. These declarations imply that a subscript for x or y must be an integer expression with a value from 1 to 9 and that a subscript for yes_no must be an integer expression whose value is from −99 to +99.

A list of character strings may be declared in a form like the following:

```
character (len = 8), dimension (0 : 17) :: char_list
```

In this example, the variable char_list is a list of 18 character strings, each of length 8.

The **shape** of an array is a list of the number of elements in each dimension. A 9 × 7 array has shape (9,7); the array char_list declared above has shape (18); and the array declared by

```
integer, dimension (9, 0:99, -99:99) :: iii
```

has shape (9,100,199). When only one number is given in a dimension declaration in place of a subscript range, it is used as the upper subscript bound and the lower bound is 1.

The shape of a scalar is a list with no elements in it. The shape of a scalar or array can be computed using the shape intrinsic function.

The declaration

```
real, dimension (:, :), allocatable :: a, b
```

indicates that the arrays a and b have two dimensions (rank 2). The colons mean that the extents along each dimension will be established later, when an allocate statement is executed.

A similar declaration using colons may occur for a dummy argument of a procedure, indicating that the shape of the dummy array is to be taken from the actual argument used when the procedure is called. This sort of dummy argument is called an **assumed-shape array**.

```
subroutine s (d)
   integer, dimension (:, :, :) :: d
```

The allocatable attribute must not be used for an array argument, but a pointer attribute may be (see Chapter 8).

The declaration of arrays also may use values of other dummy arguments to establish extents; such arrays are called **automatic arrays**. For example, the statements

```
subroutine s2 (dummy_list, n, dummy_array)
   real, dimension (:) :: dummy_list
   real, dimension (size (dummy_list)) :: local_list
   real, dimension (n, n) :: dummy_array, local_array
   real, dimension (2 * n + 1) :: longer_local_list
```

declare that the size of dummy_list is to be the same as the size of the corresponding actual argument, that the array local_list is to be the same size as dummy_list, and that dummy_array and local_array are both to be two-dimensional arrays with n x n elements. The last declaration shows that some arithmetic on other dummy arguments is permitted in calculating array bounds; these expressions may include references to certain intrinsic functions, such as size.

In the main program, an array must either be declared with constant fixed bounds or be declared allocatable and be given bounds by the execution of an allocate statement (Section 4.1.5). In the first case, our lost and stolen card program might contain the declaration

```
integer, dimension (8262) :: lost_card
```

This is not satisfactory if the number of lost cards changes frequently. In this situation, perhaps the best solution is to declare the array to have a sufficiently large upper bound so that there will always be sufficient space to hold the card numbers. Because the upper bound is fixed, there must be a variable whose value is the actual number of cards lost. Assuming that the list of lost credit cards is stored in a file connected to the standard input unit (unit=*), the following program fragment reads, counts, and prints the complete list of lost card numbers. The read statement has an iostat keyword argument whose value is set to zero if no error occurs and is set to a negative number if there is an attempt to read beyond the last data item in the file. The slightly different form of the read statement necessitated by the use of iostat is described in detail in Section 9.3, as is the iostat specifier.

```
integer, dimension (20000) :: lost_card
integer :: number_of_lost_cards, i, iostat_var

do i = 1, 20000
   read (unit = *, fmt = *, iostat = iostat_var)  &
        lost_card (i)
   if (iostat_var < 0) then
      number_of_lost_cards = i - 1
      exit
   end if
end do
print "(4i8)", lost_card (1:number_of_lost_cards)
```

Although the array lost_card is declared to have room for 20,000 entries, the print statement limits output to only those lost card numbers that actually were read from the file by specifying a range of subscripts 1 : number_of_lost_cards (see Section 4.1.6 for more details about this notation).

4.1.4 Array Constructors

Rather than assign array values one by one, it is convenient to give an array a set of values using an array constructor. An **array constructor** is a sequence of scalar values defined along one dimension only. An array constructor is a list of values, separated by commas and delimited by the pair of two-character symbols "(/" and "/)". There are three possible forms for the array constructor values:[1]

1.   A scalar expression as in

$$x (1:4) = (/ 1.2, 3.5, 1.1, 1.5 /)$$

2.   An array expression as in

$$x (1:4) = (/ a (i, 1:2), a (i+1, 2:3) /)$$

3.   An implied do loop as in

---

[1]. The array constructor uses a syntax for constructing lists similar to that of the data statement, but with more generality and expanded capability.

$$x \ (1{:}4) = (/ \ (\text{sqrt} \ (\text{real} \ (i)), \ i = 1, \ 4) \ /)$$

If there are no values specified in an array constructor, the resulting array is zero sized. The values of the components must have the same type and type parameters (kind and length). The rank of an array constructor is always one; however, the reshape intrinsic function can be used to define rank-two and greater arrays from the array constructor values. For example,

reshape ((/ 1, 2, 3, 4, 5, 6 /), (/ 2, 3 /))

is the 2 × 3 array $\begin{bmatrix} 1 & 3 & 5 \\ 2 & 4 & 6 \end{bmatrix}$.

An **implied do list** is a list of expressions, followed by something that is like an iterative control in a do statement. The whole thing is contained in parentheses. It represents a list of values obtained by writing each member of the list once for each value of the do variable replaced by a value. For example, the implied do list in the array constructor above

(sqrt (real (i)), i = 1, 4)

is the same as the list

sqrt (real (1)), sqrt (real (2)), &
sqrt (real (3)), sqrt (real (4))

The following print statement illustrates another use of an implied do list.

print *, (a (i, i), i = 1, n)

4.1.5 Dynamic Arrays

In Fortran 77, all the storage that was required during execution of a program could be determined and allocated by the compiler. This is known as **static storage allocation,** as opposed to **dynamic storage allocation,** which means that storage may be allocated or deallocated during execution of the program.

With static allocation, the size of each array must be declared at compile time, usually as the largest size anticipated in any execution of the program. With dynamic storage allocation, the program can wait until it knows *during execution* exactly what size array is needed and then allocate only that much space. Memory also can be deallocated dynamically, so that the storage used for a large array early in the program can be reused for other large arrays later in the program after the values in the first array are no longer needed.

For example, instead of relying on an end-of-file condition when reading in the list of lost cards, it is possible to keep the numbers stored in a file with the number of lost cards as the first value in the file, such as

```
8262
2718281
7389056
1098612
5459815
1484131

        .
        .
        .
1383596
```

The program can then read the first number, allocate the correct amount of space for the array, and read the lost card numbers.

```
integer, dimension (:), allocatable :: lost_card
integer :: number_of_lost_cards
integer :: allocation_status
    . . .
! The first number in the file is
! The number of lost card numbers in the
! rest of the file.
read *, number_of_lost_cards
allocate (lost_card (number_of_lost_cards),  &
          stat = allocation_status)

if (allocation_status > 0) then
   print *, "Allocation error"
      stop
end if

! Read the numbers of the lost cards
read "(i7)", lost_card
    . . .
```

In the declaration of the array lost_card, the colon is used to indicate the rank (number of dimensions) of the array, but the bounds are not pinned down until the allocate statement is executed. Because the programmer doesn't know how many lost cards there will be, there is no way to tell the compiler that information. During execution, the system must be able to create an array of any reasonable size *after* reading from the input data file the value of the variable `number_of_lost_cards`.

If there is an allocation error (insufficient memory, for example), the variable `allocation_status` is set to a nonzero value, which may be tested by the programmer.

The **deallocate statement** may be used to free the allocated storage.

Pointers, discussed in Chapter 8, provide an additional and more general facility for constructing data structures with variable sizes.

4.1.6 Array Sections

In the following statement, used in the example that tests for an end-of-file condition, a section of the array `lost_card` is printed.

```
print "(4i8)", lost_card (1:number_of_lost_cards)
```

On many occasions such as the one above, only a portion of the elements of an array is needed for a computation. It is possible to refer to a selected portion of an array, called an **array section**. A **parent array** is an aggregate of array elements, from which a section may be selected.

In the following example

```
real a (10)
   . . .
a (2:5) = 1.0
```

the parent array a has 10 elements. The array section consists of elements a (2), a (3), a (4), and a (5). The section is an array itself and the value 1.0 is assigned to all four of the elements in a (2:5).

In addition to the ordinary subscript that can select a subobject of an array, there are two other mechanisms for selecting certain elements along a particular dimension of an array. One is a subscript triplet, an example of which was shown above, and the other is a vector subscript.

The syntactic form of a **subscript triplet** is

[*expression*] : [*expression*] [: *expression*]

where each set of brackets encloses an optional item and each expression must produce a scalar integer value. The first expression gives a lower bound, the second an upper bound, and the third a stride. If the lower bound is omitted, the lower bound that was declared or allocated is used. (Note that an assumed-shape dummy array is treated as if it were declared with lower bound 1.) If the upper bound is omitted, the upper bound that was declared or allocated is used. The stride is the increment between the elements in the section referenced by the triplet notation. If omitted, it is assumed to be one. For example, if v is a one-dimensional array (list) of numbers

    v (0:4)

represents elements v (0), v (1), v (2), v (3), and v (4) and

    v (3:7:2)

represents elements v (3), v (5), and v (7).

Each expression in the subscript triplet must be scalar. The values of any of the expressions in triplet notation may be negative. The stride must not be zero. If the stride is positive, the section is from the first subscript up to the second in steps of the stride. If the stride is negative, the section is from the first subscript down to the second, decrementing by the stride.

Another way of selecting a section of an array is to use a vector subscript. A **vector subscript** is an integer array expression of rank one. For example, if iv is a list of three integers, 3, 7, and 2, and x is a list of 9 real numbers 1.1, 2.2, ..., 9.9, the value of x (iv) is the list of three numbers 3.3, 7.7, and 2.2—the third, seventh, and second elements of x.

Ordinary subscripts, triplets, and vector subscripts may be mixed in selecting an array section from a parent array. An array section may be empty.

Consider a more complicated example. If b were declared in a type statement as

    real b (10, 10, 5)

then b (1:4:3, 6:8:2, 3) is a section of b, consisting of four elements:

    b (1, 6, 3)   b (1, 8, 3)
    b (4, 6, 3)   b (4, 8, 3)

The stride along the first dimension is 3; therefore, the notation references the first subscripts 1 and 4. The stride in the second dimension is 2, so the second subscript varies by 2 and takes on values 6 and 8.

In the third dimension of b, there is no triplet notation, so the third subscript is 3 for all elements of the section. The section would be one that has a shape of (2, 2), that is, it is two dimensional, with extents 2 and 2.

To give an example using both triplet notation and a vector subscript, suppose again that b is declared as above:

```
real b (10, 10, 5)
```

then b (8:9, 5, (/ 4, 5, 4/)) is a 2 × 3 array consisting of the six values

```
b (8, 5, 4)    b (8, 5, 5)    b (8, 5, 4)
b (9, 5, 4)    b (9, 5, 5)    b (9, 5, 4)
```

If vs is a list of three integers, and vs = (/ 4, 5, 4/), the expression b (8:9, 5, vs) would have the same value. The expression b (8:9, 5, vs) cannot occur on the left side of an assignment because of the duplication of elements of b.

4.1.7 Array Assignment

Array assignment is permitted under two circumstances: when the array expression on the right has exactly the same shape as the array on the left, or when the expression on the right is a scalar. Note that, for example, if a is a 9 × 9 array, the section a (2:4, 5:8) is the same shape as a (3:5, 1:4), so the assignment

```
a (2:4, 5:8) = a (3:5, 1:4)
```

is valid, but the assignment

```
a (1:4, 1:3) = a (1:3, 1:4)
```

is not valid because even though there are 12 elements in the array on each side of the assignment, the left side has shape 4×3 and the right side has shape 3×4.

When a scalar is assigned to an array, the value of the scalar is assigned to every element of the array. Thus, for example, the statement

```
m (k+1:n, k) = 0
```

sets the elements m (k+1, k), m (k+2, k), ..., m (n, k) to zero.

4.1.8 The where Statement and Construct

The **where statement** may be used to assign values to only those elements of an array where a logical condition is true. For example, the following statement sets the elements of b to zero in those positions where the corresponding element of a is negative. The other elements of b are unchanged. a and b must be arrays of the same shape.

```
where (a < 0) b = 0
```

The logical condition in parentheses is an array of logical values conformable to each array in the assignment statement. In the example above, comparison of an array of values with a scalar produces the array of logical values.

The **where construct** permits any number of array assignments to be done under control of the same logical array, and the **elsewhere statement** within a where construct permits array assignments to be done where the logical expression is false. The following statements assign to the array a the quotient of the corresponding elements of b and c in those cases where the element of c is not zero. In the positions where the element of c is zero, the corresponding element of a is set to zero and the zero elements of c are set to 1.

```
where (c /= 0) ! c/=0 is a logical array.
    a = b / c  ! a and b must conform to c.
elsewhere
    a = 0      ! the elements of a are set to 0
               ! where they have not been set to b/c.
    c = 1      ! the 0 elements of c are set to 1.
end where
```

Within a where statement or where construct, only array assignments are permitted. The shape of all arrays in the assignment statements must conform to the shape of the logical expression following the keyword where. The assignments are executed in the order they are written—first those in the where block, then those in the elsewhere block. where constructs may not be nested.

4.1.9 Intrinsic Operators

All of the intrinsic operators and many of the intrinsic functions may be applied to arrays, operating independently on each element of the array. For example, the expression abs (a (k:n, k)) results in a one-dimensional array of $n - k + 1$ nonnegative real values. A binary operation, such as *, may be applied only to two arrays of the same shape, in which case it multiplies corresponding elements of the two arrays.

The assignment statement

```
a (k, k:n+1) = a (k, k:n+1) / pivot
```

divides each element of a (k, k:n+1) by the real scalar value pivot. In essence, a scalar value may be considered an array of the appropriate size with all its entries equal to the value of the scalar.

4.1.10 Element Renumbering in Expressions

An important point to remember about array expressions is that the elements in expression no longer have the same subscripts as the elements in the arrays that make up the expression. They are renumbered with 1 as the lower bound in each dimension. Thus, it is legal to add y (0:7) + z (-7:0), which results in an array whose eight values are considered to have subscripts 1, 2, 3, ..., 8.

The renumbering must be taken into account when referring back to the original array. Suppose v is a one-dimensional integer array that is given an initial value with the declaration

```
integer, dimension (0:6), parameter :: &
      v = (/ 3, 7, 0, -2, 2, 6, -1 /)
```

The intrinsic function maxloc returns a list of integers giving the position of the largest element of an array. maxloc (v) is (/ 2 /) because position 2 of the list v contains the largest number, 7, even though it is v (1) that has the value 7. Also, maxloc (v (2:6)) is the list (/ 4 /) because the largest entry, 6, occurs in the fourth position in the section v (2:6).

There is also an intrinsic function, minloc, whose value is the list of subscripts of a smallest element of an array. For example, if a = $\begin{bmatrix} 1 & 8 & 0 \\ 5 & -1 & 7 \\ 3 & 9 & -2 \end{bmatrix}$, the value of minloc (a) is (/3, 3/) because a (3, 3) is the smallest element of the array.

4.1.11 Exercises

1. Write a statement that declares values to be an array of 100 real values with subscripts ranging from -100 to -1.

2. Use an array constructor to assign the squares of the first 100 positive integers to a list of integers named squares. For example, squares (5) = 25.

3.   If a chess or checkers board is declared by

     ```
     character (len = 1), dimension (8, 8) :: board
     ```

the statement

     ```
     board = "W"
     ```

assigns the color white to all 64 positions. Write a statement or statements that assigns "B" to the 32 black positions. Assume that board (1, 1) is to be white so that the board is as shown in Figure 4-1.

W	B	W	B	W	B	W	B
B	W	B	W	B	W	B	W
W	B	W	B	W	B	W	B
B	W	B	W	B	W	B	W
W	B	W	B	W	B	W	B
B	W	B	W	B	W	B	W
W	B	W	B	W	B	W	B
B	W	B	W	B	W	B	W

Figure 4-1 .

4.   Suppose list is a one-dimensional array that contains n < max_size real numbers in ascending order. Write a subroutine insert (list, n, max_size, new_entry) that adds the number new_entry to the list in the appropriate place to keep the entire list sorted.

5.   Write a function that finds the angle between two three-dimensional real vectors. If $v = (v_1, v_2, v_3)$, the magnitude of v is $|v| = \sqrt{v \cdot v}$ where $\cdot$ is the vector dot product. The cosine of the angle between v and w is given by

$$\cos(\theta) = \frac{v \cdot w}{|v| \, |w|}$$

The built-in function acos (arccosine) may be used to find an angle with a given cosine.

4.2 Searching a List

The previous section describes the appropriate terminology and some of the Fortran rules concerning arrays and subscripts. This section makes a start toward illustrating the power of arrays as they are used in meaningful programs. The application throughout this section is that of checking a given credit card account number against a list of account numbers of lost or stolen cards. Increasingly more efficient programs are presented here and compared.

4.2.1 The Problem: Credit Card Checking

When a customer presents a credit card in payment for goods or services, it is desirable to determine quickly whether it can be accepted or whether it previously has been reported lost or stolen or canceled for any other reason. The subroutines in this section perform this task. See Sections 4.1.3 and 4.1.5 for ways to read the list lost_card.

4.2.2 Sequential Search through an Unordered List

The first and simplest strategy for checking a given credit card is simply to search from beginning to end through the list of canceled credit cards, card by card, either until the given account number is found in the list, or until the end of the list is reached without finding that account number. In the subroutine search_1, this strategy, called a **sequential search**, is accomplished by a do construct with exit that scans the list until the given account number is found in the list or all of the numbers have been examined.

> *Style Note:* It is good programming practice to make the searching part of the program a separate subroutine. Other versions of the credit card program in this section will be obtained by modifying this subroutine.

The two ways of exiting from the search loop both pass control to the end subroutine statement. However, they have a different effect on the dummy argument found. When the credit card being checked is not in the list, the search loop is executed until the list is exhausted. This normal completion of the do construct allows control to fall through to the end statement with the value of found still false. When the card being checked is found in the list, the logical variable found is set to true before exiting the do construct. The calling program can test the actual argument passed to the dummy variable found to decide whether the card number was found in the list. The intrinsic function size used in this subroutine returns an integer value that is the number of elements in the array lost_card.

```
subroutine search_1 (lost_card, card_number, found)

    integer, dimension (:), intent (in) :: lost_card
    integer, intent (in) :: card_number
    logical, intent (out) :: found
    integer :: i

    found = .false.
    do i = 1, size (lost_card)
       if (card_number == lost_card (i)) then
          found = .true.
          exit
       end if
    end do

end subroutine search_1
```

This subroutine makes a nice example for illustrating how individual elements of an array can be manipulated; but in Fortran 90, it is often better to think of operations for processing the array as a whole. In fact, using the built-in array functions, it is possible to do the search in one line.

```
found = any(lost_card(1:size(lost_card))==card_number)
```

The comparison

```
lost_card (1 : size (lost_card)) == card_number
```

creates a list of logical values with true in any position where the value of card_number matches a number in the list lost_card. The function any is true if any of the elements in a list of logical values is true; it is false otherwise. The intrinsic function any may be thought of as an extension of the binary operator .or. to arrays.

The basic strategy of the program search_1 is to check a credit card account number, supplied as input, against each account number, in turn, in the list of canceled or lost cards, either until a match is found or until the list is exhausted. These alternatives are not equally likely. Most credit cards offered in payment for purchases or services represent the authorized use of active, valid accounts. Thus, by far the most usual execution of the subroutine search_1 is that the entire list is searched without finding the card number provided.

The number of comparisons a program must make before accepting a credit card is some measure of the efficiency of that program. For example, when searching for an acceptable credit card in a list of 10,000 canceled credit cards, the subroutine search_1 usually makes 10,000 comparisons. On a traditional computer, the elapsed computer time for the search depends on the time it takes to make one comparison and to prepare to make the next comparison. However, on a computer with vector or parallel hardware, many comparisons may be done simultaneously and the intrinsic functions, probably written by the implementor to take advantage of this special hardware, might provide very efficient searching.

If the search must be performed on a traditional computer by making one comparison at a time, the search can be made more efficient by maintaining the list in order of increasing card number. As soon as one canceled card number examined in the search is too large, all subsequent ones will also be too large, so the search can be abandoned early. The subroutine search_2 presumes that the list is in increasing order.

```
subroutine search_2 (lost_card, card_number, found)

   integer, dimension (:), intent (in) :: lost_card
   integer, intent (in) :: card_number
   logical, intent (out) :: found
   integer :: i

   found = .false.
   do i = 1, size (lost_card)
      if (card_number <= lost_card (i)) then
         found = (card_number == lost_card (i))
         exit
      end if
   end do

end subroutine search_2
```

Before accepting a presented account number, search_1 always must search the entire list, but search_2 stops as soon as it reaches a number in the list of canceled account numbers that is larger than or equal to the presented number.

Roughly speaking, the average number of comparisons needed for an acceptance by search_2 is about half the list size, plus one additional comparison to determine whether the last entry examined was exactly the account number of the credit card being checked. For a list of 10,000 canceled cards, it would take an average of 5001 comparisons, significantly better than the 10,000 for search_1.

To a limited extent, this increased efficiency in the checking program is counterbalanced by some additional computer time needed to maintain the list of canceled credit cards in increasing order. However, the list is likely to be searched much more often than it is modified, so almost any increase in the efficiency of the checking program results, in practice, in an increase in the efficiency of the entire operation.

4.2.3 Program Notes

The sequential search loop in the subroutine search_2 is not quite as straightforward as it seems at first glance. When the presented card card_number is compared against an entry lost_card (i), three things can happen:

1. card_number is too low, in which case the search continues.

2. They match, in which case the presented card card_number has been found.

3. card_number is too high, in which case further search is futile.

The three possibilities are not equally likely. Case 1 can occur as many as 10,000 times in one search. Cases 2 and 3 can only happen once per search. It is important to test first for the most frequently occurring case. Otherwise, there will be two tests per iteration, slowing the search loop appreciably. This subroutine tests for the first case, and then, if it is false, determines whether case 2 or case 3 applies. The following if construct also does the tests in this same optimal order; but if the order of testing alternatives is changed, twice as many tests are done.

```
found = .false.
do i = 1, size (lost_card)
   if (card_number < lost_card (i)) then
      cycle
   else if (card_number == lost_card (i)) then
      found = .true.
      exit
   else
      exit
   end if
end do
```

4.2.4 Binary Search

Sequential search is a brute force technique. It works well for short lists but is very inefficient for large ones. A somewhat different strategy, **divide and conquer**, is employed in a **binary search**. Half of the list can be eliminated in one comparison by testing the middle element. Then half the remaining elements are eliminated by another test. This continues until there is only one element left; then this element is examined to see if it is the one being sought. The list must be ordered for binary search.

Table 4-2 shows how a binary search is used to try to find the number 2415495 in a list of 16 numbers. The numbers are given in increasing order in the first column. The presented number 2415495 is not in the list, but this fact plays no role in the search procedure until the very last step.

Table 4-2 A binary search that fails.

Before any comparisons	After one comparison	After two comparisons	After three comparisons	After four comparisons	Given number
1096633	1096633				
1202604	1202604				
1484131	1484131				
1627547	1627547*				
2008553	2008553	2008553			
2202646	2202646	2202646*			
2718281	2718281	2718281	2718281*	2718281 ≠	2415495
2980957*	2980957	2980957	2980957		
3269017					
4034287					
4424133					
5459815					
5987414					
7389056					
8103083					
8886110					

* An asterisk denotes the comparison entry at each stage, which is the last entry of the first half of the segment still under active consideration.

As a first step in binary searching, the list is divided in half. An asterisk follows the eighth number in column 1 because it is the last entry in the first half of the list. Since the given number 2415495 is less than (or equal to) the eighth entry 2980957, the second half of the list can be eliminated from further consideration. Column 2 shows only the first half of the original list, entries 1 through 8, retained as the segment still actively being searched.

The procedure is repeated. An asterisk follows the fourth entry in column 2 because it is the last entry in the first half of the segment of the list still actively being searched. Since the given number 2415495 is greater than the fourth number 1627547, this time it is the first half of the active segment that is eliminated and the second half (entries 5 through 8 of the original list) that is retained. This is shown in column 3 of Table 4-2.

In the next stage, the second remaining number 2202646, which was the sixth entry in the original list, is marked with an asterisk because it is the last entry of the first half of the segment still being searched. Since this number is exceeded by the given number 2415945, the second half of the segment in column 3 (entries 7 and 8) is retained as the active segment in column 4. The seventh entry of the original list, the number 2718281, is the last entry of the first half of the remaining list of two entries and thus is marked with an asterisk in column 4 to indicate its role as a comparison entry. Since the given number 2415495 is less than this, the other entry (the eighth original entry) is discarded, and column 5 shows that after four comparisons, only the seventh entry 2718281 remains as a candidate.

Since only one entry remains, a test for equality is made between the given number 2415495 and the one remaining entry 2718281. They are not equal. Thus, the given number is not in the list. Note that the previous comparisons of these two numbers were merely to determine whether the given number was less than or equal to the seventh entry.

Table 4-3 shows how the binary search works for the number 7389056, which is found in the list of 16 numbers. As before, the first column lists the original numbers with an asterisk following the last number of the first half of the list, the eighth entry. The number 7389056 is greater than the eighth entry, so the second half of the list (entries 9 to 16) is retained in column 2. A comparison of the given number 7389056 with the last entry of the first half of the segment remaining in column 2, the twelfth original entry 5459815, eliminates entries 9 through 12.

A comparison with the fourteenth entry, marked with an asterisk in column 3, eliminates the fifteenth and sixteenth entries. One more comparison of the given number 7389056 against the thirteenth entry, marked with an asterisk in column 4, eliminates that entry and leaves only the fourteenth entry 7389056. The final test for equality of the given number and the only remaining candidate in the list yields success, and it can be reported that the given number is the fourteenth entry in the list.

For the purpose of explanation, it is most convenient to use a list size that is an exact power of 2, that is, 2, 4, 8, 16, 32, ... This avoids fractions when the size of the list segment still under

Table 4-3 A binary search that is successful.

Before any comparisons	After one comparison	After two comparisons	After three comparisons	After four comparisons	Given number
1096633					
1202604					
1484131					
1627547					
2008553					
2202646					
2718281					
2980957*					
3269017	3269017				
4034287	4034287				
4424133	4424133				
5459815	5459815*				
5987414	5987414	5987414	5987414*		
7389056	7389056	7389056*	7389056	7389056 =	7389056
8103083	8103083	8103083			
8886110	8886110	8886110			

* An asterisk denotes the comparison entry at each stage, which is the last entry of the first half of the segment still under active consideration.

consideration is halved repeatedly. However, this is not essential; the use of integer division by 2 in the subroutine binary_search permits it to search a list of any length.

```
subroutine binary_search (lost_card, card_number, found)

    integer, dimension (:), intent (in) :: lost_card
    integer, intent (in) :: card_number
    logical, intent (out) :: found
    integer :: first, half, last, only

    first = 1
    last = size (lost_card)
    do
        if (first == last) exit
        half = (first + last) / 2
        if (card_number <= lost_card (half)) then
            ! Discard second half
            last = half
```

```
      else
         ! Discard first half
         first = half + 1
      end if
   end do

   ! The only remaining subscript to check is first
   ! (which is the same as last)
   only = first
   found = (card_number == lost_card (only))
end subroutine binary_search
```

When the part of the list still under consideration has been reduced to a single element by repeated bisection, the first element left is the last and only element left and the do construct is exited to test it.

4.2.5 Efficiency of a Binary Search

As before, we can get a reasonable indication of the efficiency of a search method by seeing how many times the given account number is compared against account numbers in the list of lost or stolen cards in the most usual event that the card number is not in the list.

The number of comparisons required in the binary search can be counted easily. With one data comparison, a list of items to be searched can be cut in half. When the list is reduced to one element, a final comparison determines whether that candidate is the credit card being searched for or not. Thus, with $n+1$ comparisons, it is possible to search 2^n items. Turning it around the other way, n items may be searched using $\log_2 n + 1$ comparisons. Thus, for example, 15 comparisons suffice for binary searching all lists of length up to 16,384 (= 2^{14}). This is considerably better than the 8192 comparisons needed for a sequential search! However, keep in mind that on a computer with intrinsic parallelism, it may be better to use the intrinsic functions and hope that the implementation takes advantage of the parallelism to do many comparisons simultaneously. Even if it does, whether or not it is faster than the binary search depends on the size of the list and the amount of parallelism in the system.

4.2.6 Exercise

1.   What changes need to be made to the subroutine binary_search to search a list of integers with kind 2 (Section 1.2.10)?

4.3 Sorting

Frequently it is necessary to sort a list of numbers or character strings. For example, the list list_card in the previous section must be sorted for the binary search to work. One of the simplest ways to do this is to compare every number in the list with every other number in the list and swap them if they are out of order. As with the previous examples in this chapter, the sorting is done with a subroutine so that it may be put in a library and used by many programs.

```
subroutine sort_1 (list)

    real, dimension (:), intent (inout) :: list
    integer :: i, j

    do i = 1, size (list) - 1
       do j = i + 1, size (list)
          if (list (i) > list (j))  &
                call swap (list (i), list (j))
       end do
    end do

end subroutine sort_1
```

The subroutine swap of Section 3.1.4 that exchanges the values of two variables is assumed to be available. This is a very simple algorithm for sorting, but it is very inefficient and should not be used to sort more than a few hundred items.

A second approach to sorting a list is to find the smallest number in the list and put it in the first position, then find the smallest number in the remainder of the list and put it in the second position, etc. The built-in function minloc can be used effectively for this sort.

For an array a of rank n, that is, with n subscripts, the value of minloc (a) is a one-dimensional array whose entries are the n subscript positions of a smallest element of a. As described in Section 4.1.10, if the lower bound in a particular dimension is 1, the subscript position and the subscript value are the same. If not, the actual subscript can be found by adding the declared lower bound − 1 to the subscript position. In the subroutine sort_2, the subscript of list (i:) containing a minimal element is min_loc (1) + i − 1, where min_loc is an array with one element used temporarily to store the value of minloc (list (i:)).

```
subroutine sort_2 (list)

    real, dimension (:), intent (inout) :: list
    integer :: i
    integer, dimension (1) :: min_loc

    do i = 1, size (list) - 1
        min_loc = minloc (list (i:))
        call swap (list (i), list (i + min_loc (1) - 1))
    end do

end subroutine sort_2
```

This subroutine appears to be just about as inefficient as sort_1, because execution of the minloc function involves searching through the elements of list (i:) to find the smallest one. Indeed, it may be just as inefficient; however, if it is executed on a system with parallelism, the minloc function may be faster than a sequential search.

4.3.1 Quick Sort

One of the best sorting algorithms is called "quick sort" or "partition sort". Whereas sort_1 needs to make approximately $n^2/2$ comparisons to sort n numbers, the quick sort needs approximately $n \log_2 n$ comparisons. To get an idea of the amount of improvement, for $n = 1000$ items, sort_1 would require approximately 500,000 comparisons and the quick sort would require approximately 10,000 comparisons, a ratio of 50 to 1; for $n = 1,000,000$ items, sort_1 would require approximately 500,000,000,000 comparisons and the quick sort would require approximately 100,000,000 comparisons, a ratio of 5000 to 1.

As might be expected, the quick sort is a bit more complicated. It is a divide-and-conquer algorithm like binary search. To sort a list of numbers, an arbitrary number (such as the first, last, or middle one) is chosen from the list. All the remaining numbers in turn are compared with the chosen number; the ones smaller are collected in a "smaller" set and the ones larger are collected in a "larger" set. The whole list is sorted by sorting the "smaller" set, following them with all numbers equal to the chosen number, and following them with the sorted list of "larger" numbers. Note that this last step involves using the quick sort routine recursively (Section 3.8).

```
recursive subroutine quick_sort (list)

    real, dimension (:), intent (inout) :: list
    real, dimension (size (list)) :: smaller, larger
    integer :: i,  &
          number_smaller, number_equal, number_larger
    real :: chosen

    if (size (list) > 1) then
        chosen = list (1)
        number_smaller = 0
        number_equal = 1
        number_larger = 0

        do i = 2, size (list)
            if (list (i) < chosen) then
                number_smaller = number_smaller + 1
                smaller (number_smaller) = list (i)
            else if (list (i) == chosen) then
                number_equal = number_equal + 1
            else
                number_larger = number_larger + 1
                larger (number_larger) = list (i)
            end if
        end do

        call quick_sort (smaller (1 : number_smaller))
        list (1:number_smaller) =  &
                smaller (1:number_smaller)
        list (number_smaller+1 :  &
                number_smaller+number_equal) = chosen
        call quick_sort (larger (1 : number_larger))
        list (number_smaller+number_equal+1 :) =  &
                larger (1 : number_larger)
    end if

end subroutine quick_sort
```

Although the subroutine quick_sort follows the description fairly closely and sorts with order $n \log_2 n$ comparisons, it wastes a lot of space in each subroutine call creating new smaller and larger lists. However, by clever management of the available space, the entire list can be sorted without using any arrays except the original argument list itself. In the following version of the quick sort, the "smaller" numbers are collected together by placing them at the beginning of the list and the "larger" numbers are collected together by placing them at the end of the list. Also, every effort is made to eliminate unnecessary moving or swapping of elements in the list. To do serious sorting, this version should be used.[2]

The details of the quick-sorting algorithm are still quite tricky and must be clarified further before an efficient and bug-free subroutine can be written. First, while it is possible to maintain two lists in a single one-dimensional array—the list smaller that grows from the bottom of the array list and the list larger that grows from the top of the array list—it is not possible to manage three lists in one array. Thus, the conditions for the sublists smaller and larger are relaxed to allow entries equal to the test element chosen to qualify for either of these sublists. Since these elements are the largest elements in the sublist smaller, and the smallest elements in the sublist larger, they are reunited in the middle of the array list when both sublists are sorted in place.

Second, since there are (essentially) no extra storage spaces for list elements, the only way to remove an unsuitably large element from the left (i.e., smaller) part of the list is to swap it with an unsuitably small element from the right (i.e., larger) part of the list. Each pass through the main loop of the subroutine quick_sort_1 consists of a search for an unsuitably large element on the left, a search for an unsuitably small element on the right, and a swap.

If the input list is in completely random order, it doesn't matter which element of the list is chosen as the test element. We use the middle element of the input list for two reasons: (1) one of the more likely nonrandom orders of a list is that the list is already sorted; choosing the middle element as test element provides much better splits than the first or last in this case; (2) if the test element is the middle element, both the search in the left list for a "large" element and the search in the right list for a "small" element are guaranteed not to run off the ends of the list, because the middle element will stop both searches. A test for invalid subscripts can be eliminated from these two inner loops if the test element is the middle element.

---

2. If the subroutine quick_sort is placed in a module (Chapter 7), it is possible to make quick_sort_1 a procedure internal to quick_sort. In this case, list, the array of numbers to be sorted, is known to the internal subroutine, and it is not necessary to pass it as an argument to quick_sort_1. Each time quick_sort_1 is called, it receives a left subscript and right subscript of the section of the list it is to sort, and it inherits the array variable list from the containing subroutine quick_sort. This will further improve the efficiency of the sorting process.

```fortran
subroutine quick_sort (list)

    real, dimension (:), intent (inout) :: list
    call quick_sort_1 (list, 1, size (list))

end subroutine quick_sort

recursive subroutine quick_sort_1 &
        (list, left_end, right_end)

    real, dimension (:), intent (inout) :: list
    integer, intent (in) :: left_end, right_end
    integer :: i, j
    real :: chosen, temp
    integer, parameter :: max_simple_sort_size = 6

    if (right_end < left_end + max_simple_sort_size) then
        ! Use interchange sort for small lists
        call interchange_sort (list, left_end, right_end)
    else
        ! Use partition ("quick") sort
        chosen = list ((left_end + right_end) / 2)
        i = left_end - 1; j = right_end + 1

        do
            ! Scan list from left end
            ! until element >= chosen is found
            do
                i = i + 1; if (list (i) >= chosen) exit
            end do
            ! Scan list from right end
            ! until element <= chosen is found
            do
                j = j - 1; if (list (j) <= chosen) exit
            end do
            if (i < j) then
                ! swap two out of place elements
                temp = list (i)
                list (i) = list (j)
                list (j) = temp
            else if (i == j) then
                i = i + 1; exit
```

```
            else
                exit
            end if
        end do

        if (left_end < j) &
                call quick_sort_1 (list, left_end, j)
        if (i < right_end) &
                call quick_sort_1 (list, i, right_end)
    end if

end subroutine quick_sort_1

subroutine interchange_sort (list, left_end, right_end)

    real, dimension (:), intent (inout) :: list
    integer, intent (in) :: left_end, right_end
    integer :: i, j
    real :: temp

    do i = left_end, right_end - 1
      do j = i + 1, right_end
         if (list (i) > list (j)) then
            temp = list (i)
            list (i) = list (j)
            list (j) = temp
         end if
      end do
    end do

end subroutine interchange_sort
```

4.3.2 Sorting Small Lists

The subroutine quick_sort has been made more efficient by the addition of the following statements that test if the quantity of numbers to be sorted is small and call an interchange sort if it is.

```
if (right_end < left_end + max_simple_sort_size) then
    ! Use interchange sort for small lists
    call interchange_sort (list, left_end, right_end)
```

Why be concerned about this? Quick sort rarely is used to sort such small lists, and even if it is, it is only relative efficiency that suffers:

the absolute time required to quick sort a small list is very small. The answer is that although the user might not call quick sort often to sort a very small list, because it is a divide-and-conquer technique, the quick-sort algorithm subdivides the list again and again until finally it calls itself recursively many times to sort very small lists. Thus, small inefficiencies in the quick sorting of small lists contribute many times over to form large inefficiencies in the quick sorting of large lists.

The solution is simple: for lists below a certain minimum size, `interchange_sort` is used. The subroutine `quick_sort_1` sorts all lists of size up to `max_simple_sort_size` using the compact and simple sorting algorithm of the subroutine `sort_1` for such lists. For larger lists, it uses the quick sort algorithm. Some experimenting with randomly generated large lists and different values of `max_simple_sort_size` indicates that for this simple sorting algorithm and this implementation of the quick-sort algorithm, `max_simple_sort_size` = 6 is probably the right choice.

4.3.3 Exercises

1. Modify the subroutine `quick_sort` so that a variable records the number of times two values are swapped. This provides a crude measure of the complexity of the sorting algorithm. Experiment with the program by generating 1000 numbers using the built-in subroutine `random_number` discussed in Section 3.7.1 and by varying the parameter `max_simple_sort_size`. Also collect data about actual running time using the built-in subroutine `system_clock`.

2. Execute `quick_sort` with randomly generated lists of numbers of various sizes n to see if the number of values swapped is proportional to $n \log_2 n$.

4.4 Selecting

A common problem is to find the median of a list of numbers, that is, the one that would be in the middle of the list if the list were in order. One way to do this is to sort the list and look at the element in the middle, but this is quite inefficient. The best sorting algorithms require $n \log_2 n$ steps to sort n numbers, whereas the median of n numbers can be found in n steps.

The trick is one that is often applicable to recursive procedures: solve a slightly more general problem instead. In this case the more general problem to solve is to find the number that would be in position k, $1 \le k \le n$, if a list of n numbers were in order. Then to find the median, simply find the number in position $k = n/2$.

A good algorithm to select the kth element is similar to the quick-sort algorithm. Arbitrarily pick one of the numbers in the list. As with the quick sort, separate the numbers into three collections: the numbers smaller than the chosen number, the numbers equal to the chosen number, and the numbers larger than the chosen number. Suppose the size of each of these collections is s, e, and l, respectively. If $k \le s$, the number we are looking for is in the collection of smaller numbers, and, in fact, is the kth number in that collection in order; this number can be found by applying the same selection algorithm recursively to the list of smaller numbers. If $s < k \le s+e$, then the number chosen is the one we are looking for and the search is complete. If $s+e < k$, the number we are looking for is in the collection of larger numbers; it is, in fact, the one in position $k-s-e$ in that list in order, so it can be found by recursively calling the selection procedure.

Here is the Fortran program; the selected element is returned as the value of the variable `element` and the logical variable `error` indicates if a position outside the bounds of the list is requested. The procedure `quick_select` is written as a subroutine instead of a function because it returns two values.

```
recursive subroutine quick_select  &
        (list, k, element, error)

    real, dimension (:), intent (in) :: list
    integer, intent (in) :: k
    real, intent (out) :: element
    logical, intent (out) :: error
    real, dimension (size (list)) :: smaller, larger
    integer :: i,  &
            number_smaller, number_equal, number_larger
    real :: chosen

    if (size (list) <= 1) then
        error = .not. (size (list) == 1 .and. k == 1)
        if (error) then
            element = 0.0  ! a value must be assigned
                    ! because element is intent (out)
        else
            element = list (1)
        end if
```

```
      else
        chosen = list (1)
        number_smaller = 0
        number_equal = 1
        number_larger = 0

        do i = 2, size (list)
          if (list (i) < chosen) then
              number_smaller = number_smaller + 1
              smaller (number_smaller) = list (i)
          else if (list (i) == chosen) then
              number_equal = number_equal + 1
          else
              number_larger = number_larger + 1
              larger (number_larger) = list (i)
          end if
        end do

        if (k <= number_smaller) then
          call quick_select &
                (smaller (1 : number_smaller), &
                 k, element, error)
        else if (k <= number_smaller + number_equal) then
          element = chosen
          error = .false.
        else
          call quick_select &
                (larger (1 : number_larger), &
                 k - number_smaller - number_equal, &
                 element, error)
        end if
      end if

end subroutine quick_select
```

4.4.1 Exercises

1. Modify the subroutine quick_select so that a variable records the number of times two values are compared. This provides a crude measure of the complexity of the selection algorithm. Experiment with the program by generating 1000 numbers using the built-in subroutine random_number discussed in Section 3.7.1. Also collect data about actual running time using the built-in subroutine system_clock.

2. Execute quick_select with randomly generated lists of numbers of various sizes n to see if the number of values compared is proportional to n.

3. Rewrite quick_select to reduce the amount of temporary storage used, using the second version of quick_sort in Section 4.3.1 as a model.

4. Instead of using list (1) as the value of chosen in the subroutine quick_select, use list (k). Repeat the timing experiments to see if this makes any difference. Try the experiments using both versions with a list that is already sorted.

4.5 Case Study: Solving Linear Equations

The operations of searching, sorting, and selecting discussed in the previous sections involve, by their nature, mostly operations on a single element of a list, one at a time. In many situations, particularly in numerical computations, whole arrays or sections of arrays can be processed at once. To explore an example of this type, we look at the problem of solving n simultaneous equations of the form

$$a_{11}x_1 + a_{12}x_2 + \cdots + a_{1n}x_n = b_1$$

$$a_{21}x_1 + a_{22}x_2 + \cdots + a_{2n}x_n = b_2$$

$$\vdots$$

$$a_{n1}x_1 + a_{n2}x_2 + \cdots + a_{nn}x_n = b_n$$

In matrix notation, this system of equations would be written as

$$
\begin{bmatrix}
a_{11} & a_{12} & \cdots & a_{1n} \\
a_{21} & a_{22} & \cdots & a_{2n} \\
 & & \cdot & \\
 & & \cdot & \\
 & & \cdot & \\
a_{n1} & a_{n2} & \cdots & a_{nn}
\end{bmatrix}
\begin{bmatrix}
x_1 \\
x_2 \\
\cdot \\
\cdot \\
\cdot \\
x_n
\end{bmatrix}
=
\begin{bmatrix}
b_1 \\
b_2 \\
\cdot \\
\cdot \\
\cdot \\
b_n
\end{bmatrix}
$$

Solving the equations is done by performing combinations of the following operations, none of which changes the values of the solutions. The three operations are (1) interchanging equations (which amounts to interchanging rows in the matrix of coefficients), (2) multiplying an equation (i.e., row) by a constant, and (3) adding one equation (i.e., row) to another equation. The operations of interchanging columns in the matrix of coefficients (which amounts to renaming variables) and multiplying a column by a constant (which amounts to rescaling the values of the variable represented by that column) are sometimes used in solving simultaneous linear equations, but are not used in the solution presented below.

These equations will be solved by a process called **Gaussian elimination**. Combinations of these operations are performed until the equations are in a form where all coefficients below the diagonal of the coefficient matrix are zero and all coefficients on the main diagonal are one; this constitutes the first phase of Gaussian elimination. In broad outline, what happens in this phase is that the first equation is solved for the first variable x_1 (i.e., its coefficient is made 1), and then appropriate multiples of the first equation are subtracted from each of the remaining equations to eliminate the variable x_1 from equations 2 to n. Then the second equation is solved for x_2, and multiples of it are subtracted from the remaining equations to eliminate x_2 also from equations 3 to n. Eventually, all the variables x_1, x_2, ..., x_{n-1} are eliminated from the nth equation, which can now be solved for x_n. At the end of the first phase, the set of equations takes the form

$$x_1 + c_{12}x_2 + c_{13}x_3 + \cdots + c_{1n-1}x_{n-1} + c_{1n}x_n = d_1$$
$$x_2 + c_{23}x_3 + \cdots + c_{2n-1}x_{n-1} + c_{2n}x_n = d_2$$
$$x_3 + \cdots + c_{3n-1}x_{n-1} + c_{3n}x_n = d_3$$

$$x_{n-1} + c_{n-1n}x_n = d_{n-1}$$
$$x_n = d_n$$

The second phase of Gaussian elimination is called **back substitution**. The last equation is already solved for $x_n = d_n$. The answer for x_n is substituted into the next to last equation, which contains only variables x_{n-1} and x_n after the first phase, so it can be solved for x_{n-1}. Then the answers for both x_n and x_{n-1} are substituted into the previous equation to solve for x_{n-2}, and so forth until all the variables x_n, x_{n-1}, ..., x_2 are substituted into the first equation to solve for x_1.

An equivalent form of the back-substitution phase, which is used sometimes, is to subtract appropriate multiples of the nth equation from all previous equations to eliminate x_n from equations 1 to $n-1$. Then multiples of equation $n-1$ are subtracted from equations 1 to $n-2$ to eliminate x_{n-1} from these equations. The process continues upward through the equations until each equation has only one variable, or equivalently, until every entry in the matrix of coefficients above the diagonal is zero. The equations now have the form

$$x_1 = e_1$$
$$x_2 = e_2$$

.   .

.   .

.   .

$$x_n = e_n$$

which is solved for all of its variables. In the program `solve_linear_equations`, we use the first method, substituting directly without changing the triangular matrix of coefficients to this completely diagonalized form.

If all goes well, the process of solving the system of linear equations is no more complicated than what we just described; however, a general solution must foresee and provide for all possibilities, even the possibility that the set of equations is inconsistent and has no solution.

The first potential problem is that when we try to solve the first equation for the first variable x_1, we might find that the first equation does not involve x_1 (i.e., $a_{11} = 0$). If some other equation involves x_1, that is, if some $a_{k1} \neq 0$, then we can swap the first and kth equations (to make $a_{11} \neq 0$ after the swap) so that we can solve the new first equation for x_1 and proceed. On the other hand, if no equation involves x_1, then the system of equations does not uniquely determine x_1 and we must report this as an undetermined system of equations.

A similar problem might occur when we try to solve the kth equation for x_k. If the coefficient a_{kk} is zero at this point in the computation, then we must seek a later equation, say the mth, for which $a_{mk} \neq 0$, and swap it with the kth equation before proceeding. If all remaining coefficients in the kth column are zero, then x_k is not uniquely determined.

Conventional wisdom, which we follow in this program, says that even if a_{kk} is nonzero, it is still better to swap the kth equation with that later equation for which the absolute value $|a_{mk}|$ is largest. Part of the reason is that roundoff error in calculations with the real coefficients often results in a coefficient that should be zero being calculated as a small nonzero value, but almost never results in it being calculated as a large nonzero value. Swapping a_{kk} with a_{mk}, the coefficient with the largest magnitude, greatly reduces the risk of dividing by a coefficient a_{kk} that should have been calculated as zero.

```fortran
subroutine solve_linear_equations (a, x, b, error)

    real, dimension (:, :), intent (in) :: a
    real, dimension (:), intent (out) :: x
    real, dimension (:), intent (in) :: b
    logical, intent (out) :: error
    real, dimension (size (b), size (b) + 1) :: m
    integer, dimension (1) :: max_loc
    real, dimension (size (b) + 1) :: temp_row
    integer :: n, k

    error = size (a, dim=1) /= size (b) .or.  &
            size (a, dim=2) /= size (b)
    if (error) then
       x = 0.0
    else

       n = size (b)
       m (1:n, 1:n) = a
       m (1:n, n+1) = b

       ! Triangularization phase
       triang_loop: do k = 1, n

          max_loc = maxloc (abs (m (k:n, k)))
          temp_row (k:n+1) = m (k, k:n+1)
          m (k, k:n+1) = m (k-1+max_loc(1), k:n+1)
          m (k-1+max_loc(1), k:n+1) = temp_row (k:n+1)

          if (m (k, k) == 0) then
             error = .true.
             exit triang_loop
          else
             m (k, k:n+1) = m (k, k:n+1) / m (k, k)
             m (k+1:n, k+1:n+1) = m (k+1:n, k+1:n+1) -  &
                spread (m (k, k+1:n+1), 1, n-k) *  &
                spread (m (k+1:n, k), 2, n-k+1)
          end if

       end do triang_loop
```

```
! Back substitution phase
if (error) then
    x = 0.0
else
    do k = n, 1, -1
        x (k) = m (k, n+1) -  &
                sum (m (k, k+1:n) * x (k+1:n))
    end do
end if


    end if


end subroutine solve_linear_equations
```

The array m is created in the subroutine solve_linear_ equations because the constant terms are subject to the same operations as the coefficients of the variables during the calculations of Gaussian elimination. It consists of the array a of coefficients enlarged by one column into which is placed the list of constants b. This is accomplished using the statements

```
real, dimension (size (b), size (b) + 1) :: m
n = size (b)
m (1:n, 1:n) = a
m (1:n, n+1) = b
```

Several array intrinsic functions are used in the subroutine solve_linear_equations. The size function is used to find the number of equations and variables, which is the size of the list b. The function spread takes an array and increases its dimension (i.e., number of subscripts) by one by duplicating entries along a chosen dimension. Suppose that m is the 3×4 array

```
11 12 13 14
21 22 23 24
31 32 33 34
```

then m (1, 2:4) is the one-dimensional array

```
12 13 14
```

and spread (m (1, 2:4), 1, 2) is the two-dimensional array

```
12  13  14
12  13  14
```

which consists of two copies of m (1, 2:4) spread downward, duplicating entries that differ only in the first subscript. Similarly, spread
(m (2:3, 1), 2, 3) is the array

```
21  21  21
31  31  31
```

consisting of three copies of m (2:3, 1) spread to the right, duplicating entries that differ only in the second subscript. Since these two
arrays are the same size and shape, they may be multiplied; the value
of spread (m (1, 2:4), 1, 2) * spread (m (2:3, 1), 2, 3) is the
array

```
12×21  13×21  14×21
12×31  13×31  14×31
```

Thus, the resulting value of m after executing the statement

```
m (2:3, 2:4) =                              &
                m (2:3, 2:4) -              &
        spread (m (1, 2:4), 1, 2) *  &
        spread (m (2:3, 1), 2, 3)
```

is

11	12	13	14
21	22 − 12×21	23 − 13×21	24 − 14×21
31	32 − 12×31	33 − 13×31	34 − 14×31

The intrinsic function sum finds the sum of all the elements of an
array. If a is a one-dimensional array, then the statement

```
s = sum (a)
```

gives the same result (subject to rounding errors) as the statements

```
s = 0
do i = lbound (a), ubound (a)
    s = s + a (i)
end do
```

For higher-dimensional arrays, a nested do loop is needed for each
dimension of the array to achieve the effect of the built-in function

sum. Besides the added simplicity and clarity of using the expression
sum (a) in place of nested loops, it is much easier for compilers to
recognize that sum (a) applies the same operation to the entire array
and therefore might be a suitable expression for parallel execution if
the hardware permits. The do loop versions explicitly ask for the calculations to be done in a specific order and thus may not benefit from
optimization.

Many other functions that operate on arrays are described
briefly in Appendix A.

4.6   Case Study: Calculating Probabilities

In Section 3.7, we considered the problem of calculating the probability that a throw of two dice will yield a 7 or an 11. The resulting program used the built-in subroutine random_number to generate a random number between 0 and 1. We now provide a slightly different
solution using the same built-in procedure, but with an array as the
first argument.

4.6.1   Generating an Array of Random Numbers

When the argument to the built-in subroutine random_number is a real
array, the array is filled with a collection of real numbers each greater
than or equal to 0 and less than 1. In general, the numbers are not all
the same, although, by chance, some pairs of them might be equal.

Also, in this section, we will rewrite the subroutine random_int
to return an array of integers from low to high. The subroutine
random_int calls the built-in subroutine random_number, but now
with an array as the argument. Note that the computational part of
the subroutine is identical to the scalar version presented in Section
3.7.

```
subroutine random_int (result, low, high)

    integer, dimension (:), intent (out) :: result
    integer, intent (in) :: low, high
    real, dimension (size (result)) ::  &
        uniform_random_value

    call random_number (uniform_random_value)
    result =  &
    int ((high - low + 1) * uniform_random_value + low)

end subroutine random_int
```

Using the techniques discussed in Section 7.3.1, it is possible to make the subroutine random_int a generic subroutine, so that when it is called with a scalar first argument, it returns a single scalar value, and when it is called with an array first argument, it returns an array of pseudorandom integer values.

4.6.2 Computing the Probability of a 7 or 11 Using Arrays

Using the subroutine random_int, the program to estimate the probability of rolling 7 or 11 with two dice is a bit shorter than the scalar version. We leave it to the reader to ponder whether it is easier or more difficult to understand than the scalar version.

```
program seven_11

    implicit none
    integer, parameter :: number_of_rolls = 1000
    integer, dimension (number_of_rolls) ::  &
            dice, die_1, die_2
    integer :: wins

    call random_int (die_1, 1, 6)
    call random_int (die_2, 1, 6)
    dice = die_1 + die_2
    wins = count ((dice == 7) .or. (dice == 11))

    print "(a, f6.2)",  &
    "The percentage of rolls that are 7 or 11 is", &
    100.0 * real (wins) / real (number_of_rolls)

contains

subroutine random_int . . .
    . . .

end program seven_11
```

The built-in function count returns the number of true values in any logical array; in this case the value in the array is true if the corresponding value in the array dice is 7 or 11. This version of the program seven_11 should produce an answer similar to the one produced by the scalar version.

4.6.3 Exercises

1. Use the array version of random_int to write a program that determines by simulation the percentage of times the sum of two rolled dice will be 2, 3, or 12.

2. Two dice are rolled until a 4 or 7 comes up. Use the array version of random_int to write a simulation program to determine the percentage of times a 4 will be rolled before a 7 is rolled.

3. Use the array version of random_int to write a simulation program to determine the percentage of times exactly 5 coins will be heads and 5 will be tails, if 10 fair coins are tossed simultaneously.

4. Is it reasonable to use the array version of random_int to create a program that deals a five-card poker hand? Remember that the same card cannot occur twice in a hand.

5

Character Data

In a computer program, a piece of written text is called a **character string**. Character strings have been used throughout this book to retain messages and identify information printed out but not processed in any other way. This chapter reviews this simple use of character strings and presents computer programs in which the character strings themselves are the center of interest.

5.1 Use of Character Data in Fortran Programs

5.1.1 Character String Declarations

A character string variable in a Fortran program is declared to be type character. Each object of type character has a length, which is the maximum number of characters that the string may have. For example, the declaration

```
character (len = 7) :: string_7
```

declares the variable string_7 to be a character string of length 7.

It is possible to have an array of character strings, all of the same length. The following declares string_array to be a $5 \times 9 \times 7$ array of character strings of length 20.

```
character (len = 20), dimension (5,9,7) :: string_array
```

It is possible for a character string to have length zero. It is not particularly useful to declare a variable to have length zero because such a variable could only assume one value, called the **null string**. However, the null string can arise as a result of a computation, and a variable could be declared to be length zero in a program generated by another computer program.

5.1.2 Character Kinds

Although there is a requirement for a Fortran system to support only one kind of character set, it may allow others, such as Kanji, Greek, mathematical symbols, or chemical symbols. You must consult the Fortran manual for the system you are using to see what character kinds are available and determine the number indicating each of the character kinds. For example, if you find that your system supports Greek characters and the kind for Greek is 7, it would be possible to declare the variables greek_name and greek_city with the statements

```
integer, parameter :: greek = 7
character (len = 20, kind = greek) ::  &
      greek_name, greek_city
```

Of course, it is not necessary to use the parameter greek, but it is a good idea, so that if Greek is supported on another machine but with a different kind number, only the value of the parameter greek needs to be changed to run the program on the other machine.

If the kind parameter is missing from a declaration, a default character set is assumed. In many cases, this will be the international standard character set known as ASCII. A program that prints the default character set is discussed in Section 5.1.10.

5.1.3 Character Constants

Recall that a character constant is enclosed in quotation marks (double quotes) or in apostrophes (single quotes). This makes it possible for the computer to tell the difference between the character constant "yes" and the variable yes, or between the character constant "14" and the integer constant 14.

If a character constant is to be a kind other than the default kind, it must be preceded by a kind value. For example, if kind 9 indicates strings of mathematical symbols,

9_"∫∫∫"

or

math_"∫∫∫"

where math is a named integer constant with the value 9, indicate a string of three integral signs. Note that the placement of the kind on constants is inconsistent. Integer, real, and logical constants may have a kind suffix and character constants may have a kind prefix.

5.1.4 Character Parameters

A character constant may be given a name using the parameter attribute. As a simple example, the program hello prints a character parameter or named character constant, instead of a literal character constant.

```
program hello
   implicit none
   character (len = *), parameter :: &
         message = "Hello, I am a computer."
   print *, message
end program hello

run hello

Hello, I am a computer.
```

Note that the name of the character parameter must be declared, just like a character variable, but the length may be declared as an asterisk indicating that the length is to be determined from the value of the string. Dummy arguments and function results also can have their length designated as an asterisk, indicating that their length will be determined by declarations in the calling program.

5.1.5 Assigning Values to Character Variables

A variable that has been declared to be a character string may be assigned a value that is a character string. A simple example is provided by the following program that assigns a string to a character variable used in a print statement instead of executing alternative print statements containing different messages.

```
program test_sign
   implicit none
   real :: number
   character (len = 8) :: sign

   read *, number
   if (number > 0) then
      sign = "positive"
   else if (number == 0) then
      sign = "zero"
   else
      sign = "negative"
   end if
   print *, number, "is ", sign
end program test_sign

run test_sign

  -2.3000000 is negative
```

5.1.6 Length of a Character String

The **length** of a character string is the number of characters in the string. The length of a Fortran character string is fixed and is never negative. Each blank occurring in the string is counted in its length. The built-in function len gives the length of a character string. Thus,

```
len ("love") = 4
len ("Good morning.") = 13
len (" ") = 1
len ("   ") = 4
len ("bg7*5 ad") = 8
```

As with other functions, the argument of the function len may be a variable or more general expression, as well as a constant.

During execution of a program, a character string variable always has its declared length. However, the length of a character string assigned to a character variable may be different from the length declared for that variable. For example, if the input number is zero in the program test_sign, the 4-character constant "zero" is assigned to the 8-character variable sign. This assignment is legal. Four blanks are added to the end of the string "zero" to make its length 8, the declared length of the variable sign. Thus, the new value of the variable sign is "zero   ".

On the other hand, if the character string to be assigned to a variable is longer than the declared length of the variable, characters are truncated from the right end of the string prior to assignment. For example, if the string name has a declared length of 3, the assignment statement

```
name = "Jonathan"
```

results in the string "Jon" being assigned to name.

The length of a character parameter (named constant) may be *, in which case the length is determined by the string assigned to it.

In a subprogram, the length of a character dummy argument may be given as an asterisk (*), which means that the length of the corresponding actual argument is to be used. Such a dummy argument is said to have **assumed length**. For example,

```
subroutine process (c)
character (len = *) :: c
```

The length of a local character string may depend on values related to the dummy arguments; such strings are called **automatic**, as they are very similar to automatic arrays (Section 4.1.3).

For example, a temporary local string can be declared to hold the value of an argument passed in.

```
subroutine ss (c)
   character (len = *), intent (in) :: c
   character (len = len (c)) :: temp_c
   temp_c = c
   . . .
```

The intrinsic function len provides information that is otherwise unobtainable in the case where a character string, such as the variable c above, is a dummy argument with its length given by an asterisk. The programmer knows the length of all other character strings from their declarations.

5.1.7 Input of Character Strings

When character strings are supplied as input data for a read statement with the default format (*), the string should be enclosed in quotes or apostrophes, just like a character constant. When using an a format, however, surrounding quotes must be omitted; any quotes among the characters read are considered to be part of the character constant. Input and output of nondefault character kinds are implementation dependent, and details must be checked in the manuals for the computer system you are using.

5.1.8 Character Collating Sequences

Every Fortran 90 system is required to support a default character kind. Other character kinds are permitted, but not required. Many computers use the standard 128-character ASCII character set. The acronym ASCII stands for "American Standard Code for Information Interchange".

Each character set has an intrinsic ordering of individual characters, derived originally from the most usual way characters were stored internally on computers that used these character sets. More recently the intrinsic ordering for characters of a specific kind, called the **collating sequence** for that character set, has been fixed by published standards, whether or not the computer uses the motivating internal representation. For example, the ASCII code is described in the ANSI standard X3.4-1986, which is the U.S. national version of the international standard ISO 646:1983. Table 5-1 shows a selection of printable characters in the ASCII collating sequence.

Table 5-1 The collating sequence for printable ASCII characters.

```
blank ! " # $ % & ' ( ) * + , - . /
0 1 2 3 4 5 6 7 8 9 : ; < = > ? @
A B C D E F G H I J K L M N O P Q R S T U V W X Y Z [ \ ] ^ _ '
a b c d e f g h i j k l m n o p q r s t u v w x y z { | } ~
```

One character is considered "less than" another character if it precedes the other character in the collating sequence for the kind of the characters. Comparison of characters of different kinds is not permitted. The result of a comparison of characters may depend on the kind.

5.1.9 The Built-In Functions ichar, char, iachar, and achar

The built-in function ichar gives an integer representing the internal code or position in the collating sequence of the character given as argument. The kind of the actual argument determines the collating sequence to be used.

The function char returns the character with a given code. The kind of the character is the default unless an optional second argument is provided indicating the kind. For example, char (20, kind =

7) and char (20, greek) would both give the character in position 20 for the character set of kind 7, assuming that greek is a named integer constant with value 7. The kind argument is identified by its keyword in the first case.

The built-in function iachar gives the integer code used to represent a given character in the ASCII collating sequence, and the built-in function achar returns the character with a given ASCII code. The actual argument for iachar must be a character of default type.

5.1.10 A Testing Technique for Character Output

The program explore_character_set will allow you to explore the collating sequence of the default kind one character at a time. You type the character code and the computer prints the character with that code. It should be run interactively.

```
program explore_character_set

! Prints the character with given character code
! in the default kind

    implicit none
    integer :: code

    print *, "Type a character code"
    read *, code
    print "(i5, 3a)", code, ">", char (code), "<"

end program explore_character_set

run explore_character_set

Type a character code
  65>a<
```

The blank character is a perfectly valid character (ASCII code 32). To better see the value of char, the value is printed surrounded by the printable characters > and <. A blank character will then conspicuously occupy the print or display position between its delimiters.

You must expect some surprises when you run the program explore_character_set. Most of the characters from 0 to 31 do not print. Some, like the line feed, char (10) in ASCII, direct the printer to perform some action rather than print a character. The delimiters > and < will help you figure out what action was taken.

Table 5-2   summarizes   executions   of   the   program
`explore_character_set`. It is the output of a program similar to
`explore_character_set` that uses loops to show the printable ASCII
characters and their corresponding codes, eight per line of output.
Codes 0 through 31 and code 127 represent special control characters
such as the "bell" character, backspace, and newline. Code 32 represents the space character.

Table 5-2 The printable ASCII characters.

32	33 !	34 "	35 #	36 $	37 %	38 &	39 '
40 (	41)	42 *	43 +	44 ,	45 -	46 .	47 /
48 0	49 1	50 2	51 3	52 4	53 5	54 6	55 7
56 8	57 9	58 :	59 ;	60 <	61 =	62 >	63 ?
64 @	65 A	66 B	67 C	68 D	69 E	70 F	71 G
72 H	73 I	74 J	75 K	76 L	77 M	78 N	79 O
80 P	81 Q	82 R	83 S	84 T	85 U	86 V	87 W
88 X	89 Y	90 Z	91 [	92 \	93]	94 ^	95 _
96 '	97 a	98 b	99 c	100 d	101 e	102 f	103 g
104 h	105 i	106 j	107 k	108 l	109 m	110 n	111 o
112 p	113 q	114 r	115 s	116 t	117 u	118 v	119 w
120 x	121 y	122 z	123 {	124 |	125 }	126 ~	

5.1.11 Comparison of Character Strings

In Fortran the comparison operators[1]

```
<, <=, ==, /=, >, >=
```

may be used to compare character values according to the intrinsic
ordering of the character kind being compared. It is not permitted to
compare character expressions of different kinds. If strings are to be
sorted on the ASCII collating sequence, the built-in functions `llt`, `lle`,
`lgt`, and `lge` may be used.

The ordering of strings is an extension of the ordinary lexicographic (i.e., dictionary) ordering of words, but uses the processor
codes to order characters other than letters. If the first character of
one character string precedes the first character of the second string
in the collating sequence, then we say the first character string is less
than the second. If the first characters are equal, the second characters are used to decide which character string is smaller. If the

---

1. Of course, the old versions of the relational operators, `.lt.`, `.le.`, `.eq.`, `.n`, `.gt.`, and
`.ge.`, still work.

second characters match also, the third characters are used to decide, and so on. The character string with the the smaller character in the first position where the two strings differ is considered the smaller character string. When character strings of different lengths are compared, the shorter one is treated as if it were padded with enough blanks at the end to make it the same length as the longer one. For example,

```
"apple" < "bug" < "cacophony" < "doldrums"

"earache" < "elephant" < "empathy" < "equine"

"phlegmatic" < "phonograph" < "photosynthetic"

"dipole" < "duplicate" == "duplicate   " < "dynamic"
```

In the first line of expressions, decisions are made on the basis of the first letter of the strings. In the second line, since each string has first letter "e", decisions are made on the basis of the relative collating position of the second letters. In the third set of comparisons, third or fourth letters differ.

From these examples, it is clear that the natural order of character strings corresponds exactly to ordinary alphabetic order when the character strings are words written either entirely in lowercase or entirely in uppercase letters.

String ordering does not take meaning into account. For example, although

```
"1" < "2" < "3" < "4"
```

as expected, it is also true that

```
"four" < "one" < "three" < "two"
```

and, worse yet

```
"12" < "2"
```

String ordering also is sensitive to upper and lower case. The two character strings

```
"word"        "WORD"
```

are not equal.

5.1.12 Substrings

Many character-processing applications require breaking down a string into individual characters or subsequences of characters. Examples are decomposing a word into letters or a sentence into words. The key idea in such a decomposition is a substring.

A **substring** of a character string is any consecutive sequence of characters in the string. For example, "J", "ne D", and "Doe" are substrings of the character string "Jane Doe", but "JDoe" is not a substring. Every character string is regarded as a substring of itself. The string of length zero (the null string) is a substring of every string; it occurs between every pair of characters and at both the beginning and end of the string. The following table indicates all the substrings of the character string "then".

Length 0: "" (the null string)
Length 1: "t" "h" "e" "n"
Length 2: "th" "he" "en"
Length 3: "the" "hen"
Length 4: "then"

5.1.13 Referencing Substrings

There is a convenient way to refer to any contiguous subsequence of characters of a character string. This is done by writing after any character variable or array element two integer expressions that give the positions of the first and last characters in the substring. These two expressions are separated by a colon and enclosed in parentheses. An example is string (k : l), where the values of k and l are positive integers less than or equal to the length of string and k ≤ l. If k > l, the result is the null string. For example if c = "crunch",

c (2 : 4) = "run"
c (1 : 6) = "crunch"
c (3 : 2) = "" (the null string)
c (2 : 7) is illegal
c (5 : 5) = "c"

The last example illustrates how to refer to a single character of a string. The program single_letters tells the computer to print, one at a time, the characters of a string supplied as input.

```
program single_letters
!  Print individually the letters of an input string
```

```
    implicit none
    integer :: k
    character (len = 10) :: string

    read "(a)", string
    print *, "Input data  string:", string

    do k = 1, len (string)
       print *, string (k : k)
    end do

    print *, "====="
end program single_letters

run single_letters

 Input data  string:SHAZAM
 S
 H
 A
 Z
 A
 M




 =====
```

There are four blank lines between "M" and "=====" in the output of the program single_letter because there are are four blank letters following the characters SHAZAM in the value of the variable string. This is because string is declared to have length 10, but SHAZAM contains only 6 characters.

5.1.14 Trimmed Length of a String

It is a nuisance that the length of a character variable is always the same regardless of its value. A definition of length that is suitable for many applications is the length of the substring that includes all characters up to and including the last nonblank character, but excluding terminal blanks. Using substrings, it is possible to write a function subprogram len_trim (trimmed length) that computes this value.

```
function len_trim (string) result (len_trim_result)

    character (len = *), intent (in) :: string
    integer :: len_trim_result, k

    len_trim_result = 0
    do k = len (string), 1, -1
        !  or until nonblank found
        if (string (k : k) /= " ") then
            len_trim_result = k
            exit
        end if
    end do

end function len_trim
```

Style Note: It is almost always a good idea to use an asterisk
as the length declaration for a dummy argument of type
character and to use the built-in function len to find its
true length when needed.

Actually, the function len_trim is a built-in function that computes exactly the same result as the one given above. In addition,
there is a built-in function trim, whose value is the given character
string with all trailing blanks removed. The value of trim (string)
is the same as string (1 : len_trim (string)) and is used in the
sample program plural in Section 5.1.17.

The program substrings_length_2 (substrings of length two)
prints all substrings of length two of any character string supplied as
input. The upper bound len_trim (string) – 1 on the do variable k
is the starting point of the last substring of length two that doesn't
contain a trailing blank.

```
program substrings_length_2
    implicit none
    character (len = 20) :: string
    integer :: k

    read "(a)", string
    print *, "Input data  string: ", string
    do k = 1, len_trim (string) - 1
        print *, string (k : k + 1)
    end do
```

```
    print *, "====="
end program substrings_length_2

run substrings_length_2

 Input data  string: High their!
 Hi
 ig
 gh
 h
  t
 th
 he
 ei
 ir
 r!
 =====
```

By adapting the method of the program substrings_length_2, we could write a program to print out all the substrings of any given length. By using a double loop, we could write a program that lists all substrings of all possible lengths. Tasks like these are provided as exercises at the end of this section.

5.1.15 Reassigning the Value of a Substring

It is possible to reassign the value of a substring without affecting the rest of the string. For instance, the three lines

```
name = "John X. Public"
initial = "Q"
name (6 : 6) = initial
```

tell the computer to change the value of the variable name from "John X. Public" to "John Q. Public". Similarly the three lines

```
name = "John Xavier Public"
new_middle_name = "Quincy"
name (6 : 11) = new_middle_name
```

direct the computer to change the value of the variable name from "John Xavier Public" to "John Quincy Public".

In reassigning the value of a substring as in the above two examples, it is necessary that the length of the new substring value exactly equal the length of the old substring value. The following example shows how to use a loop to make room for a longer replacement substring. It is assumed that the declared length of name is at least 17 characters.

```
name = "John Paul Public"
! Move last name and blank one position to the right
do letter = 16, 10, -1
   name (letter + 1 : letter + 1) = &
        name (letter : letter)
end do
! Insert middle name
name (6 : 10) = "Peter"
```

Note that it would not be correct to have the do variable count forward from 10 to 16. That loop would first move the blank in position 10 to position 11, which is what is desired. However, for the second iteration of the loop, the value of letter would be 11 and the blank just placed in position 11 would be moved to position 12. Next, the blank in position 12 would be moved to position 13. The total effect of the loop would be to put blanks in positions 11 through 17.

It is possible to replace the do block that moves the last name one position to the right with the single statement

```
name (11 : 17) = name (10 : 16)
```

This was illegal in Fortran 77 because of the overlap, but is legal in Fortran 90.

5.1.16 Finding the Position of One String in Another

There are numerous reasons for wanting to know if one string is contained as a substring in another. We might want to know if a particular letter is in a word or if a certain word is in a sentence. The built-in function index tells even more than that; it tells where to find the first instance of one character string as a substring of another. For example,

```
index ("monkey", "on")
```

is 2 because the substring "on" begins at the second letter of the string "monkey" and

```
index ("monkey", "key")
```

is 4 because the substring "key" begins at the fourth letter of "monkey".

If the string supplied as the second argument occurs more than once as a substring of the string supplied as the first argument, the function value is the location of the beginning of the leftmost occurrence, so that

```
index ("banana", "ana")
```

is 2 even though characters 4 to 6 of "banana" also are "ana". If the second argument is not a substring of the first argument, rather than calling it an error and halting, a function value of zero is used as a signal. For example,

```
index ("monkey", "off")
```

is 0. A program that calls the function index can test for the signal value zero if desired.

The function index is a built-in function in Fortran; but to provide a better understanding of how the function works, a programmer-defined version of the program follows. The intrinsic function index has an optional third argument back not implemented in this version. In the intrinsic version, when back is true, the search is from right to left.

```
function index (text, string)  result (index_result)
!  Searches for string as a substring of text.
!  If found, index is the position of the first
!  character of the leftmost occurrence of string
!  in text.  If not found, index = 0

   integer :: index_result
   character (len = *), intent (in) :: text, string
   integer left_end, right_end

   index_result = 0
   do left_end = 1, len (text) - len (string) + 1
      right_end = left_end + len (string) - 1
      if (text (left_end : right_end) == string) then
         index_result = left_end
         exit
      end if
   end do

end function index
```

5.1.17 Concatenation

The only built-in operation that can be performed on strings is **concatenation.** The concatenation of two strings is formed simply by placing one string after the other. The symbol for concatenation is two slashes (//). The concatenation operator in Fortran is less useful than it might be because strings are all fixed length. The program plural attempts to form the plural of given words by the method of putting the letter "s" at the end. Obviously, this program is not very useful as it stands, but it does illustrate the use of the concatenation operator.

```
program plural
   implicit none
   character (len = 18) :: word
   integer :: ios

   do ! until out of words
      read (*, "(a)", iostat = ios) word
      if (ios < 0) exit  ! end of file
      print *, "Input data  word: ", word
      print *, "  Plural of word: ", trim (word) // "s"
   end do
end program plural

run plural

 Input data  word: program
   Plural of word: programs
 Input data  word: programmer
   Plural of word: programmers
 Input data  word: matrix
   Plural of word: matrixs
 Input data  word: computer
   Plural of word: computers
 Input data  word: horses
   Plural of word: horsess
```

The read statement in the program plural needs both a format specification and an option that sets the integer variable ios to a negative value when attempting to read beyond the end of the file. Thus, the long form (see Chapter 9) is required. However, we still want to use the default input unit, so we could write

```
read (unit = *, fmt = "(a)", iostat = ios) word
```

If the first two options are respectively the unit number and format specifier, the introductory keyword phrases for these two options may be omitted, resulting in the shorter form

```
read (*, "(a)", iostat = ios) word
```

5.1.18 Exercises

1. What is the value of each of the following expressions?

```
len ("5 feet")
len ("alphabet")
len ("abcdefghijklmnopqrstuvwxyz")
len ("42")
```

2. List all the substrings of length 3 of the string "alphabet".

3. Write a program that reads a character string of maximum length 50 and prints all substrings of length 3. If you can't think of anything better, use as input data

```
"These are the times that try men's souls."
```

The output from this sample input should be

```
run substrings_3

The
hes
ese
 .
 .
 .
uls
ls.
```

4. Write a program that reads a character string of maximum length 50 and prints all of its substrings.

5. Write a program that sorts a list of at most 200 character strings. Each character string is at most 50 characters long and occupies the leftmost positions of one line in the input file. Use the end-of-file test to terminate reading of input data. You may be surprised at what happens if you accidentally type a blank in the leftmost column of one of the lines in the input file. Then again, after you think about it, you might not be.

6. A computer system maintains a list of valid passwords. Write a
    program that accepts an 8-character password and checks it
    against its list of valid passwords. The program should print
    "ok" if the password is in the list and "Try again" if it is not.
    Give the user two additional tries, replying with successively
    nastier messages each time the user fails to give the correct pass-
    word. **Hint:** Keep a list of responses as well as a list of pass-
    words. A sample execution might produce the following output:

    ```
    run check_password

      Welcome to the super special simulated system
      Enter your password:
    bug free
      Try again
      Enter your password:
    silicon
      Are you sure you have a password?
      Enter your password:
    fortran
      ok
    ```

7. Read a character string of maximum length 50 as input and
    print it in reverse order. Ignore trailing blanks. You must use a
    character-valued function **reverse (string)**. If the input is

    ```
    until
    ```

    the output should be

    ```
    run test_reverse

      Input data  string:  until
      litnu
    ```

8. Nicely displayed headings add impact to a document. Write a
    program to take a character string as input and print it sur-
    rounded by a border of asterisks. Again, ignore trailing blanks
    in the input. Leave one blank before the first character and
    after the last character in the display. If the input is

    ```
    Payroll Report
    ```

    the output should be

```
run border

Input data  title:  Payroll Report

*******************
* Payroll Report *
*******************
```

9. Write a logical-valued function `fortran_name` that determines whether or not its character string argument is a legal Fortran name.

10. Write a function `char_to_int` that accepts a character string and returns a vector of integers, one for each character in the string. The integer value should be 1 through 26, reflecting the position in the alphabet if the character is either an uppercase or lowercase letter; the value should be zero, otherwise. For example, `char_to_int ("e")` = (/5/) and `char_to_int ("a-z")` = (/1, 0, 26/).

11. Write a function `int_to_binary` that converts an integer to a character string that is the binary representation of the integer. Adjust the 1s and 0s in the right-hand portion of the string and pad the remainder of the string with blanks. The string should contain no insignificant zeros, except that the integer 0 should produce the string consisting of all blanks and one character "0". If the integer is negative, the first nonblank character should be a minus sign; if it is positive, the first nonblank character should be "1". In the function, the result should be declared to have length *. If the declared length of the function in the calling program is not long enough to contain the result, it should consist of all asterisks. For example, if the calling program declares `int_to_binary` to be length 5

    ```
    int_to_binary (5) = "bb101"
    int_to_binary (0) = "bbbb0"
    int_to_binary (-4) = "b-100"
    int_to_binary (77) = "*****"
    ```

5.2 Text Analysis

There are numerous reasons for examining text in minute detail, word by word and letter by letter. One of the reasons is to determine the authorship of an historical or literary work. Such quantities as the average length of a word or the frequency of usage of certain letters can be important clues. Computers have been useful in studying text from this viewpoint.

5.2.1 Blanking Out Punctuation

We start with some routines that perform simple text manipulation processes. The subroutine blank_punct (blank out punctuation) uses the substring value reassignment facility and the intrinsic function index. Keep in mind that a function value zero means the function index has determined that the second supplied argument is not a substring of the first supplied argument. The subroutine blank_punct regards any character besides a letter or a blank as a "punctuation mark" to be blanked out.

The program test_bp (test blank out punctuation) is intended to show how the subroutine blank_punct works.

```
program test_bp
   implicit none
   character (len = 100) ::  &
        text = "Suppress5$,superfluous*/3punctuation."

   call blank_punct (text)
   print *, text

contains

subroutine blank_punct (text)
! Blank out punctuation
! Retain only letters and blanks

   implicit none
   character (len = *), intent (inout) :: text
   character (len = *), parameter :: letter_or_b =  &
        "ABCDEFGHIJKLMNOPQRSTUVWXYZ" //  &
        "abcdefghijklmnopqrstuvwxyz "
   integer :: i

   ! Replace any character that is not a blank
   ! or letter with a blank
```

```
      do i = 1, len_trim (text)
        if (index (letter_or_b, text (i : i)) == 0) then
          text (i : i) = " "
        end if
      end do
  end subroutine blank_punct

  end program test_bp

  run test_bp
```

Suppress   superfluous   punctuation

A slightly different version of the subroutine blank_punct uses the verify built-in function. The verify function scans the first argument, checking that each character in the string is also in the string that is the second argument. If each character in the first argument is also in the second, the value of the function is 0. Otherwise, the value of the function is the character position of the leftmost character in the first argument that is not in the second argument. For example the value of verify ("banana", "nab") is 0 and the value of verify ("banana", "ab") is 3, the position in "banana" of the first "n".

```
  subroutine blank_punct (text)
  ! blank out punctuation
  ! retain only letters and blanks

    character (len = *), intent (inout) :: text
    character (len = *), parameter :: letter_or_b = &
        "ABCDEFGHIJKLMNOPQRSTUVWXYZ" // &
        "abcdefghijklmnopqrstuvwxyz "
    integer :: i

    ! Replace any character that is not a blank
    ! or letter with a blank
    do
        i = verify (text, letter_or_b)
        if (i == 0) exit
        text (i : i) = " "
    end do
  end subroutine blank_punct
```

The subroutine `blank_punct` needs a character string of length 53 that does not fit conveniently on one line. The concatenation operator is used at the line break so that leading blanks on the continuation line, inserted for readability, are not part of the character constant. Another way to do this is to use a continuation line with an ampersand (Section 1.4.1):

```
character (len = *), parameter :: letter_or_b =  &
    "ABCDEFGHIJKLMNOPQRSTUVWXYZ&
    &abcdefghijklmnopqrstuvwxyz "
```

5.2.2 Excising a Character from a String

When a character of a string is blanked out, as by the subroutine `blank_punct`, that character is replaced by a blank and the length of the character string remains unchanged. When a character is *excised* from a string, not only is the character removed, but also all of the characters to the right of the excised character are moved one position to the left. Thus, when a character is excised from a string, the trimmed length (that is, not including trailing blanks) of the string is decreased by one. Of course, the declared total length of the string cannot change in Fortran and so a blank is added as the rightmost character. The character in position c of `name` can be excised by the statement

```
name (c :) = name (c + 1 :)
```

A blank is added because `name (c + 1 :)` is one character shorter than `name (c :)`.

The subroutine `compress_bb` (compress double blanks) removes all double blanks from a string except those that occur at the right end. It is called by a program `words` that lists all the words in a string; the program `words` is discussed in the next subsection.

```
subroutine compress_bb (text)
!  Removes double blanks, except at right end
   character (len = *), intent (inout) :: text
   integer :: i
```

```
      do
          i = index (trim (text), "  ")
          if (i == 0) exit
          text (i :) = text (i + 1 :)
      end do
  end subroutine compress_bb
```

5.2.3 Listing All the Words

We now turn our attention to the problem of listing all the words in a text. For this purpose, the program words regards a substring as a word if and only if it consists entirely of letters and both the character immediately before it (if any) and the character immediately after it (if any) are not letters. The computer does not consult a dictionary to see whether the word has been approved by a lexicographer.

```
  program words
      implicit none
      character (len = 200) :: text
      integer :: end_of_word

      read "(a)", text
      print *, "Input data  text: ", text

      ! Blanking out the punctuation,
      ! compressing the multiple blanks,
      ! and ensuring that the first character is a letter
      ! are pre-editing tasks to simplify the job.
      call blank_punct (text)
      call compress_bb (text)
      text = adjustl (text)

      ! Print all the words.
      if (len_trim (text) == len (text)) then
         print *, text
      else
        ! Each word is followed by exactly one blank.
        do ! until all words are printed
            if (len_trim (text) == 0) exit
            end_of_word = index (text, " ") - 1
            print *, text (1 : end_of_word)
```

```
              ! Discard word just printed
              text = text (end_of_word + 2 :)
          end do
      end if
  end program words

  run words

      Input data  text: Then, due to illness*, he resigned.
      Then
      due
      to
      illness
      he
      resigned
```

If the string supplied as input to the program words contains no letters, the pre-editing provides a string of all blanks to the do block that prints all the words. The do block exits correctly on the first iteration without printing any words because the trimmed length is zero. In the usual case, however, a word starts at position 1 of text and stops immediately before the first blank. The computer prints the word and discards it and the blank immediately following it, so that the next word to be printed begins at location 1 of the resulting character string.

Even after the subroutines blank_punct and compress_bb are called, it is possible that the first character of the string is a blank. Application of the built-in function adjustl shifts the string to the left to eliminate any leading blanks, filling in the end of the string with a blank for each position shifted.

5.2.4 Average Word Length

To compute the average length of words in a given text, it is necessary to determine both the total number of letters in the text and the total number of words. The most direct way that comes to mind is used by the program avg_word_len_1 (average word length, version 1).

```
  program avg_word_len_1
      Initialize word count and letter count to zero
      Read text
```

```
    Start scan at leftmost character of the text
    Do until end of text is reached
        Locate the beginning and end of a word
        If no more words then exit the loop
        Increase the letter count by the number of letters
            in the word
        Increase the word count by 1
    print "average word length = ",  &
            letter count / word count
end program avg_word_len_1
```

After reading in the text, the computer starts to look for the first word at the extreme left. Blanks, commas, and other nonletters are passed over to find the beginning of a word. Then letters are counted until the first nonletter is reached, such as a blank or punctuation mark which signals the end of the word. These steps are repeated for each word in the text. Each time it locates a word, the computer increases the letter count by its length and the word count by one.

The refinement of avg_word_len_1 is straightforward. It uses the intrinsic function scan that works like verify, except that it looks for the first occurrence of any character from a set of given characters, in this case the alphabetic characters.

```
program avg_word_len_1
!   Calculate the average word length of input text

    implicit none
    character (len = 200) :: text
    integer word_begin, word_end
    integer word_count, letter_count
    character (len = *), parameter :: alphabet =  &
            "ABCDEFGHIJKLMNOPQRSTUVWXYZ" //  &
            "abcdefghijklmnopqrstuvwxyz"

    letter_count = 0
    word_count = 0
    read "(a)", text
    print *, "Input data  text: ", trim (text)

    do  ! until no more words
        word_begin = scan (text, alphabet)
        if (word_begin == 0) exit
        text = text (word_begin :)
        word_end = verify (text, alphabet) - 1
```

```
        if (word_end == -1) word_end = len (text)
        letter_count = letter_count + word_end
        word_count = word_count + 1
        text = text (word_end + 2 :)
    end do

    print *, "Average word length =",  &
            real (letter_count) / word_count
end program avg_word_len_1
```

```
run avg_word_len_1
```

```
 Input data  text: Never mind the whys and wherefores.
 Average word length =    4.8333335
```

```
run avg_word_len_1
```

```
 Input data  text: I computed the average word length.
 Average word length =    4.8333335
```

The sample execution output of the program avg_word_len_1 might suggest that to use average word length as a test for authorship, one should have a fairly large sample of text.

5.2.5 Modification for a Large Quantity of Text

If the amount of text is very large, the computer might not have enough memory to hold it all at one time. Also, in some Fortran systems, there is a maximum length for character strings. For these reasons, it may be desirable to modify the program avg_word_len_1 so that it reads the text one line at a time, rather than all at once. The program avg_word_len_2 incorporates such a modification. Much of the main program avg_word_len_1 is put into the internal subroutine one_line (process one line).

```
program avg_word_len_2
!  Calculate the average word length of input text.
!  Text may have many lines, terminated by end of file.

    implicit none
    character (len = *), parameter :: alphabet =  &
        "ABCDEFGHIJKLMNOPQRSTUVWXYZ" //  &
        "abcdefghijklmnopqrstuvwxyz"
    character (len = 200) :: text
    integer :: word_count, letter_count, ios
```

```
      letter_count = 0
      word_count = 0

      do  ! until no more lines of text
         read (*, "(a)", iostat = ios) text
         if (ios < 0) exit
         print *, "Input data  text: ", trim (text)
         call one_line
      end do

      print *, "Average word length =",  &
            real (letter_count) / word_count

contains

subroutine one_line
!  Accumulate statistics on one line of input text.
      integer word_begin, word_end

      do  ! until no more words
         word_begin = scan (text, alphabet)
         if (word_begin == 0) exit
         text = text (word_begin :)
         word_end = verify (text, alphabet) - 1
         if (word_end == -1) word_end = len (text)
         letter_count = letter_count + word_end
         word_count = word_count + 1
         text = text (word_end + 2 :)
      end do

end subroutine one_line

end program avg_word_len_2

run avg_word_len_2

 Input data  text: One of the more important uses
 Input data  text: of the character manipulation
 Input data  text: capability of computers is
 Input data  text: in the analysis of text.
 Average word length =   4.8947368
```

5.2.6 Frequency of Occurrence of Letters

There are two basic ways to count the number of occurrences of each letter of the alphabet in a given text. Both ways use 27 counters, one for each letter of the alphabet and one to count all the other characters.

One way to tabulate letter frequencies in a line of text is first to scan it for all occurrences of the letter "a", then to scan it for all occurrences of the letter "b", and so on through the alphabet. This requires 26 scans of the whole line. This method is embodied in the program letter_count_1.

```
program letter_count_1
   Initialize
   do
      Read line of text
      If no more text, exit loop
      do letter = "a", "z"
         Scan line of text, counting occurrences
                of that letter (either uppercase
                or lowercase)
         Calculate the number of nonletters and
                increment nonletter total
      end do
   end do
   Print the counts
end program letter_count_1
```

The second way to count letter frequencies in a line of text is to begin with the first symbol of the text, to decide which of the 27 counters to increment, to continue with the second letter of the line of text, to see which counter to increment this time, and so on through the text. This second way is implemented by the program letter_count_2

```
program letter_count_2
   Initialize
   do
      Read a line of text
      If no more text, exit loop
```

```
        Do for each character in the line of text
            If the character is a letter then
                Increment the count for that letter
            else
                Increment the nonletter count
            end if
        end do
    end do
    Print the counts
end program letter_count_2
```

By the method of the program letter_count_1, the text must be scanned completely for each letter of the alphabet. By the method of the program letter_count_2, the text is scanned just once. Thus, the second program executes considerably faster than the first one and so only the program letter_count_2 is refined.

Unfortunately, in Fortran, the subscripts of the array of counters cannot be "a", "b", etc. A subscript must be type integer. Therefore, subscripts 1 through 26 are used to count the number of occurrences of each letter of the alphabet and subscript 0 is used to count the characters that are not letters.

```
program letter_count_2
!   Count frequency of occurrence in a text
!   of each letter of the alphabet
!   Variables:
!       count (0) = count of nonletters
!       count (1) - count (26) = counts of A/a - Z/z

    implicit none
    character (len = *), parameter :: alphabet = &
        "ABCDEFGHIJKLMNOPQRSTUVWXYZ" // &
        "abcdefghijklmnopqrstuvwxyz"
    character (len = 200) :: text
    integer, dimension (0 : 26) :: count
    integer :: ios

    count = 0  ! Set entire array to zero
```

```fortran
   do  ! until no more lines in file
      read (*, "(a)", iostat = ios) text
      if (ios < 0) exit
      print *, "Input data  text: ", trim (text)
      call count_letters
   end do

   call print_counts

contains

subroutine count_letters
!  Count letters in one line of text
   integer :: i, letter

   do i = 1, len_trim (text)
      letter = index (alphabet, text (i : i))
      if (letter > 26) letter = letter - 26
      count (letter) = count (letter) + 1
   end do
end subroutine count_letters

subroutine print_counts
!  Print the frequency counts

   integer :: letter

   print *
   print "(2a10)", "Letter", "Frequency"
   do letter = 1, 26
      print "(a10, i10)",  &
            alphabet (letter : letter), count (letter)
   end do
   print "(a10, i10)", "Other", count (0)
end subroutine print_counts

end program letter_count_2

run letter_count_2
```

```
Input data  text: One of the important text analysis
Input data  text: techniques (to determine authorship)
Input data  text: is to make a frequency count of
Input data  text: letters in the text.
```

Letter	Frequency
a	6
b	0
c	3
d	1
e	15
f	3
g	0
h	5
i	7
j	0
k	1
l	2
m	3
n	8
o	8
p	2
q	2
r	5
s	6
t	16
u	4
v	0
w	0
x	2
y	2
z	0
other	20

In the program `letter_count_2`, the two internal subroutines are used to make the main part of the program easier to read.

5.2.7 Palindromes

Another aspect of text analysis is searching for patterns. Perhaps the text repeats itself every so often, or perhaps the lengths of the words form an interesting sequence of numbers. One pattern for which we search here is called a "palindrome", which means that the text reads the same from right to left as from left to right. The word "radar" is a palindrome, for example. Liberal palindromers customarily relax the rules so that punctuation, spacing, and capitalization are ignored. To liberal palindromers, the names "Eve", "Hannah", and "Otto" are all palindromes, as is the sentence

"Able was I ere I saw Elba."

something Napoleon might have said, except that he preferred speaking French.

The program `palindrome` satisfies the most conservative palindromers. As the two sample runs show, it accepts the string

"NAT SAW I WAS TAN"

as a palindrome, but it rejects the string

"MADAM I'M ADAM"

It is easy to modify the program `palindrome` to apply a more liberal test for palindromes; simply preprocess the text as in the program `words` in Section 5.2.3. The subroutine `blank_punct` converts all non-letters to blanks, the subroutine `compress_bb` can be modified to excise all blanks, and a subroutine `fold_cases` can be written to change all lowercase letters to uppercase.

```
program palindrome
!  Tests for a palindrome

   implicit none
   character (len = 200) :: text
   integer :: i, j
   logical :: match

   read "(a)", text
   print *, "Input data  text: ", trim (text)

   j = len_trim (text)
   match = .true.
   do i = 1, j / 2
      if (text (i : i) /= text (j : j)) then
         match = .false.
         exit
      else
         j = j - 1
      end if
   end do

   if (match) then
      print *, "Palindrome"
   else
      print *, "Not a palindrome"
      print *, "Character", i, "from the left is ",  &
               c_or_blank (text (i : i))
```

```
        print *, "Character", i, "from the right is ",  &
              c_or_blank (text (j : j))
    end if

contains

function c_or_blank (c)  result (cb_result)
!  Tests if c is blank
!  Returns "blank" if it is
!  Returns c otherwise
    character (len = 5) :: cb_result
    character (len = *), intent (in) :: c

    if (c == " ") then
        cb_result = "blank"
    else
        cb_result = c
    end if
end function c_or_blank

end program palindrome

run palindrome

 Input data  text: NAT SAW I WAS TAN
 Palindrome

run palindrome

 Input data  text: MADAM I'M ADAM
 Not a palindrome
 Character 5 from the left is m
 Character 5 from the right is blank
```

5.2.8 Exercises

1. Mark Twain wrote in "The Awful German Language" (in *A Tramp Abroad*) that he heard a California student in Heidelberg say, in one of his calmest moods, that he would rather decline two drinks than one German adjective. Write a program to help out this California student. The input data consists of a German adjective, for example,

    gut

The output might be

```
run decline

Input data  adj:  gut

der gute  Mann      die gute Frau      das gute Kind
des guten Mannes  der guten Frau     des guten Kindes
dem guten Mann     der guten Frau     dem guten Kind
den guten Mann     die gute Frau      das gute Kind
```

2. In a Fortran program using the old fixed-column source form, all blanks not within a character constant are ignored. Most Fortran compilers immediately remove these blanks to simplify the processing. (a) Write a program to move all blanks that occur in an input string to the end of the string. (b) Modify the program so that blanks within matched pairs of quotes or apostrophes are not removed. If the input data is

```
do 18 i = 1, 10
```

the output should be

```
run deblank

Input data  source:  do 18 i = 1, 10
do18i=1,10
```

3. Calculate the ratio of letters in the first half of the alphabet to letters in the second half of the alphabet in an input text.

4. An alliteration is a sequence of words all starting with the same letter. Write a program `alliteration` that counts how many consecutive words in an input text start with the letter P or p. For the sample input data

```
In his popular paperback, "Party Pastimes People
Prefer", prominent polo player Paul Perkins
presents pleasing palindromes.
```

the output should be

```
run alliteration
```

14

5.3 Case Study: Expression Evaluation

In Section 3.8 it was mentioned that it is possible for recursive procedures to call each other. This is illustrated in this section with an example that also gives a little insight into how computer programs are processed, producing the answers that we expect to see when a program is run.

In this book, the syntax or form of Fortran statements is given by a very informal description. In a more official description of the language, such as in the standard document, it is important to have a more precise definition. The following definitions use notation similar to that used in the standard to describe a small part of Fortran, namely, a class of arithmetic expressions involving only nonnegative integer constants, addition (+), multiplication (*), and parentheses. A description of the notation used in the standard can be found in Appendix B.2.

The first thing to do is describe what a number is.

number	**is**	*digit*
	or	*digit number*

This says that a number is either a single digit or a digit followed by another (shorter) number. It is a recursive definition because the definition of *number* involves *number* as part of the second option. As with any recursive definition or program, there must be a way to terminate the recursion; in this case, a *number* must eventually be just a *digit*, the first choice for *number*. A digit is a single character 0, 1, ..., or 9. This is a situation in which the recursion is not very essential and a number can be described more simply as a sequence of one or more digits, but this provides a very simple example of the definitions of other syntactic objects that are a little more complicated.

The fundamental building block of an expression is called a *primary*. Primaries are the basic components out of which expressions are built; they are treated as operands and combined using arithmetic operators. In our case it is either a number or any other expression enclosed in parentheses.

primary	**is**	*number*
	or	(*expression*)

The next rule indicates how to build expressions using just primaries and multiplication to form what are called *term*s. A term is a sequence of primaries separated by the multiplication symbol (*). It can also be described recursively with the rule

term	**is**	*primary*
	or	*primary * term*

This description says that a *term* is either a *primary* by itself or a *primary* followed by the multiplication symbol and another (simpler) term. Examples of terms are

```
64
111*2222
397*43*(2899*64352)
```

In the last case one of the primaries is (2899*64352), which is an example of an expression enclosed in parentheses.

The description of an expression is similar to that of a term. An expression is a sequence of terms separated by the plus (+) operator and can be described recursively in our notation by

> *expression*   **is**   *term*
> **or**   *term + expression*

Examples of expressions are all of the example terms given in the previous list and the following as well.

```
111+2222
111+2222*33
(111+2222)*33
```

The last two are seen to be expressions in slightly different ways. For 111+2222*33, 111 is a term and 2222*33 is an expression, because it is a term consisting of two primaries separated by *. However, (111+2222)*33 consists of an expression in parentheses followed by * and the number 33. This illustrates that the syntax rules indicate how the expression is to be broken down into components, which, in turn, indicates how the value of the expression will be computed.

It is now possible to see how intertwined these definitions are. We started with the definition of a primary that involved an expression. But the definition of expression involves the definition of term, which involves the definition of primary!

It is possible to construct a program that determines if a string of characters is a legal expression as defined above. This program can be implemented using the recursive definitions directly or it can take advantage of the *tail recursion* in the definitions of *number, term,* and *expression* in order to be a little more efficient. However, it is not easy to see how to handle the second alternative in the definition of primary without a recursive call to determine if it is an expression in parentheses.

It is interesting that it is possible to write a program that is not much more complicated than one that just tests the legality of an expression, but that computes the *value* of any legal expression.

Giving the rules that determine the value of each expression specifies the *semantics* or meaning of the expression. It is easy to transform the rules given above into rules that compute the value of any expression.

A primary is either a number or an expression in parentheses; the value of a primary is either the value of the number or the value of the expression in parentheses. This sounds so simple that it may seem like it doesn't even say anything, but it does give the value of any primary in terms of its components. By the way, we will assume that the value of a number is "obvious", although it is not hard to define the value of a number in terms of its digits.

The description of the value of a term and an expression are very similar. If a term is a primary, its value is the value of the primary, which is defined in the previous paragraph. If it is *primary * term*, its value is the product of the value of the primary and the term. Similarly, the value of expression is either the value of a term or the sum of the values of a term and another expression.

We can now begin to write some of the functions that will return the value of the various kinds of expressions. Blanks are not permitted or are removed by preprocessing. Taking them in the same order as before, `primary` is a function that computes the value of a primary. We agree to return the value –1 if the string is not a legal primary. This works because only nonnegative integer constants are allowed and there is no subtraction operator.

```
recursive function primary (string)  &
      result (primary_result)

    integer :: primary_result
    character (len = *), intent (in) :: string
    integer :: ls

    ! See if it is a number
    primary_result = number (string)
    ls = len (string)
    ! If not, see if it is an expression in parens
    if (primary_result < 0 .and. ls > 0) then
       if (string (1:1) == "(" .and.  &
          string (ls:ls) == ")")  &
             primary_result =  &
                  expression (string (2 : ls - 1))
    end if

end function primary
```

The first executable statement evaluates the primary as if it were a number. If it is a number, the value is not −1 and its value is also the value of the primary. If the value is −1, the other option is that the primary is an expression enclosed in parentheses. The first and last characters are checked—if they are left and right parentheses, respectively, the expression between is evaluated and is used as the value of the primary.

To check that a string is a number, which must be a string of one or more digits, the verify function is used. It returns 0 if all the characters are digits. If the length of the string is also greater than zero, an internal read statement (Section 9.3.6) is used to convert the string of digits to an integer value.

```fortran
function number (string)  result (number_result)

    integer :: number_result
    character (len = *) :: string

    ! Check that it is one or more digits
    if (len (string) > 0 .and.  &
            verify (string, "0123456789") == 0) then
        read (string, *) number_result
    else
        number_result = -1
    end if

end function number
```

The function term that returns the value of a string if it is a term and −1 otherwise first checks to see if the string is a primary. If it is, the value of the primary is the value of the term. If it is not a primary, it must be a primary followed by * followed by another term.

```fortran
recursive function term (string)  result (term_result)

    integer :: term_result
    character (len = *), intent (in) :: string
    integer :: op

    ! Check if it is a primary
    term_result = primary (string)
    if (term_result < 0) then
```

```
            ! If not a primary,
            ! find the first * outside parens
            op = position (string, "*")
            if (op > 0)  &
                term_result =  &
                    combine (primary (string (:op-1)),  &
                            term (string (op+1:)), "*")
        end if

    end function term
```

We have made the function a bit more efficient by realizing that a primary cannot contain a multiplication sign unless it is inside parentheses. So we look for the leftmost multiplication sign that is not enclosed in parentheses. This is done by scanning the string, counting a left parenthesis as +1 and a right parenthesis as −1 and finding the first * at a place where the count is zero (and hence the parentheses to the left are balanced). The function position does this and returns 0 if it doesn't find such a multiplication symbol.

```
    function position (string, operator)  &
            result (position_result)

        integer :: position_result
        character (len = *), intent (in) :: string, operator
        integer :: p, paren_count

        position_result = 0
        paren_count = 0
        do p = 1, len (string)
            ! Can't use a case construct,
            ! because operator is a variable
            if (string (p:p) == "(") then
                paren_count = paren_count + 1
            else if (string (p:p) == ")") then
                paren_count = paren_count - 1
            else if (string (p:p) == operator .and.  &
                        paren_count == 0) then
                position_result = p
                exit
            end if
        end do

    end function position
```

It is interesting to note that a case construct cannot be used to select which operation to perform because the items in parentheses in each case statement must be *constants*; an item cannot be the character string that is the dummy argument operator.

If position is positive, the function term treats the characters to the left of the * as a primary and the characters to the right as another term, getting their values and multiplying them together if neither is −1. The function combine is used to multiply two values together, except that it returns −1 if either argument is −1. It is also used to add two values, so it takes a third argument that indicates which operation to perform.

```
function combine (x, y, operator)  &
      result (combine_result)

   integer :: combine_result
   integer, intent (in) :: x, y
   character (len = 1), intent (in) :: operator

   if (x < 0 .or. y < 0) then
      combine_result = -1
   else
      select case (operator)
         case ("+")
            combine_result = x + y
         case ("*")
            combine_result = x * y
         case default
            combine_result = -1
      end select
   end if

end function combine
```

The function expression is very similar to term. The names of the functions called are changed, and the operator passed to combine is + instead of *.

```
recursive function expression (string)  &
      result (expression_result)

   integer :: expression_result
   character (len = *), intent (in) :: string
   integer :: op
```

```
      ! check if it is a term
      expression_result = term (string)
      if (expression_result < 0) then
         ! if not a term,
         ! find the first + outside parens
         op = position (string, "+")
         if (op > 0) &
               expression_result = &
                  combine (term (string (:op-1)), &
                     expression (string (op+1:)), "+")
      end if

end function expression
```

All of these functions are internal to the program expression_evaluation that evaluates a few expressions.

```
program expression_evaluation

   implicit none
   character (len = 100) :: line
   integer :: status, value

   do
      read (*, "(a)", iostat = status) line
      if (status < 0) exit
      print *
      print *, "Input data line:  ", trim (line)
      value = expression (trim (line))
      print *, "The value of the expression is: ", value
   end do

contains

recursive function expression (string) . . .

recursive function term (string) . . .

recursive function primary (string) . . .

function number (string) . . .

function position (string, operator) . . .

function combine (x, y, operator) . . .

end program expression_evaluation
```

```
run expression_evaluation
```

```
Input data  line:  (443+29)(38+754)
The value of the expression is:  -1

Input data  line:  89+23*4
The value of the expression is:  181

Input data  line:  (((((((555)))))))
The value of the expression is:  555

Input data  line:  64+23*(5388+39)*(54*22+3302*2)
The value of the expression is:  972605296
```

5.3.1 Exercises

1. Give a recursive definition of the value of a *number* that uses the value of a digit.

2. Extend the `expression_evaluation` program to allow negative constants, subtraction, and division.

6

Structures and Derived Types

Fortran arrays allow data to be grouped, but only if all items have the same data type. It is often useful to use a structure, which is a compound object consisting of values that may be of different data types. Derived types are used to define the form of structures. It is possible to define new operations on defined types, creating abstract data types. Derived types and their operations often are defined in a module, making them globally available to many programs.

An interesting kind of structure is a recursive data structure, which can be built and manipulated using pointers. Examples of these structures in the form of linked lists and trees are found in Chapter 8.

6.1 Structures

A **structure** is a collection of values, not necessarily of the same type. The objects that make up a structure are called its **components**. The components of a structure are identified by Fortran names, whereas the elements of an array are identified by numerical subscripts.

A good example of the use of a structure might be provided by a simple text editor, such as the one supplied with many Basic programming language systems. Each line in a Basic program consists of a line number and one or more statements. When the editor is running, the program being edited could be represented in the editing program as two arrays, one to hold line numbers and one to hold the text of each line. Perhaps a better way to do this is to have a single object called line consisting of two components, an integer line_number and a character string statement. The entire program would then be an array of these structures, one for each line.

The components of a structure may be arrays or other structures. The elements of an array may be a structure. The elements of an array may not be arrays, but this functionality can be achieved with an array whose elements are structures whose only component is an array.

To give a slightly more complicated example, suppose we wish to store in our computer the contents of our little black book that contains names, addresses, phone numbers, and perhaps some remarks about each person in the book. In this case, each entry in the book can be treated as a structure containing four components: name, address, phone number, and remarks. The diagram in Figure 6-1 represents the organization of this information.

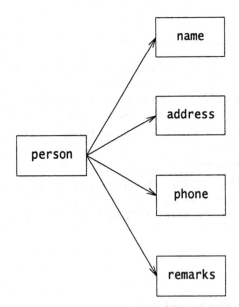

Figure 6-1 Diagram of the structure person.

The name of the structure is person, and it has four components: name, address, phone, and remarks. Sometimes one or more components might be broken down into lower-level components. For instance, if the owner of the black book wanted to contact every acquaintance in a particular city, it would be helpful to have the component address itself be a structure with components number, street, city, state, and postal zip_code. With this organization of the data, it would be possible to have a computer program scan the entries for city and state without having to look at the street address or zip code. For similar reasons, it might be convenient to subdivide each telephone number into a three-digit area code and a seven-digit local number, assuming all of the numbers are in North America. This more refined data organization is represented schematically by the structure in Figure 6-2.

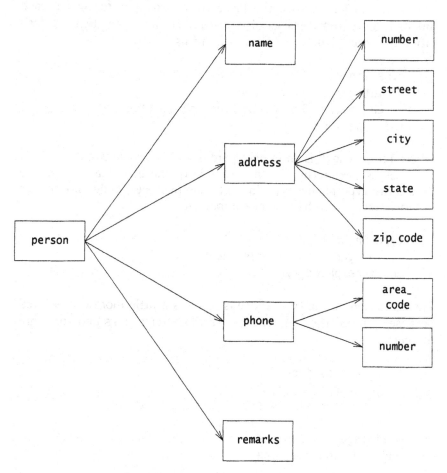

Figure 6-2 A refined structure person.

6.2 Derived Types

As was discussed in Section 1.2, there are five intrinsic Fortran data types: integer, real, complex, logical, and character. A programmer may **define** a new data type, called a **derived type**. In Fortran, a derived type can be used only to define a structure. Conversely, a structure can only occur in a program as a value of some derived type.

A **type definition** begins with the keyword **type** and is followed by the name of the type being defined. The components of the type are given in the form of ordinary type declarations. The type definition ends with the keywords **end type**, optionally followed by the name of the type being defined.

Let's start first with the Basic editor example, for which each line of the program consists of a line number and some text. A definition of a type that would be useful in this example is

```
type line
   integer :: line_number
   character (len = line_length) :: text
end type line
```

where line_length is an integer parameter (named constant).

Let us next return to the example of the little black book. To define the type phone_type in that example, area_code and number are each declared to be integer components:

```
type phone_type
   integer :: area_code, number
end type phone_type
```

The definition of the type address_type is a little more complicated because some of the components are character strings and some are integers:

```
type address_type
   integer :: number
   character (len = 30) :: street, city
   character (len = 2) :: state
   integer :: zip_code
end type address_type
```

Now that the types address_type and phone_type have been defined, it is possible to define a type suitable for one entry in the black book. Note that the names address_type and phone_type were used for the names of the types, so that the names address and phone could be used for the components of the type person_type.

```
type person_type
   character (len = 40) :: name
   type (address_type) :: address
   type (phone_type) :: phone
   character (len = 100) :: remarks
end type person_type
```

6.2.1 Exercises

1. Design a data structure suitable for information on a college student to be used by the college registrar. Write the type definitions needed for this data structure.

2. Assuming that airlines accept reservations for flights up to one year in advance, design a data structure suitable for storing information associated with each reservation. Write the type definitions needed for this data structure.

3. Design a data structure suitable to hold information on each flight to be made by an airline during the next year. Write the type definitions needed for this data structure.

4. Design a data structure suitable for a bank to keep the information on a checking account. Write the type definitions needed for this data structure.

6.3 Declaring and Using Structures

Given the type definition for line in Section 6.1 that can be used to hold a line number and one line of a Basic program, a variable new_line that could be used to represent one line of the program can then be declared by

```
type (line) :: new_line
```

As shown in this example, a variable is declared to be a derived type with a declaration that is similar to the declaration of a variable of intrinsic type, except that the name of the intrinsic type is replaced by the keyword type and the name of the type in parentheses. Note that in a type *definition*, the name of the type is not enclosed in parentheses, but in a type *declaration*, the name of the type is enclosed in parentheses.

The entire program to be edited could be represented by a single variable declared to be an array of values of type line:

```
type (line), dimension (max_lines) :: basic_program
```

With this declaration, some parts of the editor are a little easier to write and read because any operations that must be done to both a line number and the text can be expressed as a single operation on a line. For example, if two arrays were used, the print statement of a subroutine list_program might have been written

```
print "(i5, tr1, a)", line_number (1), text (1)
```

It can now be written

```
print "(i5, tr1, a)", basic_program (1)
```

where the tr (tab right) edit descriptor indicates a number of print positions to skip.

To use the type declarations for the address book, joan can be declared to be type person_type with the statement

```
type (person_type) :: joan
```

and the little black book can be declared to be an array of type person_type:

```
type (person_type), dimension (1000) :: black_book
```

In most cases, a type definition will need to be known in more than one program or procedure, so they will probably most often occur in a module (Chapter 7).

6.3.1 Referencing Structure Components

A component of a structure is referenced by writing the name of the structure followed by a percent sign (%) and then the name of the component. Suppose joan is a Fortran variable declared to be type person_type as shown above. Then Joan's address is referenced by the expression

```
joan % address
```

Style Note: Blanks are permitted, but not required, around the percent sign in a structure component reference. We usually use the blanks because it improves readability.

The object joan % address is itself a structure. If it is desired to refer to one of the components of this structure, another percent symbol is used. For example, the state Joan lives in is

```
joan % address % state
```

and her area code is

```
joan % phone % area_code
```

To see how structures can be used in a program, suppose the contents of the little black book are stored as the value of the variable black_book declared above, and suppose we want an internal subroutine that will print out the names of all persons who live in a given postal zip code. The subroutine simply goes through the entire contents of the black book, one entry at a time, and prints out the name of any person with the appropriate zip code.

```
subroutine find_zip (zip)

   integer, intent (in) :: zip
   integer :: entry

   do entry = 1, number_of_entries
      if (black_book (entry) % address % zip_code  &
         == zip) then
        print *, black_book (entry) % name
      end if
   end do

end subroutine find_zip
```

This subroutine assumes, of course, that there is a variable named number_of_entries with the appropriate value in the program that contains the subroutine find_zip.

> *Style Note:* If you use Fortran names followed by the suffix _type to name derived types, the same name without the suffix is available for variables and structure components of that type. For example, the component name can be type name_type and address can be address_type. This convention is used frequently, but not always.

6.3.2 Structure Constructors

Each derived-type declaration creates a constructor whose name is the same as that of the derived type. This constructor may be used much like a function to create a structure of the named type. The arguments are values to be placed in the individual components of the structure. For example, using the type phone_type in Section 6.2, an area code and telephone number may be assigned with the statement

```
joan % phone = phone_type (505, 2750800)
```

It is not necessary that the function arguments be constants. If joan % address has been given a value, the variable joan of type person_type can be assigned a value with the statement

```
joan = person_type ("Joan Doe", john % address,  &
        phone_type (505, fax_number - 1),  &
        "Same address as husband John")
```

6.3.3 Exercises

1. Write a program that builds a small database of friends' addresses and phone numbers by using the type definitions and declarations in this chapter. The program should prompt the user for information about each entry, keep the entries in an array and write the whole database to a file when the program is terminated. The following statements from Chapter 9 should be of interest:

    ```
    open (9, file = "pfile", status = "replace")
    write (9, fmt = "(...)") black_book (entry_number)
    close (9, status = "keep")
    ```

    The open statement establishes that any operations using input/output unit 9 will refer to the file named "pfile". "replace" indicates that a new file is to be built, replacing any existing file with the same name. "keep" indicates that the file is to be kept when the program that builds the database stops.

2. Write a program that finds entries in the database created in Exercise 1 based on information provided by the user of the program. The statement

    ```
    open (9, file = "pfile", status = "old")
    ```

    can be used to connect unit 9 to file "pfile" created by the program in the previous exercise; "old" indicates that the file is already there.

7

Modules

One way for procedures to share data is by passing values as arguments. This was discussed in Chapter 3. Passing arguments may not be the most effective way to share a large number of things among a large number of procedures, however. Just writing the lists of arguments and getting them all in the right order may be a significant chore. Also, on some systems, passing lots of arguments to procedures that are used frequently can reduce the efficiency of the program significantly.

Modules provide another way of sharing constants, variables, and type definitions.[1] Modules also provide a way of sharing procedures, as well as data; this is especially useful when building a "package" or "library" of data and procedures that may be accessible to many different programs.

A **module** is a program unit that is not executed directly, but contains data specifications and procedures that may be utilized by other program units via the use statement.

---

1. The sharing of values among procedures that was done quite awkwardly in Fortran 77 using the common statement now may be done more cleanly using modules.

7.1 Writing and Using Modules

To begin with a very simple example, one use of a module might be to include the definition of constants that are different on various computer systems. There could be a different version of this module for each Fortran compiler available at one site and the Fortran programmer could use the module appropriate for the computer being used. For example, there might be a module for the Ajax model 2002 computer that contains information such as the kind parameters that are available on the system. Part of it might look like the following:

```
module ajax_2002_parameters

    integer, parameter :: single = 4,   &
                          double = 8,   &
                          quad = 12,    &
                          short = 2,    &
                          ascii = 1
        . . .
```

A program to be run on the Ajax 2002 could include this information and use the constants to declare variables. The program could then be transported to a different computer system by simply changing the use statement to reference a different module.

```
program equation_solver

    use ajax_2002_parameters
    real (kind = quad) :: a, b, c
    integer (kind = short) :: index
    character (len = 20, kind = ascii) :: name
        . . .
    name = ascii_"john doe"
    call create_array (a, 100_short)
        . . .
```

7.1.1 Shared Data

A slightly different use of a module allows any number of procedures to share the value of a variable without making it accessible to any other procedures. Suppose, for example, that function f and subroutine s both need to manipulate the values of some array a. The array may be declared in a module and used by each of the procedures.

```
module m
   implicit none
   integer, parameter :: nr_of_unknowns = 10
   real, dimension (nr_of_unknowns,nr_of_unknowns) :: a
end module m

program p
   implicit none
   . . .
contains

subroutine s
   use m
   a = 0
   . . .
end subroutine s

function f(x)  result (f_result)
   use m
   real :: f_result
   real, intent (in) :: x
   f_result = x + a (1,1)
   . . .
end function f

end program p
```

There is only one copy of each of the variables declared in the module. If two or more procedures use the same module, all can reference the procedures and values of variables declared in their common module. In the example above, the reference to a (1,1) extracts a value from the same array that was set to zero in the subroutine s. Note that it is incorrect to redeclare the array a in either procedure that uses the module.

If it were desirable to have the array a known to all of the procedures internal to the program p, the use statement could be placed once inside the program p, just after the program statement.

7.1.2 The use Statement

The simple form of the **use statement** is just the keyword use followed by a list of the modules to be used, as illustrated by the previous examples.

However, with the use statement, there are two ways to affect the way that names in a module are accessed by another program unit. The first is that the names used in the module may be changed in the program unit using the module. This may be necessary because the program is using two or more modules that use the same name. Or it simply may be desirable to change the name to suit the taste or needs of the programmer of the program unit.

For example, in a subroutine using module m, the programmer may have to write the parameter name nr_of_unknowns many times and may decide that the name is too long. This can be fixed by renaming the variable nr_of_unknowns to the shorter name nu with the use statement.

```
use m, nu => nr_of_unknowns
```

Any number of renames may appear in the use statement.

The second way to affect the objects accessed in a module is to use the only clause in the use statement. Suppose, that from the ajax_2002_parameter module, only the values of double and quad are needed. This can be accomplished with the use statement:

```
use ajax_2002_parameters, only : double, quad
```

If, in addition, it were desirable to rename the value of the parameter double to dbl, this could be done with the statement:

```
use ajax_2002_parameters, only : dbl => double, quad
```

There can be many names, with or without renaming, in a list after the colon.

As we will see later in this chapter, it is possible for the programmer of the module to restrict the variables and procedures in the module that are accessible outside the module. This is done to "hide" implementation details in the module and is accomplished by declaring things private.

7.1.3 Shared Type Definitions and Procedures

Modules may contain procedures and type definitions that can be used by other program units. It would be reasonable, for example, to construct a module of special functions: Bessel, gamma, etc. This is done simply by placing subroutines or functions inside a module. Any program, procedure, or other module that uses that module will have access to all the procedures declared in that module, unless some have been designated as private.

However, the capability of having data, type definitions, and procedures in a module can be used in a much more sophisticated way to create "abstract data types". An abstract data type is defined by indicating what values the data may assume and what operations may be performed on the data. This is done by defining a new derived type and writing procedures to perform operations on data of the new type. Perhaps the best way to describe how all this works is to go through the steps of creating a new data type with some of its operations. This is done in Section 7.4 for the new data type big_integer.

7.1.4 The Private Attribute

As was discussed above, the use statement with the only clause provides a way to exclude some of the objects in a module while including others. Conversely, the private attribute allows the author of a module to prevent objects in the module from being used. This is useful for two reasons. First, it decreases the chances that some name used in a module that is not really necessary to be shared conflicts with a name in a program that uses it. Perhaps the more important reason is that it allows libraries containing abstract data types and procedures to be changed in some of its details without affecting programs that use the modules. For example, a library of matrix routines might be implemented using Fortran arrays. It may be decided later that it would be better to use linked lists. The change is possible only if no program using the module can access any of the details of the data representation or any of the low level procedures that process the matrices. All of the procedures to be used by others are explicitly provided in the module and are not private. The user of the library manipulates these objects only through those procedures provided.

It is possible to list types, constants, variables, and procedures in a private statement within a module. This prevents their use outside the module, which is desirable for objects that are only to be used in the module to build the functions that are intended to be exported. One simple example might be a subroutine invert_details that is called to do some of the computations necessary to invert a matrix. The matrix inversion routine would be available outside the module, but the lower-level routine would not be.

```
private :: invert_details
```

7.2 Case Study: Adaptive Numerical Integration

It is not always convenient or even possible to keep all the procedures that are needed to perform a certain task in one file. If the program becomes quite large, it is natural to split up the file simply to avoid having to deal with a very large file. More significantly, different people may be working on different parts of the program at the same time and cannot all be editing one file simultaneously. Finally, it is possible that parts of the program are already available from a library of procedures written by another person or purchased from a software vendor.

To illustrate how procedures can be kept in separate files, yet keep the example manageable, let us return to the program inte-grate from Section 3.6 that computes an approximation to a definite integral

$$\int_a^b f(x)\,dx$$

that represents the area bounded by the lines $x = a$, $x = b$, $y = 0$, and the curve $y = f(x)$, by a sum of the areas of n "inscribed" trapezoids, each of width h. The program used a function integral that takes arguments that are a function, the lower and upper limits of integration, and an integer that indicates the number of intervals to be used to form the approximating sum. The example in Section 3.6 computes

    integral (sin, a=0.0, b=3.14159, n=100)

passing the intrinsic function sin to be integrated as the first argument to the subroutine integral.

Now suppose we want to integrate a function such as

$$f(x) = e^{-x^2}$$

that is not an intrinsic function. It is not legal to pass an internal procedure as an argument, so the function f must be written as a module procedure. Or perhaps it is already written by somebody else and is contained in the module function_mod.[2]

---

2. This module shows all that needs to be done to convert a Fortran 77 external proce-dure into a module procedure: put a module statement and contains statement before the procedure and an end module statement after it.

```
module function_mod

    implicit none

contains

function f (x) result (f_result)

    real, intent (in) :: x
    real :: f_result

    f_result = exp (-x ** 2)

end function f

end module function_mod
```

The function that performs integration is generally useful, so it too should probably be placed in a module. Instead of using the previous version of the function integrate, a slightly more sophisticated recursive function is used because decreasing the width of each trapezoid may not be the most efficient way to improve the accuracy of a trapezoidal approximation. In regions where the curve $y = f(x)$ is relatively straight, trapezoids approximate the area closely, and further reductions in the width of the trapezoids produces little further reduction in the error, which is already small. In regions where the curve $y = f(x)$ bends sharply, on the other hand, the area under the curve is approximated less well by trapezoids, and it would pay to concentrate the extra work of computing the areas of thinner trapezoids in such regions.

The recursive function integral written in this section uses an **adaptive trapezoidal** method of approximating the area under a curve, requesting extra calculations through a recursive call only in those regions where the approximation by trapezoids is not yet sufficiently accurate.

Mathematicians tell us that the error $E(h)$ in approximating the area of the almost rectangular region with top boundary $y = f(x)$ by the area of one trapezoid is approximately $-1/12 f''(c) h^3$, where h is the width of the trapezoid, and c is any x value in the interval. The dependence of $E(h)$ on h^3 shows why the error drops rapidly as h decreases, and the dependence of $E(h)$ on $f''(c)$ shows why the error is smaller when $f''(x)$ is smaller, at places such as near inflection points (where the tangent line crosses the curve) where $f''(x) = 0$. If the same region is approximated by the sum of the areas of two trapezoids, each of width $h/2$, the error in each of them is approximately

$-1/12 f''(c)(h/2)^3$, or $1/8 E(h)$, but since there are two trapezoids, the total error $E(h/2)$ is approximately $1/4 E(h)$. If $T(h)$ and $T(h/2)$ are the two trapezoidal approximations and I is the exact integral, we have

$$T(h/2) - T(h) = (I - E(h/2)) - (I - E(h))$$

$$= -E(h/2) + E(h)$$

$$= -E(h/2) + 4 E(h/2)$$

$$= 3 E(h/2)$$

approximately. This formula provides a way to check whether the trapezoidal approximations are better than a specified error tolerance ε. Since

$$| E(h/2) | = \frac{1}{3} | T(h/2) - T(h) |$$

approximately, the two-trapezoid approximation is sufficiently accurate if

$$\frac{1}{3} | T(h/2) - T(h) | < \varepsilon$$

If not, then the error tolerance ε is split in two, and the adaptive trapezoidal function integral is called again to approximate the area of each half of the region to within half of the original error tolerance. Thus, only regions where the approximation error is still large are further subdivided.

```
recursive function integral (f, a, b, epsilon) &
      result (integral_result)

   real, intent (in) :: a, b, epsilon
   real :: integral_result, f
   real :: h, mid
   real :: one_trapezoid_area, two_trapezoid_area
   real :: left_area, right_area
```

```
h = b - a
mid = (a + b) /2
one_trapezoid_area = h * (f(a) + f(b)) / 2.0
two_trapezoid_area = h/2 * (f(a) + f(mid)) / 2.0 + &
                     h/2 * (f(mid) + f(b)) / 2.0
if (abs(one_trapezoid_area - two_trapezoid_area)  &
      < 3.0 * epsilon) then
   integral_result = two_trapezoid_area
else
   left_area = integral (f, a, mid, epsilon / 2)
   right_area = integral (f, mid, b, epsilon / 2)
   integral_result = left_area + right_area
end if

end function integral
```

To test the function integral, we write a small test program and a function subprogram f. The test program will evaluate

$$\int_{-4}^{4} e^{-x^2} dx$$

to an accuracy of 0.01. The curve $y = e^{-x^2}$ is an unnormalized error distribution function, used extensively in probability and statistics. Its integral is $\sqrt{\pi}$ (approximately 1.772454).

```
program integrate

   use function_mod
   use integral_mod

   implicit none

   real :: x_min, x_max
   real :: answer, pi

   pi = 4 * atan (1.0)
   x_min = -4.0; x_max = 4.0
   answer = integral (f, x_min, x_max, 0.01)
```

```
    print "(a, f11.6)",  &
        "The integral is approximately ",  &
        answer
    print "(a, f11.6)",  &
        "The exact answer is           ",  &
        sqrt (pi)

end program integrate

run integrate

The integral is approximately    1.777074
The exact answer is              1.772454
```

When parts of a program are kept in separate files, the process of compiling and running the program could be a little more complicated, although how this is done depends on the system being used. In any case, it is important to ensure that the current version of each piece of the program is the one that is used. Many systems have programs, such as *make*, that help with this task.

Comparing the adaptive trapezoidal approximation to the exact answer, we see that the difference is approximately 0.0046, which is less than the specified error tolerance 0.01. Figure 7-1 shows the approximating trapezoids used between $x = -2$ and $x = +2$ to obtain the answer; trapezoids not shown have boundary points at $x = -4, -3, -2, 2, 3,$ and 4. Notice that more trapezoids are required to keep within the error tolerance in the highly curved regions near the maximum of the function and where it first approaches zero than are required in the relatively straight regions near the two inflection points where the curve switches from concave upward to concave downward.

7.2.1 Accelerated Convergence

Even better approximations to the integral can be squeezed out of the same calculations if the returned value `integral_result` is assigned an approximation to $I = T(h/2) + E(h/2)$ instead of settling for the approximation $I = T(h/2)$.

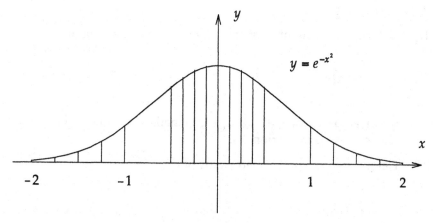

Figure 7-1 Approximating trapezoids used to calculate the integral of e^{-x^2}.

$$I = T(h/2) + E(h/2)$$

$$= T(h/2) + \frac{T(h/2) - T(h)}{3}$$

$$= \frac{4T(h/2) - T(h)}{3}$$

Using this formula in the recursive function integral in the form

```
integral_result =  &
       (4 * two_trapezoid_area - one_trapezoid_area) / 3
```

results in the same sequence of subdivisions and recursive calls, but an improved final answer of 1.772808, which differs from the exact answer, 1.772454, by approximately 0.000354.

It can be proved that this approximation formula is equivalent to approximating the area under $y = f(x)$ by the area under a parabola passing through the three points where the smaller trapezoids touch the curve. It is not surprising that parabolas can match the curve $y = f(x)$ more closely than the straight line boundaries of trapezoids, so that the resulting approximations, called **Simpson's approximations**, are more accurate for about the same number of calculated function values.

7.2.2 Exercises

1.   Determine the number of trapezoids needed to evaluate

$$\int_{-4}^{4} e^{-x^2} dx$$

to an accuracy of 0.01 using the nonadaptive integration function discussed in Section 3.6.

2.   Determine the approximate value of

$$\int_{0}^{2\pi} e^x \sin 2x\, dx$$

using both the adaptive integration method of this section and the nonadaptive integration method discussed in Section 3.6.

3.   The area under the curve $y = f(x)$ between $x = a - h$ and $x = a + h$ may be approximated by the area under a parabola passing through the three points $(a-h, f(a-h))$, $(a, f(a))$, and $(a+h, f(a+h))$. The approximation, called Simpson's approximation, is given by the formula

$$\int_{a-h}^{a+h} f(x)\, dx = \frac{h}{3}\left[f(a-h) + 4f(a) + f(a+h)\right]$$

with error $-1/90\, f''''(c) h^5$ for some c in the interval of integration.

Use these facts to write a recursive adaptive Simpson's approximation subroutine patterned on the adaptive trapezoidal approximation subroutine integral in this section. Compare the number of recursive function calls for your adaptive Simpson's approximation function with the number required to achieve the same accuracy with the adaptive trapezoidal rule.

4.   Use the accelerated convergence technique of Section 7.2.1 to improve even more the recursive adaptive Simpson's approximation subroutine written for Exercise 3.

7.3 Extending and Defining Operations

In Fortran 90, the programmer may create generic procedures, define new operators, and extend the definition of intrinsic functions, existing operators, and assignment.

7.3.1 Generic Procedures

Many intrinsic procedures are generic in that they allow arguments of different types. For example, abs will take an integer, real, or complex argument. Such generic procedures were available in Fortran 77, but the programmer could not write a new generic procedure. This can be done in Fortran 90.

In Section 3.1.4 there is a subroutine that exchanges the values of any two real variables. It would be nice to have a similar routine that swapped integer values, but the normal rules of argument matching presented in Chapter 3 indicate that the types of the dummy and actual arguments must match. This is true, but it is possible to have one procedure name swap stand for several swapping routines, each with different names. The correct routine is picked for execution based on the types of the arguments, just as for generic intrinsic functions.

Here is the swap subroutine from Section 3.1.4, but with its name changed to swap_reals.

```
subroutine swap_reals (a, b)
   real :: a, b, temp
   temp = a; a = b; b = temp
end subroutine swap_reals
```

It is easy to construct a similar subroutine swap_integers.

```
subroutine swap_integers (a, b)
   integer :: a, b, temp
   temp = a; a = b; b = temp
end subroutine swap_integers
```

The way to make them both callable by the generic name swap is to place the name swap in an interface statement and list the module procedures that can be called when the arguments match appropriately. Here is the interface block to do that.

```
interface swap
   module procedure swap_reals, swap_integers
end interface
```

When the interface block and the two subroutines are placed in a module, a program that uses the module can call swap with either two integer arguments or two real arguments. Here is the module and a program that tests the generic procedure swap.

```
module swap_module

   implicit none

   interface swap
      module procedure swap_reals, swap_integers
   end interface

contains

subroutine swap_reals (a, b)
   real :: a, b, temp
   temp = a; a = b; b = temp
end subroutine swap_reals

subroutine swap_integers (a, b)
   integer :: a, b, temp
   temp = a; a = b; b = temp
end subroutine swap_integers

end module swap_module

program test_swap

   use swap_module

   real :: x = 1.1, y = 2.2
   integer :: i = 1, j = 2

   call swap (x, y)
   print *, x, y

   call swap (i, j)
   print *, i, j

end program test_swap

run test_swap

   2.2000000    1.1000000
  2 1
```

7.3.2 Extending Assignment

When an assignment statement is executed, sometimes the data type of the expression on the right-hand side of the assignment symbol (=) is converted to the type of the variable on the left-hand side. For example, if i is integer and r is real, the assignment

```
r = i
```

causes the integer value of i to be converted to type real for assignment to r. Suppose we would like to extend this feature so that a logical value can be assigned to an integer with a false value being converted to zero and a true value converted to one when the assignment

```
i = l
```

is written with l logical and i integer. To do this, a subroutine that does the assignment must be written and an interface block must be given that indicates which subroutine does the assignment with conversion. Both of these things should be placed in a module. The subroutine that will do the conversion follows.

```
subroutine integer_gets_logical (i, l)

    integer, intent (out) :: i
    logical, intent (in) :: l

    if (l) then
       i = 1
    else
       i = 0
    end if

end subroutine integer_gets_logical
```

The interface block indicates that assignment is extended by the subroutine integer_gets_logical.

```
interface assignment (=)
    module procedure integer_gets_logical
end interface
```

Here is the complete module to accomplish this task with a program that tests it.

```
module int_logical

    interface assignment (=)
        module procedure integer_gets_logical
    end interface

contains

subroutine integer_gets_logical (i, l)

    integer, intent (out) :: i
    logical, intent (in) :: l

    if (l) then
       i = 1
    else
       i = 0
    end if

end subroutine integer_gets_logical

end module int_logical

program test_int_logical

    use int_logical
    implicit none
    integer :: i, j

    i = .false.
    print *, i
    j = (5 < 7) .and. (sin (.3) < 1.0)
    print *, j

end program test_int_logical

run test_int_logical

   0
   1
```

A subroutine that serves to define an assignment must have exactly two arguments; the first must be intent out and the second intent in.

7.3.3 Extending Operators

Suppose we now want to be able to use + in place of .or., * in place of .and., and - in place of .not. to manipulate logical values. This can be done by extending these operators, which already work with numeric operands. Functions must be written and the names of the functions placed in an interface block in a module. The interface statement contains the keyword operator in this case. Here is a complete module and program to implement and test the extension of + to logical operands.

```
module logical_plus

    interface operator (+)
       module procedure log_plus_log
    end interface

contains

function log_plus_log (x, y)  &
       result (log_plus_log_result)

    logical :: log_plus_log_result
    logical, intent (in) :: x, y

    log_plus_log_result = x .or. y

end function log_plus_log

end module logical_plus

program test_logical_plus

    use logical_plus
    implicit none
```

```
    print *, .false. + .false.
    print *, .true. + .true.
    print *, (2.2 > 5.5) + (3.3 > 1.1)

end program test_logical_plus

run test_logical_plus


F
T
T
```

Note that the parentheses in the expression in the third print statement are necessary because + has a higher precedence than >.

A function used to extend an operator must have one or two arguments (depending on the operator being extended), both of which must be intent in.

7.3.4 User-Defined Operators

In addition to extending the meaning of the Fortran built-in operators, it is possible to make up new names for operators. If we were to add the operation of testing if an integer is prime, there is probably not a good unary built-in operator that would be suitable to extend to this use. Any name consisting of from 1 to 31 letters preceded and followed by a period may be used, except for the name of a logical constant or an intrinsic operator. For example, we might pick .prime. for the name of the operator that returns true or false depending on whether its operand is a prime integer. Defining a new operator is similar to extending an existing one; its name is used in an interface statement and the function, which must have one or two intent in arguments, is named in a module procedure statement.

```
    interface operator (.prime.)
       module procedure prime
    end interface
```

This operator could now be used just like any built-in unary operator, as illustrated by the following if statement:

```
    if (.prime. b .and. b > 100) then
```

The precedence of a defined binary operator is always lower than all other operators, and the precedence of a defined unary operator is always higher than all other operators.

7.3.5 Extending Intrinsic Functions

Many programmers are surprised that the sqrt function may be used with a real or complex argument, but not with an integer argument. One possible reason is that there might be some controversy about whether the result should be an integer or real value. For example, should sqrt (5) be 2.236068, a type real approximation to the square root, or 2, the largest integer less than the real square root? The integer square root is sometimes useful; one example is in determining the upper bound on factors of an integer i. It is not hard to compute either value with the expressions sqrt (real (i)) and int (sqrt (real (i))) for any integer i, but it would be nice to just write sqrt (i). We will extend the sqrt function to take an integer argument and return an integer value. This is done by writing an interface block and the function to do the computation. Here is the interface, the function, and a brief testing program. In the program, i is increased by 0.5 to avoid any problems with roundoff.

```
module integer_sqrt

    interface sqrt
       module procedure sqrt_int
    end interface

contains

function sqrt_int (i) &
       result (sqrt_int_result)

    integer :: sqrt_int_result
    integer, intent (in) :: i

    sqrt_int_result = int (sqrt (real (i) + 0.5))

end function sqrt_int

end module integer_sqrt

program test_integer_sqrt

    use integer_sqrt
    implicit none
    integer :: i
```

```
     do i = 1, 25
        print "(2i5)", i, sqrt (i)
     end do

   end program test_integer_sqrt

   run test_integer_sqrt
```

```
    1    1
    2    1
    3    1
    4    2
    5    2
    6    2
    7    2
    8    2
    9    3
   10    3
   11    3
   12    3
   13    3
   14    3
   15    3
   16    4
   17    4
   18    4
   19    4
   20    4
   21    4
   22    4
   23    4
   24    4
   25    5
```

7.3.6 Exercises

1. Extend the subroutine swap to handle arrays of integers.

2. Write the procedure and interface block to extend assignment to allow assigning an integer to a logical variable. The logical variable should be set to true if the integer is 1 and set to false otherwise. Test the procedure with a program that uses the module.

3. Write a module that extends the == and /= operators to allow comparison of both scalar logical values and arrays of logical

values. Note that the built-in operators .eqv. and .neqv. are used for this purpose. Test the module.

4. The program seven_11 in Section 3.7.2 calls the function random_int, which produces one pseudorandom real value. The program seven_11 in Section 4.6.2 calls the function random_int, which produces an array of pseudorandom real values. Write a module that makes random_int generic in the sense that it can be called to either produce a single value or an array of values, depending on its arguments.

5. Extend the intrinsic subroutine random_integer so that it has the functionality of random_int in the previous exercise when called with an argument that is type integer. Create both the scalar version and the array version.

6. Modify the extended intrinsic subroutine random_integer of the previous exercise so that the arguments low and high are optional as was done for random_int in Exercise 5 of Section 3.7.3.

7. Modify the user-defined version of index given in Section 5.1.16 to have an optional third argument back, making it identical to the intrinsic function index. When back is true, the search proceeds backward from right to left.

7.4 Computing with Big Integers

Suppose we are interested in adding, multiplying, and dividing very large integers, possibly with hundreds of digits. This kind of capability is needed to factor large integers, a task very important in cryptography and secure communications. The Fortran intrinsic integer type has a limit on the size of numbers it can represent; the largest integer can be determined on any Fortran system as the value of the intrinsic function huge (0). A typical limit is $2^{31}-1$, which is 2,147,483,647. This problem can be solved by creating a new data type, called big_integer, deciding which operations are needed, and writing procedures that will perform the operations on values of this type. All of this will be placed in a module called big_integers so that it can be used by many programs.

7.4.1 The Type Definition for Big Integers

The first task is to decide how these large integers will be represented. Although a linked list of digits is a possibility, it seems more straightforward to use an array of ordinary Fortran integers. The only remaining thing to decide is how much of a big integer to put into each element of the array. One possibility would be to put as large a number into each element as possible. To make it easier to conceptualize with simple examples, we will store one decimal digit in each element. *However, because the abstract data type paradigm is followed, changing the representation so that larger integers are stored in each array element can be implemented easily without changing the programs using the* big_integer *package.*

The following type definition does the job. It uses a parameter nr_of_digits that has arbitrarily been set to 100; this allows decimal numbers with up to 100 digits to be represented using this scheme. The parameter nr_of_digits has the private attribute, which means it cannot be accessed outside the module.

```
integer, private, parameter :: nr_of_digits = 100

type :: big_integer
   private
   integer, dimension (0 : nr_of_digits) :: digit
end type big_integer
```

The array digit has 101 elements. digit (0) holds the units digit; digit (1) holds the tens digit; digit (2) holds the hundreds digit; and so on. The extra element in the array is used to check for overflow—if any value other than zero gets put into the largest element, that will be considered to exceed the largest big_integer value and the program will halt with an error. The private statement indicates that we don't want anybody that uses the module to be able to access the *component* digit of a variable of type big_integer; we will provide all of the operations necessary to compute with such values. The private statement is discussed in Section 7.1.4.

The next thing to do is to define some operations for big integers. The first necessary operations assign values to a big integer and print the value of a big integer. Let's take care of the printing first.

The following subroutine prints the value of a big integer. It takes advantage of the fact that each element of the array digit is one decimal digit. This subroutine print_big does not have a use statement because it will be inside the module big_integers and have access to all the data and procedures in the module.

```
subroutine print_big (b)

   type (big_integer), intent (in) :: b
   integer :: n
   character (len = 10) :: format
```

```
! Find first significant digit
do n = nr_of_digits, 1, -1
   if (b % digit (n) /= 0) exit
end do

! Set format = "(<n+1>i1)"
write (format, "(a, i6, a)") "(", n + 1, "i1)"
print format, b % digit (n : 0 : -1)
```

```
end subroutine print_big
```

The basic strategy is to print the digits in i1 format, but first the leftmost nonzero digit must be located, both to compute the multiplier in the format specification and to avoid printing long strings of leading zeros. This way, there is also no problem if the parameter nr_of_digits is changed.

Another interesting feature is that we use a formatted write to a character variable in order to convert an integer subscript to character form for inclusion in an edit descriptor. In effect, we calculate the appropriate print format on the fly.

In order to test this subroutine, we need to have a way to assign values to a big integer. One possibility is to write a procedure that will assign an ordinary Fortran integer to a big integer, but this will limit the size of the integer that can be assigned. A second possibility is to write the integer as a character string consisting of only digits 0–9 (we are not allowing negative numbers). This is done by the subroutine big_gets_char (b, c) that assigns the integer represented by c to the big integer b. If c contains a character other than one of the digits, the program halts with an error.

```
subroutine big_gets_char (b, c)

   type (big_integer), intent (out) :: b
   character (len = *), intent (in) :: c
   integer :: n, i

   if (len (c) > nr_of_digits) then
      print *, "Character string too long to assign"
      stop
   end if
```

```
      b % digit = 0
      n = 0
      do i = len (c), 1, -1
         b % digit (n) = index ("0123456789", c (i:i)) - 1
         if (b % digit (n) == -1) then
            print *, "Attempt to assign nonnumeric string"
            stop
         end if
         n = n + 1
      end do

   end subroutine big_gets_char
```

7.4.2 Putting the Procedures in a Module

Now that we have enough operations defined on big integers to at
least try out something meaningful, we next need to package them all
in a module. The module that we have created so far follows:

```
   module big_integers

      implicit none
      integer, private, parameter :: nr_of_digits = 100

      type :: big_integer
         private
         integer, dimension (0 : nr_of_digits) :: digit
      end type big_integer

   contains

   subroutine print_big (b)

      type (big_integer), intent (in) :: b
      integer :: n
      character (len = 10) :: format

      ! Find first significant digit
      do n = nr_of_digits, 1, -1
         if (b % digit (n) /= 0) exit
      end do
```

```
   ! Set format = "(<n+1>i1)"
   write (format, "(a, i6, a)") "(", n + 1, "i1)"
   print format, b % digit (n : 0 : -1)

end subroutine print_big

subroutine big_gets_char (b, c)

   type (big_integer), intent (out) :: b
   character (len = *), intent (in) :: c
   integer :: n, i

   if (len (c) > nr_of_digits) then
      print *, "Character string too long to assign"
      stop
   end if

   b % digit = 0
   n = 0
   do i = len (c), 1, -1
      b % digit (n) = index ("0123456789", c (i:i)) - 1
      if (b % digit (n) == -1) then
         print *, "Attempt to assign nonnumeric string"
         stop
      end if
      n = n + 1
   end do

end subroutine big_gets_char

end module big_integers
```

With the module available, we can write a simple program to test out the assignment and printing routines for big integers.

```
program test_big_1

   use big_integers
   type (big_integer) :: b1

   call big_gets_char (b1, "71234567890987654321")
   call print_big (b1)
```

```
        call big_gets_char (b1, "")
        call print_big (b1)

        call big_gets_char (b1, "123456789+987654321")
        call print_big (b1)

    end program test_big_1

    run test_big_1

    71234567890987654321
    0
     Attempt to assign nonnumeric string
```

7.4.3 Assigning Big Integers

The name for the function big_gets_char was picked because it converts a character string to a big integer. But this is just like intrinsic assignment that converts an integer to a real value when necessary. Indeed, it is possible to use the assignment statement to do the conversion from character to big integer. It is done by extending assignment as described in Section 7.3.2. Here is what it must look like in our case.

```
    interface assignment (=)
        module procedure big_gets_char
    end interface
```

Now any user of the module can use the assignment statement instead of calling a subroutine, which makes the program a lot easier to understand.

```
    program test_big_2

        use big_integers
        type (big_integer) :: b1

        b1 = "71234567890987654321"
        call print_big (b1)
        b1 = ""
        call print_big (b1)
```

```
b1 = "123456789+987654321"
call print_big (b1)
```

```
end program test_big_2
```

The result of running this version is identical to the previous output.

With conversion from character strings to big integers using the assignment statement, there is no need to have the subroutine big_gets_char available. This can be done by putting the name of the procedure in a private statement within the module.

```
private :: big_gets_char
```

The effect of this statement is slightly different from that of the private statement that occurs within the definition of the type big_integer. This one makes the procedure inaccessible outside the module, whereas the private statement in the type statement makes only the components of the type inaccessible outside the module. Both the type definition and the procedure are accessible inside the module.

7.4.4 Adding Big Integers

Now that we can assign to a big integer variable and print its value, it would be nice to be able to perform some computations with big integers. It can be done with a function that adds just like we do with pencil and paper, adding two digits at a time and keeping track of any carry, starting with the rightmost digits. The function big_plus_big does this.

```
function big_plus_big (x, y)  &
     result (big_plus_big_result)

  type (big_integer) :: big_plus_big_result
  type (big_integer), intent (in) :: x, y
  integer :: carry, temp_sum, n

  carry = 0
  do n = 0, nr_of_digits
    temp_sum = &
        x % digit (n) + y % digit (n) + carry
```

```
        big_plus_big_result % digit (n) =  &
              modulo (temp_sum, 10)
        carry = temp_sum / 10
    end do

    if (big_plus_big_result % digit(nr_of_digits) /= 0 &
          .or. carry /= 0) then
        print *, "Overflow adding two big integers"
        stop
    end if

end function big_plus_big
```

In mathematics, the symbols + and − are used to add and subtract integers. It is nice to do the same with big integers, and it is possible to do so by extending the generic properties of the operations already built into Fortran. Note that + already can be used to add two integers, two real values, or one of each. The intrinsic operator + also can be used to add two arrays of the same shape. In that sense, addition is already generic. We now extend the meaning of this operation to our own newly defined type, big_integer. This is done with another interface block, this time with the keyword operator, followed by the operator being extended. With the + operator available, the function itself can be made private by putting it in the same private statement with the subroutine big_gets_char.

```
interface operator (+)
    module procedure big_plus_big
end interface

private :: big_gets_char, big_plus_big
```

The use of the plus operator to add two big integers is tested by the program test_big_3.

```
program test_big_3

    use big_integers
    type (big_integer) :: b1, b2
```

```
    b1 = "1234567890987654321"
    b2 = "9876543210123456789"
    call print_big (b1 + b2)

end program test_big_3

run test_big_3

11111111101111111110
```

Using only the procedures written so far, it is not possible to use the expression b + i in a program where b is a big integer and i is an ordinary integer. To do that, we must write another function and add its name to the list of functions in the interface block for the plus operator. Similarly, it would be necessary to write a third function to handle the case i + b. Even if that is not done, the number 999 could be added to b using the statements

```
temp_big_integer = "999"
    b = b + temp_big_integer
```

Similar interface blocks and functions can be written to make the other operations utilize symbols, such as - and *. The precedence of the extended operators when used to compute with big integers is the same as when they are used to add ordinary integers. This holds true for all built-in operators that are extended. This is illustrated by the following program that tests the extended multiplication operator (the function is not shown). By looking at the last digit of the answer, it is possible to see that the multiplication is done before the addition.

```
program test_big_4

    use big_integers
    type (big_integer) :: a, b, c

    a = "1"
    b = "999999999999999999"
    c = "999999999999999999"
    call print_big (a + b * c)

end program test_big_4
```

```
run test_big_4
```

```
99999999999999999980000000000000000002
```

7.4.5 New Operators for Big Integers

In addition to extending the meaning of the Fortran built-in operators, it is possible to make up new names for operators. For example
we could define a new operator .prime., whose operand is a big integer and whose value is true if the big integer is a prime and is false
otherwise. Its name is used in an interface statement and the function.

```
interface operator (.prime.)
   module procedure prime
end interface
```

This operator could now be used just like any built in unary operator,
as illustrated by the following if-then statement:

```
if (.prime. b) then
```

7.4.6 Extending Intrinsic Functions to Big Integers

Many of the Fortran intrinsic functions manipulate numeric values
and it is reasonable to extend some of them, such as modulo or sqrt
to have big integer arguments. This is done by writing an interface
block and the function to do the computation. This is illustrated by
extending the intrinsic function huge so that when given a big integer
as argument, it returns the largest possible big integer. This function
is tested by the program test_big_5.

```
module big_integers

   implicit none
    . . .

   interface huge
      module procedure huge_big
   end interface
   private :: huge_big
    . . .

contains
    . . .
```

```
function huge_big (b)   result (huge_big_result)

   type (big_integer) :: huge_big_result
   type (big_integer), intent (in) :: b

   huge_big_result % digit (0 : nr_of_digits - 1) = 9
   huge_big_result % digit (nr_of_digits) = 0

end function huge_big
   . . .

end module big_integers

program test_big_5

   use big_integers
   type (big_integer) :: b1

   call print_big (huge (b1))

end program test_big_5

run test_big_5

99999999999999999999999999 . . .
```

There is not room enough on one line to show all 100 9s in the answer.

7.4.7 Raising a Big Integer to an Integer Power

Exponentiation, like the factorial function, has both an iterative definition and a recursive definition. They are

$$x^n = x \times x \times \cdots x \quad n \text{ times}$$

and

$$x^0 = 1$$

$$x^n = x \times x^{n-1} \quad \text{for } n > 1$$

Since Fortran has an exponentiation operator ** for real numbers, it is not necessary to write a procedure to do that. However, it may be necessary to write an exponentiation procedure for a new data type, such as our big integers. We suppose that the multiply operator (*) has been extended to form the product of two big integers. The task is to write a procedure for the module that will raise a big integer to a power that is an ordinary nonnegative integer. This time, the simple iterative procedure is presented first.

```
function big_power_int (b, i)  &
        result (big_power_int_result)

    type (big_integer) :: big_power_int_result
    type (big_integer), intent (in) :: b
    integer, intent (in) :: i
    integer :: n

    big_power_int_result = "1"
    do n = 1, i
        big_power_int_result = big_power_int_result * b
    end do

end function big_power_int
```

It would be straightforward to use the recursive factorial function as a model and construct a recursive version of the exponentiation function; but this is another example of tail recursion, and there is no real advantage to the recursive version. However, think about how you would calculate x^{18} on a calculator that does not have exponentiation as a built-in operator. The clever way is to compute x^2 by squaring x, x^4 by squaring x^2, x^8 by squaring x^4, x^{16} by squaring x^8, and finally x^{18} by multiplying the results obtained for x^{16} and x^2. This involves a lot fewer multiplications than doing the computation the hard way by multiplying x by itself 18 times. To utilize this scheme to construct a program is fairly tricky. It involves computing all of the appropriate powers x^2, x^4, x^8, ..., then multiplying together the powers that have a 1 in the appropriate position in the binary representation of n. For example, since $18 = 10010_2$, powers that need to be multiplied are 16 and 2.

It happens that there is a recursive way of doing this that is quite easy to program. It relies on the fact that x^n can be defined with the following less obvious recursive definition below. The trick that leads to the more efficient recursive exponentiation function is to think of the problem "top-down" instead of "bottom-up". That is, solve the problem of computing x^{18} by computing x^9 and squaring the result. Computing x^9 is almost as simple: square x^4 and multiply the result by x. Eventually, this leads to the problem of computing x^0, which is 1. The recursive definition we are looking for is

$$x^0 = 1$$

$$x^n = \begin{cases} (x^{\lfloor n/2 \rfloor})^2 & \text{for } n \text{ even, } n > 0 \\ (x^{\lfloor n/2 \rfloor})^2 x x & \text{for } n \text{ odd, } n > 0 \end{cases}$$

where $\lfloor \ \rfloor$ is the floor function, which for positive integers is the largest integer less than or equal to its argument. This definition can be used to construct a big_power_int function that is more efficient than the iterative version.

```
recursive function big_power_int (b, i)  &
        result (big_power_int_result)

    type (big_integer) :: big_power_int_result
    type (big_integer), intent (in) :: b
    integer, intent (in) :: i
    type (big_integer) :: temp_big

    if (i <= 0) then
        big_power_int_result = "1"
    else
        temp_big = big_power_int (b, i / 2)
        if (modulo (i, 2) == 0) then
            big_power_int_result = temp_big * temp_big
        else
            big_power_int_result = temp_big * temp_big * b
        end if
    end if

end function big_power_int
```

7.4.8 Exercises

1. Extend the the equality operator (==) and the "less than" (<) operator to compare two big integers.

2. Extend the equality operator (==) to compare a big integer with a character string consisting of digits. Hint: use extended assignment to assign the character string to a temporary big integer, then use the extended equality operator from Exercise 1 to do the comparison.

3.   Extend the multiplication operator (*) to two big integers.

4.   Use the result of the previous exercise to compute 100! = 100 × 99 × ⋯ 2 × 1. It may be necessary to increase the value of the parameter `nr_of_digits`.

5.   Extend the subtraction operator (-) so that it performs "positive" subtraction. If the difference is negative, the result should be 0.

6.   The representation of big integers used in this section is very inefficient because only one decimal digit is stored in each Fortran integer array element. It is possible to store a number as large as possible, but not so large that when two are multiplied, there is no overflow. This largest value can be determined portably on any system with the statements

```
integer, private, parameter :: &
     d = (range (0) - 1) / 2, &
     base = 10 ** d

! Base of number system is 10 ** d,
! so that each "digit" is 0 to 10**d - 1
```

On a typical system that uses 32 bits to store an integer, with one bit used for the sign, the value of the intrinsic inquiry function `range (0)` is 9 because $10^9 < 2^{31} < 10^{10}$. To ensure that there is no chance of overflow in multiplication, this number is decreased by one before dividing by 2 to determine the number of decimal digits d that can be stored in one array element `digit` of a big integer. In our example, this would set d to 4. The value of `base` is then 10 ** d, or $10^4 = 10{,}000$. With this scheme, instead of storing a number from 0 to 9 in one integer array element, it is possible to store a number from 0 to base - 1, which is 9,999 in the example. In effect, the big number system uses base 10,000 instead of base 10 (decimal).

Determine the value of `range (0)` on your system.

7.   Modify the type definition for `big_integer` module so that a number from 0 to base - 1 is stored in each element of the array. The number of elements in the array should be computed from the parameter `nr_of_digits`.

8.   Determine the largest number that can be represented as the value of a big integer using the type definition in the previous exercise.

9. Modify the procedure `big_gets_char` to use the more efficient representation of big integers.

10. Modify the procedure `print_big` to use the more efficient representation of big integers. In the format, `i1` should be replaced by `id`, where d is the number of decimal digits stored in each array element.

11. Modify the subroutine `big_plus_big` using the new type definition for `big_integer`. It is very similar to the one developed in this section, except that the base is now not 10, but `base`.

12. Extend the operator `*` to multiply a big integer by an ordinary integer.

13. Extend `huge` using the new representation. Write a test program that prints `huge (b)`.

14. Approximately n multiplications are required to compute x^n by the iterative version of the function `big_power_int`. Estimate the number of multiplications needed to compute x^n by the recursive version.

15. **Project:** Write a module to do computation with rational numbers. The rational numbers should be represented as a structure with two integers, the numerator and the denominator. Provide assignment, some input/output, and some of the usual arithmetic operators. Addition and subtraction are harder than multiplication and division, and equality is nontrivial if the rational numbers are not reduced to lowest terms.

16. Modify the module in the previous exercise to use big integers for the numerator and denominator.

17. **Project:** Write a module to manipulate big decimal numbers such as

    28447305830139375750302.374291256120923912363 6292

    using the `big_integer` module as a model.

8

Pointer Variables

In Fortran, a **pointer variable** or simply a **pointer** is best thought of as a "free-floating" name that may be associated dynamically with or "aliased to" some data object. The data object already may have one or more other names or it may be an unnamed object.

Syntactically, a pointer is just any sort of variable that has been given the pointer attribute in a declaration. A variable with the pointer attribute may be used just like any ordinary variable, but it may be used in some additional ways as well. To understand how Fortran pointers work, it is almost always better to think of them simply as aliases. This will require a change of perspective for those programmers used to treating them as memory addresses, a scheme used in other programming languages and some previous extensions of Fortran. If you tend to fall back to this, at least think of the pointers as more general "descriptors", sufficient to describe a row of a matrix, for example.

8.1 The Use of Pointers in Fortran

Each pointer in a program is in one of the three following states:

1.   It may be **undefined**, which is the condition of all pointers at the beginning of a program.

2.   It may be **null**, which means that it is not the alias of any data object.

3.   It may be **associated**, which means that it is the alias of some target data object.

The terms "disassociated" and "not associated" are used when a pointer is in state 1 or 2. However, the `associated` intrinsic inquiry function discussed later (Section 8.1.5) distinguishes between states 2 and 3 only; its arguments must not be undefined.

8.1.1 The Pointer Assignment Statement

To start with a very simple example, suppose p is a real variable with the pointer attribute, perhaps given with the declaration

```
real, pointer :: p
```

Suppose r is also a real variable. Then it is possible to make p an alias of r by the **pointer assignment statement**

```
p => r
```

For those that like to think of pointers, rather than aliases, this statement causes p to point to r.

Any variable aliased or "pointed to" by a pointer must be given the **target attribute** when declared, and the target must have the same type, kind, and rank as the pointer. However, it is not necessary that the variable have a defined value. For our example above, these requirements are met by the presence of the following declaration:

```
real, target :: r
```

A variable with the pointer attribute may be an object more complicated than a simple variable. It may be an array section or structure, for example. The following declares v to be a pointer to a one-dimensional array of reals:

```
real, dimension (:), pointer :: v
```

With v so declared, it may be used to alias any one-dimensional array of reals, including a row or column of some two-dimensional array of reals. For example,

```
v => real_array (4, :)
```

makes v an alias of the fourth row of the array real_array. Of course, real_array must have the target attribute for this to be legal.

```
real, dimension (:, :), target :: real_array
```

Once a variable with the pointer attribute is an alias for some data object, that is, it is pointing to something, it may be used in the same way that any other variable may be used. For the example above using v,

```
print *, v
```

has exactly the same effect as

```
print *, real_array (4, :)
```

and the assignment statement

```
v = 0
```

has the effect of setting all of the elements of the fourth row of the array real_array to 0.

A different version of the pointer assignment statement occurs when the right side also is a pointer. This is illustrated by the following example, in which p1 and p2 are both real variables with the pointer attribute and r is a real variable with the target attribute.

```
real, target :: r
real, pointer :: p1, p2
r = 4.7
p1 => r
p2 => p1
r = 7.4
print *, p2
```

After execution of the first assignment statement, r is a name that refers to the value 4.7:

The first pointer assignment causes p1 to be an alias for r, so that the value of the variable p1 is 4.7. The value 4.7 now has two names, r and p1, by which it may be referenced.

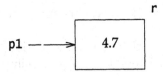

The next pointer assignment

    p2 => p1

causes p2 to be an alias for the same thing that p1 is an alias for, so the value of the variable p2 is also 4.7. The value 4.7 now has three names or aliases, r, p1, and p2.

Changing the value of r to 7.4 causes the value of both p1 and p2 also to change to 7.4 because they are both aliases of r. Thus, the next print statement

    print *, p2

prints the value 7.4.
    The pointer assignment statement

    p => q

is legal whatever the status of q. If q is undefined, p is undefined; if it is null, p is nullified; and if it is aliased to or associated with a target, p becomes associated with the same target. Note that if q is associated with some target, say t, it is not necessary that t have a defined value.

8.1.2 The Difference between Pointer and Ordinary Assignment

We can now illustrate the difference between pointer assignment, which transfers the status of one pointer to another, and ordinary assignment involving pointers. In an ordinary assignment in which pointers occur, the pointers must be viewed simply as aliases for their targets. Consider the following statements:

```
real, pointer :: p1, p2
real, target  :: r1, r2
   . . .
r1 = 1.1;  r2 = 2.2
p1 => r1;  p2 => r2
```

This produces the following situation:

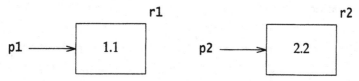

Now suppose the ordinary assignment statement

```
p2 = p1
```

is executed. This statement has exactly the same effect as the statement

```
r2 = r1
```

because p2 is an alias for r2 and p1 is an alias for r1. The situation is now:

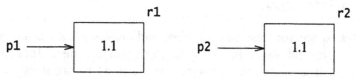

because the value 1.1 has been copied from r1 to r2. The values of p1, p2, r1, and r2 are all 1.1. Subsequent changes to r1 or p1 will have no effect on the value of r2.

If, on the other hand, the pointer assignment statement

```
p2 => p1
```

were executed instead, this statement would produce the situation

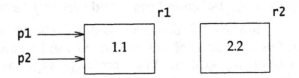

In this case, too, the values of p1, p2, and r1 are 1.1, but the value of r2 remains 2.2. Subsequent changes to p1 or r1 do change the value of p2. They do not change the value of r2.

If the target of p1 is changed to r2 by the pointer assignment statement

    p1 => r2

the target r1 and value 1.1 of p2 do not change, producing the following situation:

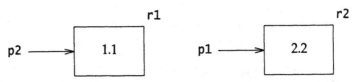

The pointer p2 remains an alias for r1; it does not remain associated with p1.

8.1.3 The allocate and deallocate Statements for Pointers

With the **allocate statement**, it is possible to create space for a value and cause a pointer variable to refer to that space. The space has no name other than the pointer mentioned in the allocate statement. For example,

    allocate (p1)

creates space for one real number and makes p1 an alias for that space. No real value is stored in the space by the allocate statement, so it is necessary to assign a value to p1 before it can be used, just as with any other real variable. As in the allocate statement for allocatable arrays, it is possible to test if the allocation is successful. This might be done with the statement

    allocate (p1, stat = allocation_status)

The statement

    p1 = 7.7

sets up the following situation.

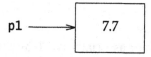

Before a value is assigned to p1, it must either be associated with an unnamed target by an **allocate** statement or be aliased with a target by a pointer assignment statement.

The **deallocate** statement throws away the space pointed to by its argument and makes its argument null (state 2). For example,

    deallocate (p1)

disassociates p1 from any target and nullifies it.

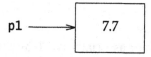

After p1 is deallocated, it must not be referenced in any situation that requires a value; however it may be used, for example, on the right side of a pointer assignment statement. If other pointer variables were aliases for p1, they, too, no longer reference a value.

8.1.4 The **nullify** Statement

At the beginning of a program, a pointer variable (just as all other variables) is not defined. A pointer variable must not be referenced to produce a value when it is not defined, but it is sometimes desirable to have a pointer variable be in the state of not pointing to anything, which might signify the last item in a linked list, for example.. This occurs when it is nullified, which creates a condition that may be tested and assigned to other pointers by pointer assignment (=>). A pointer is nullified with the **nullify statement**, which consists of the keyword `nullify` followed by the name of a pointer variable in parentheses, such as

```
nullify (p1)
```

If the target of p1 and p2 are the same, nullifying p1 does not nullify p2. On the other hand, if p1 is null, then executing the pointer assignment

```
p2 => p1
```

causes p2 to be null also.

A null pointer is not associated with any target or other pointer.

8.1.5 The associated Intrinsic Function

The **associated** intrinsic function may be used to determine if a pointer variable is pointing to, or is an alias for, another object. To use this function, the pointer variable must be defined; that is, it must either be the alias of some data object or be null. The `associated` function indicates which of these two cases is true; thus it provides the means of testing if a pointer is null.

The `associated` function may have a second argument. If the second argument is a target, the value of the function indicates whether the first argument is an alias of the second argument. If the second argument is a pointer, it must be defined; in this case, the value of the function is true if both pointers are null or if they are both aliases of the same target. For example, the expression

```
associated (p1, r)
```

indicates whether or not p1 is an alias of r, and the expression

```
associated (p1, p2)
```

indicates whether p1 and p2 are both aliases of the same thing or they are both null.

If two pointers are aliases of different parts of the same array, they are not considered to be associated. For example, the following program will print the value false.

```
program test_associated
  implicit none
  real, target, dimension (4) :: a = (/ 1, 2, 3, 4 /)
  real, pointer, dimension (:) :: p, q
  p => a (1:3)
  q => a (2:4)
  print *, associated (p, q)
end program test_associated
```

8.1.6 Dangling Pointers and Unreferenced Storage

There are two situations that the Fortran programmer must try to avoid. The first is a **dangling pointer**. This situation arises when a pointer variable is an alias for some object that gets deallocated by an action that does not involve the pointer directly. For example, if p1 and p2 are aliases, and the statement

```
deallocate (p2)
```

is executed, it is obvious that p2 is now disassociated, but the status of p1 appears to be unaffected, even though the object to which it was pointing has disappeared. A reference to p1 is now illegal and will produce unpredictable results. It is the responsibility of the programmer to keep track of the number of pointer variables referencing a particular object and to nullify each of the pointers whenever one of them is deallocated.

A related problem of **unreferenced storage** can occur when a pointer variable that is an alias of an object is nullified or set to alias something else without a deallocation. If there is no other alias for this value, it is still stored in memory somewhere, but there is no way to refer to it. This is not important if it happens to a few simple values, but if it happens many times to large arrays, the efficient management of storage could be hampered severely. In this case, it is also the responsibility of the programmer to ensure that objects are deallocated before all aliases of the object are modified. Fortran systems are not required to have runtime "garbage collection" to recover the unreferenced storage.

8.2 Linked Lists

Linked lists have many uses in a wide variety of application areas; one example in science and engineering is the use of a linked list to represent a queue in a simulation program. Lists of values can be implemented in Fortran 90 in more than one way. Perhaps the most obvious way is to use an array. Another is to use pointers and data structures to create a linked list. The choice should depend on which operations are going to be performed on the list and the relative frequency of those operations. If the only requirement is to add and delete numbers at one end of the list, as is done if the list is treated as a stack, then an array is an easy and efficient way to represent the list. If items must be inserted and deleted often at arbitrary points within the list, then a linked list is nice; with an array, many elements would have to be moved to insert or delete an element in the middle of the list. Another issue is whether storage is to be allocated all at once, using an array, or element by element in a linked list implementation. The implementation of linked lists using pointers also uses recursion effectively, but iteration also could be used.

A **linked list** of numbers (or any other objects) can be thought of schematically as a bunch of boxes, usually called *nodes*, each containing a number and a *pointer* to the box containing the next number in the list. Suppose, for example, the list contains the numbers 14, 62, and 83. In the lists discussed in this section, the numbers always will appear in numeric order, as they do in this example. Figure 8-1 contains a pictorial representation of the list.

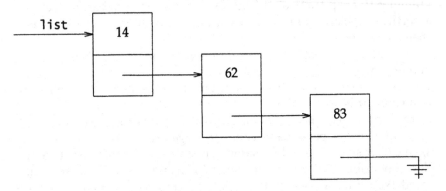

Figure 8-1 A linked list of integers.

We will illustrate the Fortran 90 techniques for manipulating linked lists by constructing a module to manipulate linked lists in which the nodes contain integers and the lists are sorted with the smallest number at the head of the list. The overall structure of the module is

```
module sorted_integer_lists_1

    type, private :: node
       integer :: value
       type (node), pointer :: next
    end type node

    type list
       private
       type (node), pointer :: first
    end type list

contains
    . . .

end module sorted_integer_lists_1
```

These declarations set up types for node, the "box" that contains a number and a pointer to the next node, and for list, which is a structure whose only component is a pointer to a node. The private specifications indicate that although the procedures and some of the types in this module will be available to any external program or procedure that uses this module, the type node will not be accessible, and the user also will not be able to access the internal structure of type list. The intent is to provide the user of the module with an **abstract data type**, that is, with the name of the list type and all necessary procedures to manipulate these lists. If it is desirable to change the implementation, we can be sure that no program has accessed the lists in any ways except those provided by the public procedures in this module.

The ability to declare which details of a module are private to the module and therefore hidden from all external users of the module, and which are public, that is, not private, and therefore available to users of the module, is important for two reasons, both of which we use in what follows.

1. In the course of implementing the module, we are free to change the details that are private, as long as we do not change the public interfaces with external procedures.

2. We will write two entirely different versions of this module that use different internal data structures for the lists, but which can be substituted for each other merely by changing the statement

```
use sorted_integer_lists_1
```

to

```
use sorted_integer_lists_2
```

Now we must decide what operations are needed. We will supply a function new that returns an empty list; a function empty (1) that returns the logical value indicating whether or not the list 1 is empty; a subroutine insert (1, number) that inserts number into list 1; a subroutine delete (1, number) that deletes one occurrence of number from a list 1, if it is there; and a subroutine print_list (1) that prints the numbers in the list in order. Some of these are pretty simple and could be done easily without a procedure, but the purpose is to include all necessary operations in the module and be able to change the implementation, as we do later in this section.

The function that returns a new empty list is relatively easy. The only tricky point is that the type list is not a pointer, but a structure whose only component is a pointer. Thus, there is no need to allocate new_result; all we need to do is nullify its pointer component first.

```
function new () result (new_result)

    type (list) :: new_result

    nullify (new_result % first)

end function new
```

With this function, the user of the module can create a new empty list and assign it to the variable x_list declared to be type list with the statement

```
x_list = new ()
```

Let's next do the subroutine that inserts a number into a list. This is a bit tricky. Suppose the list 1 has two numbers in it, 14 and 83, and we want to insert the number 62. The list is shown in Figure 8-2.

It is reasonable to move down through the list until a number in the list is found that is larger than the one to be inserted. In our example, this number is 83. Then the number 62 is inserted by creating a new node, linking the next field of the new node to the node containing 83, and finally linking the next field of the box containing

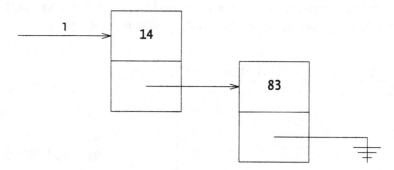

Figure 8-2 A list prior to insertion.

14 to the new box containing 62. The first two steps are easy, but to do the last step, it is necessary to have a variable that somehow references the box containing 14; but by the time we have found the number 83, unless we are careful, we no longer have anything pointing to the previous box and so cannot access it.

There are several solutions to this problem. One is to put two pointers in each box; one pointing forward in the list and one pointing backward. Another solution that we will pursue is to keep two temporary pointers as the list is traversed, one pointing at the current node and one pointing at the previous node. The latter pointer is often called a **trailing pointer**. In our example, when 83, the first number larger than 62, is found, the trailing pointer `trail_ptr` will be pointing at the box containing 14 and the other pointer, `temp_ptr`, will be pointing at the 83, as illustrated in Figure 8-3.

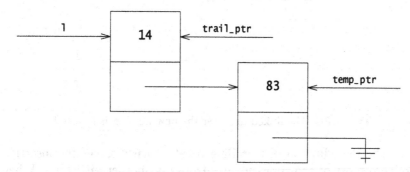

Figure 8-3 Locating the position of a new number in a linked list.

In this situation, the new number may be inserted with three statements. The first statement is

```
allocate (trail_ptr % next)
```

This statement creates a new unnamed node and sets the next pointer in the box containing 14 to point to it, as shown in Figure 8-4.

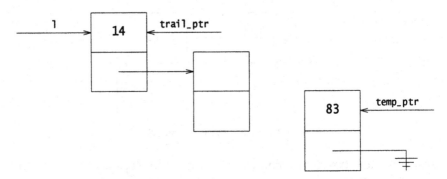

Figure 8-4 Allocating a new node for a linked list.

The other two statements put the number 62 into the `value` field of the newly created node and make its `next` field point to the node containing the number 83. The result is illustrated in Figure 8-5.

```
trail_ptr % next % value = number
trail_ptr % next % next => temp_ptr
```

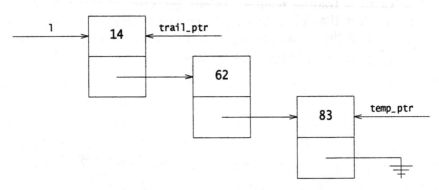

Figure 8-5 The linked list after the new number is inserted.

The introduction of a trailing pointer neatly solves the insertion problem most of the time, but it introduces another difficulty. When the list is empty, there can be no trailing pointer. One way to solve this difficulty is to treat the empty list as a special case. Instead, we will have one extra unused node at the head of each list. Since an empty list now has one (unused) node, the function `new` must be rewritten.

```
function new () result (new_result)

    type (list) :: new_result

    allocate (new_result % first)
    nullify (new_result % first % next)

end function new
```

The value of this function is represented schematically in Figure 8-6.

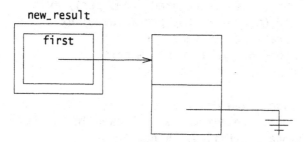

Figure 8-6 A newly created empty list.

A list 1 with a dummy node at the head containing the two numbers 14 and 83 is represented by the diagram in Figure 8-7.

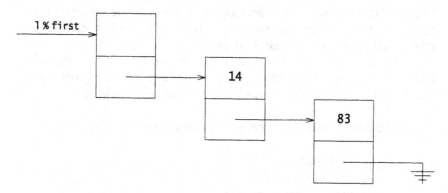

Figure 8-7 A linked list with a dummy node at the head.

As the list is traversed, the trailing pointer is initially set to point to the dummy node at the head and another pointer is set to start pointing at the rest of the list, which may be empty. We can now complete the function insert.

```
subroutine insert (1, number)

    type (list), intent (inout) :: 1
    integer, intent (in) :: number
    type (node), pointer :: trail_ptr, temp_ptr

    ! Find location to put new number
    trail_ptr => 1 % first
    temp_ptr => trail_ptr % next
    do
        if (.not. associated (temp_ptr)) exit
        if (number < temp_ptr % value) exit
        trail_ptr => temp_ptr
        temp_ptr => temp_ptr % next
    end do

    ! Insert new node
    ! Duplicate entries are allowed in the list
    allocate (trail_ptr % next)
    trail_ptr % next % value = number
    trail_ptr % next % next => temp_ptr

end subroutine insert
```

The two if tests inside the do loop in the subroutine insert cannot be replaced by a single test using .and. because if the first condition is false, making the second test is illegal.

The function that determines if a list is empty, that is, determines that only the dummy node is present, is straightforward. Recall that a pointer is not associated if it has been nullified.

```
function empty (1)  result (empty_result)

    implicit none
    type (list), intent (in) :: 1
    logical :: empty_result

    empty_result = .not. associated (1 % first % next)

end function empty
```

The subroutine to delete a number from a list, if it is there, is quite similar to the subroutine to insert. First the number must be found. Then, to delete a node, it is only necessary to adjust the next field of the node pointed to by the trailing pointer to "point around" the deleted node to the node following it. Also, it is a good idea to deallocate the space for the deleted node. If the number 62 is to be deleted, when its node is located by `temp_ptr`, the part of the list after the dummy node looks as shown in Figure 8-8.

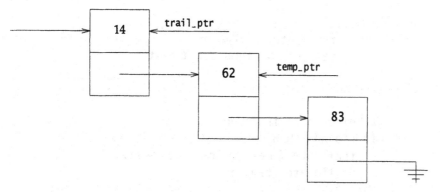

Figure 8-8 Locating a deletion position in a linked list with a dummy head.

The node containing 62 is removed from the list with the statement

```
trail_ptr % next => temp_ptr % next
```

and the node containing 62 is deallocated with the statement

```
deallocate (temp_ptr)
```

The entire subroutine follows. The third argument, found, indicates whether or not the number was found and deleted.

```
subroutine delete (l, number, found)

    type (list), intent (inout) :: l
    integer, intent (in) :: number
    logical, intent (out) :: found
    type (node), pointer :: trail_ptr, temp_ptr
```

```
! Find location to delete number
trail_ptr => l % first
temp_ptr => trail_ptr % next
do
    if (.not. associated (temp_ptr)) then
       found = .false.
       exit
    else if (number == temp_ptr % value) then
       found = .true.
       exit
    else
       trail_ptr => temp_ptr
       temp_ptr => temp_ptr % next
    end if
end do

! Delete node if found
if (found) then
    trail_ptr % next => temp_ptr % next
    deallocate (temp_ptr)
end if

end subroutine delete
```

The last subroutine needed to complete the module is one that prints the numbers in the list in order. This just involves traversing the list as in the subroutines insert and delete, except that no trailing pointer is required.

```
subroutine print_list (l)

    type (list), intent (in) :: l
    type (node), pointer :: temp_ptr

    temp_ptr => l % first % next
    do
       if (.not. associated (temp_ptr)) exit
       print *, temp_ptr % value
       temp_ptr => temp_ptr % next
    end do

end subroutine print_list
```

8.2.1 Sorting with a Linked List

With the integer list module just created, it is possible to write a simple but inefficient sorting program. The program works by reading in a file of numbers and inserting each number into a list as it is read. When all the numbers have been put into the list, it is printed, producing all the numbers in order.

```
program list_sort

    use sorted_integer_lists_1

    implicit none
    type (list) :: l
    integer :: number, ios

    l = new ()
    do
        read (*, *, iostat = ios) number
        ! a negative value for ios indicates end of file
        if (ios < 0) exit
        call insert (l, number)
    end do

    call print_list (l)

end program list_sort
```

8.2.2 Processing Lists Recursively

In this subsection we investigate how the procedures of the module sorted_integer_lists_1 would look if written using recursion. In these cases, the recursion is usually tail recursion, so, in one sense, not much is gained. However, it turns out that much of the detailed manipulation of pointers is eliminated and the recursive versions do not need a dummy node at the head of the list. This makes the routines a lot easier to write, understand, and maintain, but perhaps a little less efficient to execute on systems that have a high overhead for procedure calls.

The approach to writing recursive routines to process the list is to view the list itself as a recursive data structure. That is, a list of integers is either empty or it is an integer followed by a list of integers. This suggests that to process a list of numbers, process the first number in the list and then process the rest of the list with the same routine, quitting when the list is empty.

To view the list as a recursive data structure as described above, the object of type node now should consist of a value and another object, rest_of_list, of type list. In the module sorted_integer_lists_1, the second component of type node was a pointer to a node, but in sorted_integer_lists_2, it is an object of type list, which is slightly different; it is a structure consisting of one component that is the pointer to a node. With this change, the type definitions for the new module are

```
module sorted_integer_lists_2

    implicit none

    type list
        private
        type (node), pointer :: first
    end type list

    type, private :: node
        integer :: value
        type (list) :: rest_of_list
    end type node

contains
    . . .

end module sorted_integer_lists_2
```

With the revised type definitions, the function new may be changed back to the original version, because there is no need for a dummy node at the head of the list.

```
function new () result (new_result)

    type (list) :: new_result

    nullify (new_result % first)

end function new
```

Since the subroutines insert and delete were the most complicated, let's look at those next. The following is a recursive version of the subroutine insert.

```
recursive subroutine insert (1, number)

    type (list), intent (inout) :: 1
    integer, intent (in) :: number
    type (node), pointer :: temp_ptr

    if (.not. associated (1 % first)) then
        allocate (1 % first)
        1 % first % value = number
        nullify (1 % first % rest_of_list % first)
    else if (number < 1 % first % value) then
        ! insert at the front of the list 1
        allocate (temp_ptr)
        temp_ptr % value = number
        temp_ptr % rest_of_list = 1
        1 % first => temp_ptr
    else
        call insert (1 % first % rest_of_list, number)
    end if

end subroutine insert
```

Notice that objects of type list are assigned by ordinary assignment, not by pointer assignment because they are structures, even though their only component has the pointer attribute.

To see just one more example of a recursive routine to process the list, let's look at the subroutine print_list.

```
recursive subroutine print_list (1)

    type (list), intent (in) :: 1

    if (associated (1 % first)) then
        print *, 1 % first % value
        call print_list (1 % first % rest_of_list)
    end if

end subroutine print_list
```

Although this is just an instance of tail recursion, the procedure is quite a bit simpler than the iterative version.

Style Note: A very important point to note is that even when the procedures in the module sorted_integer_lists_1 are rewritten to be recursive, or even if arrays are used to represent the lists, creating yet another list module, a program such as list_sort that uses one of these modules does not have to be changed at all (unless the name of the module is changed). This illustrates one of the real benefits of using modules. However, the program list_sort must be recompiled using the new module.

8.2.3 Exercise

1. Use first the recursive version and then the nonrecursive version of the programs to manipulate lists of integers to construct a program that sorts integers. Experiment with each program, sorting different quantities of randomly generated integers to determine an approximate formula for the complexity of the program. Is the execution time (or some other measure of complexity, such as the number of statements executed) proportional to $n \log_2 n$? Is it proportional to n^2?

8.3 Trees

One of the big disadvantages of using a linked list to sort numbers is that the resulting program has poor expected running time. In fact, for the program list_sort, the expected running time is proportional to n^2, where n is the number of numbers to be sorted. A much more efficient sorting program can be constructed if a slightly more complicated data structure, the binary tree, is used. The resulting program, tree_sort, has an expected running time proportional to $n \log_2 n$ instead of n^2.

It is quite difficult to write nonrecursive programs to process trees, so we will think of trees as recursive structures right from the start. Using this approach, a **binary tree** of integers is either empty or is an integer, followed by two binary trees of integers, called the *left subtree* and *right subtree*.

8.3.1 Sorting with Trees

To sort numbers with a tree, we will construct a special kind of ordered binary tree with the property that the number at the "top" or "root" node of the tree is greater than all the numbers in its left subtree and less than or equal to all the numbers in its right subtree. This partitioning of the tree into a left subtree containing smaller numbers and a right subtree containing larger numbers is exactly analogous to the partitioning of a list into smaller and larger sublists that makes quicksort (Section 4.3.1) an efficient algorithm. This property will hold not only for the most accessible node at the "top" of the tree (paradoxically called the "root" of the tree), but for all nodes of the tree. To illustrate this kind of tree, suppose a file of integers contains the numbers 265, 113, 467, 264, 907, and 265 in the order given. To build an ordered binary tree containing these numbers, first start with an empty tree. Then read in the first number 265 and place it in a node at the root of the tree, as shown in Figure 8-9.

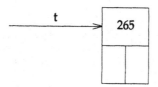

Figure 8-9 The root of a tree.

A blank box in the lower part of a node is understood to represent a null pointer.

When the next number is read, it is compared with the first. If it is less than the first number, it is placed as a node in the left subtree; if it is greater than or equal to the first number, it is placed in the right subtree. In our example, 113 < 265, so a node containing 113 is created and the left subtree pointer of the node containing 265 is set to point to it, as shown in Figure 8-10.

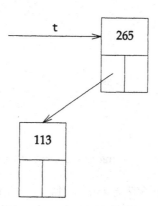

Figure 8-10 Adding the number 113 to the tree.

The next number is 467, and it is placed in the right subtree of 265 because it is larger than 265. The result is shown in Figure 8-11.

The next number is 264, so it is placed in the left subtree of 265. To place it properly within the left subtree, it is compared with 113, the occupant of the top of the left subtree. Since 264 ≥ 113, it is placed in the right subtree of the one with 113 at the top to obtain the tree shown in Figure 8-12.

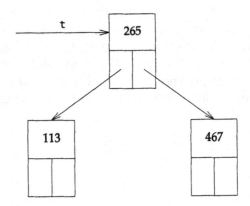

Figure 8-11 Adding the number 467 to the tree.

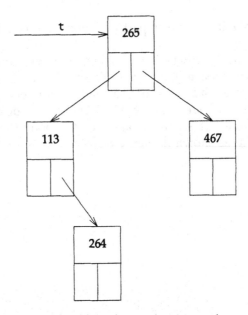

Figure 8-12 Adding the number 264 to the tree.

The next number 907 is larger than 265, so it is compared with 467 and put in the right subtree of the node containing 467, as shown in Figure 8-13.

The final number 265 is equal to the number in the root node. An insertion position is therefore sought in the right subtree of the root. Since 265 < 467, it is put to the left of 467, as shown in Figure 8-14. Notice that the two nodes containing the number 265 are not even adjacent, nor is the node containing the number 264 adjacent to either node with key 265. This doesn't matter. When the tree is printed, they will come out in the right order.

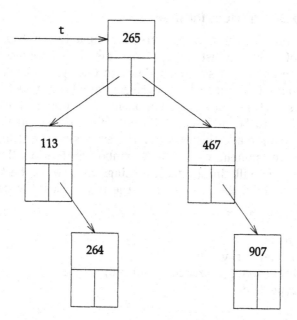

Figure 8-13 Adding the number 907 to the tree.

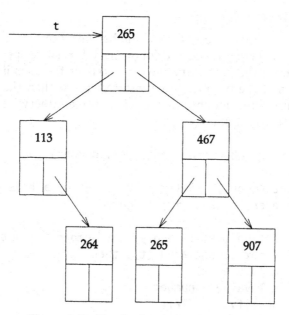

Figure 8-14 The final ordered binary tree.

8.3.2 Type Declarations for Trees

The declaration for the node of a tree is similar to the declaration for the node of a linked list, except that the node must contain two pointers, one to the left subtree and one to the right subtree. As with lists, we could have tree be a derived data type, which implies it must be a structure with one component, a pointer to the node of a tree. But just to be different, let's not put the tree operations in a module. Having made this decision, the extra syntax needed to select the pointer component using the % symbol clutters up the program enough that we will simply declare things that would be trees to be pointers to a node, the root node of the tree. Thus, the declarations needed are

```
type node
   integer :: value
   type (node), pointer :: left, right
end type node

type (node), pointer :: t
```

8.3.3 The insert Subroutine

The subroutine that inserts a new number into the tree is a straightforward implementation of the following informal recipe: if the tree is empty, make the new entry the only node of the tree; if the tree is not empty and the number to be inserted is less than the number at the root, insert the number in the left subtree; otherwise, insert the number in the right subtree.

```
recursive subroutine insert (t, number)

    type (node), pointer :: t  ! really a tree.
    integer, intent (in) :: number

    ! If (sub)tree is empty, put number at root
    if (.not. associated (t)) then
       allocate (t)
       t % value = number
       nullify (t % left)
       nullify (t % right)
```

```
! Otherwise, insert into correct subtree
else if (number < t % value) then
   call insert (t % left, number)
else
   call insert (t % right, number)
end if

end subroutine insert
```

8.3.4 Printing the Tree in Order

The recipe for printing the nodes of the tree follows from the way the tree has been built. It is simply to print in order the values in the left subtree of the root, print the value at the root node, then print in order the values in the right subtree. This subroutine is shown in the following complete program that sorts a file of integers by reading them all in, constructing an ordered binary tree, and then printing out the values in the tree in order.

```
program tree_sort
! Sorts a file of integers by building a
! tree, sorted in infix order.
! This sort has expected behavior n log n,
! but worst case (input is sorted) n ** 2.

   implicit none
   type node
      integer :: value
      type (node), pointer :: left, right
   end type node

   type (node), pointer :: t  ! A tree
   integer :: number, ios

   nullify (t)  ! Start with empty tree
   do
      read (*, *, iostat = ios) number
      if (ios < 0) exit
      call insert (t, number) ! Put next number in tree
   end do
   ! Print nodes of tree in infix order
   call print_tree (t)
```

```
contains

    recursive subroutine insert (t, number)

        type (node), pointer :: t  ! A tree
        integer, intent (in) :: number

        ! If (sub)tree is empty, put number at root
        if (.not. associated (t)) then
            allocate (t)
            t % value = number
            nullify (t % left)
            nullify (t % right)
        ! Otherwise, insert into correct subtree
        else if (number < t % value) then
            call insert (t % left, number)
        else
            call insert (t % right, number)
        end if

    end subroutine insert

    recursive subroutine print_tree (t)
    ! Print tree in infix order

        type (node), pointer :: t  ! A tree

        if (associated (t)) then
            call print_tree (t % left)
            print *, t % value
            call print_tree (t % right)
        end if

    end subroutine print_tree

end program tree_sort
```

8.3.5 Exercise

1. Experiment with the program tree_sort, sorting different
    quantities of randomly generated integers to determine an
    approximate formula for the complexity of the program. It
    should be proportional to $n \log_2 n$.

8.4 Case Study: Finding the Median

A common problem is to find the median of a set of numbers. A related problem is to find the score at the 50th percentile in a set of test scores. These can both be done with the subroutine `select` discussed in Section 4.4.

To review the method used by `select`, suppose we arbitrarily pick one number from the list. Split the list into three lists, one containing those numbers less than the number picked, a second containing the numbers equal to the number picked, and a third list containing the numbers larger than the one picked. Count the numbers, respectively s, e, and l, in each of the three lists. If the kth number is to be found and there are k or more numbers in the list of smaller numbers, then the kth number must be in that list, so the problem reduces to that of finding the kth number in the list of smaller numbers. Otherwise, if $k \leq s + e$, the sum of the sizes of the smaller and equal lists together, the number sought is equal to each number in the list of equal numbers. If neither of these cases is true, then the number sought is the $(k-s-e)$th number in the list of larger numbers.

To see how this works, suppose we are to find the fifth number (the median) of the following nine numbers: 43, 28, 56, 72, 43, 34, 62, 62, and 97. Suppose the first number 43 is picked to form the partition into smaller, equal, and larger numbers. Then the list of smaller numbers is 28, 34; the list of equal numbers is 43, 43; and the list of larger numbers is 56, 72, 62, 62, 97. Since there are only four numbers in the combined smaller and equal lists, the fifth number of the original list is the first number of the list of larger numbers. The process is applied again, let's say with 56 as the picked number. Then the list of smaller numbers is empty; the list of equal numbers is 56; and the list of larger numbers is 72, 62, 62, 97. In this case the number we are looking for is 56.

This process is described recursively and the algorithm is most easily implemented using recursion. A very important decision involves the manner in which the lists are to be represented. It is certainly possible to put the numbers in arrays as was done in Section 4.4, but the sizes of the lists are all different and it turns out that it is necessary to insert and delete numbers from the list only at one end, so a linked list is an excellent choice.

8.4.1 Stacks

A linked list for which insertions and deletions are made only at one end is called a **stack**. Stacks arise in many sorts of applications, so it is not a bad idea to have a module of routines to manipulate stacks.

We shall construct some of the procedures handy to have for manipulating stacks of integers. The structure of the module and the data types used look much like our previous list module. Also, because they are just like the previous versions, we can include in the module immediately the function new that returns an empty stack and the logical function empty that tests to see if a stack is empty.

```
module stack_of_integers

    implicit none

    type stack
        private
        type (node), pointer :: top
    end type stack

    type, private :: node
        integer :: value
        type (stack) :: rest_of_stack
    end type node

contains

function new () result (new_result)

    type (stack) :: new_result
    nullify (new_result % top)

end function new

function empty (s) result (empty_result)

    implicit none
    type (stack), intent (in) :: s
    logical :: empty_result

    empty_result = .not. associated (s % top)

end function empty
    . . .

    end module stack_of_integers
```

8.4.2 Pushing a Number onto a Stack

Insertion of a new integer into a stack is always done at the top of the stack and so is simpler than the insert procedure for a general linked list. The operation is said to **push** the integer onto the stack. This operation is implemented as a function that returns a stack modified to contain the additional element.

```
function push (s, number)  result (push_result)

    type (stack) :: push_result
    type (stack), intent (in) :: s
    integer, intent (in) :: number

    allocate (push_result % top)
    push_result % top % value = number
    push_result % top % rest_of_stack = s

end function push
```

8.4.3 Top Element of a Stack

Another natural operation is to return the number from the top of the stack. The stack should be checked to see if it is empty before the top_of operation is executed; however, the value -huge is returned if it is. The intrinsic function huge returns the largest representable number of the same type and kind as its argument.

```
function top_of (s)  result (top_of_result)

    integer :: top_of_result
    type (stack), intent (in) :: s

    if (empty (s)) then
       top_of_result = - huge (top_of_result)
    else
       top_of_result = s % top % value
    end if

end function top_of
```

This operation does not affect the stack; that is, it does not remove the top element from the stack.

8.4.4 The Rest of the Stack

Another natural operation is to **pop** a number from the top of a stack and return the stack with its top element removed as the value of the function.

```
function rest_of (s)  result (rest_of_result)

    type (stack) :: rest_of_result
    type (stack), intent (in) :: s

    if (empty (s)) then
       rest_of_result = s
    else
       rest_of_result = s % top % rest_of_stack
    end if

end function rest_of
```

Now we can concentrate on the job of writing the procedure that finds the kth number in a given list. It will be assumed that the list will be in the form of a variable of type stack. If this is not the case, it is pretty easy to convert an array of integers, for example, into a stack of integers by pushing them one by one onto an initially empty stack. As described above, the procedure select picks an arbitrary number from the list to use as the test element. In our case we pick the number at the head of the stack, because that one is most accessible. Then select forms three lists containing (a) the numbers less than the one picked, (b) the numbers equal to the one picked, and (c) the numbers greater than the one picked. Actually there is no reason to construct the list of equal numbers, but only to record how many there are. We also need to record the size of the other two lists. Then the procedure is called recursively using the appropriate sublist.

```
recursive subroutine select (s, k, number, error)

    type (stack), intent (in) :: s
    integer, intent (in) :: k
    integer, intent (out) :: number
    logical, intent (out) :: error
    type (stack) :: smaller, larger
    integer :: number_smaller, number_equal, number_larger

    if (empty (s)) then
       error = .true.
```

```
   else
      number = top_of (s)
      call split (rest_of (s), number, smaller,  &
            number_smaller, number_equal,  &
            larger, number_larger)

      if (k <= number_smaller) then
         call select (smaller, k, number, error)
      else if (k <= number_smaller + number_equal) then
         ! number is the correct value
         error = .false.
      else
         call select (larger,  &
            k - number_smaller - number_equal,  &
            number, error)
      end if
   end if

   end subroutine select
```

This procedure is a subroutine because it returns two values, the number selected and error flag that is set to true if an error occurs, such as trying to select the 47th number from a list of 12 numbers.

The only remaining task is to write a subroutine that splits the list into the three parts.

```
subroutine split (s, picked, smaller, number_smaller,  &
                  number_equal, larger, number_larger)

   type (stack), intent (in) :: s
   integer, intent (in) :: picked
   type (stack), intent (out) :: smaller, larger
   integer, intent (out) :: &
         number_smaller, number_equal, number_larger
   type (stack) :: temp_s
   integer :: number

   smaller = new ()
   larger = new ()
   number_smaller = 0
   number_equal = 1
   number_larger = 0
```

```
temp_s = s   ! so as not to modify s
do
   if (empty (temp_s)) exit
   number = top_of (temp_s)
   temp_s = rest_of (temp_s)
   if (number < picked) then
      smaller = push (smaller, number)
      number_smaller = number_smaller + 1
   else if (number > picked) then
      larger = push (larger, number)
      number_larger = number_larger + 1
   else
      number_equal = number_equal + 1
   end if
end do

end subroutine split
```

The subroutine select is tested by the program test_select.

```
program test_select

   use stack_of_integers

   integer number
   logical error
   type (stack) :: integer_stack
   integer, dimension (9) :: test_values = &
      (/ 43, 28, 56, 72, 43, 34, 62, 62, 97 /)

   integer_stack = new ()
   do i = 1, 9
      integer_stack = &
            push (integer_stack, test_values (i))
   end do

   call select (integer_stack, 5, number, error)
   print *, 5, error, number
   call select (integer_stack, 1, number, error)
   print *, 1, error, number
   call select (integer_stack, 9, number, error)
   print *, 9, error, number
```

```
call select (integer_stack, 0, number, error)
print *, 0, error, number

end program test_select

run test_select

5 f 56
1 f 28
9 f 97
0 t 28
```

8.4.5 Exercises

1. Experiment with the program select, finding the median of different quantities of randomly generated integers to determine an approximate formula for the complexity of the program. The execution time should be proportional to n.

2. A way to handle the problem of manipulating stacks of objects that are not single values, such as integers, but perhaps are large structures or arrays, is to replace the value field in each node with a pointer to the object that is to be placed in the stack. That is, instead of manipulating stacks of objects, manipulate stacks of pointers to the objects. Modify the procedures in the module stack_of_integers to process stacks of large structures or arrays of values by this scheme.

8.5 Arrays of Pointers

In Fortran, it is not possible to have an array of pointers. However, the same effect can be achieved with an array of structures, each of which has a single component that is a pointer variable.

8.5.1 A Poor Sorting Algorithm

We begin with a very simple, but very inefficient, subroutine that sorts an array of real numbers. This should never be used to sort more than a few dozen numbers, but it is pretty easy to remember and write in a hurry, if necessary. Anyway, the point of this discussion is not to get a good sorting algorithm, but show how pointers can be used.

```
subroutine bad_sort (numbers)
! Uses an inefficient sorting algorithm
! Moves type real data when swapping

   real, dimension (:), intent (inout) :: numbers
   integer :: i, j
   real :: temp

   do i = 1, size (numbers) - 1
      do j = i + 1, size (numbers)
         if (numbers (i) > numbers (j)) then
            temp = numbers (i)
            numbers (i) = numbers (j)
            numbers (j) = temp
         end if
      end do
   end do

end subroutine bad_sort
```

Let's also suppose that instead of sorting an array of real numbers, we must sort an array of large data structures, one component of which is a key that determines the order of the data in the sorted list. An example might be structures, one for each person, maintained by the U.S. Internal Revenue Service. It might be desirable to sort the structures based on social security number, for example. Thus, we may have structures of type person_type with one component being ssn, the social security number that identifies each taxpayer.

```
type person_type

   integer :: ssn
   . . . ! A lot of other stuff

end type person_type
```

The subroutine bad_sort would have to be modified to the following:

```
subroutine bad_sort (person)
! Uses inefficient sorting algorithm
! Moves whole records when swapping
```

```
type (person_type), dimension (:),  &
     intent (inout) :: person
type (person_type) :: r
integer :: i, j

do i = 1, size (person) - 1
   do j = i + 1, size (person)
      if (person (i) % ssn > person (j) % ssn) then
         r = person (i)
         person (i) = person (j)
         person (j) = r
      end if
   end do
end do

end subroutine bad_sort
```

Now we not only have a subroutine that uses an inefficient sorting algorithm, but it wastes a lot of time moving large amounts of data around every time it finds two structures out of order and swaps them.

A way around this last difficulty is to create an array of pointers to the structures and instead of moving the structures, just swap the pointers. The argument to the following function is not an array of objects of type person_type, but an array of structures containing just one component, which is a pointer to an object of type person_type.

```
type person_ptr_type
   type (person_type), pointer :: ptr
end type person_ptr_type

type (person_ptr_type), dimension (:),  &
     allocatable :: pointers
```

It is necessary to declare the array of structures of type person_type to have the target attribute.

```
type (person_type), dimension (number_of_persons),  &
     target :: person
```

First, we can set things up so that the first pointer in the array pointers points to the first structure, the second pointer points to the second structure, and so on.

```
allocate (pointers (size (person)))
do i = 1, size (person)
   pointers (i) % ptr  => person (i)
end do
```

Now we can write a subroutine that will do the sorting in the sense that it will change the array of pointers so that the first pointer points to the structure with the smallest key, the second pointer points to the structure with the second smallest key, and so on. The main argument to this sorting routine is the array of pointers, not the array of objects to be sorted.

```
subroutine bad_sort (pointers)
! Still uses inefficient algorithm
! But now moves only pointers when swapping

   type (person_ptr_type), dimension (:),  &
        intent (inout) :: pointers
   type (person_ptr_type) :: p
   integer :: i, j

   do i = 1, size (pointers) - 1
      do j = i + 1, size (pointers)
         if (pointers (i) % ptr % ssn >  &
             pointers (j) % ptr % ssn) then
            p = pointers (i)
            pointers (i) = pointers (j)
            pointers (j) = p
         end if
      end do
   end do

end subroutine bad_sort
```

As can be seen, the subroutine is pretty much the same, except that the array argument is a different type and one more indirect reference is needed to access the value of an ssn: namely, pointers (i) % ptr % ssn is used in place of number (i). Notice that ordinary assignment is used for the variable p and the elements of the array pointers because they are structures and not pointers, even though their only component is a pointer. However, when one structure with a pointer component is assigned to another structure of the same type, components that are pointers are pointer assigned.

8.5.2 A Good Sorting Algorithm for Structures

Next we combine an efficient algorithm with the pointer techniques of the previous section that replace the time-consuming action of copying large structures with the much faster operation of changing pointers to these structures. We use the better quick sort algorithm written in Section 4.3.1, modified below to use the array names of this chapter. Also, because we have been discussing "bad" sorting algorithms and have a subroutine bad_sort, we modify it to an internal subroutine bad_sublist_sort to do the sorting for very small lists, where it actually is faster than quick sort.

The modifications that need to be made are the same as those for converting the bad sorting algorithm on the same data type to a pointer algorithm on structures. Basically, we always move objects of person_ptr_type, which is a structure with one component. That component is a pointer to the structure of type person_type that we want to avoid moving. When we need to reference a key value for comparison, we do it indirectly from the array of pointers. In effect, the current ith social security number in the list is referenced by pointers (i) % ptr % ssn. The following subroutines and declarations show the modifications and the results of running a simple test of these routines.

```
module quick_sort_using_pointers

    type person_type
      integer :: ssn
    !   . . . ! A lot of other stuff
    end type person_type

    type person_ptr_type
       type (person_type), pointer :: ptr
    end type person_ptr_type

contains

subroutine quick_sort (pointers)

    type (person_ptr_type), dimension (:),  &
                         intent (inout) :: pointers
    call quick_sort_1 (1, size (pointers))

contains
```

```
recursive subroutine quick_sort_1 (left_end, right_end)

    integer, intent (in) :: left_end, right_end
    integer :: i, j
    type (person_ptr_type) :: chosen, t

    if (right_end < left_end + 6) then
        ! Use interchange sort for small lists
        call bad_sublist_sort (left_end, right_end)
    else
        ! Use partition ("quick") sort
        chosen = pointers ((left_end + right_end) / 2)
        i = left_end - 1; j = right_end + 1

        do
            ! Scan list from left end
            ! until element >= chosen is found
            do
                i = i + 1
                if (pointers (i) % ptr % ssn >=  &
                    chosen % ptr % ssn) exit
            end do
            ! Scan list from right end
            ! until element <= chosen is found
            do
                j = j - 1
                if (pointers (j) % ptr % ssn <=  &
                    chosen % ptr % ssn) exit
            end do
            if (i < j) then
                ! Swap two out of place elements
                t = pointers (i); pointers (i) = pointers (j);
                pointers (j) = t
            else if (i == j) then
                i = i + 1; exit
            else
                exit
            end if
        end do
```

```fortran
         if (left_end < j) call quick_sort_1 (left_end, j)
         if (i < right_end) call quick_sort_1 (i, right_end)
      end if

end subroutine quick_sort_1

subroutine bad_sublist_sort (left_end, right_end)

   implicit none
   integer, intent (in) :: left_end, right_end
   integer :: i, j
   type (person_ptr_type) :: t

   do i = left_end, right_end - 1
      do j = i + 1, right_end
         if (pointers (i) % ptr % ssn > &
             pointers (j) % ptr % ssn) then
            t = pointers (i); pointers (i) = pointers (j)
            pointers (j) = t
         end if
      end do
   end do

end subroutine bad_sublist_sort

end subroutine quick_sort

end module quick_sort_using_pointers

program quick_program

   use quick_sort_using_pointers

   integer, parameter :: number_of_persons = 16

   type (person_type), dimension (number_of_persons), &
         target :: person
   type (person_ptr_type), dimension (:), &
         allocatable :: pointers
```

```
      read *, person
      print *, "Input data: ssn"

      do i = 1, number_of_persons
         print *, person (i) % ssn
      end do

      ! Set up pointers
      allocate (pointers (size (person)))
      do i = 1, size (person)
         pointers (i) % ptr => person (i)
      end do

      call quick_sort (pointers)

      print *; print *, "Sorted by SSN:"
      do i = 1, number_of_persons
         print *, pointers (i) % ptr % ssn
      end do

end program quick_program

run quick_program

 Input data: ssn
 2980957
 3269017
 1202604
 2718281
 8103083
 2202646
 8886110
 2008553
 4424133
 1627547
 4034287
 5459815
 7389056
 1096633
 1484131
 5987414
```

Sorted by SSN:
1096633
1202604
1484131
1627547
2008553
2202646
2718281
2980957
3269017
4034287
4424133
5459815
5987414
7389056
8103083
8886110

9

Input and Output

The facilities needed to do simple input and output tasks were described in Chapter 1, and many examples of these statements were discussed throughout the other chapters. Sometimes it is necessary to use the more sophisticated input/output features of Fortran, which are probably superior to those found in any other high level language. This chapter describes in some detail these features, including direct access input/output, nonadvancing input/output, the use of internal files, file connection statements, the `inquire` statement, file positioning statements, and formatting.

The input/output statements are

```
read
print
write
open
close
inquire
backspace
endfile
rewind
```

The read, write, and print statements are the ones that do the actual data transfer; the open and close statements deal with the connection between an input/output unit and a file; the inquire statement provides the means to find out things about a file or unit; and the backspace, endfile, and rewind statements affect the position of the file.

Because this chapter is needed only for the more sophisticated kinds of input and output, it is organized a little bit differently from other chapters. The first part contains a discussion of some fundamental ideas needed for a thorough understanding of how Fortran input/output works. The next part of the chapter contains a description and examples of the special kinds of data transfer statements. Then there is a discussion of the open, close, inquire, backspace, rewind, and endfile statements. The final part contains a more detailed description of formatting than that provided in Chapter 1.

Input and output operations deal with collections of data called **files**. The data are organized into **records**, which may correspond to lines on a computer terminal, lines on a printout, or parts of a disk file. The descriptions of records and files in this chapter are to be considered abstractions and do not necessarily represent the way data is stored physically on any particular device. For example, a Fortran program may produce a file of answers. This file might be printed, and the only remaining physical representation of the file would be the ink on the paper. Or it might be written onto magnetic tape and remain there for a few years, eventually to be erased when the tape is used to store other information.

The general properties of records are discussed first.

9.1 Records

There are two kinds of records, data records and endfile records. A **data record** is a sequence of values. Thus, a data record may be represented schematically as a collection of small boxes, each containing a value, as shown in Figure 9-1.

Figure 9-1 Schematic representation of the values in a record.

The values in a data record may be represented in one of two ways: formatted or unformatted. If the values are characters readable by a person, each character is one value and the data is **formatted**. For example, the statement

```
write (*, "(i1, a, i2)") 6, ",", 11
```

would produce a record containing the four character values "6" ","
"1", and "1". In this case, the record might be represented schematically as Figure 9-2.

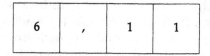

Figure 9-2 A formatted record with four character values.

   Unformatted data consists of values usually represented just as
they are stored in computer memory. For example, if integers are
stored using an eight-bit binary representation, execution of the statement

```
write (9) 6, 11
```

might produce an unformatted record that looks like Figure 9-3.

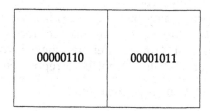

Figure 9-3 An unformatted record with two integer values.

9.1.1 Formatted Records

A **formatted record** is one that contains only formatted data. A formatted record may be created by a person typing at a terminal or by
a Fortran program that converts values stored internally into character strings that form readable representations of those values. When
formatted data is read into the computer, the characters must be converted to the computer's internal representation of values, which is
often a binary representation. Even character values may be converted from one character representation in the record to another
internal representation. The length of a formatted record is the number of characters in it; the length may be zero.

9.1.2 Unformatted Records

An **unformatted record** is one that contains only unformatted data. Unformatted records usually are created by running a Fortran program, although, with the knowledge of how to form the bit patterns correctly, they could be created by other means. Unformatted data often requires less space on an external device. Also, it is usually faster to read and write unformatted data because no conversion is required. However, it is not as suitable for reading by humans, and usually it is not suitable for transferring data from one computer to another because the internal representation of values is machine dependent. The length of an unformatted data record depends on the number of values in it, but is measured in some processor-dependent units such as as machine words; the length may be zero. The length of an unformatted record that will be produced by a particular output list may be determined by the `inquire` statement (Section 9.6.2).

9.1.3 Endfile Records

The other kind of record is the **endfile record**, which, at least conceptually, has no values and has no length. There can be at most one endfile record in a file and it must be the last record of a file. It is used to mark the end of a file.

An endfile record may be written explicitly by the programmer using the `endfile` statement. An endfile record also is written implicitly when the last data transfer statement involving the file was an output statement, the file has not been repositioned, and

1.   a backspace statement is executed,

2.   a `rewind` statement is executed, or

3.   the file is closed.

9.1.4 Record Length

In some files, the lengths of the records are fixed in advance of data being put in the file; in others, it depends on how data is written to the file. For external formatted advancing sequential output (Section 9.3.4), a record ends whenever a slash (/) edit descriptor is encountered and at the conclusion of each input/output operation (`write` or `print`).

9.1.5 Printing of Formatted Records

Sometimes output records are sent to a device that interprets the first character of the record as a control character. This is usually the case with line printers. If a formatted record is printed on such a device, the first character of the record is not printed but instead is used to control vertical spacing. The remaining characters of the record, if any, are printed in one line beginning at the left margin.

The first character of such a record must be of default character type and determines vertical spacing, as shown in Table 9-1.

Table 9-1 Carriage control characters.

Character	Vertical spacing before printing
Blank	One line (single spacing)
0	Two lines (double spacing)
1	To first line of next page (begin new page)
+	No advance (overprint on top of old line)

If there are no characters in the record, a blank line is printed.

Sometimes it is difficult to determine if the first character of each record is going to be interpreted as a carriage control character. On some systems it is done on terminals and on some it is not. The first character in a record is almost always interpreted in this way by line printers and probably rarely so interpreted prior to storing on a disk or magnetic tape. The only way to know is to read the manual for the system you are using or to experiment.

9.2 Files

A **file** is a collection of records. A file may be represented schematically with each box representing a record, as shown in Figure 9-4.

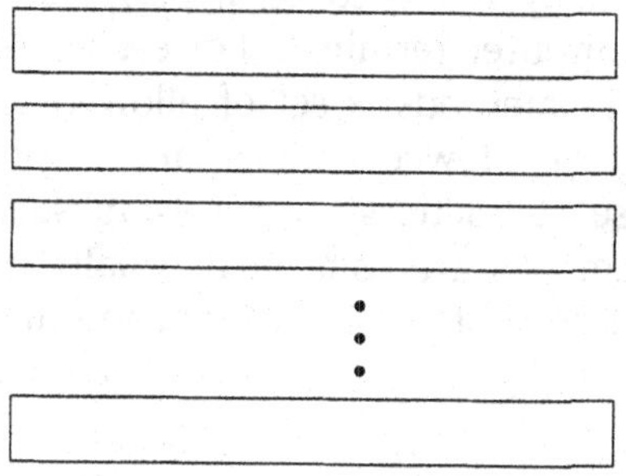

Figure 9-4 Schematic representation of records in a file.

The records of a file must be either all formatted or all unformatted, except that the file may contain an endfile record as the last record. A file may have a name, but the length of the names and the characters that may be used in the names depend on the system being used. The set of names that are allowed often is determined by the operating system as well as the Fortran compiler.

A distinction is made between files that are located on an external device, such as a disk, and files in memory accessible to the program. The two kinds of files are

1.   External files

2.   Internal files

The use of the files is illustrated schematically in Figure 9-5.

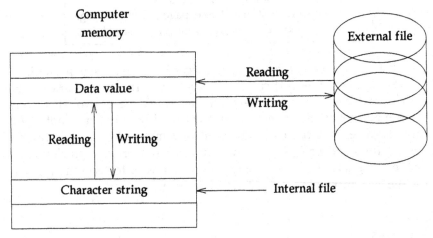

Figure 9-5 Internal and external files.

9.2.1 External Files

An external file usually is stored on a peripheral device, such as a tape, a disk, or a computer terminal. For each external file, there is a set of allowed access methods, a set of allowed forms (formatted or unformatted), a set of allowed actions, and a set of allowed record lengths. How these characteristics are established is dependent on the computer system you are using, but usually they are determined by a combination of requests by the user of the file and actions by the operating system.

9.2.2 Internal Files

Internal files are stored in memory as values of character variables. The character values may be created using all the usual means of assigning character values or they may be created with an output statement using the variable as an internal file. If the variable is a scalar, the file has just one record; if the variable is an array, the file has one record for each element of the array. The length of the record is the number of characters declared or assumed for the character variable. Only formatted sequential access is permitted on internal files. For example, if char_array is an array of two character strings declared by

```
character (len = 7), dimension (2) :: char_array
```

the statement

```
write (char_array, "(f7.5, /, f7.5)") 10/3.0, 10/6.0
```

produces the same effect as the assignment statements

```
char_array (1) = "3.33333"
char_array (2) = "1.66667"
```

9.2.3 Existence of Files

Certain files are known to the processor and are available to an executing program; these files are said to **exist** at that time. For example, a file may not exist because it is not anywhere on the disks accessible to a system. A file may not exist for a particular program because the user of the program is not authorized to access the file. For example, Fortran programs usually are not permitted to access special system files, such as the operating system or the compiler, in order to protect them from user modification. The inquire statement may be used to determine whether or not a file exists.

In addition to files that are made available to programs by the processor for input, output, and other special purposes, programs may create files needed during and after program execution. When the program creates a file, it is said to exist, even if no data has been written into it. A file no longer exists after it has been deleted. Any of the input/output statements may refer to files that exist for the program at that point during execution. Some of the input/output statements (inquire, open, close, write, print, rewind, and endfile) may refer to files that do not exist. For example, a write statement may create a file that does not exist and put data into that file. An internal file always exists.

9.2.4 File Access Methods

There are two access methods for external files:

1. Sequential access

2. Direct access

Sequential access to the records in the file begins with the first record of the file and proceeds sequentially to the second record, and then to the next record, record by record. The records are accessed in the order that they appear in the file. It is not possible to begin at some particular record within the file without reading from the current record down to that record in sequential order.

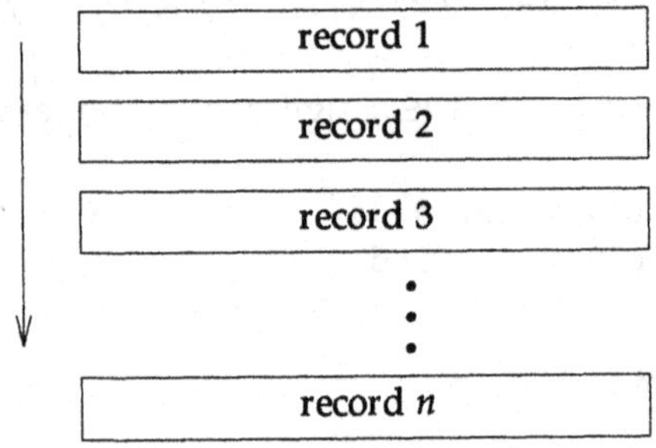

```
┌─────────────────────┐
│      record 1       │
├─────────────────────┤
│      record 2       │
├─────────────────────┤
│      record 3       │
├─────────────────────┤
│         •           │
│         •           │
│         •           │
│      record n       │
└─────────────────────┘
```

Figure 9-6 Sequential access.

When a file is being accessed sequentially, the records are read and written sequentially. For example, if the records are written in any arbitrary order using direct access and then read using sequential access, the records are read beginning with record number one of the file, regardless of when it was written.

When a file is accessed directly, the records are selected by record number. Using this identification, the records may be read or written in any order. For example, it is possible to write record number 47 first, then write record number 13. In a new file, this produces a file represented by Figure 9-7. Either record may be read without first accessing the other.

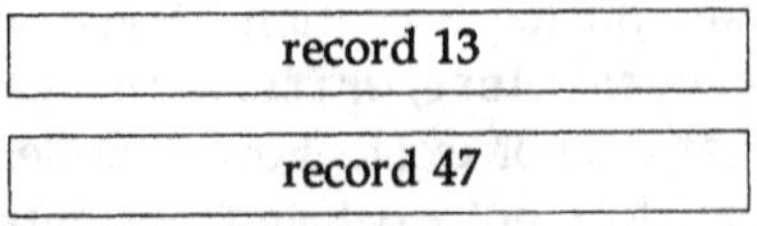

```
┌─────────────────────┐
│      record 13      │
├─────────────────────┤
│      record 47      │
└─────────────────────┘
```

Figure 9-7 A file written using direct access.

The following rules apply when accessing a file directly:

1. If a file is to be accessed directly, all of the records must be the same length.

2. It is not possible to delete a record using direct access.

3. List-directed formatting and nonadvancing input/output are prohibited.

4. An internal file must not be accessed directly.

Each file has a set of permissible access methods, which usually means that it may be accessed either sequentially or directly. However, it is possible that a file may be accessed by either method. The actual file access method used to read or write the file must be one of the allowed access methods for the file; it is established when the file is connected to a unit (Section 9.2.7). The same file may be accessed sequentially by a program, then disconnected and later accessed directly by the same program, if both types of access are permitted for the file.

9.2.5 File Position

Each file being processed by a program has a **position**. During the course of program execution, records are read or written, causing the position of the file to change. Also, there are Fortran statements that cause the position of a file to change; an example is the backspace statement.

The **initial point** is the point just before the first record. The **terminal point** is the point just after the last record. If the file is empty, the initial point and the terminal point are the same.

A file may be positioned between records. In the example pictured in Figure 9-9, the file is positioned between records 2 and 3. In this case, record 2 is the preceding record and record 3 is the next record. Of course, if a file is positioned at its initial point, there is no preceding record, and there is no next record if it is positioned at its terminal point.

There may be a current record during execution of an input/output statement or after completion of a nonadvancing input/output statement as shown in Figure 9-10, where record 2 is the current record.

When there is a current record, the file is positioned at the initial point of the record, between values in a record, or at the terminal point of the record as illustrated in Figure 9-11.

An internal file is always positioned at the beginning of a record just prior to data transfer.

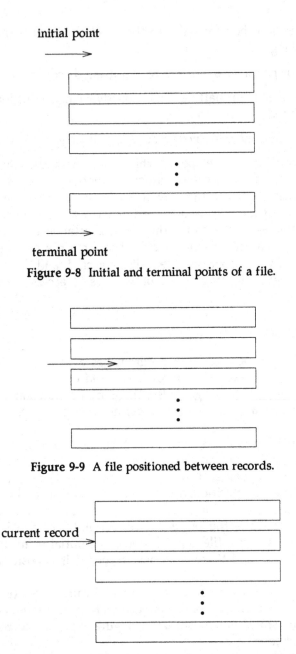

initial point

terminal point

Figure 9-8 Initial and terminal points of a file.

Figure 9-9 A file positioned between records.

current record

Figure 9-10 A file positioned within a current record.

9.2.6 Advancing and Nonadvancing I/O

Advancing input/output is record oriented. Completion of an input/output operation always positions the file at the end of a record. **Nonadvancing input/output** is character oriented. After

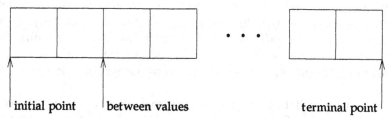

initial point · between values · terminal point

Figure 9-11 Positions within a record of a file.

reading and writing, the file position may be between characters within a record.

Nonadvancing input/output is restricted to use with external sequential formatted files and may not be used with list-directed formatting.

9.2.7 Units and File Connection

Input/output statements refer to a particular file by specifying its **unit**. For example, the read and write statements do not refer to a file directly, but refer to a unit number, which must be connected to a file. The unit number for an external file is a nonnegative integer. The name of an internal file also is called a unit; it is a character variable. In the following examples, 5 and char_string are units.

```
read (unit = 5) a
write (char_string, fmt = "(i3)") k
```

Some rules and restrictions for units are:

1. The unit * specifies a processor determined unit number. On input, it is the same unit number that the processor would use if a read statement appeared without the unit number. On output, it is the same unit number that the processor would use if a print statement appeared without the unit number. The unit specified by an asterisk may be used only for formatted sequential access.

2. File positioning, file connection, and inquiry must use external files.

3. A unit number identifies one and only one unit in a Fortran program. That is, a unit number is global to an entire program; a particular file may be connected to unit 9 in one procedure and referred to through unit 9 in another procedure.

Only certain unit numbers may be used on a particular computing system. The unit numbers that may be used are said to **exist**.

Some unit numbers on some processors are always used for data input (for example, unit 5), others are always used for output (for example, unit 6). Input/output statements must refer to units that exist, except for those that close a file or inquire about a unit. The inquire statement may be used to determine whether or not a unit exists.

To transfer data to or from an external file, the file must be connected to a unit. Once the connection is made, most input/output statements use the unit number instead of using the name of the file directly. An internal file always is connected to the unit that is the name of the character variable. There are two ways to establish connection between a unit and an external file:

1.   Execution of an open statement in the executing program

2.   Preconnection by the operating system

Only one file may be connected to a unit at any given time. If the unit is disconnected after its first use on a file, it may be reconnected later to another file or it may be reconnected later to the same file. A file that is not connected to a unit may not be used in any statement except the open, close, or inquire statements. Some units may be preconnected to files for each Fortran program by the operating system, without any action necessary by the program. For example, on most systems, units 5 and 6 are always preconnected to the default input and default output files, respectively. Preconnection of units also may be done by the operating system when requested by the user in the operating system command language. In either of these cases, the user program does not require an open statement to connect the file; it is preconnected.

9.2.8 Error, End-of-File, and End-of-Record Conditions

During execution of input/output statements, error conditions can occur. Error conditions may be checked by using the iostat= specifier on many input/output statements. Each error condition will result in some positive value for the iostat variable, but the values used will depend on the computer system being used. Examples of errors are attempting to open a file that does not exist or attempting to read input consisting of letters when the input variable is type integer. When such an error occurs, the value of the iostat variable may be tested and alternative paths selected.

If a read statement attempts to read an endfile record, the iostat variable will be set to some negative value. It will also be set to a negative value when reading beyond the end of a record with a nonadvancing read statement. These conditions cannot both occur at the same time.

If there is both an error condition and either an end-of-file or end-of-record condition, the iostat variable will be set to a positive value to indicate that an error has occurred.[1]

The program count_lines counts the number of lines in a file and illustrates the use of iostat to determine when the end of the file is encountered. The sample run shows what happens when the input to the program is the program itself.

```
run count_lines

The input file is:

    program count_lines

    implicit none

    character (len = 100) :: line
    integer :: count, status

    count = 0
    print *, "The input file is:"
    print *

    do
        read (*, "(a)", iostat = status) line
        if (status < 0) exit
        write (*, "(t6, a)") trim (line)
        count = count + 1
    end do

    print *
    print *, "The file contains", count, "lines."
    end program count_lines

The file contains 21 lines.
```

The intrinsic function trim removes trailing blank characters on the output lines.

---

1. In Fortran 77 and Fortran 90, error and end-of-file conditions can also be checked using the end= and err= specifiers with a label (Section 10.3.3).

9.3 Data Transfer Statements

The **data transfer statements** are the read, write, and print statements. In previous chapters we have seen examples of various kinds of data transfer statements. The general forms for the data transfer statements are as follows. Optional parts of a statement appear in square brackets.

> read (*io-control-spec-list*) [*input-item-list*]
> read *format* [, *input-item-list*]
> write (*io-control-spec-list*) [*output-item-list*]
> print *format* [, *output-item-list*]

Some examples of data transfer statements are

```
read (iostat = is, unit = 9) x
write (6, rec = 14) y
read "(f10.2)", z
print *, zt
```

9.3.1 The Format Specifier

The **format specifier** (*format* in the syntax for the print statement and the short form of the read statement) may be a character expression indicating **explicit formatting** (Section 9.8), or an asterisk (*) indicating list-directed or default formatting.[2]

9.3.2 The Control Information List

The input/output control specification list must contain a unit specifier of the form

> [unit] = *io-unit*

and may contain at most one each of the following optional items:

> [fmt =] *format*
> rec = *scalar-int-expr*
> iostat = *scalar-default-int-variable*
> advance = *scalar-default-char-expr*
> size = *scalar-default-int-variable*

The input/output unit must be a nonnegative integer expression indicating an external unit connected to a file, an asterisk indicating a processor-dependent external unit, or a character variable of default

---

2. The format statement (Section 10.3.2) also has been used for many years to indicate the format specifier; it is no longer necessary with the introduction of other forms in Fortran 77.

type indicating an internal unit. If the keyword unit does not appear with the unit specifier, then the unit specifier must be the first item in the list. In this case, the keyword fmt= may be omitted from the format, and this item must be second in the list.

The allowed forms of a format are the same within a control information list as they are in the print statement and the short form of the read statement.

There are lots of additional rules about which combinations of these items may occur; some of these rules will be covered in the discussion of various types of data transfer statements in the following sections.

9.3.3 The Input/Output List

The input/output list consists basically of variables in a read statement and expressions in a write or print statement. In addition, in any of the statements, the input/output list may contain an input/output implied do list, described in Section 4.1.4.

9.3.4 External Formatted Advancing Sequential Access I/O

The title of this section is a mouthful, but this is the kind of input/output that has been illustrated throughout the book. For formatted input and output, the file consists of characters. These characters are converted into representations suitable for storing in computer memory during input and converted from an internal representation to characters on output. When a file is accessed sequentially, records are processed in the order in which they appear in the file. Advancing input/output means that the file is positioned after the end of the last record read or written when the input/output is finished.

The general form for input/output statements is given later in this chapter, but templates that may be used to construct explicitly formatted sequential access data statements are

```
read ( [ unit = ] unit-number &
      , [ fmt = ] format &
      [ , iostat = scalar-default-int-variable ] &
      [ , advance = scalar-default-char-expr ] &
      ) [ input-list ]

read format [ , input-list ]
```

```
write ( [ unit = ] unit-number &
       , [ fmt = ] format &
       [ , iostat = scalar-default-int-variable ] &
       [ , advance = scalar-default-char-expr ] &
       ) [ output-list ]
```

print *format* [, output-list]

The symbols fmt= may be omitted only if unit= is omitted. The *format* may be a character expression whose value is a format specification, or an asterisk indicating list-directed default formatting. For advancing input/output, the expression in the advance= specifier must evaluate to yes, if it is present; nonadvancing input/output is discussed in Section 9.3.5. The advance= specifier must not be present if the format is an asterisk designating list-directed formatting.

Examples of formatted reading are

```
read (5, fmt_100) a, b, c (1 : 40)
read (9, fmt = "(2f20.5)", iostat = iend) x, y
read (unit = 5, fmt = "(5e20.0)", advance = "yes")  &
      y (1 : kk)
read *, x, y
```

Examples of formatted writing are

```
write (9, fmt_103, iostat = is) a, b, c, s
write (unit = 7, fmt = *) x
write (*, "(f10.5)") x
print "(a, e14.6)", " y = ", y
```

When an advancing sequential access input/output statement is executed, reading or writing of data begins with the next character in the file. If a previous input/output statement was a nonadvancing statement, the next character transferred may be in the middle of a record, even if the statement being executed is an advancing statement. The difference between the two is that an advancing input/output statement always leaves the file positioned at the end of the record when the data transfer is completed.

The iostat specifier may be used to check for an end-of-file or an error condition.

9.3.5 Nonadvancing Data Transfer

Like advancing input/output, the file is read or written beginning with the next character; however, nonadvancing input/output leaves the file positioned after the last character read or written, rather than skipping to the end of the record. Nonadvancing input/output is sometimes called *partial record* or *stream* input/output. It may be used only with explicitly formatted external files connected for sequential access. It may not be used with list-directed input/output.

Templates that may be used to construct nonadvancing input/output statements are

```
read ( [ unit = ] unit-number &
     , [ fmt = ] format &
     , advance = scalar-default-char-expr &
     [ , size = scalar-default-int-variable ] &
     [ , iostat = scalar-default-int-variable ] &
     ) [ input-list ]

write ( [ unit = ] unit-number &
      , [ fmt = ] format &
      , advance = scalar-default-char-expr &
      [ , iostat = scalar-default-int-variable ] &
      ) [ output-list ]
```

The scalar character expression in the advance= specifier must evaluate to no for nonadvancing input/output. The symbols fmt= may be omitted only if unit= is omitted. The format is a character expression whose value is a format specification; it must not be an asterisk designating list-directed formatting.

The size= variable is assigned the number of characters read on input. It does not count trailing blanks used for padding during an input operation when the pad= specifier is yes (Section 9.4.3).

Examples of nonadvancing data transfer statements are

```
advance_indicator = "no"
read (5, fmt_100, advance=advance_indicator) a, b, c
read (9, fmt="(a)", advance="no", &
      size=rec_size, iostat=ios) line
write (6, "(i1)", advance=advance_indicator) n
write (unit=6, fmt=fmt_200, advance="no") x (1:n)
```

The iostat specifier may be used to check for an end-of-file, end-of-record, or error condition.

One of the important uses of nonadvancing input/output occurs when the size of the records is not known. To illustrate this, the following program counts the number of characters in a file, reading the input one character at a time. iostat values for end-of-record and end-of-file are required to be negative, but are otherwise processor dependent. The values −2 and −1 are typical, but the manual for your system should be consulted.

```
program char_count
   implicit none
   integer, parameter :: end_of_record = -2
   integer, parameter :: end_of_file = -1
   character (len = 1) :: c
   integer :: count, ios

   count = 0
   do
      read (*, "(a)", advance = "no", iostat = ios) c
      if (ios == end_of_record) then
         cycle
      else if (ios == end_of_file) then
         exit
      else
         count = count + 1
      end if
   end do

   print *, "The number of characters in the file is", &
            count
end program char_count
```

Another obvious use is to print part of a line at one place in a program and finish the line later. If things are implemented properly, it also should be possible to use nonadvancing input/output to supply a prompt to a terminal and have the user type in data on the same line. This is not absolutely guaranteed, because many systems consider input from a terminal and output to the terminal to involve two different files. Here is a simple example:

```
program test_sign
   implicit none
   integer :: number
   write (*, "(a)", advance = "no")  &
        "Type in any integer: "
   read *, number
   write (*, "(a, i9, a)", advance = "no")  &
        "The number ", number, " is "
   if (number > 0) then
      print *, "positive."
   else if (number == 0) then
      print *, "zero."
```

```
    else
        print *, "negative."
    end if
end program test_sign

run test_sign

Type in any integer: 36
The number          36 is  positive.
```

9.3.6 Data Transfer on Internal Files

Transferring data from machine representation to characters or from characters back to machine representation can be done between two variables in an executing program. A formatted sequential access input or output statement is used; list-directed formatting is permitted. The format is used to interpret the characters. The internal file and the internal unit are the same character variable.

Templates that may be used to construct data transfer statements on an internal file are

read ([unit =] *default-char-variable* &
    , [fmt =] *format* &
    [, iostat = *scalar-default-int-variable*] &
) [*input-list*]

write ([unit =] *default-char-variable* &
    , [fmt =] *format* &
    [, iostat = *scalar-default-int-variable*] &
) [*output-list*]

The optional symbols fmt= may be omitted only if unit= is omitted. Examples of data transfer statements on internal files are

```
read (char_24, fmt_1, iostat = io_err) mary, x, j, name
write (unit = char_var, fmt = *) x
```

Some rules and restrictions for using internal files are:

1. The unit must be a default character variable that is not an array section with a vector subscript.

2. Each record of an internal file is a scalar character variable.

3. If the file is an array or an array section, each element of the array or section is a scalar character variable and thus a record.

The order of the records is the order of the array elements (for arrays of rank two and greater, the first subscript varies most rapidly). The length of the record, which must be the same for each record, is the length of one array element.

4.   If the character variable is an array or part of an array that has the allocatable attribute, the variable must be allocated before its use as an internal file.

5.   If the number of characters written is less than the length of the record, the remaining characters are set to blank. If the number of characters is greater than the length of the record, the remaining characters are truncated.

6.   The records in an internal file are assigned values when the record is written. An internal file also may be assigned a value by a character assignment statement, or some other means.

7.   To read a record in an internal file, it must be defined.

8.   An internal file is always positioned at the beginning before a data transfer occurs.

9.   Only formatted sequential access is permitted on internal files. List-directed formatting is permitted.

10. File connection, positioning, and inquiry must not be used with internal files.

11. The use of the iostat specifier is the same as for external files.

12. On input, blanks are treated the same as for an external file with a blank= specifier having the value null, and records are padded with blanks if necessary.

13. On list-directed output, character constants are delimited with either quote or apostrophes.

As a simple example of the use of internal files, the following write statement converts the value of the integer variable n into the character string s of length 10:

```
write (s, "(i10)") n
```

If n = 999, the string s would be "*bbbbbbb*999", where "*b*" represents a blank character. To make the conversion behave a little differently, we can force the first character of s to be a sign (Section 9.8.17) and make the rest of the characters digits, using as many leading zeros as necessary (Section 9.8.5).

```
write (s, "(sp, i10.9)") n
```

Now if n = 999, the string s will have the value "+000000999".

Another use of internal input/output is to read data from a file directly into a character string, examine it to make sure it has the proper form for the data that is supposed to be read, then read it with formatting conversion from the internal character string variable to the variables needed to hold the data. To keep the example simple, suppose that some input data record is supposed to contain 10 integer values, but they have been entered into the file as 10 integers separated by colons. List-directed input requires that the numbers be separated by blanks or commas. One option is to read in the data, examine the characters one at a time, and build the integers; but list-directed input will do everything except find the colon separators. So another possibility is to read in the record, change the colons to commas, and use an internal list-directed read statement to convert the character string into 10 integer values.

```
character (len = 100) internal_record
integer, dimension (10) :: numbers
integer :: colon_position
   . . .
read (*, "(a)") internal_record
do
    colon_position = index (internal_record, ":")
    if (colon_position == 0) exit
    internal_record (colon_position:colon_position) = ","
end do
read (internal_record, fmt = *) numbers
```

Of course, in a real program, some error checking should be done to make sure that the internal record has the correct format after the colons are converted to commas.

Another example of formatted writing to an internal file occurs in Section 7.4.1, in which this feature is used to construct a format specification tailored to the exact length of the output data of a later print statement.

9.3.7 Unformatted Input/Output

For unformatted input and output, the file usually consists of values stored using the same representation used in program memory. This means that no conversion is required during input and output. Unformatted input/output may be done using both sequential and direct access. It is always advancing.

Direct access is indicated by the presence of a rec= specifier; sequential access occurs when no rec= specifier is present.

Templates that may be used to construct unformatted access data statements are

```
read ( [ unit = ] unit-number &
       [ , rec = record-number ] &
       [ , iostat = scalar-default-int-variable ] &
     ) [ input-list ]
```

```
write ( [ unit = ] unit-number &
        [ , rec = record-number ] &
        [ , iostat = scalar-default-int-variable ] &
      ) [ output-list ]
```

Examples of unformatted access reading are

```
read (5) a, b, c (1:n, 1:n)
read (unit = 9, rec = 14, iostat = iend) x, y
read (5) y
```

Examples of unformatted access writing are

```
write (9, iostat = is) a, b, c, s
write (iostat = status, unit = 7) x
write (9, rec = next_record_number) x
```

The record number given by the rec= specifier is a scalar integer expression whose value indicates the number of the record to be read or written.

If the access is sequential, the file is positioned at the beginning of the next record prior to data transfer and positioned at the end of the record when the input/output is finished, because nonadvancing unformatted input/output is not permitted.

The iostat specifier may be used in the same way it is used for formatted input/output.

Unformatted access is very useful when creating a file of data that must be saved from one execution of a program and used for a later execution of the program. Suppose, for example that a program deals with the inventory of a large number of automobile parts. The data for each part (in our simple example) consists of the part number and the quantity in stock.

```
type part
   integer :: id_number, qty_in_stock
end type part

type (part), dimension (10000) :: part_list
integer :: number_of_parts
```

Suppose the integer variable `number_of_parts` records the number of different parts that are stored in the array `part_list`. At the end of the program, the number of parts and the entire part list can be saved in the file named `part_file` with the following statements:

```
open (unit = 9, file = "part_file",  &
      position = "rewind", form = "unformatted",  &
      action = "write")
write (9), number_of_parts,  &
      part_list (1:number_of_parts)
```

At the beginning of the next execution of the program, the inventory can be read back into memory with the statements:

```
open (unit = 9, file = "part_file",  &
      position = "rewind", form = "unformatted",  &
      action = "read", status = "old")
read (9), number_of_parts, part_list (1:number_of_parts)
```

See Section 9.4 for the description of the open statement.

9.3.8 Direct Access Data Transfer

When a file is accessed directly, the record to be processed is the one given by the record number in a `rec=` specifier. The file may be formatted or unformatted.

Templates that may be used to construct direct access data statements are

```
read ( [ unit = ] unit-number &
       [ , [ fmt = ] format ] &
       , rec = record-number &
       [ , iostat = scalar-default-int-variable ] &
     ) [ input-list ]
```

```
write ( [ unit = ] unit-number ] &
       [ , [ fmt = ] format ] &
       , rec = record-number &
       [ , iostat = scalar-default-int-variable ] &
       ) [ output-list ]
```

fmt= may be omitted only if unit= is omitted. The *format* must not be an asterisk.

Examples of direct access input/output statements are

```
read (7, fmt_x, rec = 32) a
read (unit = 10, rec = 34, iostat = io_status) a, b, d
write (8, "(2f15.5)", rec = n + 2) x, y
```

The iostat specifier is used just as it is with sequential access.

To illustrate the use of direct access files, let us consider the simple automobile parts example used in Section 9.3.7 to illustrate unformatted input/output. In this example, suppose that the parts list is so large that it is not feasible to read the entire list into memory. Instead, each time information about a part is needed, just the information about that one part is read from an external file. To do this in a reasonable amount of time, the file must be stored on a device such as a disk, where each part is accessible as readily as any other. Analogous but more realistic examples might involve the bank accounts for all customers of a bank or tax information on all tax payers in one country. This time a structure is not needed, because the only information in the file is the quantity on hand. The part identification number is used as the record number of the record in the file used to store the information for the part having that number. Also, the array is not needed because the program deals with only one part at a time.

Suppose we just need a program that looks up the quantity in stock for a given part number. This program queries the user for the part number, looks up the quantity on hand by reading one record from a file, and prints out that quantity.

```
program part_info
   implicit none
   integer :: part_number, qty_in_stock

   print *, "Enter part number"
   read *, part_number
```

```
open (unit = 9, file = "part_file",  &
      access = "direct",  recl = 10,  &
      form = "unformatted",  &
      action = "read",  status = "old")
read (unit = 9, rec = part_number) qty_in_stock
print *, "The quantity in stock is", qty_in_stock
end program part_info
```

Of course, the program could be a little more sophisticated by using a loop to repeat the process of asking for a part number and providing the quantity in stock. Also, there must be other programs that create and maintain the file that holds the database of information about the parts. A more complex organization for the file may be necessary if the range of legal part numbers greatly exceeds the actual number of different parts for which information is saved.

9.4 The open Statement

The **open statement** establishes a connection between a unit and an external file and determines the connection properties. After this is done, the file can be used for data transfers (reading and writing) using the unit number. It is not necessary to execute an open statement for files that are preconnected to a unit.

The open statement may appear anywhere in a program and, once executed, the connection of the unit to the file is valid in the main program or any subprogram for the remainder of that execution, unless a `close` statement affecting the connection is executed.

If a file is connected to one unit, it may not be connected to a different unit at the same time.

9.4.1 Changing the Connection Properties

Execution of an open statement may change the properties of a connection that is already established. The properties that may be changed are those indicated by `blank=`, `delim=`, and `pad=` specifiers. If new values for `blank=`, `delim`, and `pad` are specified, these will be used in subsequent data transfer statements; otherwise, the old ones will be used. In addition an open statement affecting an existing connection also may contain an `iostat=` specifier.

9.4.2 Syntax Rule for the open Statement

The form of the open statement is

open (*connect-spec-list*)

where the permissible connection specifications are

> [unit =] *external-file-unit*
> access = *scalar-default-char-expr*
> action = *scalar-default-char-expr*
> blank = *scalar-default-char-expr*
> delim = *scalar-default-char-expr*
> file = *file-name-expr*
> form = *scalar-default-char-expr*
> iostat = *scalar-default-int-variable*
> pad = *scalar-default-char-expr*
> position = *scalar-default-char-expr*
> recl = *scalar-int-expr*
> status = *scalar-default-char-expr*

Examples are

> open (status = "scratch", unit = 9, iostat = ios)
> open (8, file = "plot_data", access = "direct")

Some rules and restrictions for the open statement are

1. An external unit number is required. If the keyword unit= is omitted, the external unit must be the first item in the list.

2. A specifier may appear at most once in any open statement.

3. The file= specifier must appear if the status is old, new, or replace; the file= specifier must not appear if the status is scratch.

4. The character expression established for many of the specifiers must contain permitted values in a list of alternative values as described below. For example, old, new, unknown, replace, and scratch are permitted for the status= specifier; any other combination of letters is not permitted. Trailing blanks in any specifier are ignored.

9.4.3 The Connection Specifiers

iostat=   The iostat specifier must be a default integer variable. It is given a value that is a positive integer if there is an error condition while executing the open statement and zero if there is no error.

file=   The file= specifier indicates the name of the file to be connected. If the name is omitted, the connection could be made to a processor-determined file.

status=   The value of the status= specifier must be old, new, unknown, replace, or scratch. old refers to a file that must exist. new refers to a file that must not exist. unknown refers to a processor-dependent status. If the status is replace and the file does not exist, it is created and given a status of old. If the status is replace and the file does exist, it is deleted, a new file is created with the same name, and its status is changed to old. scratch refers to a scratch file that exists only until termination of execution of the program or until a close is executed on that unit. Scratch files must be unnamed. replace is recommended when it is not certain if there is an old version, but it is to be replaced if there is one.

access=   The value of the access= specifier must be direct or sequential. direct refers to direct access. sequential refers to sequential access. The method must be an allowed access method for the file. If the file is new, the allowed access methods given to the file must include the one indicated. If the access is direct, there must be a recl= specifier to specify the record length.

form=   The value of the form= specifier must be formatted or unformatted. formatted indicates that all records will be formatted. unformatted indicates that all records will be unformatted. If the file is connected for direct access, the default is unformatted. If the file is connected for sequential access, the default is formatted. If the file is new, the allowed forms given to the file must include the one indicated.

recl=   The recl= specifier has a positive value that specifies the length of each record if the access method is direct or the maximum length of a record if the access method is sequential. If the file is connected for formatted input/output, the length is the number of characters. If the file is connected for unformatted input/output, the length is measured in processor-dependent units. The length may, for example, be the number of computer words. If the file exists, the length of the record specified must be an allowed record length. If the file does not exist, the file is created with the specified length as an allowed length.

blank=

The blank= specifier has a value that is null or zero and may be specified only for files connected for formatted input/output. If there is no blank specifier, the default is null. If null is specified, all blanks in numeric fields are ignored; a field of all blanks would evaluate to zero. If zero is specified, all blanks except leading blanks are interpreted as zero.

position=

The value of the position= specifier must be asis, rewind, or append. asis leaves the file position unchanged for a connected file and unspecified for a file that is not connected. rewind positions the file at its initial point. append positions the file at the terminal point or just before an endfile record, if there is one. The file must be connected for sequential access. If the file is new, it is positioned at its initial point. The default value is asis, permitting an open statement to change other connection properties of a file that is already connected without changing its position.

action=

The value of the action= specifier must be read, write, or readwrite. read indicates that write, print, and endfile statements are prohibited. write indicates that read statements are prohibited. readwrite indicates that any input/output statement is permitted. The default is readwrite.

delim=

The value of the delim= specifier must be apostrophe, quote, or none. apostrophe and quote indicate that the delimiting character for character constants written in list-directed formatting is the apostrophe or quotation mark, respectively. In this case, an occurrence of the designated character within a character constant will be doubled. none indicates that character constants will not be delimited. The default is none. The specifier is permitted only for a file connected for formatted input/output; it is ignored for formatted input.

pad=

The pad= specifier has a value yes or no. yes means that blank padding is used when the input list requires more data than the record contains. no means that the input list must contain the data that the input list and formatting require. The default is yes.

9.5 The close Statement

Execution of a **close statement** terminates the connection of a file to a unit. Any connections not closed explicitly by a close statement are closed by the operating system when the program terminates. The form of the close statement is

close (*close-spec-list*)

The items in the close specification list may be selected from

[unit =] *external-file-unit*
iostat = *scalar-default-int-variable*
status = *scalar-default-char-expr*

Examples are

close (9)
close (iostat = ir, status = "keep", unit = 8)

Some rules for the close statement are

1. An external unit number is required. If the keyword unit is omitted, the external unit must be the first item in the list.

2. A close statement may refer to a unit that is not connected or does not exist, but it has no effect. This is not considered an error.

3. The status= specifier must have a value that is keep or delete. If it is keep, the file continues to exist after closing the file. If it has the value of delete, the file will not exist after closing the file. The default value is keep, except that the default for scratch files is delete.

4. The rules for the iostat= specifier are the same as for the open statement.

5. A specifier must not appear more than once in a close statement.

6. Connections that have been closed may be reopened at a later point in an executing program. The new connection may be to the same or to a different file.

9.6 The inquire Statement

The inquire statement provides the capability of determining information about a file's existence, connection, access method, or other properties during execution of a program. For each property inquired about, a scalar variable of default kind is supplied; that variable is given a value that answers the inquiry. The variable may be tested and optional execution paths selected in a program based on the answer returned. The inquiry specifiers are indicated by keywords in the `inquire` statement. A file inquiry may be made by unit number, by the file name, or by an output list that might be used in an unformatted direct access output statement.

The values of the character items (except name) are always in uppercase.

9.6.1 Syntax Rule for the `inquire` Statement

The form of an inquiry by unit number or file name is

    inquire (*inquiry-spec-list*)

An **inquiry by unit** must include the following in the inquiry specification list:

    [unit =] *external-file-unit*

If the keyword `unit` is omitted, it must be the first item in the list.

An **inquiry by name** must include the following in the inquiry specification list:

    file = *file-name*

The expression for the file name may refer to a file that is not connected or does not exist. The value for the file name must be acceptable to the system. An `inquire` statement must not have both a file specifier and a unit specifier.

In addition, the inquiry specification list may contain the following items. The type of the item following the keyword is indicated; each item following the keyword and equals sign must be a scalar variable of default kind.

    access = *character*
    action = *character*
    blank = *character*
    delim = *character*
    direct = *character*
    exist = *logical*
    form = *character*
    formatted = *character*
    iostat = *integer*
    name = *character*
    named = *logical*
    nextrec = *integer*

```
number = integer
opened = logical
position = character
read = character
readwrite = character
recl = integer
sequential = character
unformatted = character
write = character
pad = character
```

Examples of the inquire statement are

```
inquire (9, exist = ex)
inquire (file = "t123", opened = op, access = ac)
```

9.6.2 The iolength Inquiry

The form of an inquire statement used to determine the length of an output item list is

```
inquire ( iolength = scalar-default-int-variable ) &
    output-item-list
```

The length value returned in the scalar integer variable will be an acceptable value that can be used later as the value of the recl= specifier in an open statement to connect a file whose records will hold the data indicated by the output list of the inquire statement.

An example of this form of the inquire statement is

```
inquire (iolength = iolen)  x, y, cat
```

9.6.3 Specifiers for Inquiry by Unit or File Name

This section describes the syntax and effect of the inquiry specifiers that may appear in the unit and file forms of the inquire statement. The values returned in the inquiry specification list are those current at that point in the execution of the program.

The iostat inquiry specifier indicates error condition information about the inquiry statement execution itself. If an error condition occurs, all the inquiry specifiers are undefined except the iostat specifier.

exist=   If the inquiry is by unit, the logical variable indicates whether or not the unit exists. If the inquiry is by file, the logical variable indicates whether or not the file exists.

opened=
If the inquiry is by unit, the logical variable indicates whether or not the unit is connected to some file. If the inquiry is by file, the logical variable indicates whether or not the file is connected to some unit.

number=
The value returned is the number of the unit connected to the file. If there is no unit connected to the file, the value is -1.

named=
The scalar logical value is true if and only if the file has a name.

name=
The value is the name of the file if the file has a name; otherwise the designated variable becomes undefined. The processor may return a name different from the one given in the file= specifier by the program, because a user identifier or some other processor requirement for file names may be added. The name returned will be acceptable for use in a subsequent open statement. The case (upper or lower) used is determined by the processor.

access=
The value returned is SEQUENTIAL if the file is connected for sequential access, DIRECT if the file is connected for direct access, or UNDEFINED if the file is not connected.

sequential=
The value returned is YES if sequential access is an allowed method, NO if sequential access is not an allowed method, or UNKNOWN if the processor does not know if sequential access is allowed.

direct=
The value returned is YES if direct access is an allowed method, NO if direct access is not an allowed method, or UNKNOWN if the processor does not know if direct access is allowed.

form=
The value returned is FORMATTED if the file is connected for formatted input/output, UNFORMATTED if the file is connected for unformatted input/output, or UNDEFINED if the file is not connected.

formatted=
The value returned is YES if formatted input/output is permitted for the file, NO if formatted input/output is not permitted for the file, or UNKNOWN if the processor cannot determine if formatted input/output is permitted for the file.

unformatted=   The value returned is YES if unformatted input/output is permitted for the file, NO if unformatted input/output is not permitted for the file, or UNKNOWN if the processor cannot determine if unformatted input/output is permitted for the file.

recl=   The integer value returned is the maximum record length of the file. For a formatted file, the length is in characters. For an unformatted file or a file with non-default characters, the length is in processor-dependent units. If the file does not exist, the specified variable becomes undefined.

nextrec=   The integer value returned is one more than the last record number read or written in a file connected for direct access. If no records have been processed, the value is 1. The specified variable becomes undefined if the file is not connected for direct access or if the file position is indeterminate because of a previous error condition.

blank=   The value returned is NULL if null blank control is in effect, ZERO if zero blank control is in effect, or UNDEFINED if the file is not connected for formatted input/output or if the file is not connected at all.

position=   The value returned is REWIND if the file is connected with its position at the initial point, APPEND if the file is connected with its position at the end point, ASIS if the file is connected without any position change, or UNDEFINED if the file is not connected, is connected for direct access, or if any repositioning has occurred since the file was connected.

action=   The value returned is READ if the file is connected limiting the access to input, WRITE if the file is connected limiting the access to output, READWRITE if the file is connected for input and output, or UNDEFINED if the file is not connected.

read=   The value returned is YES if read is one of the allowed actions for the file, NO if read is not one of the allowed actions for the file, or UNKNOWN if the processor is unable to determine if read is one of the allowed actions for the file.

write=   The value returned is YES if write is one of the allowed actions for the file, NO if write is not one of the allowed actions for the file, or UNKNOWN if the processor is unable to determine if write is one of the allowed actions for the file.

readwrite=   The value returned is YES if input and output are allowed for the file, NO if input and output are not both allowed for the file, or UNKNOWN if the processor is unable to determine if input and output are allowed for the file.

delim=   The value returned indicates the way character strings in list-directed formatted output will be delimited. It is APOSTROPHE if an apostrophe is used as the delimiter, QUOTE if the quotation mark is used as the delimiter, NONE if there is no delimiting character, or UNDEFINED if the file is not connected or the file is not connected for formatted input/output.

pad=   The value returned is NO if the file was connected with the pad= specifier set to no; otherwise, it is YES.

9.6.4 Table of Values Assigned by inquire

Table 9-2 indicates the values assigned to the various variables by the execution of an inquire statement.

9.7 File Positioning Statements

Execution of a data transfer usually changes the position of a file. In addition, there are three statements whose main purpose is to change the position of a file. Changing the position backwards by one record is called **backspacing**. Changing the position to the beginning of the file is called **rewinding**. The endfile statement writes an endfile record and positions the file after the endfile record.

The syntax of the file positioning statements is

```
backspace external-file-unit
backspace ( position-spec-list )
rewind external-file-unit
rewind ( position-spec-list )
endfile external-file-unit
endfile ( position-spec-list )
```

A position specification may by either of the following:

```
[ unit = ] external-file-unit
iostat = scalar-default-int-variable
```

Table 9-2 Values assigned by the inquire statement.

Specifier	Inquire by file		Inquire by unit	
	Unconnected	Connected	Connected	Unconnected
access=	UNDEFINED	SEQUENTIAL or DIRECT		UNDEFINED
action=	UNDEFINED	READ, WRITE, or READWRITE		UNDEFINED
blank=	UNDEFINED	NULL, ZERO, or UNDEFINED		UNDEFINED
delim=	UNDEFINED	APOSTROPHE, QUOTE, NONE, or UNDEFINED		UNDEFINED
direct=	UNKNOWN	YES, NO, or UNKNOWN		UNKNOWN
exist=	true if file exists, false otherwise		true if unit exists, false otherwise	
form=	UNDEFINED	FORMATTED or UNFORMATTED		UNDEFINED
formatted=	UNKNOWN	YES, NO, or UNKNOWN		UNKNOWN
iostat=	0 for no error, a positive integer for an error			
name=	Filename (may not be same as file= value)		Filename if named, else undefined	Undefined
named=	true		true if file named, false otherwise	false
nextrec=	Undefined	If direct access, next record #; else undefined		Undefined
number=	-1	Unit number		-1
opened=	false	true		false
pad=	YES	YES or NO		YES
position=	UNDEFINED	REWIND, APPEND, ASIS, or UNDEFINED		UNDEFINED
read=	UNKNOWN	YES, NO, or UNKNOWN		UNKNOWN
readwrite=	UNKNOWN	YES, NO, or UNKNOWN		UNKNOWN
recl=	Undefined	If direct access, record length; else maximum record length		Undefined
sequential=	UNKNOWN	YES, NO, or UNKNOWN		UNKNOWN
unformatted=	UNKNOWN	YES, NO, or UNKNOWN		UNKNOWN
write=	UNKNOWN	YES, NO, or UNKNOWN		UNKNOWN
iolength=	recl= value for output-item-list			

Examples of file positioning statements are

```
backspace 9
backspace (iostat = status, unit = 8)
rewind (unit = 10)
endfile (10, iostat = ierr)
endfile (11)
```

As with the other input/output statements, if the keyword unit is omitted, that specifier must be first in the list. There must be an external unit specifier.

Rules and restrictions for file positioning statements:

1.   The backspace, rewind, and endfile statements may be used only to position external files.

2.   The external file unit number is required.

3.   The files must be connected for sequential access.

9.7.1 The backspace Statement

Execution of a **backspace statement** causes the file to be positioned before the current record if there is a current record, or before the preceding record if there is no current record. If there is no current record and no preceding record, the position of the file is not changed. If the preceding record is an endfile record, the file becomes positioned before the endfile record. If a **backspace** statement causes the implicit writing of an endfile record and if there is a preceding record, the file becomes positioned before the record that precedes the endfile record.

If the file is already at its initial point, a **backspace** statement does not affect it. Backspacing over records written using list-directed formatting is prohibited.

9.7.2 The rewind Statement

A **rewind statement** positions the file at its initial point. Rewinding has no effect on the position of a file already at its initial point.

9.7.3 The endfile Statement

The **endfile statement** writes an endfile record and positions the file after the endfile record written. Writing records past the endfile record is prohibited. After executing an **endfile** statement, it is necessary to execute a **backspace** or a **rewind** statement to position the file before the endfile record prior to reading or writing the file.

9.8 Formatting

Data usually is stored in memory as the values of variables in some binary form. For example, the integer 6 may be stored as 0000000000000110, where the 1s and 0s represent bits. On the other hand, formatted data records in a file consist of characters. Thus, when data is read from a formatted record, it must be converted from characters to the internal representation, and when data is written to a formatted record, it must be converted from the internal representation into a string of characters. A **format specification** provides the information needed to determine how these conversions are to be performed. The format specification is basically a list of **edit descriptors**, one for each data value in the input/output list of the data transfer statement.

A format specification is written as a character string.[3] The character expression, when evaluated, must be a valid format specification including the parentheses. Using these methods is called **explicit formatting**.

There is also list-directed formatting. Formatting (that is, conversion) occurs without specifically providing the editing information usually contained in a format specification. In this case, the editing or formatting is implicit. List-directed editing, also called default formatting, is explained in Section 9.8.19.[4]

Some rules and restrictions pertaining to format specifications are:

1. Any information may appear following the last right parenthesis in the format; this has no effect.

2. If the expression is a character array, the format is derived in array element order.

3. If the expression is an array element, the format must be entirely contained within that element.

9.8.1 Format Specifications

The items that make up a format specification are **edit descriptors**, which may be **data edit descriptors** or **control edit descriptors**. Each data list item must have a corresponding data edit descriptor; other descriptors control spacing, tabulation, etc. Character string edit

---

3. A format specification also can be given in a format statement, which is described in Section 10.3.2.

4. Namelist formatting, another sort of implicit formatting, is described briefly in Section 10.3.1.

descriptors and the d and g edit descriptors are discussed in Sections 10.3.4 to 10.3.6.

Each format item has one of the following forms:

[r] *data-edit-desc*
control-edit-desc
[r] (*format-item-list*)

where r is an integer literal constant called a **repeat factor**; it must be a positive integer with no kind parameter value.

Examples:

```
read (*, "(5e10.1, i10)") max_values, k
print "(a, 2i5)", "the two values are: ", n (1), n (2)
```

The data edit descriptors have the forms shown in Table 9-3, where w specifies the width of the field, m the minimum number of digits written, d the number of decimal places, and e the number of digits in the exponent.

Table 9-3 Data Edit Descriptors.

Descriptor	Data type
i w [. m]	decimal integer
b w [. m]	binary integer
o w [. m]	octal integer
z w [. m]	hexadecimal integer
f w . d	real, positional form
e w . d [e e]	real, exponential form
en w . d [e e]	real, engineering form
es w . d [e e]	real, scientific form
l w	logical
a [w]	character ("alphabetic")

w and e must be positive integer literal constants and d and m must be nonnegative integer literal constants. None of them may include a kind parameter. The value of m, d, and e may be restricted further by the value of w.

In each case, w designates the width of the field in the file, that is, the number of characters transferred to or from the file. Also, as explained in Sections 9.8.5 to 9.8.8 and Sections 9.8.12 to 9.8.13, in the description of each edit descriptor, m is the number of digits in the number field, d is the number of digits after the decimal point, and e is the number of digits in the exponent.

The control edit descriptors have the forms shown in Table 9-4. n is a positive integer literal constant with no kind parameter.

Table 9-4 Control Edit Descriptors.

Descriptor	Function
t *n*	tab to position *n*
tl *n*	tab left *n* positions
tr *n*	tab right *n* positions
[*r*] /	next record
:	stop formatting if list exhausted
s	default printing of plus sign
sp	print plus sign
ss	suppress plus sign
bn	ignore blanks in numeric fields
bz	treat blanks as zeros in numeric fields

9.8.2 Formatted Data Transfer

When formatted data transfer is taking place, the next item in the input/output list is matched up with the next data edit descriptor to determine the form of conversion between the internal representation of the data and the string of characters in the formatted record. Before this matching process occurs, the input/output list is considered to be expanded by writing out each element in an array and each component in a structure, and expanding any implied dos. Analogously, the repeated edit descriptors are considered to be expanded, and the whole specification is considered to be repeated as often as necessary to accommodate the entire list, as explained below regarding the use of parentheses. Let's take an example:

```
print "(i5, 2(i3, tr1, i4), i5)", i, n (1:4), j
```

The expanded input/output list would be

```
i, n (1), n (2), n (3), n (4), j
```

and the expanded list of edit descriptors would be

```
i5, i3, tr1, i4, i3, tr1, i4, i5
```

As the formatting proceeds, each input/output list item is read or written with a conversion as specified by its corresponding data edit descriptor. Note that complex data type items require two real data edit descriptors. The control edit descriptors affect the editing process at the point they occur in the list of edit descriptors.

An empty format specification such as ( ) is restricted to input/output statements without a list of items. The effect on input is that one record is skipped in the input file. The effect on output is that no characters are written to the record.

Control edit descriptors do not require a corresponding data item in the list. When the data items are completely processed, any control edit descriptors occurring next in the expanded list of edit descriptors are processed and then the formatting terminates.

9.8.3 Parentheses in a Format Specification

The action indicated by encountering a right parenthesis in a format specification depends on the nesting level. The rules are the following:

1. When the rightmost right parenthesis is encountered and there are no more data items, input/output terminates.

2. When the rightmost right parenthesis is encountered and there are more data items, the format is searched backward first until a right parenthesis is encountered, then back to the matching left parenthesis. If there is no other right parenthesis except the outermost one, format control reverts to the left parenthesis at the beginning of the format specification. A slash edit descriptor is considered to occur after processing the rightmost right parenthesis and before processing the left parenthesis.

3. If there is a repeat factor encountered when reverting to the left parenthesis, the repeat before the parenthesis is reused.

4. Sign control and blank interpretation are not affected. They remain in effect for the duration of the format processing.

This process is illustrated by the following two cases:

```
print "(a, i5)", "x", 1, "y", 2, "z", 3
```

is equivalent to

```
print "(a, i5, /, a, i5, /, a, i5)",  &
      "x", 1, "y", 2, "z", 3
```

and

```
print "(a, (i5))", "x", 1, 2, 3
```

is equivalent to

```
print "(a, i5, /, i5, /, i5)", "x", 1, 2, 3
```

9.8.4 Numeric Editing

The edit descriptors that cover numeric editing are i, b, o, z, f, e, en, and es. The following rules apply to all of them.

On input:

1. Leading blanks are not significant.

2. Within a field, the way blanks are interpreted is dependent on defaults for preconnected or internal files, the blank= specifier, and any bn or bz blank control edit descriptors in effect. The default is to ignore blanks; the blank= specifier may establish a different default for a file, and the bn and bz edit descriptors may override that default during the execution of part or all of one input/output statement.

3. Plus signs may be omitted in the input data.

4. In numeric fields that have a decimal point and correspond to f, e, en, or es edit descriptors, the decimal point in the input field overrides placement of the decimal point indicated by the edit descriptor.

On output:

1. A positive or zero internal value may have a plus sign, depending on the sign edit descriptors used.

2. The number is right justified in the field. Leading blanks may be inserted.

3. If the number or the exponent is too large for the field width specified in the edit descriptor, the output field is filled with asterisks. The processor must not produce asterisks when elimination of optional characters (such as the optional plus sign indicated by the sp edit descriptor) will allow the output to fit into the output field.

9.8.5 Integer Editing

The integer edit descriptors are

$iw[.m]$
$bw[.m]$
$ow[.m]$
$zw[.m]$

w is the field width; m is the least number of digits to be output. m has no affect on an input field. If m is omitted, its default value is 1. The value of m must not exceed the value of w. Leading zeros pad an integer field to the value of m. The field on output consists of an optional sign (except for b, o, and z edit descriptors) and the magnitude of the integer number without leading zeros, except in the case of padding to the value of m. Blanks are output only if the magnitude is zero and $m = 0$.

i editing produces a decimal integer using the digits 0–9; b editing produces a binary integer using the digits 0 and 1; o editing produces an octal integer using the digits 0–7; and z editing produces a hexadecimal integer using the digits 0–9 and the letters A–F, representing 10–15.

Input. The character string in the file must be an optionally signed integer constant using only the digits permitted by the edit descriptor.

Output. The field consists of leading blanks, followed by an optional sign, followed by the unsigned value of the integer. At least one digit must be output unless m is 0 and the output value is 0.

Example:

```
read (5, "(i5, b8)") i, j
```

If the input field is

bbb2401110101

i is read using the integer i5 edit descriptor. j is read with a b8 edit descriptor, where the digits allowed are 0 and 1. The resulting values of i and j are 24 and 117, respectively.

9.8.6 Real Editing

The forms of the edit descriptors for real values are

```
fw.d
ew.d[ee]
enw.d[ee]
esw.d[ee]
```

9.8.7 The f Edit Descriptor

f editing converts to or from a string of w digits with d places after the decimal point. d must not be greater than w. The number may be signed.

Input. If the input field contains a decimal point, the value of d has no effect. If there is no decimal point, a decimal point is inserted in front of the rightmost d digits. There may be more digits in the number than the processor can use. On input, the number may contain an e indicating an exponent value.

Output. The number is an optionally signed real number with a decimal point, rounded to d digits after the decimal point. If the number is less than one, the processor may place a zero in front of the decimal point. At least one zero must be output if no other digits would appear. If the number does not fit into the output field, the entire field is filled with asterisks.

Example:

```
read (5, "(f10.2, f10.3)") x, y
```

If the input field is

*bbbb*6.42181234567890

the values assigned to x and y are 6.4218 and 1234567.89, respectively. The value of d (indicating two digits after the decimal point) is ignored for x because the input field contains a decimal point.

9.8.8 The e Edit Descriptor

For e editing, the field representing the floating-point number contains w characters, including an exponent. d and e must not be greater than the length, w.

Input. The form is the same as for f editing, where e may indicate an exponent.

Output. The form of the output field is

$[\pm]\,[0]\,.\,x_1 x_2 \cdots x_d exp$

Example: if y = –212.12 and z = 26592.12,

```
write (6, "(2e15.3)") y, z
```

produces the output record

bbbbb–0.212E+03*bbbbbb*0.266E+05

9.8.9 The en Edit Descriptor

en is the engineering edit descriptor.

Input. The form is the same as for f editing.

Output. The output of the number is in the form of engineering notation, where the exponent is divisible by three and the $1 \le$ |mantissa| < 1000, except when the output value is 0.

Example:

```
write (6, "(en12.3)") b
```

The form of the output field is

$$[\pm]\, yyy.x_1x_2 \cdots x_d exp$$

where yyy is nonzero representing 1, 2, or 3 digits, and exp is a signed integer that is divisible by 3; the sign must be present in the exponent.

Examples of output using the en descriptor are found in Table 9-5.

Table 9-5 Examples of output using the en edit descriptor.

Internal value	Output field using ss, en12.3
6.421	6.421E+00
-.5	-500.000E-03
.0217	21.700E-03
4721.3	4.721E+03

9.8.10 The es Edit Descriptor

es is the scientific edit descriptor.

Input. The form is the same as for f editing.

Output. The output of the number is in the form of scientific notation; $1 \le |\text{mantissa}| < 10$, except when the output value is 0.[5]

Example:

```
write (6, "(es12.3)") b
```

The form of the output field is

$$[\pm]\, y.x_1x_2 \cdots x_d exp$$

where y is nonzero and exp is a signed integer; the sign must be present in the exponent.

Examples of output using the es edit descriptor are found in Table 9-6.

---

5. The effect of the es edit descriptor could be achieved in Fortran 77 with the use of the 1p edit descriptor. However, the 1p edit descriptor affects all following real edit descriptors, often with results not intended or expected by the programmer.

Table 9-6 Examples of output using the es edit descriptor.

Internal value	Output field using ss, es12.3
6.421	6.421E+00
-.5	-5.000E-01
.0217	2.170E-02
4721.3	4.721E+03

9.8.11 Complex Editing

Editing of complex numbers requires two real edit descriptors, one for the real part and one for the imaginary part. Different edit descriptors may be used for the two parts. Data read for a complex quantity is converted by the rules of conversion for assignment to complex; the kinds of both parts of a complex quantity are made the same. Other controls and characters may be inserted between the specification for the real and imaginary parts.

Example:

```
complex cm (2)
read (5, "(4e7.2)") cm (:)
write (6, "(2 (f7.2, a, f7.2, a))") &
    real (cm (i)), " + ", aimag (cm (i)), "i ", i = 1, 2
```

If the input record is

bb55511bbb2146$bbbb$100$bbbb$621

the values assigned to cm (1) and cm (2) are $555.11 + 21.46i$ and $1 + 6.21i$, respectively, and the output record is

b555.11b+bbb21.46$bi\,bbbb$1.00b+$bbbb$6.21$bi\,b$

9.8.12 Logical Editing

The edit descriptor used for logical editing is

lw

w is the field width.

Input. The input field for a logical value consists of any number of blanks, followed by an optional period, followed by t or f, either uppercase or lowercase, followed by anything. Valid input fields for true include t, True, .TRUE., .T, and thursday_afternoon, although the last is poor practice.

Output. The output field consists of $w-1$ leading blanks, followed by T or F.

Example:

```
write (6, "(2l7)") l1, l2
```

If l1 and l2 are true and false, respectively, the output record will be

*bbbbbb*T*bbbbbb*F

9.8.13 Character Editing

The edit descriptor for character editing is

a[*w*]

w is the field width measured in characters. If *w* is omitted, the length of the data object being read in or written out is used as the field width.

Input. Let *len* be the length of the data object being read. If *w* is greater than *len*, the rightmost *len* characters in the input field are read. If *w* is less than *len*, the input is padded with blanks on the right. If the character datum is not the default kind, the character used for padding is processor dependent.

Output. If *w* is greater than *len*, blanks are added on the left. If *w* is less than *len*, the leftmost *w* characters will appear in the output field. Unlike numeric fields, asterisks are not written if the data does not fit in the specified field width.

Example:

```
character (len = *), parameter :: &
        slogan = "Save the river"
write (*, "(a)") slogan
```

produces the output record

Save*b*the*b*river

9.8.14 Position Editing

Position edit descriptors control tabbing left or right in the record before the next list item is processed. The edit descriptors for tabbing are:[6]

---

6. The position edit descriptor *n*x, used prior to the introduction of the tab edit descriptors in Fortran 77, is equivalent to t*rn*.

t*n*   tab to position *n*
t1*n*   tab left *n* positions
tr*n*   tab right *n* positions

n must be an unsigned integer constant with no kind parameter.

The t*n* edit descriptor positions the record just before character *n*, so that if a character is put into or taken from the record, it will be the *n*th character in the record. tr*n* moves right *n* characters. t1*n* moves left *n* characters.

If, because of execution of a nonadvancing input/output statement, the file is positioned within a record at the beginning of an input/output statement, left tabbing may not position that record any farther left than the position of the file at the start of the input/output operation.

Input. The t descriptor may position either forward or backward. A position to the left of the current position allows input to be processed twice.

Output. The positioning does not transmit characters and does not by itself cause the record to be shorter or longer. Positions that are skipped are blank filled, unless filled later in the processing. A character may be replaced by the action of subsequent descriptors, but the positioning descriptors do not carry out the replacement.

Examples: if x = 12.66 and y = −8654.123,

```
print "(f9.2, tr6, f9.3)", x, y
```

produces the record

```
bbbb12.66bbbbbb-8654.123
```

```
print "(f9.2, t7, f9.3)", x, y
```

produces the record

```
bbbb12-8654.123
```

9.8.15 Slash (/) Editing

The current record is ended when a slash is encountered in a format specification. The slash edit descriptor consists of the single slash character (/).

Input. If the file is connected for sequential access, the file is positioned at the beginning of the next record. The effect is to skip the remainder of the current record. For direct access, the record number is increased by one. A record may be skipped entirely on input.

Output. If the file is connected for sequential access, the file is positioned at the beginning of a new record. For direct access, the record number is increased by one, and this record becomes the current record. An empty record is blank filled.

Example: if a = 1.1, b = 2.2, and c = 3.3,

```
print "(f5.1, /, 2f6.1)", a, b, c
```

produces two records

```
bb1.1
bbb2.2bbb3.3
```

9.8.16 Colon Editing

The colon edit descriptor consists of the single colon character (:).

If the list of items in the formatted read or write statement is exhausted, a colon stops format processing at that point. It has no effect if there is more data.

Example:

```
fmt_spec = "(3f5.1, :, ""stop"")"
write (6, fmt_spec) a, b, c
```

produces

```
bb1.1bb2.2bb3.3
```

The characters stop are not printed because the output list is exhausted when the colon edit descriptor is processed.

Example: if a = 1.1, b = 2.2, and c = 3.3,

```
fmt_spec = "(3 (f5.1, :, "",""))"
write (6, fmt_spec) a, b, c
```

produces

```
bb1.1,bb2.2,bb3.3
```

Because of the colon edit descriptor, a comma is not written after the third number.

9.8.17 Sign Editing

Sign editing applies to numeric fields only; it controls the printing of the plus sign. It only applies to output. The sign edit descriptors are

s	optional plus is processor dependent
sp	optional plus must be printed
ss	optional plus must not be printed

The s edit descriptor indicates that the printing of an optional plus sign is up to the processor; it is the default. sp indicates that an optional plus sign must be printed. ss indicates that an optional plus sign must not be printed. The occurrence of these descriptors applies until another one (s, sp, ss) is encountered in the format specification.

Example: if x (1) = 1.46 and x (2) = 234.1217,

```
write (6, "(sp, 2f10.2)") x (1:2)
```

produces the record

bbbbb+1.46*bbb*+234.12

9.8.18 Blanks in Numeric Fields

Blanks other than leading blanks may be interpreted as zeros or ignored as determined by the blank edit descriptors:

bn	ignore blanks in numeric input fields
bz	treat blanks in numeric input fields as zeros

The interpretation is for input fields only; output fields are not affected. See the interpretation of blanks specifier in the blank= keyword in the open statement. If the blank= specifier is null, the blanks are ignored and treated as if they were not in the input field. If, however, a bz is encountered in the format specification, the blanks are interpreted as zeros in succeeding numeric fields. A bn or bz edit descriptor overrides the blank= specifier for the duration of the current read statement.

Example:

```
read (5, "(i5, bz, i5)") n1, n2
```

If the input record is

*b*9*b*9*b*9*b*9*b*9

the values assigned to n1 and n2 are 99 and 90909, respectively.

9.8.19 List-Directed Formatting

List-directed formatting, also called **default formatting,** is selected by using an asterisk (*) in place of an explicit format specification in a read, write, or print statement. List-directed editing occurs based on the type of each list item.

Example:

```
read (5, *) a, b, c
```

Some rules and restrictions relating to list-directed formatting are:

1. List-directed formatting cannot be used with direct access or nonadvancing input/output.

2. The record consists of values and value separators.

3. If there are no list items, an input record is skipped or an output record that is empty is written.

    Values. The values allowed are

null	a null value as in , , (no value between separators)
c	an unsigned literal constant without a kind parameter
r*c	r repetitions of the constant c
r*	r repetitions of the null value

where r is a string of digits.

Separators. The separators allowed are

,	a comma, optionally preceded or followed by contiguous blanks
/	a slash, optionally preceded or followed by contiguous blanks
	a blank between two nonblank values

Input. Input values generally are accepted as list-directed input if they are accepted in explicit formatting with an edit descriptor. There are some exceptions. They are

1. The type must agree with the next item in the list.

2. Blank editing (the blank= specifier) is not allowed and blanks are never zeros.

3. Embedded blanks are not allowed, except within a character constant and around the comma or parentheses of a complex constant.

4. Complex items in the list include the parentheses for a complex constant. They are not treated as two reals, as is done with data edit descriptors. Blanks may occur before or after the comma. An example is

(1.2, 5.666)

5. Logical items must not use value separators as the optional characters following the t or f.

6. Character constants must be delimited by quotes or apostrophes. When a character constant is continued beyond the current record, the end of the record must not be between any quotes or apostrophes that are doubled because they are the same character as the character constant delimiter. Value separators may be representable characters in the constant.

7. If *len* is the length of the next input list item, w is the length of a character constant in the input, and if

$len \leq w$ the leftmost *len* characters of the constant are used
$len > w$ the w characters of the constant are used and
the field is blank filled on the right

Null Values. A null value is encountered if

1. There is no value between separators.

2. The record begins with a value separator.

3. The $r*$ form is used.

Rules and restrictions:

1. An end of record does not signify a null value.

2. The null value does not change the next list item; however, the following value will be matched with the following list item.

3. In complex number input, the entire constant may be null, but not one of the parts.

4. If a slash terminates the input, the rest of the list items are treated as though a null value had been read. This applies to the remaining items in an array.

Example:

```
real x (4)
read (5, *) i, x (:)
```

If the input record is

b6,,2.418 /

the result is that i = 6, x (1) is unchanged, and x (2) = 2.418. x (3) and x (4) are unchanged.

Output. List-directed output uses the same conventions that are used for list-directed input. There are a few exceptions that are noted below for each of the intrinsic types. Blanks and commas are used as separators except for certain character constants that may contain a separator as part of the constant. The processor begins new records as needed, at any point in the list of output items. A new record does not begin in the middle of a number, except that complex numbers may be separated between the real and the imaginary parts. Very long character constants are the exception; they may be split across record boundaries. Slashes and null values are never output. Each new record begins with a blank for carriage control, except for continued delimited character constants. The processor has the option of using the repeat factor, $r * c$.

Integer. The effect is as though a suitable iw edit descriptor were used.

Real. The effect is as though an f or an e edit descriptor were used. The output result depends on the magnitude of the number, and the processor has some discretion in this case.

Complex. The real and imaginary parts are enclosed in parentheses and separated by a comma (with optional blanks surrounding the comma). If the length of the complex number is longer than a record, the processor may separate the real and imaginary parts on two records.

Logical. List-directed output prints T or F depending on the value of the logical data object.

Character. Character constants are output based on the value of the delim= specifier in the open statement for that unit. If there is no delimiter specified, or delim = none:

1.   Character constants are not delimited.

2.   Character constants are not surrounded by value separators.

3.   Only one quote or apostrophe is output for each quote and apostrophe embedded in the character constant.

4.   A blank is inserted in new records for carriage control for a continued character constant.

If the delimiter is quote or apostrophe

1.   Character constants are delimited.

2.   Character constants are surrounded by value separators.

3.   Embedded delimiters are doubled in the output.

4. Optional kind parameters and underscores are allowed if applicable.

5. No blank is inserted in a new record for carriage control for a continued constant.

10

Redundant Features

Because Fortran is one of the oldest commonly used high-level languages, there are many features that should be considered redundant or even perhaps obsolete in the sense that they should not be used in constructing new programs. However, lots of programs that have used these features are still being compiled and run. As a Fortran programmer, you may be asked to modify or convert a program containing these features and should know something about what they do. This chapter contains a brief description of these features with some guidelines for converting the features to more modern ones.

There are two kinds of "redundant" or "out of fashion" features. The standard itself lists a few of these features as **obsolescent**, which indicates that they might be removed from some future version of the standard. Features are in this category only if there were replacements for them already in Fortran 77. Others are redundant in the sense that there are newer features that are better designed and safer to use.

Most of the features in this chapter have superior replacements in Fortran 90. Some of these features are useful in some circumstances, but those situations occur rarely. If there is a need to use these features and it is necessary to obtain more detailed information about them, you should consult the standard itself or a more complete reference work such as the *Fortran 90 Handbook* by Adams, Brainerd, Martin, Smith, and Wagener, McGraw-Hill, 1992.

10.1 Going Against the Flow

10.1.1 Labels

A Fortran statement may be preceded by a **label**, which is a string of digits. The label is used to refer to the statement from other places within the same program unit. Any digits that occur at the beginning of a statement must constitute a label because no statement can begin with a digit. Leading zeros are insignificant in a label, so that the labels 11, 011, and 0011 are all considered to be the same label, but 01, 10, and 100 are all different labels. One of the digits in a label must be nonzero.

The use of labels is rarely necessary with the introduction in Fortran 90 of modern control constructs and the introduction in Fortran 77 of character string format specifications.

10.1.2 The Arithmetic if Statement

An example of an **arithmetic if statement** is

```
if (x - y) 100, 200, 300
```

Any expression may occur within the parentheses. The expression is evaluated. If it is negative, control is transferred to the first label (100); if it is zero, control is transferred to the second label (200); if it is positive, control is transferred to the third label (300). The if construct or if statement should be used to replace the three-branch arithmetic if statement.

10.1.3 Old Forms of the do Loop and the continue Statement

The do statement may have a label following the keyword do, in which case, the loop ends with a statement having that label, rather than with an end do statement. The end do statement is new in Fortran 90, but prior to that, careful programmers used the continue statement to end do loops. The **continue statement** has no effect. It may be used anywhere, but its most common use was to host the label that marked the end of a do loop. A do loop may end with many different kinds of statements, however, and more than one do loop may terminate with the same statement, as in

```
do 10 i = 1, 100
   do 10 j = 1, 100
10    a (i, j) = i + j
```

This example is straightforward, but when a program contains branches to the terminating statement, either from within the inner loop or from within the outer loop, it is very difficult to tell what is going on.

All such forms of the do loop can be rewritten using the do construct, the exit statement, and the cycle statement. For example, the statements above can be rewritten as

```
do i = 1, 100
   do j = 1, 100
      a (i, j) = i + j
   end do
end do
```

10.1.4 Real do Variables

do variables that are type real may be used, but this is considered poor practice by some people. Because of the possibility of roundoff error with real values, do constructs with real do variables do not always execute the expected number of times. Such loops can be replaced by those using integer do variables. For example,

```
do r = 0.1, 0.9, 0.1
   . . .
end do
```

can be rewritten as

```
do i = 1, 9
   r = 0.1 * i
   . . .
end do
```

10.1.5 The Alternate Return

It is possible to use a label preceded with an asterisk (*) as an actual argument in a subroutine call, such as

```
call subr_alt (x, y, *100, *200, *300)
```

The subroutine `subr_alt` must have an asterisk as its third, fourth, and fifth arguments. If a `return` statement containing an expression is executed in the subroutine, that expression is evaluated getting an integer value, say n. Back in the calling program, a branch is made to the nth label in the list of labels that are arguments. For example, if the statement

```
return 2
```

is executed in the subroutine `subr_alt`, a branch is made to the statement with label 200 in the calling program.

A better scheme is to use an integer variable to return a value to the calling program and let the calling program test the value and perform the necessary operations. For example,

```
call subr_alt (x, y, return_code)
select case (return_code)
    . . .
```

10.1.6 The go to Statement

The **go to statement** causes a simple transfer of control to the statement with the label following the keyword go to. For example,

```
go to 87122
```

causes a branch to the statement with label 87122. This labeled statement must be in the same main program or procedure as the go to statement. There are a few cases for which the go to statement can be effective, but almost all of the time, an `if` construct, do construct, `exit` statement, `cycle` statement, or `select case` construct should be used instead.

10.1.7 The Computed go to Statement

The **computed go to statement** involves an integer expression and a list of labels. The expression is evaluated, giving a value n. Then a branch is made to the nth label in the list. For example,

```
go to (100, 200, 300) i
```

causes a branch to the statement labeled 100, 200, or 300, depending on whether the value of i is 1, 2, or 3, respectively. Other control constructs usually can be used to replace the computed go to statement. For example,

```
select case (i)
   case (1)
      . . .
   case (2)
      . . .
   case (3)
      . . .
end select
```

10.1.8 The assign and Assigned go to Statements

The **assign** statement

```
assign 200 to i
```

allows the use of the value of i as a label. For example, it could be used in an input/output statement to specify that 200 is the label of a format statement.

```
write (*, fmt = i) x, y, z
```

The assign statement also can be used to assign the label of a branch target to an integer variable that can then be used in as assigned go to statement.

The simple form of the **assigned go to statement** looks just like the ordinary go to except that a variable is used in place of the label. The variable must be assigned a label as its value using the assign statement, and the label must be on a statement to which a branch can be made.

```
go to i
```

A list of labels in parentheses is permitted after the variable, in which case the value of one of those labels must be the label currently assigned to the variable.

```
go to i (100, 200, 300)
```

10.1.9 The do while Statement

Although the do while version of the do construct was added in Fortran 90, it is redundant because it provides only the special case of exiting a loop at the top, whereas the exit statement allows an exit from any point in the loop. A consistent use of the exit statement makes the exit condition explicit and all loops with exit will look similar. The statement

```
do while (.not. converged)
```

can be replaced by

```
do
    if (converged) exit
```

or even

```
do; if (converged) exit
```

if you like the looks of this better. Moreover, these forms explicitly reference the condition of exit rather than its negation.

10.1.10 The pause Statement

The **pause statement** was used to suspend execution of a program so that the console lights could be examined and the "run" button pushed again to resume execution of the program. The same thing can be accomplished using a `write` statement to the user followed by a `read` statement to wait until the user responds, so it has very little functionality not provided by other features.

10.2 Data

10.2.1 The implicit Statement

The `implicit` statement may be used to indicate that each undeclared variable has a type based on its first letter. For example

```
implicit real (a-z)
```

indicates that all undeclared variables are to be of type real, and

```
implicit integer (a-k, m-z), logical (l)
```

indicates that all undeclared variables beginning with the letter l are to be of type logical and all other undeclared variables are to be of type integer.

If there is no implicit none statement in a program unit, all undeclared variables have a type determined as if the program unit contained the following implicit statement:

```
implicit real (a-h, o-z), integer (i-n)
```

That is, all variables beginning with the letters i, j, k, l, m, or n are of type integer and all others are of type real. An implicit statement can be used to override some of the default typing so that, for example, if a program contained only the following single implicit statement:

```
implicit complex (c)
```

all undeclared variables beginning with the letters i-n would be of type integer, those beginning with the letter c would be of type complex, and all others would be of type real.

There is no other feature that is equivalent to implicit typing; it is simply a poor programming practice to use it. Its use leads to errors that are often difficult to detect.

10.2.2 Attribute Statements

Each of the following attributes may occur in a type declaration, but they also have a statement form.

```
allocatable
dimension
intent
intrinsic
optional
parameter
pointer
private
public
save
target
```

For example, x can be declared a real array with the target attribute using the real, dimension, and target statement.

```
real x
dimension x (20, 30)
target x
```

Use of the attribute forms, rather than the statement forms, is recommended.

```
real, dimension (20, 40), target :: x
```

10.2.3 Type Declaration Statements

Variables can be declared in myriad ways, particularly if they are type character, arrays, or have a specified kind parameter. Here are a few of the equivalent ways to declare the variable name to be a 4 × 5 array of character strings, each of length 20.

```
character name (4, 5) * 20
character name (4, 5) * (20)
character :: name (4, 5) * (20)
character * 20 name (4, 5)
character * (20) name (4, 5)
character * (20) :: name (4, 5)
character (len = 20) :: name (4, 5)
character (len = 20), dimension (4, 5) :: name
character, dimension (4, 5) :: name * 20
character, dimension (4, 5) :: name * (20)
```

If, in addition, the variable name is to have kind type parameter kanji (assumed to be an integer parameter), there are the following options:

```
character (kind = kanji) :: name (4, 5) * 20
character (kind = kanji) :: name (4, 5) * (20)
character (20, kanji) :: name (4, 5)
character (20, kind = kanji) :: name (4, 5)
character (len=20, kind=kanji), dimension (4,5) :: name
character (kind=kanji, len=20), dimension (4,5) :: name
```

The meaning of all of these different forms should be apparent to the knowledgeable reader of other programs, but when new programs are written or old ones revised, one style of declarations should be used consistently, as is done in this book.

10.2.4 The data Statement

The **data statement** provides a way to give variables initial values. The syntax is a bit unusual, but the following examples should allow you to understand how to interpret a **data** statement. The **data** statement is not needed as variables may be initialized in a type statement, as described in Section 1.3.1, or with an assignment statement.

```
character (len = 10)  name
integer, dimension (0:9) :: miles
real, dimension (100, 100) :: skew
type person
   integer :: age
   character (len = 20) :: name
end type person
type (person) my_name, your_name
data name / 'john doe' /, miles / 10 * 0 /
data ((skew (k,j), j=1,k), k=1,100) / 5050*0.0 /
data ((skew (k,j), j=k+1,100), k=1,99) / 4950*1.0 /
data my_name / person (21, 'john smith') /
data your_name%age, your_name%name / 35,'fred brown' /
```

The character variable name is initialized with the value john doe with padding on the right because the length of the constant is less than the length of the variable. All ten elements of the integer array miles are initialized to zero. The two-dimensional array skew is initialized so that the lower triangle of skew is zero and the strict upper triangle is one. The structures my_name and your_name are declared using the derived type person. my_name is initialized by a structure constructor. your_name is initialized by supplying a separate value for each component.

Note that a data statement may contain implied do loops similar to those that may occur in array constructors and input/output lists.

A data statement is one of the few places that binary, octal, and hexadecimal constants may occur, so if you want to initialize an integer using a constant of one of these forms, the data statement is the only choice.

```
integer :: n
data n / z"ffff" /  ! initializes n to hexadecimal ffff
```

10.2.5 The Double Precision Data Type

One of the kinds of reals corresponds to what is called **double precision**. Variables of this type also can be declared using the double precision type statement. Constants of this type are written with an exponent letter "d" instead of "e", as in the example

```
5.67d-22.
```

10.2.6 Hollerith Data

Prior to Fortran 77, it was possible to assign characters to variables of other data types with a constant that begins with a character count and the letter h, as in the string

```
4hwalt
```

This was removed from Fortran 77, but the h edit descriptor, which looks just like the Hollerith constant, was kept. All uses of Hollerith data and h edit descriptors can be replaced with the use of the character data type and the a edit descriptor.

10.2.7 Common Blocks

Common blocks provide a mechanism for creating values that can be shared between program units. How values get shared using common blocks depends on the arrangement of variables in the common blocks. Although the names of the common blocks themselves are global, none of the variables within the blocks are global; values are shared between two variables simply by the fact that they occupy corresponding positions within the same common block. Suppose the following common statements occur within two subroutines named s1 and s2.

```
subroutine s1
   common / cmn / a, b (2)
   . . .

subroutine s2
   common / cmn / c, x
   complex c
   . . .
```

Because c is complex, it corresponds to two real values, so a in s1 shares values with the real part of c in s2. Similarly b (1) in s1 corresponds to the imaginary part of c in s2, and b (2) in s1 corresponds to x in s2. Many programmers who use common blocks try to ensure that common statements declaring the same common blocks in two different program units are identical; this avoids complicated sharing mechanisms as illustrated above and errors that are difficult to detect.

All uses of common blocks can be replaced by modules and other Fortran 90 features.

10.2.8 The equivalence Statement

The **equivalence statement** establishes a value-sharing scheme within a program unit in much the same way the common blocks do in different program units. For example,

```
complex z
real x (2), y (2)
equivalence (x, z), (y (1), x (2))
```

cause x (1) and the real part of z to share storage and cause x (2), y (1), and the imaginary part of z to share storage.

The introduction of modules, dynamic storage allocation, pointers, structures, and the intrinsic function transfer makes the use of equivalence unnecessary.

10.2.9 The sequence Statement

A type definition may contain the **sequence statement**, consisting of just the keyword sequence. This indicates that the storage for the components of the structure being defined are laid out in a specific way, allowing structures of that type to work with other features depending on storage layout, such as equivalence and common. It also allows types in different programs to be equivalent.

```
type polar
    sequence
    real rho, theta
end type polar
```

Type definitions can always be put in a module if they are to be shared.

10.2.10 Block Data Program Unit

A **block data program unit** provides a mechanism to initialize data in common blocks. It may contain only type definitions, type declarations, and common, data, dimension, equivalence, implicit, intrinsic, parameter, pointer, save, target, and use statements. The use of modules makes the use of block data program units unnecessary.

10.3 Input/Output

10.3.1 Namelist Input/Output

Namelist input/output accomplishes two different things. It provides a mechanism for naming the objects that may occur in an input/output list (as you might expect), but only in namelist input/output statements. It also provides a mechanism whereby the input data may contain values for only a portion of the variables in the input list. Here are two very simple examples.

```
integer :: i
real, dimension (3) :: a
character (len = 3) :: char
complex :: x
logical :: 11
namelist / token / i, a, char, x, 11
read (*, nml = token)
```

If the input record is

```
&token a(1:2) = 2*1.0 11 = t char = "nop" x = (2.4,0.0)/
```

results of the read are

i	unchanged
a (1)	1.0
a (2)	1.0
a (3)	unchanged
char	nop
x	(2.4, 0.0)
11	true

To illustrate namelist output

```
integer :: i = 20
real :: x = 2.468
       . . .
namelist / turn / i, x
write (*, nml = turn)
```

produces the output record

```
&TURN I = 20, X =    2.4679999/
```

Although namelist input/output has been around for a long time in the form of vendor extensions, it was added to standard

Fortran only recently. It can be useful in some circumstances, but it is an extremely poorly designed feature and there are many restrictions on its use with other features of Fortran, so it is best not to use it unless absolutely necessary. Identified output is easy to produce, and null input values on list directed input provide an alternative means to read values for only some of the items in an input/output list. However, there is no other substitute for namelist's keyword-identified input values.

10.3.2 The format Statement

Perhaps the most common use of a label is with a **format statement**. This provides an alternative (and formerly the only) way to have one format be used by several input/output statements. In the statements

```
print 15, x, " and ", n
15 format (f5.1, a, i4)
```

the format specification is placed in a **format** statement. The digits 15 in the **print** and **format** statements form a statement label. They identify the **format** statement so that the **print** statement can refer to it.

As illustrated by the example above, the **format** statement consists of the keyword **format** followed by a format specification. **format** statements are not executable statements. Thus, they do not have to appear immediately following the **print** statements that reference them. However, this is a reasonable place for **format** statements that are used only once. If several **print** statements use the same **format** statement, many programmers put the **format** statement at the end of the program. The same effect is achieved in Fortran 90 by assigning the format specification to a character variable.

10.3.3   err=, end=, and eor= Specifiers

The end= and eor= specifiers may be followed by a label in an input statement to check for an end of file or an end of record. The err= specifier can be used in most input/output statements to check for an error condition. If such a condition occurs, a branch is taken to the label indicated.

```
read (*, fmt = "(a)", end = 88, err = 999) line_of_text
```

Each of these conditions can be checked using the iostat= specifier.

10.3.4 Character String Edit Descriptors

A **character string edit descriptor** consists of a character constant placed in a format. The character string edit descriptors are

> ' *characters* '
> " *characters* "
> *n*h *characters*

When the character edit descriptor is reached in output, the value of the character constant is inserted in the output. The Hollerith descriptor *n*h . . . may be used to print the *n* characters following the h. These edit descriptors must not be used on input.

To print one of the delimiting characters in the output field, use two consecutive apostrophes or quotes. The field width is basically the length of the character constant, but doubled quotes or apostrophes are counted as single characters.

Example:

```
write (6, 110) temp
110 format (15h temperature = , f13.6)
```

produces the record

> *b*temperature*b*=*bbbb*32.120001

So also do the statements

```
write (6, 120) temp
120 format (' temperature = ', f13.6)
```

which avoids counting characters in the Hollerith constant. The following equivalent ways to produce the record were available in Fortran 77:

```
write (6, '('' temperature = '', f13.6)') temp

chrfmt = '('' temperature = '', f13.6)'
write (6, chrfmt) temp

write (6, '(a, f13.6)') ' temperature = ', temp
```

As illustrated by the last example, character string edit descriptors may be replaced with the a edit descriptor and the character constant is placed in the input/output list, where all other data values are placed.

If a character string edit descriptor occurs in a format specification that is a literal constant delimited by apostrophes, two apostrophes must be written to represent each apostrophe in the format specification. If a format specification is, in turn, a character constant delimited by apostrophes, there must be two apostrophes for each delimiter and each apostrophe within the constant must be represented by four apostrophes. See the example below. The use of quote marks for delimiters is similar. One way to avoid problems is to use delimiters different from the characters within the format specification, if possible. However, the best way to avoid the problem is to put the character expression in the input/output list instead of the format specification as shown in the second example.

Example:

```
print '(''I can''''t hear you'')'

print "(a)", "I can't hear you"
```

10.3.5 The d Edit Descriptor

The **d edit descriptor** is similar to the e edit descriptor, except that on output, constants are written using D as the exponent letter instead of E.

10.3.6 The g Edit Descriptor

The **g edit descriptor** may be used to edit values of each of the Fortran data types. It is sometimes a small convenience to use the same letter, and with real values, g editing selects between e and f editing, based on the value to be printed. However, using i, e, f, l, or a edit descriptors provides some checking that the data types are all correct. For real convenience, list-directed formatting is available.

Example: if x = 87.532 and 1 is false,

```
print "(2g10.1)", x, 1
```

produces the output

*bbbbbb*87.6*bbbbbbbbbb*F

10.3.7 The x Edit Descriptor

The **position edit descriptor** nx skips n characters in a record. It is the same as tr$n$.

10.3.8 Scale Factors

The **p edit descriptor** is designed to allow numbers to be computed in a range different from their actual values. For example, a collection of data consisting of very small values could all be multiplied by 10^{100} when read in and divided by the same value when printed. Unfortunately, the p edit descriptor only changes the values in some cases. For e output editing, it just changes the form of the number without changing its value. This effect was used to improve the form of printed output, but programmers often have been surprised that it affects all e and f edit descriptors following it in the format. The rules indicating when the scale factor actually changes values and when it does not are very strange, so this edit descriptor is best avoided. The en and es edit descriptors can be used to produce output in a more desirable format.

Consider the following example:

```
read (*, "(3p, f5.0)") x
write (*, "(e20.5)") x
write (*, "(3p, e20.5)") x
write (*, "(f20.5)") x
write (*, "(3p, f20.5)") x
```

When this program is run with the following input

```
10.23
```

the resulting output is

```
        0.10230E-01
        102.300E-04
             0.01023
            10.23000
```

Note that when the value 10.23 is read, it is converted to the internal value 0.01023 by multiplying by 10^{-3}. In the first three cases, the value printed is the same value as the internal value—only its format is different. Only when it is printed with f editing and the 3p scale factor does it come out with a value that is the same as the input.

10.4 Procedures

10.4.1 Intrinsic Functions

Intrinsic functions that can be used with only one data type have been superceded by generic versions. For example, the function cabs finds the absolute value of a complex number, but the function abs can be used to find the absolute value of a number of any numeric data type. It is always best to use the generic version. Some of the nongeneric intrinsic functions cannot be passed as an argument to a procedure. Other intrinsic functions, such as mod, have equivalent replacements.

10.4.2 The Statement Function

It is possible to define and use a function in a program, subroutine, or function by giving a one-line definition of a **statement function**. A statement function must come before any executable statements. An example is

```
program statement_function_example

    f (x) = x ** 2 - 1
    . . .
    y = f (a + 2 * b)
    . . .

    end program statement_function_example
```

If more than one statement is needed to define the function, a statement function cannot be used. All uses of statement functions can be replaced by internal functions.

10.4.3 External Procedures and the external Statement

Internal procedures and module procedures were introduced in Fortran 90. Before that, all procedures were **external procedures**. They are completely independent of any other parts of the program and can be compiled separately from any other part of the program. The following partial example shows a typical organization of a program with two external subroutines.

```
program p
   . . .
   call s1 (x)
   . . .
   call s2
   . . .
end program p

subroutine s1 (x)
   . . .
end subroutine s1

subroutine s2
   . . .
end subroutine s2
```

The subroutines could be kept in separate files, or the whole program, including the subroutines, could be kept in one file and compiled together. The same options are available with module procedures.

In certain circumstances, such as when passing a procedure as an argument, it is necessary to indicate that a procedure is external to the program referencing it. This is done with the external statement.

```
external s1, s2
```

10.4.4 Interface Blocks

With the more powerful argument passing facilities in Fortran 90, it is often required that a calling program know several things about an external procedure that it calls. For example, the characteristics of the arguments must be known when optional or keyword arguments are used. For internal procedures and module procedures, all this information is available to any calling program that knows about the procedure. For external procedures, the information is provided by putting it in an **interface block**. The interface block basically contains all of the information about the procedure arguments and the result, in the case of a function. For example, if the subroutine big_gets_char in the example module big_integers in Section 7.4 were not in a module, but written as an external procedure, any program that wanted to invoke it using assignment would need to include an interface block like the following:

```
interface assignment (=)
   subroutine big_gets_char (b, c)

      use big_integers
      implicit none
      type (big_integer), intent (out) :: b
      character (len = *), intent (in) :: c

   end subroutine big_gets_char
end interface
```

Note that the use statement is needed in the external subroutine big_gets_char and the interface block because it would not be internal to the module big_integers and information such as the type declaration for big_integer would not be available. Also the implicit none statement is needed both places for similar reasons.

Putting procedures either in a module or another program unit makes things so much easier that it really is not necessary to use external procedures in any new or revised programs.

10.4.5 The entry Statement

The **entry statement** allows one program unit to define more than one procedure. This may be useful when two procedures share some computations but still are different. A classic example is the computation of the trigonometric functions sine and cosine. Cosines of certain angles are computed as sines of related angles, and vice versa. In the following simple example, $g(x) = f(x)$ and $h(x) = f(|x|)$:

```
function h (x)
   xx = abs (x)
   go to 10
entry g (x)
   xx = x
10 h = f (xx)
end function h
```

Internal procedures can be used to replace the use of the entry statement.

10.5 Miscellaneous

10.5.1 Fixed Source Form

There is a second format that may be used to write Fortran programs. With **fixed source form**, positions 1–5 can be used only for labels; position 6, if it contains any character except a blank or zero, indicates that the line is a continuation of the previous line; and the main part of the statement must fall in positions 7–72. Positions 73 to the end of the record are ignored. A c or * in position one indicates that the entire line is a comment. The exclamation point (!) may be used to indicate comments, just as it does in the free source form used in this book. The semicolon (;) may be used to separate statements. Blank characters are insignificant in fixed source form, which is a major difference. Many older Fortran programs are written in fixed source form, which was once the only acceptable form and the only standard form until the adoption of Fortran 90.

Each program unit must use one form or the other; they cannot be mixed. There must be some way for the programmer to indicate whether a program unit is written in fixed form or written in free form, but that mechanism varies from one system to another. Check the manual for the system you are using to see how this is done.

Program units in fixed source form may be modified to be compatible with free source form by three changes:

1. All cs or asterisks in position 1 are replaced with exclamation marks (!).

2. All continuation characters in position 6 are replaced with ampersands (&), and ampersands are inserted in the previous (noncomment) line of the statement in position 73.

3. If ignored characters appear in positions 73 to the end of the line, an exclamation point is inserted before them.

After such modifications, the program unit will still have the look and feel of fixed source form, but will be *both legal fixed source form and legal free source form*. This is useful during the awkward period of changeover from Fortran 77 to Fortran 90, when some programs must run under Fortran 77 systems.

10.5.2 Assumed-Size Arrays

An **assumed-size array** is a dummy argument for which the upper bound in the last dimension is declared to be an asterisk (*). This indicates that the extent of the array in that dimension, and hence its size, is not known. It is up to the programmer to make sure that elements of the assumed-size dummy argument match up correctly with the corresponding actual argument.

All uses of assumed-size arrays can be replaced by uses of assumed-shape arrays, in which all bounds are assumed from the actual argument by declaring the bounds to be a colon (:).

10.5.3 include Line

An **include line** contains the keyword `include` and a character literal constant without a kind parameter. The meaning of the constant is not specified, but probably is a file name on most systems. The include line is replaced by included text, such as the contents of a specified file.

Although the include line might be useful in some simple cases, the use of modules is recommended instead.

10.5.4 Vendor Extensions

In many respects, any features in the Fortran system provided by a vendor that are not in the standard should be treated as obsolete, however new they may be. Every Fortran compiler is required to have a mechanism that will flag all nonstandard syntax. This feature always should be enabled during development and debugging.

Vendor extensions never should be used for the programmers' convenience or to achieve a small gain in efficiency. Use of such extensions will prevent the program from being run on different systems, perhaps even those provided later by the same vendor.

There are some circumstances in which it is necessary to use vendor extensions to standard Fortran in a program. One is to construct programs that are not possible to write in standard Fortran. Examples might be some real-time processing applications or a program that must manipulate special registers of a computer. The other use of nonstandard features is to achieve major improvements in efficiency on sections of code that use very large amounts of computing resources. Examples of this are provided by vendor extensions to access special vector-processing hardware. Fortran now has array processing facilities that should eliminate most of these uses. However, some machines now have special facilities for synchronous and asynchronous parallel processing, and it might be necessary to introduce special language facilities to utilize these facilities most effectively.

If it is really necessary to use vendor extensions, do it only in those parts of the program that require them, and document their use thoroughly. Isolate these parts of the program into small procedures as much as possible.

Intrinsic Procedures

There are four classes of intrinsic procedures: inquiry functions, elemental functions, transformational functions, and subroutines.

A.1 Intrinsic Functions

An **intrinsic function** is an inquiry function, an elemental function, or a transformational function. An **inquiry function** is one whose result depends on the properties of its principal argument other than the value of this argument; in fact, the argument value may be undefined. An **elemental function** is one that is specified for scalar arguments but may be applied to array arguments, as described in Section A.2. All other intrinsic functions are **transformational functions**; they almost all have one or more array-valued arguments or an array-valued result.

Generic names of intrinsic functions are given in Sections A.4 to A.11. In most cases, generic functions accept arguments of more than one type and the type of the result is the same as the type of the arguments. **Specific names** of intrinsic functions with corresponding generic names are listed in Section A.12.

If an intrinsic function is used as an actual argument to a procedure, its specific name must be used, and it may be referenced in the procedure only with scalar arguments. If an intrinsic function does not have a specific name, it must not be used as an actual argument.

A.2 Elemental Intrinsic Procedures

A.2.1 Elemental Intrinsic Function Arguments and Results

If a generic name or a specific name is used to reference an elemental intrinsic function, the shape of the result is the same as the shape of the argument with the greatest rank. If the arguments are all scalar, the result is scalar. For those elemental intrinsic functions that have more than one argument, all arguments must be conformable (i.e., have the same shape). In the array-valued case, the values of the elements, if any, of the result are the same as would have been obtained if the scalar-valued function had been applied separately, in any order, to corresponding elements of each argument. Arguments called kind must always be specified as scalar integer initialization expressions, which are essentially expressions whose primaries are constants or are references to certain intrinsic functions. These expressions must evaluate to a processor supported kind number.

A.2.2 Elemental Intrinsic Subroutine Arguments

If a generic name is used to reference an elemental intrinsic subroutine, either all actual arguments must be scalar or all intent (out) arguments must be arrays of the same shape, and the remaining arguments must be conformable with them. In the case that the intent (out) arguments are arrays, the values of the elements, if any, of the results are the same as would be obtained if the subroutine with scalar arguments were applied separately, in any order, to corresponding elements of each argument.

A.3 Positional Arguments or Argument Keywords

All intrinsic procedures may be invoked with either positional arguments or argument keywords. The descriptions in Sections A.4 to A.11 give the keyword names and positional sequence. A keyword is required for an argument only if a preceding optional argument is omitted or a preceding actual argument is specified using a keyword. For example, a reference to cmplx may be written in the form cmplx (real_part, complex_part, m) or in the form cmplx (y = complex_part, kind = m, x = real_part).

Many of the argument keywords have names that are indicative of their usage. For example,

kind	Describes the kind of the result
string, string_a	An arbitrary character string
back	Indicates a string scan is to be from right to left (backward)
mask	A mask that may be applied to the arguments
dim	A selected dimension of an array argument

A.4 Argument Presence Inquiry Function

The inquiry function present permits an inquiry to be made about the presence of an actual argument associated with a dummy argument that has the optional attribute. Its result is logical.

present (a)	Argument presence

A.5 Numeric, Mathematical, Character, and Logical Procedures

A.5.1 Numeric Functions

The elemental functions int, real, dble, and cmplx perform type conversions. The elemental functions aimag, conjg, aint, anint, nint, abs, mod, sign, dim, dprod, modulo, floor, ceiling, max, and min perform simple numeric operations.

abs (a)	Absolute value
aimag (z)	Imaginary part of a complex number
aint (a, kind) Optional kind	Truncation to whole number
anint (a, kind) Optional kind	Nearest whole number
ceiling (a)	Least integer greater than or equal to number
cmplx (x, y, kind) Optional y, kind	Conversion to complex type
conjg (z)	Conjugate of a complex number
dble (a)	Conversion to double precision real type
dim (x, y)	Positive difference; max (x-y, 0)
dprod (x, y)	Double precision real product
int (a, kind) Optional kind	Conversion to integer type
floor (a)	Greatest integer less than or equal to number
max (a1, a2, a3,...) Optional a3,...	Maximum value
min (a1, a2, a3,...) Optional a3,...	Minimum value
mod (a, p)	Remainder function; a-int(a/p)*p; if nonzero, mod(a,p) has the sign of a

modulo (a, p)	Modulo function; a-floor(a/p)*p; if nonzero, modulo(a,p) has the sign of p
nint (a, kind) Optional kind	Nearest integer
real (a, kind) Optional kind	Conversion to real type
sign (a, b)	Absolute value of a with the sign of b

A.5.2 Mathematical Functions

The elemental functions sqrt, exp, log, log10, sin, cos, tan, asin, acos, atan, atan2, sinh, cosh, and tanh evaluate elementary mathematical functions.

acos (x)	Arccosine
asin (x)	Arcsine
atan (x)	Arctangent
atan2 (y, x)	Arctangent of y/x
cos (x)	Cosine
cosh (x)	Hyperbolic cosine
exp (x)	Exponential
log (x)	Natural logarithm
log10 (x)	Common logarithm (base 10)
sin (x)	Sine
sinh (x)	Hyperbolic sine
sqrt (x)	Square root
tan (x)	Tangent
tanh (x)	Hyperbolic tangent

A.5.3 Character Functions

The elemental functions ichar, char, lge, lgt, lle, llt, iachar, achar, index, verify, adjustl, adjustr, scan, and len_trim perform character operations. The transformational function repeat returns repeated concatenations of a character string argument. The transformational function trim returns the argument with trailing blanks removed.

achar (i)	Character in given position in ASCII collating sequence
adjustl (string)	Adjust left; move leading blanks to end
adjustr (string)	Adjust right; move trailing blanks to beginning
char (i, kind) Optional kind	Character in given position in processor collating sequence
iachar (c)	Position of a character in ASCII collating sequence
ichar (c)	Position of a character in processor collating sequence
index (string, substring, back) Optional back	Starting position of a substring
len_trim (string)	Length without trailing blank characters
lge (string_a, string_b)	Lexically greater than or equal

lgt (string_a, string_b)	Lexically greater than
lle (string_a, string_b)	Lexically less than or equal
llt (string_a, string_b)	Lexically less than
repeat (string, ncopies)	Repeated concatenation
scan (string, set, back)	Scan a string for any character
Optional back	in a set of characters
trim (string)	Remove trailing blank characters
verify (string, set, back)	Find a character in a string
Optional back	not in a set of characters

A.5.4 Character Inquiry Function

The inquiry function len returns the length of a character entity. The value of the argument to this function need not be defined. It is not necessary for a processor to evaluate the argument of this function if the value of the function can be determined otherwise.

len (string)	Length of a character entity

A.5.5 Logical Function

The elemental function logical converts between objects of type logical with different kind parameter values.

logical (l, kind)	Convert between objects of type logical
Optional kind	with different kind type parameters

A.5.6 Kind Functions

The inquiry function kind returns the kind parameter value of an integer, real, complex, logical, or character entity. The transformational function selected_real_kind returns the real kind parameter value that has at least the decimal precision and exponent range specified by its arguments. The transformational function selected_int_kind returns the integer kind parameter value that has at least the decimal exponent range specified by its argument.

kind (x)	Kind parameter value
selected_int_kind (r)	Integer kind parameter value,
	sufficient for integers with r digits
selected_real_kind (p, r)	Real kind parameter value,
Optional p, r	given decimal precision and range

A.6 Numeric Manipulation and Inquiry Functions

The numeric manipulation and inquiry functions are described in terms of a model for the representation and behavior of numbers on a processor. The model has parameters which are determined so as to make the model best fit the machine on which the executable program is executed.

A.6.1 Models for Integer and Real Data

The model set for integer i is defined by

$$i = s \times \sum_{k=1}^{q} w_k \times r^{k-1}$$

where r is an integer exceeding one, q is a positive integer, each w_k is a nonnegative integer less than r, and s is +1 or -1. The model set for real x is defined by

$$x = \begin{cases} 0 & or \\ s \times b^e \times \sum_{k=1}^{p} f_k \times b^{-k}, \end{cases}$$

where b and p are integers exceeding one; each f_k is a nonnegative integer less than b, except f_1 which is also nonzero; s is +1 or -1; and e is an integer that lies between some integer maximum e_{max} and some integer minimum e_{min} inclusively. For $x = 0$, its exponent e and digits f_k are defined to be zero. The integer parameters r and q determine the set of model integers, and the integer parameters b, p, e_{min}, and e_{max} determine the set of model floating point numbers. The parameters of the integer and real models are available for each integer and real data type implemented by the processor. The parameters characterize the set of available numbers in the definition of the model. The numeric manipulation and inquiry functions provide values related to the parameters and other constants related to them. Examples of these functions in this section use the models

$$i = s \times \sum_{k=1}^{31} w_k \times 2^{k-1}$$

and

$$x = 0 \quad or \quad s \times 2^e \times \left[\frac{1}{2} + \sum_{k=2}^{24} f_k \times 2^{-k} \right], \quad -126 \le e \le 127$$

A.6.2 Numeric Inquiry Functions

The inquiry functions radix, digits, minexponent, maxexponent, precision, range, huge, tiny, and epsilon return scalar values related to the parameters of the model associated with the type and type parameters of the arguments. The value of the arguments to these functions need not be defined, pointer arguments may be disassociated, and array arguments need not be allocated.

digits (x)	Number of significant digits p in the model
epsilon (x)	Number that is almost negligible compared to one
huge (x)	Largest number in the model
maxexponent (x)	Maximum exponent in the model; e_{max}
minexponent (x)	Minimum exponent in the model; e_{min}
precision (x)	Decimal precision
radix (x)	Base of the model; b
range (x)	Decimal exponent range; floor(log10(huge(x)))
tiny (x)	Smallest positive number in the model

A.6.3 Floating Point Manipulation Functions

The elemental functions exponent, scale, nearest, fraction, set_exponent, spacing, and rrspacing return values related to the components of the model values (Section A.6.1) associated with the actual values of the arguments.

exponent (x)	Exponent part e of a model number
fraction (x)	Fractional part of a number
nearest (x, s)	Nearest different processor number in given direction
rrspacing (x)	Reciprocal of the relative spacing of model numbers near given number
scale (x, i)	Multiply a real by its base to an integer power
set_exponent (x, i)	Set exponent part of a number
spacing (x)	Absolute spacing of model numbers near given number

A.7 Bit Manipulation and Inquiry Procedures

The bit manipulation procedures consist of a set of ten functions and one subroutine. Logical operations on bits are provided by the functions ior, iand, not, and ieor; shift operations are provided by the functions ishft and ishftc; bit subfields may be referenced by the function ibits and by the subroutine mvbits; single-bit processing is provided by the functions btest, ibset, and ibclr.

For the purposes of these procedures, a bit is defined to be a binary digit w located at position k of a nonnegative integer scalar object based on a model nonnegative integer defined by

$$j = \sum_{k=0}^{s-1} w_k \times 2^k$$

and for which w_k may have the value 0 or 1. An example of a model number compatible with the examples used in Section A.6.1 would have $s = 32$, thereby defining a 32-bit integer.

An inquiry function bit_size is available to determine the parameter s of the model. The value of the argument of this function need not be defined. It is not necessary for a processor to evaluate the argument of this function if the value of the function can be determined otherwise.

Effectively, this model defines an integer object to consist of s bits in sequence numbered from right to left from 0 to $s-1$. This model is valid only in the context of the use of such an object as the argument or result of one of the bit manipulation procedures. In all other contexts, the model defined for an integer in Section A.6.1 applies. In particular, whereas the models are identical for $w_{s-1} = 0$, they do not correspond for $w_{s-1} = 1$ and the interpretation of bits in such objects is processor dependent.

bit_size (i)	Number of bits in the model; s
btest (i, pos)	Bit testing
iand (i, j)	Logical and
ibclr (i, pos)	Clear bit
ibits (i, pos, len)	Bit extraction
ibset (i, pos)	Set bit
ieor (i, j)	Exclusive or
ior (i, j)	Inclusive or
ishft (i, shift)	Logical shift
ishftc (i, shift, size)	Circular shift
Optional size	
not (i)	Logical complement

A.8 Transfer Function

The function transfer specifies that the physical representation of the first argument is to be treated as if it were one of the type and type parameters of the second argument with no conversion. Results are processor dependent.

transfer (source, mold, size)	Treat first argument as if
Optional size	of type of second argument
	If mold is scalar, result is scalar.
	If mold is an array, result is rank one
	with size of source or size (if present)

A.9 Array Intrinsic Functions

The array intrinsic functions perform the following operations on arrays: vector and matrix multiplication, numeric or logical computation that reduces the rank, array structure inquiry, array construction, array manipulation, and geometric location.

A.9.1 The Shape of Array Arguments

The transformational array intrinsic functions operate on each array argument as a whole. The shape of the corresponding actual argument must therefore be defined; that is, the actual argument must be an array section, an assumed-shape array, an explicit-shape array, a pointer that is associated with a target, an allocatable array that has been allocated, or an array-valued expression. It must not be an assumed-size array.

Some of the inquiry intrinsic functions accept array arguments for which the shape need not be defined. Assumed-size arrays may be used as arguments to these functions; they include the function lbound and certain references to size and ubound.

A.9.2 Mask Arguments

Some array intrinsic functions have an optional mask argument that is used by the function to select the elements of one or more arguments to be operated on by the function. Any element not selected by the mask need not be defined at the time the function is invoked.

The mask affects only the value of the function, and does not affect the evaluation, prior to invoking the function, of arguments that are array expressions.

A mask argument must be of type logical.

A.9.3 Vector and Matrix Multiplication Functions

The matrix multiplication function matmul operates on two matrices, or on one matrix and one vector, and returns the corresponding matrix-matrix, matrix-vector, or vector-matrix product. The arguments to matmul may be numeric (integer, real, or complex) or logical arrays. On logical matrices and vectors, matmul performs Boolean matrix multiplication (that is, multiplication is .and. and addition is .or.).

The dot product function dot_product operates on two vectors and returns their scalar product. The vectors are of the same type (numeric or logical) as for matmul. For logical vectors, dot_product returns the Boolean scalar product.

dot_product (vector_a, vector_b)	Dot product of two rank-one arrays
matmul (matrix_a, matrix_b)	Matrix multiplication

A.9.4 Array Reduction Functions

The array reduction functions sum, product, maxval, minval, count, any, and all perform numerical, logical, and counting operations on arrays. They may be applied to the whole array to give a scalar result or they may be applied over a given dimension to yield a result of rank reduced by one. The optional dim argument selects which subscript is reduced. By use of a logical mask that is conformable with the given array, the computation may be confined to any subset of the array (for example, the positive elements).

all (mask, dim) Optional dim	True if all values are true
any (mask, dim) Optional dim	True if any value is true
count (mask, dim) Optional dim	Number of true elements in an array
maxval (array, dim, mask) Optional dim, mask	Maximum value in an array
minval (array, dim, mask) Optional dim, mask	Minimum value in an array
product (array, dim, mask) Optional dim, mask	Product of array elements
sum (array, dim, mask) Optional dim, mask	Sum of array elements

A.9.5 Array Inquiry Functions

The function allocated returns a value true if the array argument is currently allocated, and returns false otherwise. The functions size, shape, lbound, and ubound return, respectively, the size of the array, the shape, and the lower and upper bounds of the subscripts along each dimension. The size, shape, or bounds must be defined.

The values of the array arguments to these functions need not be defined.

allocated (array)	Array allocation status
lbound (array, dim) Optional dim	Lower dimension bounds of an array
shape (source)	Shape of an array or scalar
size (array, dim) Optional dim	Total number of elements in an array
ubound (array, dim) Optional dim	Upper dimension bounds of an array

A.9.6 Array Construction Functions

The functions merge, spread, pack, and unpack construct new arrays
from the elements of existing arrays. merge combines two conformable arrays into one array by an element-wise choice based on a logical
mask. spread constructs an array from several copies of an actual
argument (spread does this by adding an extra dimension, as in form-
ing a book from copies of one page). pack and unpack, respectively,
gather and scatter the elements of a one-dimensional array from and
to positions in another array where the positions are specified by a
logical mask.

merge (tsource,
       fsource, mask)
	Merge under mask
	     Where mask is true, result is tsource,
	     elsewhere result is fsource

pack (array, mask, vector)
     Optional vector
	Pack an array into an array of rank one
	     under a mask. Result size is count(mask).
	     If vector is present, result is padded
	     with terminal elements of vector
	     to size(vector).

spread (source, dim, ncopies)	Replicates array by adding a dimension

unpack (vector, mask,
       field)
	Unpack an array of rank one into an array
	     under a mask. Where mask is true,
	     elements of field are replaced
	     by elements of vector.
	     result has shape of mask.

A.9.7 Array Reshape Function

reshape produces an array with the same elements as its argument,
but with a different shape.

reshape (source, shape,
       pad, order)
    Optional pad, order
	Reshape an array

A.9.8 Array Manipulation Functions

The functions transpose, eoshift, and cshift manipulate arrays.
transpose performs the matrix transpose operation on a two-
dimensional array. The shift functions leave the shape of an array
unaltered but shift the positions of the elements parallel to a specified
dimension of the array. These shifts are either circular (cshift), in
which case elements shifted off one end reappear at the other end, or
end-off (eoshift), in which case specified boundary elements are
shifted into the vacated positions.

cshift (array, shift, dim) Optional dim	Circular shift

eoshift (array, shift,
      boundary, dim)
  Optional boundary, dim
	End-off shift

transpose (matrix)	Transpose of an array of rank two

A.9.9 Array Location Functions

The functions maxloc and minloc return the location (subscripts) of an element of an array that has maximum and minimum values, respectively. By use of an optional logical mask that is conformable with the given array, the reduction may be confined to any subset of the array. The size of the returned value is the rank of the array.

maxloc (array, mask) Optional mask	Location of a maximum value in an array
minloc (array, mask) Optional mask	Location of a minimum value in an array

A.10 Pointer Association Status Inquiry Function

The function associated tests whether a pointer is currently associated with any target, with a particular target, or with the same target as another pointer.

associated (pointer, target) Optional target	Association status or comparison

A.11 Intrinsic Subroutines

Intrinsic subroutines are supplied by the processor and have the special definitions given in this section. An intrinsic subroutine is referenced by a call statement that uses its name explicitly. The name of an intrinsic subroutine must not be used as an actual argument.

A.11.1 Date and Time Subroutines

The subroutines date_and_time and system_clock return integer data from the date and real-time clock. The time returned is local, but there are facilities for finding out the difference between local time and Coordinated Universal Time.

date_and_time (date, time,
      zone, values)
  Optional date, time,
      zone, values
	Obtain date and time
	  date="ccyymmdd"
	  time="hhmmss.sss"
	  values=(/year, month, day, gmt_min,
	    hr,min,sec,msec/)

system_clock (count,
     count_rate, count_max)
	Obtain data from the system clock
	  count_rate is in counts per second.

Optional count, count_rate,
    count_max

A.11.2 Pseudorandom Numbers

The subroutine random_number returns a pseudorandom number
greater than or equal to 0.0 and less than 1.0 or an array of pseudorandom numbers. The subroutine random_seed initializes or restarts
the pseudorandom number sequence.

random_number (harvest)   Returns pseudorandom number
random_seed (size, put, get)   Initializes or restarts the
    Optional size, put, get   pseudorandom number generator

A.11.3 Bit Copy Subroutine

The subroutine mvbits copies a bit field from a specified position in
one integer object to a specified position in another.

mvbits (from, frompos,   Copies bits from one integer to another
    len, to, topos)

A.12 Specific Names for Intrinsic Functions

Specific Name	Generic Name	Argument Type
abs (a)	abs (a)	default real
acos (x)	acos (x)	default real
aimag (z)	aimag (z)	default complex
aint (a)	aint (a)	default real
alog (x)	log (x)	default real
alog10 (x)	log10 (x)	default real
• amax0 (a1,a2,a3,...) Optional a3,...	real (max (a1, a2,a3,...)) Optional a3,...	default integer
• amax1 (a1,a2,a3,...) Optional a3,...	max (a1, a2,a3,...) Optional a3,...	default real
• amin0 (a1,a2,a3,...) Optional a3,...	real (min (a1, a2,a3,...)) Optional a3,...	default integer
• amin1 (a1,a2,a3,...) Optional a3,...	min (a1, a2,a3,...) Optional a3,...	default real
amod (a,p)	mod (a,p)	default real
anint (a)	anint (a)	default real
asin (x)	asin (x)	default real
atan (x)	atan (x)	default real
atan2 (y,x)	atan2 (y,x)	default real
cabs (a)	abs (a)	default complex
ccos (x)	cos (x)	default complex
cexp (x)	exp (x)	default complex

• char (i)	char (i)	default integer
clog (x)	log (x)	default complex
conjg (z)	conjg (z)	default complex
cos (x)	cos (x)	default real
cosh (x)	cosh (x)	default real
csin (x)	sin (x)	default complex
csqrt (x)	sqrt (x)	default complex
dabs (a)	abs (a)	double precision real
dacos (x)	acos (x)	double precision real
dasin (x)	asin (x)	double precision real
datan (x)	atan (x)	double precision real
datan2 (y,x)	atan2 (y,x)	double precision real
dcos (x)	cos (x)	double precision real
dcosh (x)	cosh (x)	double precision real
ddim (x,y)	dim (x,y)	double precision real
dexp (x)	exp (x)	double precision real
dim (x,y)	dim (x,y)	default real
dint (a)	aint (a)	double precision real
dlog (x)	log (x)	double precision real
dlog10 (x)	log10 (x)	double precision real
• dmax1 (a1,a2,a3,...) Optional a3,...	max (a1,a2,a3,...) Optional a3,...	double precision real
• dmin1 (a1,a2,a3,...) Optional a3,...	min (a1,a2,a3,...) Optional a3,...	double precision real
dmod (a,p)	mod (a,p)	double precision real
dnint (a)	anint (a)	double precision real
dprod (x,y)	dprod (x,y)	default real
dsign (a,b)	sign (a,b)	double precision real
dsin (x)	sin (x)	double precision real
dsinh (x)	sinh (x)	double precision real
dsqrt (x)	sqrt (x)	double precision real
dtan (x)	tan (x)	double precision real
dtanh (x)	tanh (x)	double precision real
exp (x)	exp (x)	default real
• float (a)	real (a)	default integer
iabs (a)	abs (a)	default integer
• ichar (c)	ichar (c)	default character
idim (x,y)	dim (x,y)	default integer
• idint (a)	int (a)	double precision real
idnint (a)	nint (a)	double precision real
• ifix (a)	int (a)	default real
index (string, substring)	index (string, substring)	default character
• int (a)	int (a)	default real
isign (a,b)	sign (a,b)	default integer
len (string)	len (string)	default character
• lge (string_a, string_b)	lge (string_a, string_b)	default character
• lgt (string_a, string_b)	lgt (string_a, string_b)	default character
• lle (string_a, string_b)	lle (string_a, string_b)	default character
• llt (string_a, string_b)	llt (string_a, string_b)	default character

• max0 (a1,a2,a3,...)	max (a1,a2,a3,...)	default integer
Optional a3,...	Optional a3,...	
• max1 (a1,a2,a3,...)	int (max (a1,a2,a3,...))	default real
Optional a3,...	Optional a3,...	
• min0 (a1,a2,a3,...)	min (a1,a2,a3,...)	default integer
Optional a3,...	Optional a3,...	
• min1 (a1,a2,a3,...)	int (min (a1,a2,a3,...))	default real
Optional a3,...	Optional a3,...	
mod (a,p)	mod (a,p)	default integer
nint (a)	nint (a)	default real
• real (a)	real (a)	default integer
sign (a,b)	sign (a,b)	default real
sin (x)	sin (x)	default real
sinh (x)	sinh (x)	default real
• sngl (a)	real (a)	double precision real
sqrt (x)	sqrt (x)	default real
tan (x)	tan (x)	default real
tanh (x)	tanh (x)	default real

• These specific intrinsic function names must not be used as an actual argument. However, they may be enclosed in a function subprogram of a different name and be passed that way.

B

Syntax Rules

This appendix contains two parts. The first part is an extraction of all syntax rules and constraints in the order in which they occur in the Fortran standard. The second part is a cross reference with an entry for each terminal symbol and each nonterminal symbol in the syntax rules.

B.1 Notation Used in the Syntax Rules

Syntax rules are used to help describe the form that Fortran lexical tokens, statements, and constructs may take. These syntax rules are expressed in a variation of Backus-Naur form (BNF) in which

1. Characters from the Fortran character set are to be written as shown, except where otherwise noted.

2. Lowercase italicized letters and words (often hyphenated and abbreviated) represent general syntactic classes for which specific syntactic entities must be substituted in actual statements.

Some common abbreviations used in syntactic terms are

stmt	for	statement	*attr*	for	attribute
expr	for	expression	*decl*	for	declaration
spec	for	specifier	*def*	for	definition
int	for	integer	*desc*	for	descriptor
arg	for	argument	*op*	for	operator

3. The syntactic metasymbols used are

is	introduces a syntactic class definition
or	introduces a syntactic class alternative
[ ]	encloses an optional item
[ ] ...	encloses an optionally repeated item which may occur zero or more times
■	continues a syntax rule

4. Each syntax rule is given a unique identifying number of the form R*snn*, where *s* is a one- or two-digit section number of the Fortran standard and *nn* is a two-digit sequence number within that section. The syntax rules are distributed as appropriate throughout the text, and are referenced by number as needed. Some rules in Sections 2 and 3 of the Fortran standard are more fully described in later sections; in such cases, the section number *s* is the number of the later section where the rule is repeated.

5. The syntax rules are not a complete and accurate syntax description of Fortran, and cannot be used to generate automatically a Fortran parser; where a syntax rule is incomplete, it is accompanied by the corresponding constraints.

6. A **constraint** is a restriction on the syntax rule that is capable of being checked by a compiler. Standard-conforming Fortran compilers must have the capability of detecting all deviations from the rules and the constraints given in this appendix.

An example of the use of syntax rules is

> *int-literal-constant*   **is** *digit* [*digit*] ...

The following forms are examples of forms for an integer literal constant allowed by the above rule:

digit
digit digit
digit digit digit digit
digit digit digit digit digit digit digit digit

When specific entities are substituted for *digit*, actual integer literal constants might be

```
4
67
1999
10243852
```

B.1.1 Assumed Syntax Rules

To minimize the number of additional syntax rules and convey appropriate constraint information, the following rules are assumed. The letters "*xyz*" stand for any legal syntactic class phrase.

xyz-list	**is** *xyz* [, *xyz*] ...
xyz-name	**is** *name*
scalar-xyz	**is** *xyz*

Contraint:
scalar-xyz must be scalar.

B.1.2 Syntax Conventions and Characteristics

1. Any syntactic class name ending in "*-stmt*" follows the source form statement rules: it must be delimited by end-of-line or semicolon and may be labeled unless it forms part of another statement (such as an if or where statement). Conversely, everything considered to be a source form statement is given a "*-stmt*" ending in the syntax rules.

2. The rules on statement ordering are described rigorously in the definition of *program-unit* (R202-R216). Expression hierarchy is described rigorously in the definition of *expr* (R723).

3. The suffix "*-spec*" is used consistently for specifiers, such as keyword type parameters, keyword actual arguments, and input/output statement specifiers. It also is used for type declaration attribute specifications (for example, "*array-spec*" in R512), and in a few other cases.

4. When reference is made to a type parameter, including the surrounding parentheses, the term "selector" is used. See, for example, "*length-selector*" (R507) and "*kind-selector*" (R505).

5. The term "*subscript*" (for example, R615, R616, and R617) is used consistently in array definitions.

B.2 Syntax Rules and Constraints

Each of the following sections contains the syntax rules and constraints from one section of the Fortran standard.

B.2.1 Introduction

B.2.2 Fortran Terms and Concepts

R201	*executable-program*	**is**	*program-unit*
			[*program-unit*] ...
R202	*program-unit*	**is**	*main-program*
		or	*external-subprogram*
		or	*module*
		or	*block-data*
R1101	*main-program*	**is**	[*program-stmt*]
			[*specification-part*]
			[*execution-part*]
			[*internal-subprogram-part*]
			end-program-stmt
R203	*external-subprogram*	**is**	*function-subprogram*
		or	*subroutine-subprogram*
R1215	*function-subprogram*	**is**	*function-stmt*
			[*specification-part*]
			[*execution-part*]
			[*internal-subprogram-part*]
			end-function-stmt
R1219	*subroutine-subprogram*	**is**	*subroutine-stmt*
			[*specification-part*]
			[*execution-part*]
			[*internal-subprogram-part*]
			end-subroutine-stmt
R1104	*module*	**is**	*module-stmt*
			[*specification-part*]
			[*module-subprogram-part*]
			end-module-stmt
R1110	*block-data*	**is**	*block-data-stmt*
			[*specification-part*]
			end-block-data-stmt
R204	*specification-part*	**is**	[*use-stmt*] ...
			[*implicit-part*]
			[*declaration-construct*] ...
R205	*implicit-part*	**is**	[*implicit-part-stmt*] ...
			implicit-stmt
R206	*implicit-part-stmt*	**is**	*implicit-stmt*
		or	*parameter-stmt*
		or	*format-stmt*
		or	*entry-stmt*
R207	*declaration-construct*	**is**	*derived-type-def*
		or	*interface-block*
		or	*type-declaration-stmt*
		or	*specification-stmt*
		or	*parameter-stmt*
		or	*format-stmt*
		or	*entry-stmt*
		or	*stmt-function-stmt*

R208 *execution-part* **is** *executable-construct*
                               [*execution-part-construct*] ...

R209 *execution-part-construct* **is** *executable-construct*
                                    or *format-stmt*
                                    or *data-stmt*
                                    or *entry-stmt*

R210 *internal-subprogram-part* **is** *contains-stmt*
                                          internal-subprogram
                                          [*internal-subprogram*] ...

R211 *internal-subprogram* **is** *function-subprogram*
                              or *subroutine-subprogram*

R212 *module-subprogram-part* **is** *contains-stmt*
                                        module-subprogram
                                        [*module-subprogram*] ...

R213 *module-subprogram* **is** *function-subprogram*
                            or *subroutine-subprogram*

R214 *specification-stmt* **is** *access-stmt*
                             or *allocatable-stmt*
                             or *common-stmt*
                             or *data-stmt*
                             or *dimension-stmt*
                             or *equivalence-stmt*
                             or *external-stmt*
                             or *intent-stmt*
                             or *intrinsic-stmt*
                             or *namelist-stmt*
                             or *optional-stmt*
                             or *pointer-stmt*
                             or *save-stmt*
                             or *target-stmt*

R215 *executable-construct* **is** *action-stmt*
                               or *case-construct*
                               or *do-construct*
                               or *if-construct*
                               or *where-construct*

R216 *action-stmt* **is** *allocate-stmt*
                      or *assignment-stmt*
                      or *backspace-stmt*
                      or *call-stmt*
                      or *close-stmt*
                      or *computed-goto-stmt*
                      or *continue-stmt*
                      or *cycle-stmt*
                      or *deallocate-stmt*
                      or *endfile-stmt*
                      or *end-function-stmt*
                      or *end-program-stmt*
                      or *end-subroutine-stmt*
                      or *exit-stmt*
                      or *goto-stmt*
                      or *if-stmt*
                      or *inquire-stmt*
                      or *nullify-stmt*
                      or *open-stmt*
                      or *pointer-assignment-stmt*
                      or *print-stmt*
                      or *read-stmt*
                      or *return-stmt*
                      or *rewind-stmt*

		or	*stop-stmt*
		or	*where-stmt*
		or	*write-stmt*
		or	*arithmetic-if-stmt*
		or	*assign-stmt*
		or	*assigned-goto-stmt*
		or	*pause-stmt*

Constraint: An *execution-part* must not contain an *end-function-stmt*, *end-program-stmt*, or *end-subroutine-stmt*.

B.2.3 Characters, Lexical Tokens, and Source Form

R301	*character*	**is**	*alphanumeric-character*
		or	*special-character*
R302	*alphanumeric-character*	**is**	*letter*
		or	*digit*
		or	*underscore*
R303	*underscore*	**is**	_
R304	*name*	**is**	*letter* [*alphanumeric-character*] ...

Constraint: The maximum length of a *name* is 31 characters.

R305	*constant*	**is**	*literal-constant*
		or	*named-constant*
R306	*literal-constant*	**is**	*int-literal-constant*
		or	*real-literal-constant*
		or	*complex-literal-constant*
		or	*logical-literal-constant*
		or	*char-literal-constant*
		or	*boz-literal-constant*
R307	*named-constant*	**is**	*name*
R308	*int-constant*	**is**	*constant*

Constraint: *int-constant* must be of type integer.

R309	*char-constant*	**is**	*constant*

Constraint: *char-constant* must be of type character.

R310	*intrinsic-operator*	**is**	*power-op*
		or	*mult-op*
		or	*add-op*
		or	*concat-op*
		or	*rel-op*
		or	*not-op*
		or	*and-op*
		or	*or-op*
		or	*equiv-op*
R708	*power-op*	**is**	**
R709	*mult-op*	**is**	*
		or	/
R710	*add-op*	**is**	+
		or	–
R712	*concat-op*	**is**	//
R714	*rel-op*	**is**	.eq.
		or	.ne.
		or	.lt.
		or	.le.
		or	.gt.
		or	.ge.
		or	==
		or	/=
		or	<

			or <=
			or >
			or >=
R719	*not-op*	**is**	.not.
R720	*and-op*	**is**	.and.
R721	*or-op*	**is**	.or.
R722	*equiv-op*	**is**	.eqv.
		or	.neqv.
R311	*defined-operator*	**is**	*defined-unary-op*
		or	*defined-binary-op*
		or	*extended-intrinsic-op*
R704	*defined-unary-op*	**is**	. *letter* [*letter*] ... .
R724	*defined-binary-op*	**is**	. *letter* [*letter*] ... .
R312	*extended-intrinsic-op*	**is**	*intrinsic-operator*

Constraint: A *defined-unary-op* and a *defined-binary-op* must not contain more than 31 letters and must not be the same as any *intrinsic-operator* or *logical-literal-constant*.

| R313 | *label* | **is** *digit* [*digit* [*digit* [*digit* [*digit*]]]] |

Constraint: At least one digit in a *label* must be nonzero.

B.2.4 Intrinsic and Derived Data Types

R401	*signed-digit-string*	**is**	[*sign*] *digit-string*
R402	*digit-string*	**is**	*digit* [*digit*] ...
R403	*signed-int-literal-constant*	**is**	[*sign*] *int-literal-constant*
R404	*int-literal-constant*	**is**	*digit-string* [_ *kind-param*]
R405	*kind-param*	**is**	*digit-string*
		or	*scalar-int-constant-name*
R406	*sign*	**is**	+
		or	-

Constraint: The value of *kind-param* must be nonnegative.
Constraint: The value of *kind-param* must specify a representation method that exists on the processor.

R407	*boz-literal-constant*	**is**	*binary-constant*
		or	*octal-constant*
		or	*hex-constant*

Constraint: A *boz-literal-constant* may appear only in a data statement.

| R408 | *binary-constant* | **is** | b ' *digit* [*digit*] ... ' |
| | | **or** | b " *digit* [*digit*] ... " |

Constraint: *digit* must have one of the values 0 or 1.

| R409 | *octal-constant* | **is** | o ' *digit* [*digit*] ... ' |
| | | **or** | o " *digit* [*digit*] ... " |

Constraint: *digit* must have one of the values 0 through 7.

R410	*hex-constant*	**is**	z ' *hex-digit* [*hex-digit*] ... '
		or	z " *hex-digit* [*hex-digit*] ... "
R411	*hex-digit*	**is**	*digit*
		or	a
		or	b
		or	c
		or	d
		or	e
		or	f
R412	*signed-real-literal-constant*	**is**	[*sign*] *real-literal-constant*
R413	*real-literal-constant*	**is**	*significand* [*exponent-letter exponent*] [_ *kind-param*]
		or	*digit-string exponent-letter exponent* [_ *kind-param*]

R414	significand	is	digit-string . [digit-string]
		or	. digit-string
R415	exponent-letter	is	e
		or	d
R416	exponent	is	signed-digit-string

Constraint: If both kind-param and exponent-letter are present, exponent-letter must be e.

Constraint: The value of kind-param must specify an approximation method that exists on the processor.

R417	complex-literal-constant	is	(real-part , imag-part)
R418	real-part	is	signed-int-literal-constant
		or	signed-real-literal-constant
R419	imag-part	is	signed-int-literal-constant
		or	signed-real-literal-constant
R420	char-literal-constant	is	[kind-param _] ' [rep-char] ... '
		or	[kind-param _] " [rep-char] ... "

Constraint: The value of kind-param must specify a representation method that exists on the processor.

R421	logical-literal-constant	is	.true. [_ kind-param]
		or	.false. [_ kind-param]

Constraint: The value of kind-param must specify a representation method that exists on the processor.

R422	derived-type-def	is	derived-type-stmt
			[private-sequence-stmt] ...
			component-def-stmt
			[component-def-stmt] ...
			end-type-stmt

R423	private-sequence-stmt	is	private
		or	sequence
R424	derived-type-stmt	is	type [[, access-spec] ::] type-name

Constraint: The same private-sequence-stmt must not appear more than once in a given derived-type-def.

Constraint: If sequence is present, all derived types specified in component definitions must be sequence types.

Constraint: An access-spec (5.1.2.2) or a private statement within the definition is permitted only if the type definition is within the specification part of a module.

Constraint: If a component of a derived type is of a type declared to be private, either the derived type definition must contain the private statement or the derived type must be private.

Constraint: A derived type type-name must not be the same as the name of any intrinsic type nor the same as any other accessible derived type type-name.

R425	end-type-stmt	is	end type [type-name]

Constraint: If end type is followed by a type-name, the type-name must be the same as that in the corresponding derived-type-stmt.

R426	component-def-stmt	is	type-spec [[, component-attr-spec-list] ::] ■
			■ component-decl-list
R427	component-attr-spec	is	pointer
		or	dimension (component-array-spec)

Constraint: No component-attr-spec may appear more than once in a given component-def-stmt.

Constraint: If the pointer attribute is not specified for a component, a type-spec in the component-def-stmt must specify an intrinsic type or a previously defined derived type.

Constraint: If the pointer attribute is specified for a component, a type-spec in the component-def-stmt must specify an intrinsic type or any accessible derived type including the type being defined.

R428 *component-array-spec* **is** *explicit-shape-spec-list*
            or *deferred-shape-spec-list*
R429 *component-decl*   **is** *component-name* [(*component-array-spec*)] ■
             ■ [* *char-length*]

Constraint: If the pointer attribute is not specified, each *component-array-spec* must be an *explicit-shape-spec-list*.

Constraint: If the pointer attribute is specified, each *component-array-spec* must be a *deferred-shape-spec-list*.

Constraint: The * *char-length* option is permitted only if the type specified is character.

Constraint: A *char-length* in a *component-decl* or the *char-selector* in a *type-spec* (5.1, 5.1.1.5) must be a constant specification expression (7.1.6.2).

Constraint: Each bound in the *explicit-shape-spec* (R428) must be a constant specification expression (7.1.6.2).

R430 *structure-constructor* **is** *type-name* (*expr-list*)
R431 *array-constructor*   **is** (/ *ac-value-list* /)
R432 *ac-value*   **is** *expr*
            or *ac-implied-do*
R433 *ac-implied-do*   **is** (*ac-value-list* , *ac-implied-do-control*)
R434 *ac-implied-do-control* **is** *ac-do-variable* = *scalar-int-expr* , ■
             ■ *scalar-int-expr* [, *scalar-int-expr*]
R435 *ac-do-variable*   **is** *scalar-int-variable*

Constraint: *ac-do-variable* must be a named variable.

Constraint: Each *ac-value* expression in the *array-constructor* must have the same type and type parameters.

B.2.5 Data Object Declarations and Specifications

R501 *type-declaration-stmt* **is** *type-spec* [[, *attr-spec*] ... ::] *entity-decl-list*
R502 *type-spec*   **is** `integer` [*kind-selector*]
            or `real` [*kind-selector*]
            or `double precision`
            or `complex` [*kind-selector*]
            or `character` [*char-selector*]
            or `logical` [*kind-selector*]
            or `type` (*type-name*)
R503 *attr-spec*   **is** `parameter`
            or *access-spec*
            or `allocatable`
            or `dimension` (*array-spec*)
            or `external`
            or `intent` (*intent-spec*)
            or `intrinsic`
            or `optional`
            or `pointer`
            or `save`
            or `target`
R504 *entity-decl*   **is** *object-name* [(*array-spec*)] ■
             ■ [* *char-length*] [= *initialization-expr*]
            or *function-name* [(*array-spec*)] [* *char-length*]
R505 *kind-selector*   **is** ([`kind` =] *scalar-int-initialization-expr*)

Constraint: The same *attr-spec* must not appear more than once in a given *type-declaration-stmt*.

Constraint: The *function-name* must be the name of an external function, an intrinsic function, a function dummy procedure, or a statement function.

Constraint: The = *initialization-expr* must appear if the statement contains a parameter attribute (5.1.2.1).

Constraint: If = *initialization-expr* appears, a double colon separator must appear before the *entity-decl-list*.

Constraint: The = *initialization-expr* must not appear if *object-name* is a dummy argument, a function result, an object in a named common block unless the type declaration is in a block data program unit, an object in blank common, an allocatable array, a pointer, an external name, an intrinsic name, or an automatic object.

Constraint: The * *char-length* option is permitted only if the type specified is character.

Constraint: The `allocatable` attribute may be used only when declaring an array that is not a dummy argument or a function result.

Constraint: An array declared with a pointer or an `allocatable` attribute must be specified with an *array-spec* that is a *deferred-shape-spec-list* (5.1.2.4.3).

Constraint: An *array-spec* for a *function-name* that does not have the pointer attribute must be an *explicit-shape-spec-list*.

Constraint: An *array-spec* for a *function-name* that does have the pointer attribute must be a *deferred-shape-spec-list*.

Constraint: If the `pointer` attribute is specified, the target, intent, external, or `intrinsic` attribute must not be specified.

Constraint: If the `target` attribute is specified, the pointer, external, intrinsic, or parameter attribute must not be specified.

Constraint: The `parameter` attribute must not be specified for dummy arguments, pointers, allocatable arrays, functions, or objects in a common block.

Constraint: The `intent` and `optional` attributes may be specified only for dummy arguments.

Constraint: An entity must not have the `public` attribute if its type has the `private` attribute.

Constraint: The save attribute must not be specified for an object that is in a common block, a dummy argument, a procedure, a function result, or an automatic data object.

Constraint: An entity must not have the `external` attribute if it has the `intrinsic` attribute.

Constraint: An entity in a *type-declaration-stmt* must not have the `external` or `intrinsic` attribute specified unless it is a function.

Constraint: An array must not have both the `allocatable` attribute and the `pointer` attribute.

Constraint: An entity must not be given explicitly any attribute more than once in a scoping unit.

Constraint: The value of *scalar-int-initialization-expr* must be nonnegative and must specify a representation method that exists on the processor.

R506   *char-selector*   **is**   *length-selector*
                                         or   (`len` = *type-param-value* , ■
                                                 ■ `kind` = *scalar-int-initialization-expr*)
                                         or   (*type-param-value* , ■
                                                   ■ [`kind` =] *scalar-int-initialization-expr*)
                                         or   (`kind` = *scalar-int-initialization-expr* ■
                                                   ■ [, `len` = *type-param-value*])

R507   *length-selector*   **is**   ([`len` =] *type-param-value*)
                                         or   * *char-length* [,]

R508   *char-length*   **is**   (*type-param-value*)
                                         or   *scalar-int-literal-constant*

Constraint: The optional comma in a *length-selector* is permitted only in a *type-spec* in a *type-declaration-stmt*.

Constraint: The optional comma in a *length-selector* is permitted only if no double colon separator appears in the *type-declaration-stmt*.

Constraint: The value of *scalar-int-initialization-expr* must be nonnegative and must specify a representation method that exists on the processor.

Constraint: The *scalar-int-literal-constant* must not include a *kind-param*.

R509   *type-param-value*   **is**   *specification-expr*
                                    or   *

Constraint: A function name must not be declared with an asterisk *type-param-value* if the function is an internal or module function, array-valued, pointer-valued, or recursive.

R510   *access-spec*   **is**   `public`
                                    or   `private`

Constraint: An *access-spec* attribute may appear only in the scoping unit of a module.

R511   *intent-spec*   **is**   `in`
                                    or   `out`
                                    or   `inout`

Constraint: The `intent` attribute must not be specified for a dummy argument that is a dummy procedure or a dummy pointer.

R512   *array-spec*   **is**   *explicit-shape-spec-list*
                                    or   *assumed-shape-spec-list*
                                    or   *deferred-shape-spec-list*
                                    or   *assumed-size-spec*

Constraint: The maximum rank is seven.

R513   *explicit-shape-spec*   **is**   [*lower-bound* :] *upper-bound*
R514   *lower-bound*   **is**   *specification-expr*
R515   *upper-bound*   **is**   *specification-expr*

Constraint: An explicit-shape array whose bounds depend on the values of nonconstant expressions must be a dummy argument, a function result, or an automatic array of a procedure.

R516   *assumed-shape-spec*   **is**   [*lower-bound*] :
R517   *deferred-shape-spec*   **is**   :
R518   *assumed-size-spec*   **is**   [*explicit-shape-spec-list* ,] [*lower-bound* :] *

Constraint: The function name of an array-valued function must not be declared as an assumed-size array.

R519   *intent-stmt*   **is**   `intent` (*intent-spec*) [::] *dummy-arg-name-list*

Constraint: An *intent-stmt* may appear only in the *specification-part* of a subprogram or an interface body (12.3.2.1).

Constraint: *dummy-arg-name* must not be the name of a dummy procedure or a dummy pointer.

R520   *optional-stmt*   **is**   `optional` [::] *dummy-arg-name-list*

Constraint: An *optional-stmt* may occur only in the scoping unit of a subprogram or an interface body.

R521   *access-stmt*   **is**   *access-spec* [[::] *access-id-list*]
R522   *access-id*   **is**   *use-name*
                                    or   *generic-spec*

Constraint: An *access-stmt* may appear only in the scoping unit of a module. Only one accessibility statement with an omitted *access-id-list* is permitted in the scoping unit of a module.

Constraint: Each *use-name* must be the name of a named variable, procedure, derived type, named constant, or namelist group.

Constraint: A module procedure that has a dummy argument or function result of a type that has `private` accessibility must have `private` accessibility and must not have a generic identifier that has `public` accessibility.

R523   *save-stmt*   **is**   `save` [[::] *saved-entity-list*]
R524   *saved-entity*   **is**   *object-name*
                                    or   / *common-block-name* /

Constraint: An *object-name* must not be a dummy argument name, a procedure name, a function result name, an automatic data object name, or the name of an entity in a common block.

Constraint: If a save statement with an omitted saved entity list occurs in a scoping unit, no other explicit occurrence of the save attribute or save statement is permitted in the same scoping unit.

R525   *dimension-stmt*   is   dimension [::] *array-name* (*array-spec*) ■
                                      ■ [, *array-name* (*array-spec*)] ...

R526   *allocatable-stmt*   is   allocatable [::] *array-name* ■
                                      ■ [(*deferred-shape-spec-list*)] ■
                                      ■ [, *array-name* [(*deferred-shape-spec-list*)]] ...

Constraint: The *array-name* must not be a dummy argument or function result.
Constraint: If the dimension attribute for an *array-name* is specified elsewhere in the scoping unit, the *array-spec* must be a *deferred-shape-spec-list*.

R527   *pointer-stmt*   is   pointer [::] *object-name* ■
                                      ■ [(*deferred-shape-spec-list*)] ■
                                      ■ [, *object-name* [(*deferred-shape-spec-list*)]] ...

Constraint: The intent attribute must not be specified for an *object-name*.
Constraint: If the dimension attribute for an *object-name* is specified elsewhere in the scoping unit, the *array-spec* must be a *deferred-shape-spec-list*.
Constraint: The parameter attribute must not be specified for an *object-name*.

R528   *target-stmt*   is   target [::] *object-name* [(*array-spec*)] ■
                                      ■ [, *object-name* [(*array-spec*)]] ...

Constraint: The parameter attribute must not be specified for an *object-name*.

R529   *data-stmt*   is   data *data-stmt-set* [[,] *data-stmt-set*] ...
R530   *data-stmt-set*   is   *data-stmt-object-list* / *data-stmt-value-list* /
R531   *data-stmt-object*   is   *variable*
                                 or   *data-implied-do*
R532   *data-stmt-value*   is   [*data-stmt-repeat* *] *data-stmt-constant*
R533   *data-stmt-constant*   is   *scalar-constant*
                                 or   *signed-int-literal-constant*
                                 or   *signed-real-literal-constant*
                                 or   *structure-constructor*
                                 or   *boz-literal-constant*
R534   *data-stmt-repeat*   is   *scalar-int-constant*
R535   *data-implied-do*   is   (*data-i-do-object-list* , *data-i-do-variable* = ■
                                      ■ *scalar-int-expr* , *scalar-int-expr* [, *scalar-int-expr*])
R536   *data-i-do-object*   is   *array-element*
                                 or   *scalar-structure-component*
                                 or   *data-implied-do*

Constraint: The *array-element* must not have a constant parent.
Constraint: The *scalar-structure-component* must not have a constant parent.

R537   *data-i-do-variable*   is   *scalar-int-variable*

Constraint: *data-i-do-variable* must be a named variable.
Constraint: The data statement repeat factor must be positive or zero. If the data statement repeat factor is a named constant, it must have been declared previously in the scoping unit or made accessible by use association or host association.
Constraint: If a *data-stmt-constant* is a *structure-constructor*, each component must be an initialization expression.
Constraint: In a *variable* that is a *data-stmt-object*, any subscript, section subscript, substring starting point, and substring ending point must be an initialization expression.
Constraint: A variable whose name or designator is included in a *data-stmt-object-list* or a *data-i-do-object-list* must not be: a dummy argument, made accessible by use association or host association, in a named common block unless the data statement is in a block data program unit, in a blank common block, a function name, a function result name, an automatic object, a pointer, or an allocatable array.

Constraint: In an *array-element* or a *scalar-structure-component* that is a *data-i-do-object*, any subscript must be an expression whose primaries are either constants or do variables of the containing *data-implied-dos*, and each operation must be intrinsic.

Constraint: A *scalar-int-expr* of a *data-implied-do* must involve as primaries only constants or do variables of the containing *data-implied-dos*, and each operation must be intrinsic.

R538 *parameter-stmt*   **is** parameter (*named-constant-def-list*)

R539 *named-constant-def* **is** *named-constant* = *initialization-expr*

R540 *implicit-stmt*   **is** implicit *implicit-spec-list*
                              or implicit none

R541 *implicit-spec*   **is** *type-spec* (*letter-spec-list*)

R542 *letter-spec*   **is** *letter* [- *letter*]

Constraint: If implicit none is specified in a scoping unit, it must precede any parameter statements that appear in the scoping unit and there must be no other implicit statements in the scoping unit.

Constraint: If the minus and second letter appear, the second letter must follow the first letter alphabetically.

R543 *namelist-stmt*   **is** namelist / *namelist-group-name* / ■
                               ■ *namelist-group-object-list* ■
                               ■ [[,] / *namelist-group-name* / ■
                               ■ *namelist-group-object-list*] ...

R544 *namelist-group-object* **is** *variable-name*

Constraint: A *namelist-group-object* must not be an array dummy argument with a nonconstant bound, a variable with nonconstant character length, an automatic object, a pointer, a variable of a type that has an ultimate component that is a pointer, or an allocatable array.

Constraint: If a *namelist-group-name* has the public attribute, no item in the *namelist-group-object-list* may have the private attribute.

R545 *equivalence-stmt*   **is** equivalence *equivalence-set-list*

R546 *equivalence-set*   **is** (*equivalence-object* , *equivalence-object-list*)

R547 *equivalence-object* **is** *variable-name*
                                or *array-element*
                                or *substring*

Constraint: An *equivalence-object* must not be a dummy argument, a pointer, an allocatable array, an object of a nonsequence derived type or of a sequence derived type containing a pointer at any level of component selection, an automatic object, a function name, an entry name, a result name, a named constant, a structure component, or a subobject of any of the preceding objects.

Constraint: Each subscript or substring range expression in an *equivalence-object* must be an integer initialization expression (7.1.6.1).

Constraint: If an *equivalence-object* is of type default integer, default real, double precision real, default complex, default logical, or numeric sequence type, all of the objects in the equivalence set must be of these types.

Constraint: If an *equivalence-object* is of type default character or character sequence type, all of the objects in the equivalence set must be of these types.

Constraint: If an *equivalence-object* is of a derived type that is not a numeric sequence or character sequence type, all of the objects in the equivalence set must be of the same type.

Constraint: If an *equivalence-object* is of an intrinsic type other than default integer, default real, double precision real, default complex, default logical, or default character, all of the objects in the equivalence set must be of the same type with the same kind type parameter value.

R548 *common-stmt*   **is** common [/ [*common-block-name*] /] ■
                               ■ *common-block-object-list* ■
                               ■ [[,] / [*common-block-name*] /] ■
                               ■ *common-block-object-list*] ...

R549   *common-block-object*   **is** *variable-name* [(*explicit-shape-spec-list*)]
Constraint: Only one appearance of a given *variable-name* is permitted in all *common-block-object-list*s within a scoping unit.
Constraint: A *common-block-object* must not be a dummy argument, an allocatable array, an automatic object, a function name, an entry name, or a result name.
Constraint: Each bound in the *explicit-shape-spec* must be a constant specification expression (7.1.6.2).
Constraint: If a *common-block-object* is of a derived type, it must be a sequence type (4.4.1).
Constraint: If a *variable-name* appears with an *explicit-shape-spec-list*, it must not have the pointer attribute.

B.2.6 Use of Data Objects

R601   *variable*   **is** *scalar-variable-name*
                             or *array-variable-name*
                             or *subobject*
Constraint: *array-variable-name* must be the name of a data object that is an array.
Constraint: *array-variable-name* must not have the parameter attribute.
Constraint: *scalar-variable-name* must not have the parameter attribute.
Constraint: *subobject* must not be a subobject designator (for example, a substring) whose parent is a constant.
R602   *subobject*   **is** *array-element*
                             or *array-section*
                             or *structure-component*
                             or *substring*
R603   *logical-variable*   **is** *variable*
Constraint: *logical-variable* must be of type logical.
R604   *default-logical-variable* **is** *variable*
Constraint: *default-logical-variable* must be of type default logical.
R605   *char-variable*   **is** *variable*
Constraint: *char-variable* must be of type character.
R606   *default-char-variable*   **is** *variable*
Constraint: *default-char-variable* must be of type default character.
R607   *int-variable*   **is** *variable*
Constraint: *int-variable* must be of type integer.
R608   *default-int-variable*   **is** *variable*
Constraint: *default-int-variable* must be of type default integer.
R609   *substring*   **is** *parent-string* (*substring-range*)
R610   *parent-string*   **is** *scalar-variable-name*
                             or *array-element*
                             or *scalar-structure-component*
                             or *scalar-constant*
R611   *substring-range*   **is** [*scalar-int-expr*] : [*scalar-int-expr*]
Constraint: *parent-string* must be of type character.
R612   *data-ref*   **is** *part-ref* [% *part-ref*] ...
R613   *part-ref*   **is** *part-name* [(*section-subscript-list*)]
Constraint: In a *data-ref*, each *part-name* except the rightmost must be of derived type.
Constraint: In a *data-ref*, each *part-name* except the leftmost must be the name of a component of the derived type definition of the type of the preceding *part-name*.
Constraint: In a *part-ref* containing a *section-subscript-list*, the number of *section-subscripts* must equal the rank of *part-name*.
Constraint: In a *data-ref*, there must not be more than one *part-ref* with nonzero rank. A *part-name* to the right of a *part-ref* with nonzero rank must not have the pointer attribute.

R614   *structure-component*   **is** *data-ref*
Constraint: In a *structure-component*, there must be more than one *part-ref* and the right-
most *part-ref* must be of the form *part-nume*.
R615   *array-element*   **is** *data-ref*
Constraint: In an *array-element*, every *part-ref* must have rank zero and the last *part-ref*
must contain a *subscript-list*.
R616   *array-section*   **is** *data-ref* [(*substring-range*)]
Constraint: In an *array-section*, exactly one *part-ref* must have nonzero rank, and either
the final *part-ref* has a *section-subscript-list* with nonzero rank or another
part-ref has nonzero rank.
Constraint: In an *array-section* with a *substring-range*, the rightmost *part-name* must be of
type character.
R617   *subscript*   **is** *scalar-int-expr*
R618   *section-subscript*   **is** *subscript*
        or *subscript-triplet*
        or *vector-subscript*
R619   *subscript-triplet*   **is** [*subscript*] : [*subscript*] [: *stride*]
R620   *stride*   **is** *scalar-int-expr*
R621   *vector-subscript*   **is** *int-expr*
Constraint: A *vector-subscript* must be an integer array expression of rank one.
Constraint: The second *subscript* must not be omitted from a *subscript-triplet* in the last
dimension of an assumed-size array.
R622   *allocate-stmt*   **is** allocate (*allocation-list* ■
        ■ [, stat = *stat-variable*])
R623   *stat-variable*   **is** *scalar-int-variable*
R624   *allocation*   **is** *allocate-object* [(*allocate-shape-spec-list*)]
R625   *allocate-object*   **is** *variable-name*
        or *structure-component*
R626   *allocate-shape-spec*   **is** [*allocate-lower-bound* :] *allocate-upper-bound*
R627   *allocate-lower-bound*   **is** *scalar-int-expr*
R628   *allocate-upper-bound*   **is** *scalar-int-expr*
Constraint: Each *allocate-object* must be a pointer or an allocatable array.
Constraint: The number of *allocate-shape-specs* in an *allocate-shape-spec-list* must be the
same as the rank of the pointer or allocatable array.
R629   *nullify-stmt*   **is** nullify (*pointer-object-list*)
R630   *pointer-object*   **is** *variable-name*
        or *structure-component*
Constraint: Each *pointer-object* must have the pointer attribute.
R631   *deallocate-stmt*   **is** deallocate (*allocate-object-list* ■
        ■ [, stat = *stat-variable*])
Constraint: Each *allocate-object* must be a pointer or an allocatable array.

B.2.7 Expressions and Assignment

R701   *primary*   **is** *constant*
        or *constant-subobject*
        or *variable*
        or *array-constructor*
        or *structure-constructor*
        or *function-reference*
        or (*expr*)
R702   *constant-subobject*   **is** *subobject*
Constraint: *subobject* must be a subobject designator whose parent is a constant.
Constraint: A *variable* that is a *primary* must not be an assumed-size array.
R703   *level-1-expr*   **is** [*defined-unary-op*] *primary*

R704   *defined-unary-op*   **is**   . *letter* [*letter*] ... .
Constraint: A *defined-unary-op* must not contain more than 31 letters and must not be
        the same as any *intrinsic-operator* or *logical-literal-constant*.

R705   *mult-operand*   **is**   *level-1-expr* [*power-op mult-operand*]
R706   *add-operand*   **is**   [*add-operand mult-op*] *mult-operand*
R707   *level-2-expr*   **is**   [[*level-2-expr*] *add-op*] *add-operand*
R708   *power-op*   **is**   **
R709   *mult-op*   **is**   *
                         or /
R710   *add-op*   **is**   +
                         or –
R711   *level-3-expr*   **is**   [*level-3-expr concat-op*] *level-2-expr*
R712   *concat-op*   **is**   //
R713   *level-4-expr*   **is**   [*level-3-expr rel-op*] *level-3-expr*
R714   *rel-op*   **is**   .eq.
                         or .ne.
                         or .lt.
                         or .le.
                         or .gt.
                         or .ge.
                         or ==
                         or /=
                         or <
                         or <=
                         or >
                         or >=
R715   *and-operand*   **is**   [*not-op*] *level-4-expr*
R716   *or-operand*   **is**   [*or-operand and-op*] *and-operand*
R717   *equiv-operand*   **is**   [*equiv-operand or-op*] *or-operand*
R718   *level-5-expr*   **is**   [*level-5-expr equiv-op*] *equiv-operand*
R719   *not-op*   **is**   .not.
R720   *and-op*   **is**   .and.
R721   *or-op*   **is**   .or.
R722   *equiv-op*   **is**   .eqv.
                         or .neqv.
R723   *expr*   **is**   [*expr defined-binary-op*] *level-5-expr*
R724   *defined-binary-op*   **is**   . *letter* [*letter*] ... .
Constraint: A *defined-binary-op* must not contain more than 31 letters and must not be
        the same as any *intrinsic-operator* or *logical-literal-constant*.

R725   *logical-expr*   **is**   *expr*
Constraint: *logical-expr* must be type logical.

R726   *char-expr*   **is**   *expr*
Constraint: *char-expr* must be type character.

R727   *default-char-expr*   **is**   *expr*
Constraint: *default-char-expr* must be of type default character.

R728   *int-expr*   **is**   *expr*
Constraint: *int-expr* must be type integer.

R729   *numeric-expr*   **is**   *expr*
Constraint: *numeric-expr* must be of type integer, real or complex.

R730   *initialization-expr*   **is**   *expr*
Constraint: An *initialization-expr* must be an initialization expression.

R731   *char-initialization-expr* **is**   *char-expr*
Constraint: A *char-initialization-expr* must be an initialization expression.

R732   *int-initialization-expr* **is**   *int-expr*

Constraint: An *int-initialization-expr* must be an initialization expression.

R733   *logical-initialization-expr*   **is**   *logical-expr*

Constraint: A *logical-initialization-expr* must be an initialization expression.

R734   *specification-expr*   **is**   *scalar-int-expr*

Constraint: The *scalar-int-expr* must be a restricted expression.

R735   *assignment-stmt*   **is**   *variable* = *expr*

Constraint: A *variable* in an *assignment-stmt* must not be an assumed-size array.

R736   *pointer-assignment-stmt*   **is**   *pointer-object* => *target*

R737   *target*   **is**   *variable*
                         or *expr*

Constraint: The *pointer-object* must have the `pointer` attribute.

Constraint: The *variable* must have the `target` attribute or be a subobject of an object with the `target` attribute, or it must have the `pointer` attribute.

Constraint: The *target* must be of the same type, type parameters, and rank as the pointer.

Constraint: The *target* must not be an array section with a vector subscript.

Constraint: The *expr* must deliver a pointer result.

R738   *where-stmt*   **is** `where` (*mask-expr*) *assignment-stmt*

R739   *where-construct*   **is** *where-construct-stmt*
                                 [*assignment-stmt*] ...
                                 [*elsewhere-stmt*
                                  [*assignment-stmt*] ...]
                               end-where-stmt

R740   *where-construct-stmt*   **is** `where` (*mask-expr*)

R741   *mask-expr*   **is** *logical-expr*

R742   *elsewhere-stmt*   **is** `elsewhere`

R743   *end-where-stmt*   **is** `end where`

Constraint: In each *assignment-stmt*, the *mask-expr* and the variable being defined must be arrays of the same shape.

Constraint: The *assignment-stmt* must not be a defined assignment.

B.2.8 Execution Control

R801   *block*   **is** [*execution-part-construct*] ...

R802   *if-construct*   **is** *if-then-stmt*
                                block
                             [*else-if-stmt*
                                 block] ...
                           [*else-stmt*
                                 block]
                                end-if-stmt

R803   *if-then-stmt*   **is** [*if-construct-name* :] `if` (*scalar-logical-expr*) `then`

R804   *else-if-stmt*   **is** `else if` (*scalar-logical-expr*) `then` [*if-construct-name*]

R805   *else-stmt*   **is** `else` [*if-construct-name*]

R806   *end-if-stmt*   **is** `end if` [*if-construct-name*]

Constraint: If the *if-then-stmt* of an *if-construct* is identified by an *if-construct-name*, the corresponding *end-if-stmt* must specify the same *if-construct-name*. If the *if-then-stmt* of an *if-construct* is not identified by an *if-construct-name*, the corresponding *end-if-stmt* must not specify an *if-construct-name*. If an *else-if-stmt* or *else-stmt* is identified by an *if-construct-name*, the corresponding *if-then-stmt* must specify the same *if-construct-name*.

R807   *if-stmt*   **is** `if` (*scalar-logical-expr*) *action-stmt*

Constraint: The *action-stmt* in the *if-stmt* must not be an *if-stmt*, *end-program-stmt*, *end-function-stmt*, or *end-subroutine-stmt*.

R808	*case-construct*	**is**	*select-case-stmt* 　[*case-stmt* 　　*block*] ... 　*end-select-stmt*
R809	*select-case-stmt*	**is**	[*case-construct-name* :] select case (*case-expr*)
R810	*case-stmt*	**is**	case *case-selector* [*case-construct-name*]
R811	*end-select-stmt*	**is**	end select [*case-construct-name*]

Constraint:　If the *select-case-stmt* of a *case-construct* is identified by a *case-construct-name*, the corresponding *end-select-stmt* must specify the same *case-construct-name*. If the *select-case-stmt* of a *case-construct* is not identified by a *case-construct-name*, the corresponding *end-select-stmt* must not specify a *case-construct-name*. If a *case-stmt* is identified by a *case-construct-name*, the corresponding *select-case-stmt* must specify the same *case-construct-name*.

R812	*case-expr*	**is**	*scalar-int-expr*
		or	*scalar-char-expr*
		or	*scalar-logical-expr*
R813	*case-selector*	**is**	(*case-value-range-list*)
		or	default

Constraint:　No more than one of the selectors of one of the case statements may be default.

R814	*case-value-range*	**is**	*case-value*
		or	*case-value* :
		or	: *case-value*
		or	*case-value* : *case-value*
R815	*case-value*	**is**	*scalar-int-initialization-expr*
		or	*scalar-char-initialization-expr*
		or	*scalar-logical-initialization-expr*

Constraint:　For a given *case-construct*, each *case-value* must be of the same type as *case-expr*. For character type, length differences are allowed, but the kind type parameters must be the same.

Constraint:　A *case-value-range* using a colon must not be used if *case-expr* is of type logical.

Constraint:　For a given *case-construct*, the *case-value-ranges* must not overlap; that is, there must be no possible value of the *case-expr* that matches more than one *case-value-range*.

R816	*do-construct*	**is**	*block-do-construct*
		or	*nonblock-do-construct*
R817	*block-do-construct*	**is**	*do-stmt* 　*do-block* 　*end-do*
R818	*do-stmt*	**is**	*label-do-stmt*
		or	*nonlabel-do-stmt*
R819	*label-do-stmt*	**is**	[*do-construct-name* :] do *label* [*loop-control*]
R820	*nonlabel-do-stmt*	**is**	[*do-construct-name* :] do [*loop-control*]
R821	*loop-control*	**is**	[,] *do-variable* = *scalar-numeric-expr* , ■ 　■ *scalar-numeric-expr* [, *scalar-numeric-expr*]
		or	[,] while (*scalar-logical-expr*)
R822	*do-variable*	**is**	*scalar-variable*

Constraint:　The *do-variable* must be a named scalar variable of type integer, default real, or double precision real

Constraint:　Each *scalar-numeric-expr* in *loop-control* must be of type integer, default real, or double precision real

R823	*do-block*	**is**	*block*
R824	*end-do*	**is**	*end-do-stmt*
		or	*continue-stmt*
R825	*end-do-stmt*	**is**	end do [*do-construct-name*]

Constraint: If the *do-stmt* of a *block-do-construct* is identified by a *do-construct-name*, the corresponding *end-do* must be an *end-do-stmt* specifying the same *do-construct-name*. If the *do-stmt* of a *block-do-construct* is not identified by a *do-construct-name*, the corresponding *end-do* must not specify a *do-construct-name*.

Constraint: If the *do-stmt* is a *nonlabel-do-stmt*, the corresponding *end-do* must be an *end-do-stmt*.

Constraint: If the *do-stmt* is a *label-do-stmt*, the corresponding *end-do* must be identified with the same *label*.

R826 *nonblock-do-construct* **is** *action-term-do-construct*
                                   or *outer-shared-do-construct*

R827 *action-term-do-construct* **is** *label-do-stmt*
                                          do-body
                                          do-term-action-stmt

R828 *do-body* **is** [*execution-part-construct*] ...

R829 *do-term-action-stmt* **is** *action-stmt*

Constraint: A *do-term-action-stmt* must not be a *continue-stmt*, a *goto-stmt*, a *return-stmt*, a *stop-stmt*, an *exit-stmt*, a *cycle-stmt*, an *end-function-stmt*, an *end-subroutine-stmt*, an *end-program-stmt*, an *arithmetic-if-stmt*, or an *assigned-goto-stmt*.

Constraint: The *do-term-action-stmt* must be identified with a label and the corresponding *label-do-stmt* must refer to the same label.

R830 *outer-shared-do-construct* **is** *label-do-stmt*
                                        do-body
                                        shared-term-do-construct

R831 *shared-term-do-construct* **is** *outer-shared-do-construct*
                                     or *inner-shared-do-construct*

R832 *inner-shared-do-construct* **is** *label-do-stmt*
                                        do-body
                                        do-term-shared-stmt

R833 *do-term-shared-stmt* **is** *action-stmt*

Constraint: A *do-term-shared-stmt* must not be a *goto-stmt*, a *return-stmt*, a *stop-stmt*, an *exit-stmt*, a *cycle-stmt*, an *end-function-stmt*, an *end-subroutine-stmt*, an *end-program-stmt*, an *arithmetic-if-stmt*, or an *assigned-goto-stmt*.

Constraint: The *do-term-shared-stmt* must be identified with a label and all of the *label-do-stmts* of the *shared-term-do-construct* must refer to the same label.

R834 *cycle-stmt* **is** `cycle` [*do-construct-name*]

Constraint: If a *cycle-stmt* refers to a *do-construct-name*, it must be within the range of that *do-construct*; otherwise, it must be within the range of at least one *do-construct*.

R835 *exit-stmt* **is** `exit` [*do-construct-name*]

Constraint: If an *exit-stmt* refers to a *do-construct-name*, it must be within the range of that *do-construct*; otherwise, it must be within the range of at least one *do-construct*.

R836 *goto-stmt* **is** `go to` *label*

Constraint: The *label* must be the statement label of a branch target statement that appears in the same scoping unit as the *goto-stmt*.

R837 *computed-goto-stmt* **is** `go to` (*label-list*) [,] *scalar-int-expr*

Constraint: Each *label* in *label-list* must be the statement label of a branch target statement that appears in the same scoping unit as the *computed-goto-stmt*.

R838 *assign-stmt* **is** `assign` *label* `to` *scalar-int-variable*

Constraint: The *label* must be the statement label of a branch target statement or *format-stmt* that appears in the same scoping unit as the *assign-stmt*.

Constraint: *scalar-int-variable* must be named and of type default integer.

R839 *assigned-goto-stmt* **is** `go to` *scalar-int-variable* [[,] (*label-list*)]

Constraint: Each *label* in *label-list* must be the statement label of a branch target statement that appears in the same scoping unit as the *assigned-goto-stmt*.

Constraint: *scalar-int-variable* must be named and of type default integer.

R840   *arithmetic-if-stmt*   **is**   if (*scalar-numeric-expr*) *label* , *label* , *label*

Constraint: Each *label* must be the label of a branch target statement that appears in the same scoping unit as the *arithmetic-if-stmt*.

Constraint: The *scalar-numeric-expr* must not be of type complex.

R841   *continue-stmt*   **is**   continue

R842   *stop-stmt*   **is**   stop [*stop-code*]

R843   *stop-code*   **is**   *scalar-char-constant*

                                   or   *digit* [*digit* [*digit* [*digit* [*digit*]]]]

Constraint: *scalar-char-constant* must be of type default character.

R844   *pause-stmt*   **is**   pause [*stop-code*]

B.2.9   Input/Output Statements

R901   *io-unit*   **is**   *external-file-unit*

                                   or   *

                                   or   *internal-file-unit*

R902   *external-file-unit*   **is**   *scalar-int-expr*

R903   *internal-file-unit*   **is**   *default-char-variable*

Constraint: The *default-char-variable* must not be an array section with a vector subscript.

R904   *open-stmt*   **is**   open (*connect-spec-list*)

R905   *connect-spec*   **is**   [unit =] *external-file-unit*

                                   or   iostat = *scalar-default-int-variable*

                                   or   err = *label*

                                   or   file = *file-name-expr*

                                   or   status = *scalar-default-char-expr*

                                   or   access = *scalar-default-char-expr*

                                   or   form = *scalar-default-char-expr*

                                   or   recl = *scalar-int-expr*

                                   or   blank = *scalar-default-char-expr*

                                   or   position = *scalar-default-char-expr*

                                   or   action = *scalar-default-char-expr*

                                   or   delim = *scalar-default-char-expr*

                                   or   pad = *scalar-default-char-expr*

R906   *file-name-expr*   **is**   *scalar-default-char-expr*

Constraint: If the optional characters unit= are omitted from the unit specifier, the unit specifier must be the first item in the *connect-spec-list*.

Constraint: Each specifier must not appear more than once in a given *open-stmt*; an *external-file-unit* must be specified.

Constraint: The *label* used in the err= specifier must be the statement label of a branch target statement that appears in the same scoping unit as the open statement.

R907   *close-stmt*   **is**   close (*close-spec-list*)

R908   *close-spec*   **is**   [unit =] *external-file-unit*

                                   or   iostat = *scalar-default-int-variable*

                                   or   err = *label*

                                   or   status = *scalar-default-char-expr*

Constraint: If the optional characters unit= are omitted from the unit specifier, the unit specifier must be the first item in the *close-spec-list*.

Constraint: Each specifier must not appear more than once in a given *close-stmt*; an *external-file-unit* must be specified.

Constraint: The *label* used in the err= specifier must be the statement label of a branch target statement that appears in the same scoping unit as the close statement.

R909	*read-stmt*	**is**	read (*io-control-spec-list*) [*input-item-list*]
		or	read *format* [, *input-item-list*]
R910	*write-stmt*	**is**	write (*io-control-spec-list*) [*output-item-list*]
R911	*print-stmt*	**is**	print *format* [, *output-item-list*]
R912	*io-control-spec*	**is**	[unit =] *io-unit*
		or	[fmt =] *format*
		or	[nml =] *namelist-group-name*
		or	rec = *scalar-int-expr*
		or	iostat = *scalar-default-int-variable*
		or	err = *label*
		or	end = *label*
		or	advance = *scalar-default-char-expr*
		or	size = *scalar-default-int-variable*
		or	eor = *label*

Constraint: An *io-control-spec-list* must contain exactly one *io-unit* and may contain at most one of each of the other specifiers.

Constraint: An end=, eor=, or size= specifier must not appear in a *write-stmt*.

Constraint: The *label* in the err=, eor=, or end= specifier must be the statement label of a branch target statement that appears in the same scoping unit as the data transfer statement.

Constraint: A *namelist-group-name* must not be present if an *input-item-list* or an *output-item-list* is present in the data transfer statement.

Constraint: An *io-control-spec-list* must not contain both a *format* and a *namelist-group-name*.

Constraint: If the optional characters unit= are omitted from the unit specifier, the unit specifier must be the first item in the control information list.

Constraint: If the optional characters fmt= are omitted from the format specifier, the format specifier must be the second item in the control information list and the first item must be the unit specifier without the optional characters unit=.

Constraint: If the optional characters nml= are omitted from the namelist specifier, the namelist specifier must be the second item in the control information list and the first item must be the unit specifier without the optional characters unit=.

Constraint: If the unit specifier specifies an internal file, the *io-control-spec-list* must not contain a rec= specifier or a *namelist-group-name*.

Constraint: If the rec= specifier is present, an end= specifier must not appear, a *namelist-group-name* must not appear, and the *format*, if any, must not be an asterisk specifying list-directed input/output.

Constraint: An advance= specifier may be present only in a formatted sequential input/output statement with explicit format specification (10.1) whose control information list does not contain an internal file unit specifier.

Constraint: If an eor= specifier is present, an advance= specifier also must appear.

R913	*format*	**is**	*default-char-expr*
		or	*label*
		or	*
		or	*scalar-default-int-variable*

Constraint: The *label* must be the label of a format statement that appears in the same scoping unit as the statement containing the format specifier. ·

R914	*input-item*	**is**	*variable*
		or	*io-implied-do*
R915	*output-item*	**is**	*expr*
		or	*io-implied-do*
R916	*io-implied-do*	**is**	(*io-implied-do-object-list* , *io-implied-do-control*)
R917	*io-implied-do-object*	**is**	*input-item*
		or	*output-item*

R918   *io-implied-do-control*   **is** *do-variable* = *scalar-numeric-expr* , ■
                                       ■ *scalar-numeric-expr* [, *scalar-numeric-expr*]

Constraint: A *variable* that is an *input-item* must not be an assumed-size array.

Constraint: The *do-variable* must be a scalar of type integer, default real, or double precision real.

Constraint: Each *scalar-numeric-expr* in an *io-implied-do-control* must be of type integer, default real, or double precision real.

Constraint: In an *input-item-list*, an *io-implied-do-object* must be an *input-item*. In an *output-item-list*, an *io-implied-do-object* must be an *output-item*.

R919   *backspace-stmt*   **is** backspace *external-file-unit*
                            or backspace (*position-spec-list*)

R920   *endfile-stmt*   **is** endfile *external-file-unit*
                            or endfile (*position-spec-list*)

R921   *rewind-stmt*   **is** rewind *external-file-unit*
                            or rewind (*position-spec-list*)

R922   *position-spec*   **is** [unit =] *external-file-unit*
                            or iostat = *scalar-default-int-variable*
                            or err = *label*

Constraint: The *label* in the err= specifier must be the statement label of a branch target statement that appears in the same scoping unit as the file positioning statement.

Constraint: If the optional characters unit= are omitted from the unit specifier, the unit specifier must be the first item in the *position-spec-list*.

Constraint: A *position-spec-list* must contain exactly one *external-file-unit* and may contain at most one of each of the other specifiers.

R923   *inquire-stmt*   **is** inquire (*inquire-spec-list*)
                            or inquire (iolength = *scalar-default-int-variable*) ■
                                        ■ *output-item-list*

R924   *inquire-spec*   **is** [unit =] *external-file-unit*
                            or file = *file-name-expr*
                            or iostat = *scalar-default-int-variable*
                            or err = *label*
                            or exist = *scalar-default-logical-variable*
                            or opened = *scalar-default-logical-variable*
                            or number = *scalar-default-int-variable*
                            or named = *scalar-default-logical-variable*
                            or name = *scalar-default-char-variable*
                            or access = *scalar-default-char-variable*
                            or sequential = *scalar-default-char-variable*
                            or direct = *scalar-default-char-variable*
                            or form = *scalar-default-char-variable*
                            or formatted = *scalar-default-char-variable*
                            or unformatted = *scalar-default-char-variable*
                            or recl = *scalar-default-int-variable*
                            or nextrec = *scalar-default-int-variable*
                            or blank = *scalar-default-char-variable*
                            or position = *scalar-default-char-variable*
                            or action = *scalar-default-char-variable*
                            or read = *scalar-default-char-variable*
                            or write = *scalar-default-char-variable*
                            or readwrite = *scalar-default-char-variable*
                            or delim = *scalar-default-char-variable*
                            or pad = *scalar-default-char-variable*

Constraint: An *inquire-spec-list* must contain one file= specifier or one unit= specifier, but not both, and at most one of each of the other specifiers.

Constraint: In the inquire by unit form of the inquire statement, if the optional characters unit= are omitted from the unit specifier, the unit specifier must be the first item in the *inquire-spec-list*.

B.2.10 Input/Output Editing

R1001 *format-stmt*   is   format *format-specification*
R1002 *format-specification* is   ([*format-item-list*])
Constraint: The *format-stmt* must be labeled.
Constraint: The comma used to separate *format-items* in a *format-item-list* may be omitted as follows: (a) between a p edit descriptor and an immediately following f, e, en, es, d, or g edit descriptor (10.6.5), (b) before a slash edit
descriptor when the optional repeat specification is not present (10.6.2), (c)
after a slash edit descriptor, or (d) before or after a colon edit descriptor
(10.6.3).
R1003 *format-item*   is   [*r*] *data-edit-desc*
                               or   *control-edit-desc*
                               or   *char-string-edit-desc*
                               or   [*r*] (*format-item-list*)
R1004 *r*   is   *int-literal-constant*
Constraint: *r* must be positive.
Constraint: *r* must not have a kind parameter specified for it.
R1005 *data-edit-desc*   is   i *w* [. *m*]
                               or   b *w* [. *m*]
                               or   o *w* [. *m*]
                               or   z *w* [. *m*]
                               or   f *w* . *d*
                               or   e *w* . *d* [e *e*]
                               or   en *w* . *d* [e *e*]
                               or   es *w* . *d* [e *e*]
                               or   g *w* . *d* [e *e*]
                               or   l *w*
                               or   a [*w*]
                               or   d *w* . *d*
R1006 *w*   is   *int-literal-constant*
R1007 *m*   is   *int-literal-constant*
R1008 *d*   is   *int-literal-constant*
R1009 *e*   is   *int-literal-constant*
Constraint: *w* and *e* must be positive.
Constraint: *w*, *m*, *d*, and *e* must not have kind parameters specified for them.
R1010 *control-edit-desc*   is   *position-edit-desc*
                               or   [*r*] /
                               or   :
                               or   *sign-edit-desc*
                               or   *k* p
                               or   *blank-interp-edit-desc*
R1011 *k*   is   *signed-int-literal-constant*
Constraint: *k* must not have a kind parameter specified for it.
R1012 *position-edit-desc*   is   t *n*
                               or   tl *n*
                               or   tr *n*
                               or   *n* x
R1013 *n*   is   *int-literal-constant*
Constraint: *n* must be positive.
Constraint: *n* must not have a kind parameter specified for it.
R1014 *sign-edit-desc*   is   s
                               or   sp
                               or   ss
R1015 *blank-interp-edit-desc* is   bn
                               or   bz

R1016   *char-string-edit-desc*   **is**   *char-literal-constant*
                                      or   *c* h *rep-char* [*rep-char*] ...
R1017   *c*   **is**   *int-literal-constant*
Constraint: *c* must be positive.
Constraint: *c* must not have a kind parameter specified for it.
Constraint: The *rep-char* in the ch form must be of default character type.
Constraint: The *char-literal-constant* must not have a kind parameter specified for it.

B.2.11 Program Units

R1101   *main-program*   **is**   [*program-stmt*]
                                      [*specification-part*]
                                      [*execution-part*]
                                      [*internal-subprogram-part*]
                                      end-program-stmt
R1102   *program-stmt*   **is**   program *program-name*
R1103   *end-program-stmt*   **is**   end [program [*program-name*]]
Constraint: In a *main-program*, the *execution-part* must not contain a return statement or an entry statement.
Constraint: The *program-name* may be included in the *end-program-stmt* only if the optional *program-stmt* is used and, if included, must be identical to the *program-name* specified in the *program-stmt*.
Constraint: An automatic object must not appear in the *specification-part* (R204) of a main program.
R1104   *module*   **is**   *module-stmt*
                                      [*specification-part*]
                                      [*module-subprogram-part*]
                                      end-module-stmt
R1105   *module-stmt*   **is**   module *module-name*
R1106   *end-module-stmt*   **is**   end [module [*module-name*]]
Constraint: If the *module-name* is specified in the *end-module-stmt*, it must be identical to the *module-name* specified in the *module-stmt*.
Constraint: A module *specification-part* must not contain a *stmt-function-stmt*, an *entry-stmt*, or a *format-stmt*.
Constraint: An automatic object must not appear in the *specification-part* (R204) of a module.
R1107   *use-stmt*   **is**   use *module-name* [, *rename-list*]
                                      or   use *module-name* , only : [*only-list*]
R1108   *rename*   **is**   *local-name* => *use-name*
R1109   *only*   **is**   *access-id*
                                      or   [*local-name* =>] *use-name*
Constraint: Each *access-id* must be a public entity in the module.
Constraint: Each *use-name* must be the name of a public entity in the module.
R1110   *block-data*   **is**   *block-data-stmt*
                                      [*specification-part*]
                                      end-block-data-stmt
R1111   *block-data-stmt*   **is**   block data [*block-data-name*]
R1112   *end-block-data-stmt* **is** end [block data [*block-data-name*]]
Constraint: The *block-data-name* may be included in the *end-block-data-stmt* only if it was provided in the *block-data-stmt* and, if included, must be identical to the *block-data-name* in the *block-data-stmt*.
Constraint: A *block-data* *specification-part* may contain only use statements, type declaration statements, implicit statements, parameter statements, derived-type definitions, and the following specification statements: common, data, dimension, equivalence, intrinsic, pointer, save, and target.

Constraint: A type declaration statement in a *block-data specification-part* must not contain `allocatable`, `external`, `intent`, `optional`, `private`, or `public` attribute specifiers.

B.2.12 Procedures

R1201	*interface-block*	**is**	*interface-stmt*
			[*interface-body*] ...
			[*module-procedure-stmt*] ...
			end-interface-stmt
R1202	*interface-stmt*	**is**	`interface` [*generic-spec*]
R1203	*end-interface-stmt*	**is**	`end interface`
R1204	*interface-body*	**is**	*function-stmt*
			[*specification-part*]
			end-function-stmt
		or	*subroutine-stmt*
			[*specification-part*]
			end-subroutine-stmt
R1205	*module-procedure-stmt*	**is**	`module procedure` *procedure-name-list*
R1206	*generic-spec*	**is**	*generic-name*
		or	`operator (` *defined-operator* `)`
		or	`assignment (` = `)`

Constraint: An *interface-body* must not contain an *entry-stmt*, *data-stmt*, *format-stmt*, or *stmt-function-stmt*.

Constraint: The `module procedure` specification is allowed only if the *interface-block* has a *generic-spec* and has a host that is a module or accesses a module by use association; each *procedure-name* must be the name of a module procedure that is accessible in the host.

Constraint: An *interface-block* must not appear in a `block data` program unit.

Constraint: An *interface-block* in a subprogram must not contain an *interface-body* for a procedure defined by that subprogram.

Constraint: A *procedure-name* in a *module-procedure-stmt* must not be one which previously had been established to be associated with the *generic-spec* of the *interface-block* in which it appears, either by a previous appearance in an *interface-block* or by use or host association.

R1207	*external-stmt*	**is**	`external` *external-name-list*
R1208	*intrinsic-stmt*	**is**	`intrinsic` *intrinsic-procedure-name-list*

Constraint: Each *intrinsic-procedure-name* must be the name of an intrinsic procedure.

R1209	*function-reference*	**is**	*function-name* ([*actual-arg-spec-list*])

Constraint: The *actual-arg-spec-list* for a function reference must not contain an *alt-return-spec*.

R1210	*call-stmt*	**is**	`call` *subroutine-name* [([*actual-arg-spec-list*])]
R1211	*actual-arg-spec*	**is**	[*keyword* =] *actual-arg*
R1212	*keyword*	**is**	*dummy-arg-name*
R1213	*actual-arg*	**is**	*expr*
		or	*variable*
		or	*procedure-name*
		or	*alt-return-spec*
R1214	*alt-return-spec*	**is**	`*` *label*

Constraint: The *keyword* = must not appear if the interface of the procedure is implicit in the scoping unit.

Constraint: The *keyword* = may be omitted from an *actual-arg-spec* only if the *keyword* = has been omitted from each preceding *actual-arg-spec* in the argument list.

Constraint: Each *keyword* must be the name of a dummy argument in the explicit interface of the procedure.

Constraint: A *procedure-name actual-arg* must not be the name of an internal procedure or of a statement function and must not be the generic name of a procedure (12.3.2.1, 13.1).

Constraint: The *label* used in the *alt-return-spec* must be the statement label of a branch target statement that appears in the same scoping unit as the *call-stmt*.

R1215 *function-subprogram*   **is** *function-stmt*
                                              [*specification-part*]
                                              [*execution-part*]
                                              [*internal-subprogram-part*]
                                              end-function-stmt

R1216 *function-stmt*   **is** [*prefix*] function *function-name* ■
                                      ■ ([*dummy-arg-name-list*]) [result (*result-name*)]

Constraint: If result is specified, the *function-name* must not appear in any specification statement in the scoping unit of the function subprogram.

R1217 *prefix*   **is** *type-spec* [recursive]
                     or recursive [*type-spec*]

R1218 *end-function-stmt*   **is** end [function [*function-name*]]

Constraint: If result is specified, *result-name* must not be the same as *function-name*.

Constraint: function must be present on the *end-function-stmt* of an internal or module function.

Constraint: An internal function must not contain an entry statement.

Constraint: An internal function must not contain an *internal-subprogram-part*.

Constraint: If a *function-name* is present on the *end-function-stmt*, it must be identical to the *function-name* specified in the *function-stmt*.

R1219 *subroutine-subprogram*   **is** *subroutine-stmt*
                                               [*specification-part*]
                                               [*execution-part*]
                                               [*internal-subprogram-part*]
                                               end-subroutine-stmt

R1220 *subroutine-stmt*   **is** [recursive] subroutine *subroutine-name* ■
                                        ■ ([[*dummy-arg-list*])]

R1221 *dummy-arg*   **is** *dummy-arg-name*
                        or *

R1222 *end-subroutine-stmt*   **is** end [subroutine [*subroutine-name*]]

Constraint: subroutine must be present on the *end-subroutine-stmt* of an internal or module subroutine.

Constraint: An internal subroutine must not contain an entry statement.

Constraint: An internal subroutine must not contain an *internal-subprogram-part*.

Constraint: If a *subroutine-name* is present on the *end-subroutine-stmt*, it must be identical to the *subroutine-name* specified in the *subroutine-stmt*.

R1223 *entry-stmt*   **is** entry *entry-name* [([*dummy-arg-list*]) ■
                                  ■ [result (*result-name*)]]

Constraint: If result is specified, the *entry-name* must not appear in any specification statement in the scoping unit of the function program.

Constraint: An *entry-stmt* may appear only in an *external-subprogram* or *module-subprogram*. An *entry-stmt* must not appear within an *executable-construct*.

Constraint: result may be present only if the *entry-stmt* is contained in a function subprogram.

Constraint: Within the subprogram containing the *entry-stmt*, the *entry-name* must not appear as a dummy argument in the function or subroutine statement or in another entry statement and it must not appear in an external or intrinsic statement.

Constraint: A *dummy-arg* may be an alternate return indicator only if the entry statement is contained in a subroutine subprogram.

Constraint: If result is specified, *result-name* must not be the same as *entry-name*.

R1224 *return-stmt*   **is** return [*scalar-int-expr*]

Constraint: The *return-stmt* must be contained in the scoping unit of a function or subroutine subprogram.

Constraint: The *scalar-int-expr* is allowed only in the scoping unit of a subroutine subprogram.

R1225   *contains-stmt*   **is**   contains

R1226   *stmt-function-stmt*   **is**   *function-name* ([*dummy-arg-name-list*]) = *scalar-expr*

Constraint: The *scalar-expr* may be composed only of constants (literal and named), references to scalar variables and array elements, references to functions and
function dummy procedures, and intrinsic operators. If a reference to a
statement function appears in *scalar-expr*, its definition must have been
provided earlier in the scoping unit and must not be the name of the statement function being defined.

Constraint: Named constants in *scalar-expr* must have been declared earlier in the scoping unit or made accessible by use or host association. If array elements
appear in *scalar-expr*, the parent array must have been declared as an array
earlier in the scoping unit or made accessible by use or host association. If
a scalar variable, array element, function reference, or dummy function
reference is typed by the implicit typing rules, its appearance in any subsequent type declaration statement must confirm this implied type and the
values of any implied type parameters.

Constraint: The *function-name* and each *dummy-arg-name* must be specified, explicitly or
implicitly, to be scalar data objects.

Constraint: A given *dummy-arg-name* may appear only once in any *dummy-arg-name-list*.

Constraint: Each scalar variable reference in *scalar-expr* may be either a reference to a
dummy argument of the statement function or a reference to a variable
local to the same scoping unit as the statement function statement.

B.2.13 Intrinsic Procedures

B.2.14 Scope, Association, and Definition

B.3 Cross References

The following is a cross reference of all syntactic symbols used in the
BNF, giving the rule in which they are defined and all rules in which
they are referenced.

The symbols are sorted alphabetically within three categories:
nonterminal symbols that are defined, nonterminal symbols that are
not defined, and terminal symbols. Note that except for those ending
with -*name*, the only undefined nonterminal symbols are *letter*, *digit*,
special-character, and *rep-char*. Symbols ending with -*name* are defined
by the rule:

    xyz-name   **is**   *name*

Before processing the cross references, all occurrences of -*list* and
scalar- in the symbol names were removed.

Symbol	Defined in	Referenced in
ac-do-variable	R435	R434
ac-implied-do	R433	R432

Symbol	Defined in	Referenced in		
ac-implied-do-control	R434	R433		
ac-value	R432	R431	R433	
access-id	R522	R521	R1109	
access-spec	R510	R424	R503	R521
access-stmt	R521	R214		
action-stmt	R216	R215	R807	R829	R833
action-term-do-construct	R827	R826		
actual-arg	R1213	R1211		
actual-arg-spec	R1211	R1209	R1210	
add-op	R710	R310	R707	
add-operand	R706	R706	R707	
allocatable-stmt	R526	R214		
allocate-lower-bound	R627	R626		
allocate-object	R625	R624	R631	
allocate-shape-spec	R626	R624		
allocate-stmt	R622	R216		
allocate-upper-bound	R628	R626		
allocation	R624	R622		
alphanumeric-character	R302	R301	R304	
alt-return-spec	R1214	R1213		
and-op	R720	R310	R716	
and-operand	R715	R716		
arithmetic-if-stmt	R840	R216		
array-constructor	R431	R701		
array-element	R615	R536	R547	R602	R610
array-section	R616	R602		
array-spec	R512	R503	R504	R525	R528
assign-stmt	R838	R216		
assigned-goto-stmt	R839	R216		
assignment-stmt	R735	R216	R738	R739
assumed-shape-spec	R516	R512		
assumed-size-spec	R518	R512		
attr-spec	R503	R501		
backspace-stmt	R919	R216		
binary-constant	R408	R407		
blank-interp-edit-desc	R1015	R1010		
block	R801	R802	R808	R823
block-data	R1110	R202		
block-data-stmt	R1111	R1110		
block-do-construct	R817	R816		
boz-literal-constant	R407	R306	R533	
c	R1017	R1016		
call-stmt	R1210	R216		
case-construct	R808	R215		
case-expr	R812	R809		
case-selector	R813	R810		
case-stmt	R810	R808		
case-value	R815	R814		
case-value-range	R814	R813		
char-constant	R309	R843		
char-expr	R726	R731	R812	
char-initialization-expr	R731	R815		
char-length	R508	R429	R504	R507
char-literal-constant	R420	R306	R1016	
char-selector	R506	R502		
char-string-edit-desc	R1016	R1003		
char-variable	R605			
character	R301			

Symbol	Defined in	Referenced in			
close-spec	R908	R907			
close-stmt	R907	R216			
common-block-object	R549	R548			
common-stmt	R548	R214			
complex-literal-constant	R417	R306			
component-array-spec	R428	R427	R429		
component-attr-spec	R427	R426			
component-decl	R429	R426			
component-def-stmt	R426	R422			
computed-goto-stmt	R837	R216			
concat-op	R712	R310	R711		
connect-spec	R905	R904			
constant	R305	R308	R309	R533	R610	R701
constant-subobject	R702	R701			
contains-stmt	R1225	R210	R212		
continue-stmt	R841	R216	R824		
control-edit-desc	R1010	R1003			
cycle-stmt	R834	R216			
d	R1008	R1005			
data-edit-desc	R1005	R1003			
data-i-do-object	R536	R535			
data-i-do-variable	R537	R535			
data-implied-do	R535	R531	R536		
data-ref	R612	R614	R615	R616	
data-stmt	R529	R209	R214		
data-stmt-constant	R533	R532			
data-stmt-object	R531	R530			
data-stmt-repeat	R534	R532			
data-stmt-set	R530	R529			
data-stmt-value	R532	R530			
deallocate-stmt	R631	R216			
declaration-construct	R207	R204			
default-char-expr	R727	R905	R906	R908	R912	R913
default-char-variable	R606	R903	R924		
default-int-variable	R608	R905	R908	R912	R913	R922
		R923	R924		
default-logical-variable	R604	R924			
deferred-shape-spec	R517	R428	R512	R526	R527
defined-binary-op	R724	R311	R723		
defined-operator	R311	R1206			
defined-unary-op	R704	R311	R703		
derived-type-def	R422	R207			
derived-type-stmt	R424	R422			
digit-string	R402	R401	R404	R405	R413	R414
dimension-stmt	R525	R214			
do-block	R823	R817			
do-body	R828	R827	R830	R832	
do-construct	R816	R215			
do-stmt	R818	R817			
do-term-action-stmt	R829	R827			
do-term-shared-stmt	R833	R832			
do-variable	R822	R821	R918		
dummy-arg	R1221	R1220	R1223		
e	R1009	R1005			
else-if-stmt	R804	R802			
else-stmt	R805	R802			
elsewhere-stmt	R742	R739			
end-block-data-stmt	R1112	R1110			

Symbol	Defined in	Referenced in			
end-do	R824	R817			
end-do-stmt	R825	R824			
end-function-stmt	R1218	R216	R1204	R1215	
end-if-stmt	R806	R802			
end-interface-stmt	R1203	R1201			
end-module-stmt	R1106	R1104			
end-program-stmt	R1103	R216	R1101		
end-select-stmt	R811	R808			
end-subroutine-stmt	R1222	R216	R1204	R1219	
end-type-stmt	R425	R422			
end-where-stmt	R743	R739			
endfile-stmt	R920	R216			
entity-decl	R504	R501			
entry-stmt	R1223	R206	R207	R209	
equiv-op	R722	R310	R718		
equiv-operand	R717	R717	R718		
equivalence-object	R547	R546			
equivalence-set	R546	R545			
equivalence-stmt	R545	R214			
executable-construct	R215	R208	R209		
executable-program	R201				
execution-part	R208	R1101	R1215	R1219	
execution-part-construct	R209	R208	R801	R828	
exit-stmt	R835	R216			
explicit-shape-spec	R513	R428	R512	R518	R549
exponent	R416	R413			
exponent-letter	R415	R413			
expr	R723	R430	R432	R701	R723	R725
		R726	R727	R728	R729	R730
		R735	R737	R915	R1213	R1226
extended-intrinsic-op	R312	R311			
external-file-unit	R902	R901	R905	R908	R919	R920
		R921	R922	R924		
external-stmt	R1207	R214			
external-subprogram	R203	R202			
file-name-expr	R906	R905	R924		
format	R913	R909	R911	R912	
format-item	R1003	R1002	R1003		
format-specification	R1002	R1001			
format-stmt	R1001	R206	R207	R209	
function-reference	R1209	R701			
function-stmt	R1216	R1204	R1215		
function-subprogram	R1215	R203	R211	R213	
generic-spec	R1206	R522	R1202		
goto-stmt	R836	R216			
hex-constant	R410	R407			
hex-digit	R411	R410			
if-construct	R802	R215			
if-stmt	R807	R216			
if-then-stmt	R803	R802			
imag-part	R419	R417			
implicit-part	R205	R204			
implicit-part-stmt	R206	R205			
implicit-spec	R541	R540			
implicit-stmt	R540	R205	R206		
initialization-expr	R730	R504	R539		
inner-shared-do-construct	R832	R831			
input-item	R914	R909	R917		

Symbol	Defined in	Referenced in				
inquire-spec	R924	R923				
inquire-stmt	R923	R216				
int-constant	R308	R534				
int-expr	R728	R434	R535	R611	R617	R620
		R621	R627	R628	R732	R734
		R812	R837	R902	R905	R912
		R1224				
int-initialization-expr	R732	R505	R506	R815		
int-literal-constant	R404	R306	R403	R508	R1004	R1006
		R1007	R1008	R1009	R1013	R1017
int-variable	R607	R435	R537	R623	R838	R839
intent-spec	R511	R503	R519			
intent-stmt	R519	R214				
interface-block	R1201	R207				
interface-body	R1204	R1201				
interface-stmt	R1202	R1201				
internal-file-unit	R903	R901				
internal-subprogram	R211	R210				
internal-subprogram-part	R210	R1101	R1215	R1219		
intrinsic-operator	R310	R312				
intrinsic-stmt	R1208	R214				
io-control-spec	R912	R909	R910			
io-implied-do	R916	R914	R915			
io-implied-do-control	R918	R916				
io-implied-do-object	R917	R916				
io-unit	R901	R912				
k	R1011	R1010				
keyword	R1212	R1211				
kind-param	R405	R404	R413	R420	R421	
kind-selector	R505	R502				
label	R313	R819	R836	R837	R838	R839
		R840	R905	R908	R912	R913
		R922	R924	R1214		
label-do-stmt	R819	R818	R827	R830	R832	
length-selector	R507	R506				
letter-spec	R542	R541				
level-1-expr	R703	R705				
level-2-expr	R707	R707	R711			
level-3-expr	R711	R711	R713			
level-4-expr	R713	R715				
level-5-expr	R718	R718	R723			
literal-constant	R306	R305				
logical-expr	R725	R733	R741	R803	R804	R807
		R812	R821			
logical-initialization-expr	R733	R815				
logical-literal-constant	R421	R306				
logical-variable	R603					
loop-control	R821	R819	R820			
lower-bound	R514	R513	R516	R518		
m	R1007	R1005				
main-program	R1101	R202				
mask-expr	R741	R738	R740			
module	R1104	R202				
module-procedure-stmt	R1205	R1201				
module-stmt	R1105	R1104				
module-subprogram	R213	R212				
module-subprogram-part	R212	R1104				
mult-op	R709	R310	R706			

Symbol	Defined in	Referenced in			
mult-operand	R705	R705	R706		
n	R1013	R1012			
name	R304	R307			
named-constant	R307	R305	R539		
named-constant-def	R539	R538			
namelist-group-object	R544	R543			
namelist-stmt	R543	R214			
nonblock-do-construct	R826	R816			
nonlabel-do-stmt	R820	R818			
not-op	R719	R310	R715		
nullify-stmt	R629	R216			
numeric-expr	R729	R821	R840	R918	
octal-constant	R409	R407			
only	R1109	R1107			
open-stmt	R904	R216			
optional-stmt	R520	R214			
or-op	R721	R310	R717		
or-operand	R716	R716	R717		
outer-shared-do-construct	R830	R826	R831		
output-item	R915	R910	R911	R917	R923
parameter-stmt	R538	R206	R207		
parent-string	R610	R609			
part-ref	R613	R612			
pause-stmt	R844	R216			
pointer-assignment-stmt	R736	R216			
pointer-object	R630	R629	R736		
pointer-stmt	R527	R214			
position-edit-desc	R1012	R1010			
position-spec	R922	R919	R920	R921	
power-op	R708	R310	R705		
prefix	R1217	R1216			
primary	R701	R703			
print-stmt	R911	R216			
private-sequence-stmt	R423	R422			
program-stmt	R1102	R1101			
program-unit	R202	R201			
r	R1004	R1003	R1010		
read-stmt	R909	R216			
real-literal-constant	R413	R306	R412		
real-part	R418	R417			
rel-op	R714	R310	R713		
rename	R1108	R1107			
return-stmt	R1224	R216			
rewind-stmt	R921	R216			
save-stmt	R523	R214			
saved-entity	R524	R523			
section-subscript	R618	R613			
select-case-stmt	R809	R808			
shared-term-do-construct	R831	R830			
sign	R406	R401	R403	R412	
sign-edit-desc	R1014	R1010			
signed-digit-string	R401	R416			
signed-int-literal-constant	R403	R418	R419	R533	R1011
signed-real-literal-constant	R412	R418	R419	R533	
significand	R414	R413			
specification-expr	R734	R509	R514	R515	
specification-part	R204	R1101	R1104	R1110	R1204	R1215
		R1219			

Symbol	Defined in	Referenced in			
specification-stmt	R214	R207			
stat-variable	R623	R622	R631		
stmt-function-stmt	R1226	R207			
stop-code	R843	R842	R844		
stop-stmt	R842	R216			
stride	R620	R619			
structure-component	R614	R536	R602	R610	R625	R630
structure-constructor	R430	R533	R701		
subobject	R602	R601	R702		
subroutine-stmt	R1220	R1204	R1219		
subroutine-subprogram	R1219	R203	R211	R213	
subscript	R617	R618	R619		
subscript-triplet	R619	R618			
substring	R609	R547	R602		
substring-range	R611	R609	R616		
target	R737	R736			
target-stmt	R528	R214			
type-declaration-stmt	R501	R207			
type-param-value	R509	R506	R507	R508	
type-spec	R502	R426	R501	R541	R1217
underscore	R303	R302			
upper-bound	R515	R513			
use-stmt	R1107	R204			
variable	R601	R531	R603	R604	R605	R606
		R607	R608	R701	R735	R737
		R822	R914	R1213		
vector-subscript	R621	R618			
w	R1006	R1005			
where-construct	R739	R215			
where-construct-stmt	R740	R739			
where-stmt	R738	R216			
write-stmt	R910	R216			
array-name		R525	R526		
array-variable-name		R601			
block-data-name		R1111	R1112		
case-construct-name		R809	R810	R811	
common-block-name		R524	R548		
component-name		R429			
digit		R302	R313	R402	R408	R409
		R411	R843		
do-construct-name		R819	R820	R825	R834	R835
dummy-arg-name		R519	R520	R1212	R1216	R1221
		R1226			
entry-name		R1223			
external-name		R1207			
function-name		R504	R1209	R1216	R1218	R1226
generic-name		R1206			
if-construct-name		R803	R804	R805	R806
int-constant-name		R405			
intrinsic-procedure-name		R1208			
letter		R302	R304	R542	R704	R724
local-name		R1108	R1109		
module-name		R1105	R1106	R1107	
namelist-group-name		R543	R912		
object-name		R504	R524	R527	R528
part-name		R613			
procedure-name		R1205	R1213		

Symbol	Defined in	Referenced in			
program-name	R1102	R1103			
rep-char	R420	R1016			
result-name	R1216	R1223			
special-character	R301				
subroutine-name	R1210	R1220	R1222		
type-name	R424	R425	R430	R502	
use-name	R522	R1108	R1109		
variable-name	R544	R547	R549	R601	R610
	R625	R630			
"	R408	R409	R410	R420	
%	R612				
'	R408	R409	R410	R420	
(	R417	R427	R429	R430	R433
	R502	R503	R504	R505	R506
	R507	R508	R519	R525	R526
	R527	R528	R535	R538	R541
	R546	R549	R609	R613	R616
	R622	R624	R629	R631	R701
	R738	R740	R803	R804	R807
	R809	R813	R821	R837	R839
	R840	R904	R907	R909	R910
	R916	R919	R920	R921	R923
	R1002	R1003	R1206	R1209	R1210
	R1216	R1220	R1223	R1226	
(/	R431				
)	R417	R427	R429	R430	R433
	R502	R503	R504	R505	R506
	R507	R508	R519	R525	R526
	R527	R528	R535	R538	R541
	R546	R549	R609	R613	R616
	R622	R624	R629	R631	R701
	R738	R740	R803	R804	R807
	R809	R813	R821	R837	R839
	R840	R904	R907	R909	R910
	R916	R919	R920	R921	R923
	R1002	R1003	R1206	R1209	R1210
	R1216	R1220	R1223	R1226	
*	R429	R504	R507	R509	R518
	R532	R709	R901	R913	R1214
	R1221				
**	R708				
+	R406	R710			
,	R417	R424	R426	R433	R434
	R501	R506	R507	R518	R525
	R526	R527	R528	R529	R535
	R543	R546	R548	R622	R631
	R821	R837	R839	R840	R909
	R911	R916	R918	R1107	
-	R406	R542	R710		
.	R414	R704	R724	R1005	
.and.	R720				
.eq.	R714				
.eqv.	R722				
.false.	R421				
.ge.	R714				
.gt.	R714				
.le.	R714				

Symbol	Defined in	Referenced in			
.lt.		R714			
.ne.		R714			
.neqv.		R722			
.not.		R719			
.or.		R721			
.true.		R421			
/		R524	R530	R543	R548	R709
		R1010			
/)		R431			
//		R712			
/=		R714			
:		R513	R516	R517	R518	R611
		R619	R626	R803	R809	R814
		R819	R820	R1010	R1107	
::		R424	R426	R501	R519	R520
		R521	R523	R525	R526	R527
		R528			
<		R714			
<=		R714			
=		R434	R504	R505	R506	R507
		R535	R539	R622	R631	R735
		R821	R905	R908	R912	R918
		R922	R923	R924	R1206	R1211
		R1226			
==		R714			
=>		R736	R1108	R1109		
>		R714			
>=		R714			
a		R411	R1005		
access		R905	R924		
action		R905	R924		
advance		R912			
allocatable		R503	R526		
allocate		R622			
assign		R838			
assignment		R1206			
b		R408	R411	R1005	
backspace		R919			
blank		R905	R924		
block		R1111	R1112		
bn		R1015			
bz		R1015			
c		R411			
call		R1210			
case		R809	R810		
character		R502			
close		R907			
common		R548			
complex		R502			
contains		R1225			
continue		R841			
cycle		R834			
d		R411	R415	R1005	
data		R529	R1111	R1112	
deallocate		R631			
default		R813			
delim		R905	R924		
dimension		R427	R503	R525	

Symbol	Defined in	Referenced in			
direct		R924			
do		R819	R820	R825	
double		R502			
e		R411	R415	R1005	
else		R804	R805		
elsewhere		R742			
en		R1005			
end		R425	R743	R806	R811	R825
		R912	R1103	R1106	R1112	R1203
		R1218	R1222			
endfile		R920			
entry		R1223			
eor		R912			
equivalence		R545			
err		R905	R908	R912	R922	R924
es		R1005			
exist		R924			
exit		R835			
external		R503	R1207		
f		R411	R1005		
file		R905	R924		
fmt		R912			
form		R905	R924		
format		R1001			
formatted		R924			
function		R1216	R1218		
g		R1005			
go		R836	R837	R839	
h		R1016			
i		R1005			
if		R803	R804	R806	R807	R840
implicit		R540			
in		R511			
inout		R511			
inquire		R923			
integer		R502			
intent		R503	R519		
interface		R1202	R1203		
intrinsic		R503	R1208		
iolength		R923			
iostat		R905	R908	R912	R922	R924
kind		R505	R506		
l		R1005			
len		R506	R507		
logical		R502			
module		R1105	R1106	R1205	
name		R924			
named		R924			
namelist		R543			
nextrec		R924			
nml		R912			
none		R540			
nullify		R629			
number		R924			
o		R409	R1005		
only		R1107			
open		R904			
opened		R924			

Symbol	Defined in	Referenced in			
operator		R1206			
optional		R503	R520		
out		R511			
p		R1010			
pad		R905	R924		
parameter		R503	R538		
pause		R844			
pointer		R427	R503	R527	
position		R905	R924		
precision		R502			
print		R911			
private		R423	R510		
procedure		R1205			
program		R1102	R1103		
public		R510			
read		R909	R924		
readwrite		R924			
real		R502			
rec		R912			
recl		R905	R924		
recursive		R1217	R1220		
result		R1216	R1223		
return		R1224			
rewind		R921			
s		R1014			
save		R503	R523		
select		R809	R811		
sequence		R423			
sequential		R924			
size		R912			
sp		R1014			
ss		R1014			
stat		R622	R631		
status		R905	R908		
stop		R842			
subroutine		R1220	R1222		
t		R1012			
target		R503	R528		
then		R803	R804		
tl		R1012			
to		R836	R837	R838	R839
tr		R1012			
type		R424	R425	R502	
unformatted		R924			
unit		R905	R908	R912	R922 R924
use		R1107			
where		R738	R740	R743	
while		R821			
write		R910	R924		
x		R1012			
z		R410	R1005		
-		R303	R404	R413	R420 R421

Index

A

a edit descriptor 37, 176
abs function 379
abstract data type 225, 267
access
   direct 308, 322, 323
   sequential 308, 315, 322
access= specifier 326, 331
achar function 176, 380
acos function 380
action= specifier 326, 331
actual argument 104
adaptive trapezoidal integration
   227
adjustl function 194, 380
adjustr function 380
advance= specifier 314
advancing input/output 310,
   315
aimag function 379

aint function 379
all function 386
allocatable attribute 134
allocatable statement 361
allocate statement 134, 138,
   262
allocated function 386
allocation
   memory 137
allocation status 138, 262
alternate return 357
anint function 379
any function 386
apostrophe 3, 9, 172, 352, 368
apostrophe edit descriptor 368
argument
   actual 104
   agreement 104
   dummy 100, 104
   intent 110
   keyword 108, 378